# The Doctrine and Covenants Speaks

Volume 2

# The Doctrine and Covenants Speaks

Volume 2

by
Roy W. Doxey

Published by
Deseret Book Company
Salt Lake City, Utah
1979

Library of Congress Catalog Card No. 64-57862

# Dedication

To the General Presidency of the Relief Society of The Church of Jesus Christ of Latter-day Saints —Belle S. Spafford, Marianne C. Sharp, Louise W. Madsen—and the faithful women over whom they preside.

# Preface

After centuries of spiritual darkness, revelation was again received when Joseph Smith beheld the Father and the Son in the spring of 1820. Although the record of the First Vision is not a section in the Doctrine and Covenants, though it is mentioned in the "Explanatory Introduction" of each single copy of this book of scripture, it is the foundation of all revelation received in this dispensation. The loss of the priesthood, the fulness of the gospel, and the Church of Jesus Christ brought the need for a restoration of the authority, principles, and organization by which salvation might be received. The great apostasy from the gospel of Jesus Christ and the restoration of the salvation-oriented Church were prophesied by Old and New Testament prophets. Although the four standard works of The Church of Jesus Christ of Latter-day Saints—the Holy Bible, the Book of Mormon, The Doctrine and Covenants, and The Pearl of Great Price—constitute the authorized, accepted scriptures of this dispensation, the Doctrine and Covenants is the standard work which is particularly the modern book of scripture. The revelations in the Doctrine and Covenants provide clarity and understanding of the principles of salvation, including the higher ordinances of the gospel essential for exaltation in the celestial kingdom.

Because of the unique status of the Doctrine and Covenants in this dispensation, it is a major source of inspiration and guidance for members of the Church. In 1967, the material in Volume I of *The Doctrine and Covenants Speaks* was published by permission of the General Presidency of the Relief Society of the Church, since it was written for the theology department of that organization. This second volume, consisting of discussions about Sections 71 through 136, is also published with permission of the Relief Society. While this material was being written and since then, many members of the Church have expressed the wish that it would be published in book form. The publication of Volume II brings to a conclusion the work of 13 years.

Appreciation is expressed to Gaye Davis and Kay Rice for typing the manuscript.

It is sincerely hoped that the contents of these two volumes will continue to serve the purpose for which they were written—to instruct in the great truths of the Doctrine and Covenants, that faith in God, his Son Jesus Christ, and in the divine mission of the Prophet Joseph Smith, might be furthered.

Roy W. Doxey

Brigham Young University
Provo, Utah
January, 1970

# Contents

## Chapter 1

# MISSIONARY SERVICE

### (Doctrine and Covenants Sections 71, 73, 74, and 75)

Following the four November 1831 conferences, Oliver Cowdery and John Whitmer left for Jackson County, Missouri, in obedience to Revelation. (D&C Section 69.) Joseph Smith resumed the revision of the Bible with Sidney Rigdon acting as scribe. (*Documentary History of the Church* 1:238; also known as the *History of the Church* by Joseph Smith, quoted hereafter as *DHC*.) A month before this, Ezra Booth, mentioned in Section 64:15, apostatized and set out to bring harm to the Prophet and to the Church. His efforts to do both of these apparently met with partial success. In the first instance, it was some of his efforts and his participation in mob action against the Prophet that brought physical harm to the Prophet. (*DHC* 1:261-265.) His attack against the Church and its members was made in a series of nine letters published by the *Ohio Star* (Ravenna, Ohio). They consisted of slanderous denunciations and falsehoods concerning Joseph and the Church. (Section 71.)

In view of these efforts of Satan to thwart the work of the kingdom, the Prophet and Sidney were called by revelation to preach the gospel in the regions adjacent to Kirtland. (D&C 71:1-3.) An indication of the message delivered by these two missionaries on this special mission from December 1831 until the 10th of January 1832, is given in the Prophet's journal. He said it was a vindication of the cause of the Redeemer, that the day of vengeance was coming upon this generation, and that prejudice and darkness caused some to persecute the true Church. Much of the bigotry caused by the apostate's letters was allayed through this mission.

The revelation counseled these brethren to confound their enemies both in public and private, with the promise that their opponents would be shamed. (*Ibid.*, v. 7.) It is worthy to note that when the Lord's servants are attacked, it is tantamount to attacking the Lord. (*Ibid.*, v. 8.)

### Preach the Gospel

The commandment to participate in debate was given to the Prophet because of the unusual circumstances noted above. The Lord, on the other hand, had counseled his servants to preach the first principles, to obtain the Spirit that it might convey the truth to the hearer, and thus make known the message of this dispensation. (D&C 33; 34; 42:12-17.)

An experience of the Prophet in October 1833 is an excellent example of the present counsel of the General Authorities that missionaries should not indulge in debate or argument, but they should preach the simple principles by the Spirit. While in Canada with Sidney Rigdon at the house of Freeman Nickerson's brother, the latter desired to match his Bible learning with that of the Prophet in an attempt to disprove Joseph Smith as a prophet. One night the opportunity came when Freeman Nickerson placed the Bible on the table and said, "There! Now, go to it!" The Prophet took up the challenge by telling the simple but powerful and convincing account of the restoration of the gospel. The Spirit of the Lord was so manifest in his testimony that opposition no longer remained. By the aid of Freeman's brother, meetings were held that resulted in fourteen baptisms, including the Nickerson who was determined to show the Prophet wrong. (John Henry Evans, *Joseph Smith an American Prophet*, pp. 86-88.)

## Lack of Success in Opposition

The Lord's work was not restored to fail. The kingdom of God is on the earth in the form of the Church, and the Lord has planned that it shall never be destroyed nor given to another people, but it shall stand forever. (Daniel 2:44.) In Section 71, an aspect of this foreknown eventuality is given in verses 9 and 10:

> Verily, thus saith the Lord unto you—there is no weapon that is formed against you shall prosper;
>
> And if any man lift his voice against you he shall be confounded in mine own due time.

It is apparent that this assurance of defeat for those who lift their voices in opposition to the Prophet includes not only the experiences of the missionaries of 1831-32, but of any time. To speak against the Prophet of this dispensation is the same as warring against the Church which he established, and also against God.

Published opposition was not the only "weapon" used against the Prophet and the Saints. Physical persecution has been a common means of attempting to thwart the purpose of the Lord. Despite the adversary's "weapons," the work of God has rolled on until today the voice of opposition is largely submerged by the prophesied, inevitable progress of successful endeavors.

## Commandments Are True

Obedience to truth is the prescription for happiness here and eternal joy in the life to come. The Lord admonished the Prophet and Sidney Rigdon to keep the commandments for they are true. (D&C 71:11.) The knowledge of truth is given by the Spirit which the missionary is counseled to receive and to teach by. President Joseph F. Smith stated the importance of adhering to the truth in these words:

Our hope of salvation must be founded upon the truth, the whole truth, and nothing but the truth, for we cannot build upon error and ascend into the courts of eternal truth and enjoy the glory and exaltation of the kingdom of our God. That cannot be done. (*Conference Report,* October 1917, page 3.)

Section 73 is one of the shortest revelations in the Doctrine and Covenants. After performing missionary work in several Ohio cities not far from Kirtland, Joseph Smith was commanded by this revelation to continue the work of revising the Bible which was interrupted by the mission call of Section 71. This was an undertaking which began in New York State and was set aside as other matters needed immediate attention. In a subsequent chapter some of the contributions of this work will be indicated. For the present, however, it should be known that many important contributions have been made to our understanding of the Bible as a result of that "translation."

An interesting expression, "gird up your loins and be sober," is found in verse 6 of Section 73. The admonition "gird up your loins" means to be prepared for a journey, or for a certain work. In this sense it is found in the hymn "Come, Come Ye Saints." In this scripture, we are informed that it is to be understood as used by Peter, "Gird up the loins of your minds." (I Peter 1:13.) In other words, the mind should be free from those things which deter one from the work at hand. To be sober means to be of a serious mind. (*Doctrine and Covenants Commentary*, page 431.)

## Section 75 — Introduction

At the conclusion of a conference held in Amherst, Ohio, a number of the elders asked the Prophet to inquire of the Lord concerning their specific duties in bringing people to a sense of their condition. In recording this fact the Prophet quoted a scripture that emphasizes that everyone sins and, therefore, is in need of repentance. (D&C 33:4; *DHC* 1:242-243.)

The opening verses of Section 75 may be applied to the thousands of missionaries of this dispensation. In these five verses the missionary is commissioned to proclaim the Lord's gospel in earnestness, eschewing idleness, and to be mighty in that proclamation. The earnest missionary's message should be delivered as the sound of a trumpet. This expression alludes to the sounds of this instrument that can be heard far and wide with mighty blasts. Such an allusion seems to carry with it the importance of the message since it is to be made known without shame or diffidence on the part of the Lord's servant. The following testimony of President Brigham Young is typical of those who have received the truth and made it part of their lives:

> When I first commenced preaching, I made up my mind to declare the things that I understood, fearless of friends and threats, and regardless of caresses. They were nothing to me, for if it was my duty to rise before a congregation of strangers and say that the Lord lives, that He has revealed Himself in this our day, that He has given to us a Prophet, and brought forth the new and everlasting covenant for the restoration of Israel, and if that was all I could say, I must be just as satisfied as though I could get up and talk for hours . . .
>
> With regard to preaching, let a man present himself before the Saints, or go into the world before the nobles and great men of the earth, and let him stand up full of the Holy Ghost, full of the power of God, and though he may use words and sentences in an awkward style, he will convince and convert more, of the truth, than can the most polished orator destitute of the Holy Ghost; for that Spirit will prepare the minds of the people to receive the truth, and the spirit of the speaker will influence the hearers so that they will feel it. (*Journal of Discourses* 4:21.)

Missionaries are promised by the Lord that if they labor faithfully, they "shall be laden with many sheaves, and crowned with honor, and glory, and immortality, and eternal life" (D&C 75:5.)

## Missionary Assignments

Section 75 contains many missionary assignments. (D&C 75:6-17, 30-36.) The names of some of these elders are well known in our history, such as Orson Hyde, Orson Pratt, Hyrum Smith, and others; but some are mentioned about whom little is known. This does not mean, however, that their labors were not as acceptable to the Lord nor that their reward will not be as great as the well-known. The promise of eternal glory is for all the faithful, whether apostle or elder. Each will be judged by his performance in accordance with his opportunities for service. (On pages 435-436, 439-440, of the *Doctrine and Covenants Commentary* will be found biographical sketches of the elders referred to in Section 75.)

How should these elders find success in their missionary labors? This was the question which they desired the Prophet to ask of the Lord. The answer was that they should pray to the Lord that he might give the comforter which would teach the things that were necessary for them to have. (D&C 75:10-11.) This is the way of the true missionary. Circumstances vary due to the area, people, and the particular circumstances at the moment of contacting the prospective investigator. Divine guidance is the answer in all of these cases; nonetheless, the missionary is to study the people and the culture. The key to receiving the benefits of the Holy Ghost is prayer. The Lord does not give if the person does not knock. The missionary is given the promise that through his faithfulness the Lord will be with him to the end. (*Ibid.*, vss. 13-14.) Others are told that by their faithfulness they shall overcome all things resulting in their being lifted up at the last day. (*Ibid.*, v. 16.) These promises enforce the truth that constancy and devotion to duty are the keys to receiving eternal life, or exaltation.

President Anthon H. Lund said: "Our religion is one in which we are called upon to show our faith by our works." As an example of this truism, missionary calls made upon the Church membership are most appropriate. The question as to how much pay will be received for this service is far from the mind of the Latter-day Saint. The impelling motive is one of duty, that the glorious message of the gospel may be shared with others. Distance or place is not a consideration, but rather it is, "I'll go where you want me to go, dear Lord."

## Missionary Procedures

In missionary language, the "going from house to house" is known as "tracting." (D&C 75:18.) When the missionary is received into a house, he is counseled to leave his blessing with that house. (*Ibid.*, v. 19.) The gospel is the blessing, although the prayer in the home for the benefit of the host is a direct way in which this counsel may be followed.

The missionaries in the day of judgment will be judges of the houses that reject them, and it will be more tolerable for the heathen in that day than for those who rejected them. (D&C 75:21-22.) As President John Taylor has pointed out, judgment, under God, is committed to Christ; then to the Twelve Apostles; and then to the saints, including certain officers in the Priesthood. (*Mediation and Atonement*, Chapter 22.) President Charles W. Penrose said:

. . . The great judgment that is to come will not be altogether performed by one individual sitting upon a great white throne and passing judgment upon the millions upon millions of the earth's inhabitants. God's house is a house of order, and the Lord will have agents appointed as he has now behind the veil as well as in the flesh, and when the great judgment comes, all will be judged according to their works, and the books will be opened, and the Book of Life will be scanned and the man's acts and the women's acts upon the earth will be disclosed, and we will all confess in our souls that the judgment is just and righteous, because it will be uttered and delivered by one having authority and the seal of God will be upon it. (*Conference Report*, October 1916, page 24.)

Another testimony to this effect is given in the *Doctrine and Covenants Commentary*, page 440.

The idea that it will be more tolerable for the heathen in the day of judgment than for those who reject the gospel suggests that since the heathen will be assigned to the terrestrial kingdom (D&C 45:54; 76:72), the willfully corrupt may be in a lesser kingdom. Unless the missionary does his work faithfully, he may be accused by those whom he neglected. (*Ibid.*, 43:19-20.)

## Assist in the Work

The members of the Church in 1832 were placed under the responsibility of assisting the families of the missionaries who could not sustain them. (*Ibid.*, 75:24-25.) In case there were some who could not go on missions, they should provide for their families and would "in nowise lose his [their] crown." However, they were admonished to labor in the Church. (*Ibid.*, v. 28.) Activity in the kingdom is an essential in obtaining the blessings of heaven.

In keeping with the commandment to provide for one's family, the virtue of industry is demanded. Idleness is a sin. There is always something for the person to do in the Church; there is always opportunity to improve one's mind by study. Idleness means neglect and waste, both of which are opposed to the spirit and letter of the gospel. (*Ibid.*, v. 29.)

## Section 74 — Background

While translating the Bible, a question was raised about one of Paul's statements concerning an aspect of marriage relations. Section 74 is an interpretation of

I Corinthians 7:14. It appears that in the Corinth branch of the Church there arose the question of whether or not the convert should leave the non-member husband or wife. Paul's counsel was that this should not be done because a sanctifying effect was brought in the home by the member of the Church. It was maintained by some that if the wife should leave her husband because of his not being a member, she should also leave the children. Paul declared against such a doctrine, which brings us to the real message of the Section—"little children are holy, being sanctified through the atonement of Jesus Christ." (*Ibid.*, 74:7.)

This passage and others in our modern books of scripture (*Ibid.*, 29:46-48) have cleared away some of the false doctrines that grew up during the period of apostasy regarding the salvation of little children. By revelation to Joseph Smith, children who die before the age of accountability—eight years—are saved in the celestial kingdom through the atonement of Jesus Christ.

## Chapter 2

# THE VISION

### (Section 76:1-49)

Of all the revelations received by the Prophet Joseph Smith concerning man and, particularly, his destiny, probably none other equals Section 76. In discussing the latter-day books of scripture, President Wilford Woodruff made the following statement:

> . . . When I read these solemn, these eternal declarations made through the mouth of Joseph Smith, my heart swells with gratitude and praise to God, my heavenly Father. I consider that the Doctrine and Covenants, our Testament, contains a code of the most solemn, the most Godlike proclamations ever made to the human family. I will refer to the "Vision" alone, as a revelation which gives more light, more truth, and more principle than any revelation contained in any other book we ever read. It makes plain to our understanding our present condition, where we came from, why we are here, and where we are going to. Any man may know through that revelation what his part and condition will be. For all men know what laws they keep, and the laws which men keep here will determine their position hereafter; they will be preserved by those laws and receive the blessings which belong to them. (*Journal of Discourses* 22:146-147.)

On the day this great revelation was received, February 16, 1832, the Prophet wrote his own evaluation of what the Lord had made known to him. The purity of this revelation:

> . . . witnesses the fact that that document is a transcript from the records of the eternal world. The sublimity of the ideas; the purity of the language; the scope for action; the continued duration for completion, in order that the heirs of salvation may confess the Lord and bow the knee; the rewards for faithfulness, and the punishments for sins, are so much beyond

the narrow-mindedness of men, that every honest man is constrained to exclaim: *"It came from God."* (*DHC* 1:252-253.)

The foregoing statements suggest to the reader what is in store for him as he reads Section 76. Surely, when one compares the ideas of the post-death life, which were extant in the Prophet's day and which are also present today, with this revelation and related revelations, one must acknowledge that man's uninspired conceptions of the future life were truly narrow and severe. How, actually, is it possible for man to know of the future except from Him who knows the future of mankind? This whole problem of why man exists, whether or not there is purpose in life, and man's destiny, has piqued man's curiosity over the ages. There comes to most people at some time in their lives serious consideration of these important questions.

### How Received

While Joseph Smith was revising the Bible by inspiration, aided by Sidney Rigdon as scribe, the Lord touched the eyes of their understandings (D&C 76:19) and, in open vision, they beheld the glories of the eternal worlds, and the darkness reigning in the regions of the damned.

The work of "translating" the gospel of John, fifth chapter, verse 29, was the impetus for the inquiry which brought forth the Lord's answer to their query regarding the resurrection of the hosts of mankind, both good and evil, mentioned in that verse. (D&C 76:15.) This revelation brought forth the truth regarding man's destiny. In general, "Christianity" taught that hope for the blessings of heaven was denied those who did not believe in Jesus Christ, and that an everlasting doom awaited the unbeliever, regardless of the opportunity or lack of opportunity for acknowledging Christ. Such a belief would raise questions regarding the resurrection of all people, rather than a favored few. The flood of truth received through this revelation regarding a resurrection for the "evil" as well as the "good" brought the true gospel's message of hope to the world.

An account of some details concerning the receiving of this revelation is given by Elder Philo Dibble, as follows:

The vision which is recorded in the Book of Doctrine and Covenants was given at the house of "Father Johnson," in Hiram, Ohio, and during the time that Joseph and Sidney were in the spirit and saw the heavens open, there were other men in the room, perhaps twelve, among whom I was one during a part of the time—probably two-thirds of the time,—I saw the glory and felt the power, but did not see the vision.

The events and conversation, while they were seeing what is written (and many things were seen and related that are not written), I will relate as minutely as is necessary.

Joseph would, at intervals, say: "What do I see?" as one might say while looking out the window and beholding what all in the room could not see. Then he would relate what he had seen or what he was looking at. Then Sidney replied, "I see the same." Presently Sidney would say "What do I see?" and would repeat what he had seen or was seeing, and Joseph would reply, "I see the same."

This manner of conversation was repeated at short intervals to the end of the vision, and during the whole time not a word was spoken by any other person. Not a sound nor motion made by anyone but Joseph and Sidney, and it seemed to me that they never moved a joint or limb during the time I was there, which I think was over an hour, and to the end of the vision.

Joseph sat firmly and calmly all the time in the midst of a magnificent glory, but Sidney sat limp and pale, apparently as limber as a rag, observing which, Joseph remarked, smilingly, "Sidney is not used to it as I am." (*Juvenile Instructor* 27:303-304.)

## Eternal Progression

The first ten verses of Section 76 reveal the great blessings that are promised the faithful. The revelation opens with the proclamation that beside Jesus Christ there is no Savior. There follows a message of assurance to those who will accept him as their Savior. It is based upon the revealed truth that Jesus is infinite in his knowledge, his ways, and his purposes, which never fail. (Verses 2-3.)

Notwithstanding the Lord God has passed through an earth life as we are now doing, it is true he is the same from eternity to eternity. (Verse 4.) The ultimate destiny of the exalted is eternal progression, reserved for those who "serve me (God) in righteousness and in truth unto the end." (Verse 5.) As President Joseph Fielding Smith has explained:

> . . . From eternity to eternity means from the spirit existence through the probation which we are in, and then back again to the eternal existence which will follow. Surely this is everlasting, for when we receive the resurrection, we will never die. (*Doctrines of Salvation* 1:12.)

For those who are determined to endure faithfully, there is the promise of increased knowledge concerning God's ways, his purposes, even the hidden things of his kingdom. In this life man may learn many of the mysteries of the kingdom. But even so, he learns only an infinitesimal amount of what there is to learn.

## Vision of God and Christ

Following the reason for receiving the "Vision" (D&C 76:11-18), again the eyes of Joseph Smith and Sidney Rigdon were opened to understand God's glory. Latter-day Saints are the most richly blessed people in all the world. No other people have so much support for their belief in God and his purposes. In addition to the grandeur of the First Vision received in the spring of 1820, this revelation stands as a monument of assurance that men in our generation have received a sight-knowledge of Deity. Surrounding the throne of God were concourses of angels, the sanctified who were seen to worship him. Then these brethren recorded what has come to be one of the great testimonies of the latter days:

> And now, after the many testimonies which have been given of him, this is the testimony, last of all, which we give of him: That he lives!
>
> For we saw him, even on the right hand of God; and we heard the voice bearing record that he is the Only Begotten of the Father—
>
> That by him, and through him, and of him, the worlds are and were created, and the inhabitants thereof are begotten sons and daughters unto God. (Verses 22-24.)

Joseph Smith was not alone in receiving this testimony. Two men, seeing the same things, give the lie to some claims that the testimonies of Joseph Smith were false, for, as the scriptures say, "In the mouth of two or three witnesses shall every word be established." (2 Cor. 13:1.)

Many things may be learned from this testimony: (1) Joseph Smith was not a fraud. He subsequently went to a martyr's grave in defense of his knowledge of God and His purposes in the eternities; (2) earth's inhabitants are the begotten sons and daughters of God; (3) not only are we of this earth his children, but also other worlds are inhabited by his spirit offspring; (4) the real basis for the brotherhood of man, which, if accepted, could bring peace and understanding among men, must be founded upon this knowledge; (5) a true understanding of why we should be obedient to gospel principles is discovered in our relationship to God and the purpose of this life.

## The Past

Section 76 reveals the past as well as the future. (Verses 12-13.) Next in vision these brethren beheld the time when Lucifer rebelled against the Father and the Son and thus became the fallen one. (Verses 25-27.) He is known as the one who sought to take the kingdom from the Father and the Son. (D&C 76:28, 29, 36-38.) His purpose is to overcome those who follow righteousness. Lucifer's efforts are expressed in terms of warfare, even assaults from all quarters—he "encompasseth them round about." (Verse 29.) The notion that Satan exists only in the minds of men is denied by this revelation. The testimony of the Prophet and Sidney Rigdon is that Lucifer is a real spirit-being whose influence is felt for evil and whose mission is to despoil, lead into degradation, overcome the saints, and eventually, claim as his own all who will succumb to his enticements. (2 Nephi 28.)

## Satan's Victory—Sons of Perdition

Section 76 (verses 30-39) gives the answer to two questions regarding the class known as the sons of perdition. Who are the sons of perdition? What is their fate? Concerning the first question, the revelation says that they have known God's power and then, knowingly, deny that power. (Verse 31.)

When one is endowed with the Spirit to know the existence of God, having great understanding of the principles of exaltation, and then denies this knowledge, he sins against the Holy Ghost that opened the heavens to him. This constitutes blasphemy against the Holy Ghost and puts the Savior to open shame. Such a person brings upon himself everlasting condemnation. (Verses 31-35.) Jesus said that all sins might be forgiven, including speaking against him, but to sin against the Holy Ghost was unforgivable. (Matt. 12:31-32.) Why is this so? Even though the Son is manifest in a vision or dream, it does not impress the soul as does the testimony of the Holy Ghost. It is Spirit speaking to spirit that gives greater conviction than a vision; therefore, the condemnation is greater. (Smith, Joseph Fielding: *Improvement Era*, July 1955, pp. 494-495.) The Prophet Joseph Smith says of this class:

All sins shall be forgiven, except the sin against the Holy Ghost; for Jesus will save all except the sons of perdition. What must a man do to commit the unpardonable sin? He must receive the Holy Ghost, have the heavens opened unto him, and know God, and then sin against Him. After a man has sinned against the Holy Ghost, there is no repentance for him. He has got to say that the sun does not shine while he sees it; he has got to deny Jesus Christ when the heavens have been opened unto him, and to deny the plan of salvation with his eyes open to the truth of it; and from that time he begins to be an enemy. This is the case with many apostates of the Church of Jesus Christ of Latter-day Saints. (*Teachings of the Prophet Joseph Smith,* page 358.)

It should be noted that when this sin is committed it is done in full knowledge and not in ignorance.

## Fate of Sons of Perdition

As already noted, the sons of perdition will never receive forgiveness in this world nor in the world to come. (D&C 76:34.) It should be remembered that the sons of perdition discussed in this chapter are those sons of God who have come to mortality and not the unembodied spirits who followed Lucifer in the premortal world. Both of these classes—the mortal sons of perdition and the spirit sons of perdition—suffer the second death, which is complete, or total banishment from God's presence forever. (*Teachings of the Prophet Joseph Smith*, page 24.) Adam became spiritually dead when he sinned, as do we, but the spiritual or second death suffered by the sons of perdition, comes by blasphemy against the Holy Ghost. This penalty brings death as to things pertaining unto righteousness. (D&C 29:41.) Repentance is not possible for these persons because they have lost the power of turning from their sins since the atonement of Christ is no longer effective for their salvation.

Due to a misunderstanding of Section 76, verses 38 and 39, some have believed that the sons of perdition will not receive their bodies in the resurrection. This belief does not agree, however, with what the Lord has revealed about the resurrection. (Verses 16-17.) The interpretation of verses 38 and 39 of Section 76 is expressed by President George Q. Cannon:

> A careful reading of these verses, however, and especially of the preceding paragraphs, will show that the Lord does not, in this language, exclude even the sons of perdition from the resurrection. It is plain that the intention is to refer to them explicitly as the only ones on whom the second death shall have any power "for all the rest shall be brought forth by the resurrection of the dead, through the triumph and the glory of the lamb." This excluded class are the only ones on whom the second death shall have any power, and "the only ones who shall not be redeemed in the due time of the Lord after the sufferings of his wrath." (*Juvenile Instructor* 35:123, Feb. 15, 1900.)

## No Glory Kingdom

Latter-day Saints are prone to consider that there will be only three kingdoms after everyone is resurrected, because three degrees of glory are mentioned specifically in the scriptures. (1 Cor. 15:40-42.) The Lord has revealed that the place of the sons of perdition is also known as a kingdom, but it is of no glory. (D&C 88:24.)

The exact conditions of that kingdom are unknown. That it is a place of endless duration is clear. No man living can understand the fate of this class because the Lord has said that only those who are partakers of that punishment will understand its end, width, height, depth, and misery. (*Ibid.*, 76:44-48.) Notice what the Prophet said:

> Say to the brothers Hulet and to all others, that the Lord never authorized them to say that the devil, his angels or the sons of perdition, should ever be restored; for their state of destiny was not revealed to man, is not revealed, nor ever shall be revealed, save to those who are made partakers thereof: Consquently those who teach this doctrine, have not received it of the Spirit of the Lord. Truly Brother Oliver declared it to be

the doctrine of devils. We therefore command that this doctrine be taught no more in Zion. (*DHC* 1:355.)

## Satan's Defeat

Despite the fact that there will be few who will become sons of perdition, Satan will have gained a victory over that number. On the other hand, his victory over the vast host of mankind will be only partial, for all of the rest will find some degree of glory in the kingdoms prepared for them. Many will not have realized their full potential as sons and daughters of God, but only a measure of God's honor. The judgment rendered at the time of the resurrection will be just, for it will be according to one's works. (D&C 19:3; 128:8.)

The creeds of men, developed over the centuries without revelation from heaven, have pictured God as banishing the sinner forever in a hell where punishment is endured eternally. This doom was believed to be incurred by the vast majority of mankind. The notion that there were only "heaven" and "hell," without an intermediate state of preparation for immortality or resurrection, gave rise to a doctrine of salvation incompatible with the teachings of the gospel of Jesus Christ. The saved were wafted into heaven, while the sinner went to hell, lost forever. (*Doctrine and Covenants Commentary*, page 453.)

## The Gospel Plan

In contradiction to this erroneous and unjust concept of God's justice, the message of The Church of Jesus Christ of Latter-day Saints proclaims the doctrine that our Father in heaven is solicitous for all of his children and has provided the means whereby they may receive, if not all, a part of his glory. This however, comes only by their placing themselves in accord with divine laws, either in mortality or in the spirit world. We learn:

And this is the gospel, the glad tidings, which the voice out of the heavens bore record unto us—

That he came into the world, even Jesus, to be crucified for the world, and to bear the sins of the world, and to sanctify the world, and to cleanse it from all unrighteousness;

That through him all might be saved whom the Father had put into his power and made by him;

Who glorifies the Father, and saves all the works of his hands, except those sons of perdition who deny the Son after the Father has revealed him.

Wherefore, he saves all except them. . . . (D&C 76:40-44.)

## Chapter 3

## THE VISION (continued)

### (Section 76:50-119)

Jesus Christ was crucified to save the world from sin. (D&C 76:40-42.) By this redemptive act he made it possible for every man to be resurrected from the grave. (D&C 88:27-32.) In addition to universal salvation—the resurrection—the atonement of Christ provides a spiritual life for the individual who will be obedient to the fulness of the gospel. This spiritual life brings the obedient back into the presence of God from which they were excluded by sin after arriving at the years of accountability. (D&C 29:41; John 5:24; 11:25-26; D&C 68:25-27.)

### Many Mansions

All who have lived, do live, or ever will live upon this earth are the begotten sons and daughters of God. God's solicitude for them is boundless. Through his merciful plan provision is made for the salvation of all men, except the sons of perdition. Contrasted with the erroneous notion that belief in Christ without works is sufficient for a place with God, the plan just mentioned appeals to us as one of justice and mercy. This is more evident when we realize that those who have not had the opportunity to accept Christ may do so in the spirit world. To say, however, that all men are to be saved does not mean that all will receive equal status with God. Considering the differences that exist in knowledge, faith, and righteousness, it would be unjust to save everyone on the same level. In declaring this doctrine, the Prophet Joseph Smith said:

My text is on the resurrection of the dead, which you will find in the 14th Chapter of John (Verses 1-2)—"In my Father's house are many mansions." It should be—"In my Father's kingdom are many kingdoms," in order that ye may be heirs of God and joint-heirs with me. I do not believe the Methodist doctrine of sending honest men and noble-minded men to hell, along with the murderer and the adulterer. . . . But I have an order of things to save the poor fellows at any rate, and get them saved; for I will send men to preach to them in prison and save them if I can.

There are mansions for those who obey a celestial law, and there are other mansions for those who come short of the law, every man in his own order. There is baptism, etc. for those to exercise who are alive, and baptism for the dead who die without the knowledge of the Gospel. (*DHC* 6:365.)

We have just learned that Jesus taught that there are gradations in "heaven." Paul also received a vision of the kingdoms of glory for resurrected man. (1 Cor. 15:40-41.)

The principle of reward and punishment is given in this New Testament scripture: "He which soweth sparingly shall reap also sparingly; and he which soweth bountifully shall reap also bountifully." (2 Cor. 9:6.)

## Celestial Kingdom

In verses 50 through 53 of Section 76, the Lord reveals those who are eligible to receive the highest heaven mentioned in the scriptures. In the words of Joseph Smith, entrance into the celestial kingdom is possible for those who follow these instructions:

. . . I will proceed to tell you what the Lord requires of all people, high and low, rich and poor, male and female, ministers and people, professors of religion and non-professors, in order that they may enjoy the Holy Spirit of God to a fulness and escape the judgments of God, which are almost ready to burst upon the nations of the earth. Repent of all your sins, and be baptized in water for the remission of them, in the name of the Father, and of the Son, and of the Holy Ghost, and receive the ordinance of the laying on of the hands of him who is ordained and sealed unto this power, that ye may receive the Holy Spirit of God; and this is according to the Holy Scriptures, and the Book of Mormon; and the only way that man can enter into the celestial kingdom. These are the requirements of the new covenant, or first principles of the Gospel of Christ; then "Add to your faith, virtue; and to virtue, knowledge; and to knowledge, temperance; and to temperance, patience; and to patience, godliness; and to godliness, brotherly kindness; and to brotherly kindness, charity [or love]; for if these things be in you, and abound, they make you that ye shall neither be barren nor unfruitful, in the knowledge of our Lord Jesus Christ." (*DHC* 1:314-315. See also II Peter 1:5-8.)

## Celestial Exaltation

As there are three kingdoms of glory—celestial, terrestrial, and telestial—so there are many gradations or levels of reward within these great heavens. In the celestial kingdom there are three heavens or degrees. The Lord has told us that in order for us to receive the highest of these, we must meet all of the requirements of the gospel.

> In the celestial glory there are three heavens or degrees;
>
> And in order to obtain the highest, a man must enter into this order of the priesthood [meaning the new and everlasting covenant of marriage];
>
> And if he does not, he cannot obtain it.
>
> He may enter into the other, but that is the end of his kingdom; he cannot have an increase. (D&C 131:1-4.)

The highest of these three degrees in the celestial kingdom is attained by those who receive exaltation. (D&C 132:21-24.) In addition to obedience to the first principles of the gospel, noted above in the scriptures and the Prophet's statement, one must enter into temple marriage (the new and everlasting covenant of marriage), remain just and true, and receive the seal of the Holy Ghost. (D&C 132:19.) This truth mentioned by Paul (1 Cor. 11:11) emphasizes the necessity that every Latter-day Saint understand the importance of temple marriage, the sealing of husband and wife by the authority of the Holy Priesthood. Without this ordinance, though one is married by the civil law, there is no exaltation.

## All Things Are Theirs

Section 76 continues the description of the celestial kingdom by indicating that there will be those in that glory who belong to the Church of the Firstborn. Keeping in mind that this refers to man's condition after the resurrection and not in this life, we learn that all things are given to the obedient by the Father. They become priests and kings, having received a fulness of the Father's glory as the Church of the Firstborn. To enter into the preparations for this glory, the Melchizedek Priesthood is necessary for the male and blessings of the Priesthood are received by his faithful wife in the temple marriage. When "all things" are bestowed upon them, they become gods, even the sons of God, joint-heirs with Christ. (D&C 76:54-61; 84:35-38; Romans 8:16-17.)

## Exaltation - the Goal

Latter-day Saints are prone to refer to the attainment of the celestial kingdom as the highest objective available in the gospel plan. From the foregoing discussion of eternal life, it should be evident that entrance in the celestial kingdom will not necessarily bring a fulness of powers and glory. If, in using the term celestial glory or kingdom, is meant exaltation in that kingdom, then that is the highest objective. On the other hand, if one ignores that there are different degrees in the celestial kingdom and the highest "heaven" is possible only by obedience to all of the commandments, including temple marriage and its covenants, the expression is misleading.

## Celestial Glory

All who receive the celestial kingdom receive celestial glory, for they are in the presence of God and Christ forever. (D&C 76:62.) These are they who shall come with the Christ at his coming and will receive the first resurrection. Their bodies are celestial, like God's body, compared with the sun in brightness. (Verses 63-70.)

Exaltation in that kingdom is given to all who will meet the requirements—keeping all the commandments. Positions in the Church do not necessarily qualify one for this great blessing. President George Albert Smith expressed it this way:

> One of the beautiful things to me in the Gospel of Jesus Christ is that it brings us all to a common level. It is not necessary for a man to be a president of a stake, or a member of the Quorum of the Twelve, in order to attain a high place in the celestial kingdom. The humblest member of the Church, if he keeps the commandments of God, will obtain an exaltation just as much as any other man in the celestial kingdom. The beauty of the Gospel of Jesus Christ is that it makes us all equal in as far as we keep the commandments of the Lord. In as far as we observe to keep the laws of the Church we have equal opportunities for exaltation. As we develop faith and righteousness our light is made to shine as a guide and blessing to those with whom we mingle. (*Conference Report*, October 1933, p. 25.)

## Opportunity for All

One of the most informative revelations received by the Prophet Joseph Smith was given in the Kirtland Temple on January 21, 1836. The Prophet said that he saw the blazing throne of God in the celestial kingdom, which was like circling flames of fire. There he saw some who had not received an opportunity to receive the gospel in this life, and the explanation of their being in that kingdom. A "voice" declared that all who died without an opportunity to know the gospel and accept it while on the earth will have the privilege in the spirit world.

If they would have received the gospel while on the earth, given the opportunity, they will be heirs of the celestial kingdom upon acceptance of it in the spirit world. The great truth is proclaimed that the Lord "will judge all men according to their works, according to the desire of their hearts." (*DHC* 2:380-381.)

## According to Works

To every man there is given opportunity. But all men will not abide the full law that will bring the greatest blessing. Some will have lost the opportunity for exaltation and the celestial kingdom because they did not abide the law to which they were responsible in mortality. The merciful plan of the Father is described by Joseph Smith as follows:

> But while one portion of the human race is judging and condemning the other without mercy, the Great Parent of the universe looks upon the whole of the human family with a fatherly care and paternal regard; He views them as His offspring, and without any of those contracted feelings that influence the children of men, causes "His sun to rise on the evil and on the good, and sendeth rain on the just and on the unjust." He holds the reins of judgment in His hands; He is a wise Lawgiver, and will judge all men, not according to the narrow, contracted notions of men, but, "according to the deeds done in the body whether they be good or evil," or whether these deeds were done in England, America, Spain, Turkey, or India. He will judge them, "not according to what they have not, but according to what they have," those who have lived without law, will be judged without law, and those who have a law, will be judged by that law. We need not doubt the wisdom and intelligence of the great Jehovah; He will award judgment or mercy to all nations according to their several deserts, their means of obtaining intelligence, the laws by which they are governed, the facilities afforded them of obtaining correct information, and His inscrutable designs in relation to the human family; and when the designs of God shall be made manifest, and the curtain of futurity be withdrawn, we shall all of us eventually have to confess that the Judge of all the earth has done right. (*DHC* 4:595-596.)

## Salvation of Children

In the same vision in the Kirtland Temple, revealing an opportunity for everyone to hear the gospel either in this life or in the spirit world, the "voice" declared the following to Joseph Smith:

> And I also behold that all children who die before they arrive at the years of accountability, are saved in the celestial kingdom of heaven. (*DHC* 2:381.)

This truth is in harmony with and gives meaning to verse 67 of Section 76, wherein it is given that those in the celestial kingdom will constitute "an innumerable company of angels."

## Terrestrial Kingdom

The next vision seen by Joseph Smith and Sidney Rigdon was that of the terrestrial kingdom. Differing from the celestial kingdom as the moon differs in glory from the sun, those of this kingdom will also consist of an innumerable host. (D&C 76:91-92, 96-98, 71.) Those of the terrestrial kingdom are described as "honorable men of the earth, who were blinded by the craftiness of men." They lived the law to which they were responsible on the earth, but they did not receive the fulness on the earth nor in the spirit world. In this kingdom there will also be those who "died without the law." (D&C 76:72-75.)

In addition to those mentioned, there will be some Latter-day Saints who were honorable in their lives, but who were indifferent to the fulness of the truth. Expressed in the language of the revelation, they were "not valiant in the testimony of Jesus; wherefore, they obtain not the crown over the kingdom of our God." (D&C 76:79.) It was their privilege to obtain that crown, but the spirit of apathy toward the work of the Lord gained ascendancy in their lives.

Terrestrial beings will have the presence of Jesus Christ. (D&C 76:77.) In the absence of specific scriptural statement it is reasonable to believe that there are degrees within the terrestrial and also that advancement within that kingdom is possible. (James E. Talmage, *Articles of Faith*, p. 409.)

## Telestial Kingdom

In the lowest of the three degrees of glory—the telestial—there will be innumerable gradations or degrees. (D&C 76:98; 1 Cor. 15:41.) In this kingdom will be assigned those who are described as the wicked of the earth—liars, sorcerers, adulterers. They are those who reject the gospel and the testimony of Jesus Christ and the prophets. They are the followers of man-made systems, who persist in their abominable ways. (D&C 76:99-106, 81-85.) It is these who will come from their graves in the first part of the second or general resurrection at the end of the millennium.

Although coming under this condemnation, they have been cleansed in the spirit world and are prepared to enter a glory "which surpasseth all understanding." (Verse 89.) In their kingdom they will receive the Holy Spirit through the ministry of terrestrial beings and of angels appointed to minister in the telestial world. (Verses 86, 88.) The number who will inherit this glory will be as numerous as the sand upon the seashore. (Verse 109.)

The specific ordinances, if there be such, to enter into the telestial and terrestrial kingdoms have not been revealed. The initiatory ordinances of water baptism and the laying on of hands for the gift of the Holy Ghost, and other ordinances known to the Latter-day Saint, are for the celestial kingdom only.

## Greatness of the Gospel

An example of the magnanimity of the gospel is given in the case of the terrestrial beings, some of whom are honorable "Christians" who believe that the greatest reward of obedience is to be in the presence of Christ. If honorable, they will receive their present desire because they live only that law which will give them the terrestrial glory. On the other hand, those enlightened "Christians" who did not live their law, will find themselves in the telestial kingdom; yet the "unenlightened" heathens living their law will be given the chance to accept the terrestrial law. If they do, then their place of future abode will be the terrestrial kingdom.

When reference is made to these groups of terrestrials and telestials, it should be remembered that the Lord will give to all men an opportunity to hear the gospel of Jesus Christ. The chance for celestial glory is open to all. (D&C 1:2; 128:5.)

## Conclusion

It is very gratifying to us who desire the salvation of mankind, and whose work it is to labor for their uplifting, who have been specially called of God and appointed to work under the Captain of our salvation for the redemption of the whole human race, to know by the revelations of God that the time will come, in some future state of existence if not in this, when every soul that can be redeemed will be brought out of darkness and sorrow, and hell, and death, and be placed where they can enjoy existence, to glorify God and obey His commandments. . . . The laws of God are eternal; they are forever and ever; they are inflexible; and it is only by obedience to law that exaltation can be secured. In this condition we are learning to be obedient to law—such law as God has revealed; also to the wholesome rules and regulations that are established in the governments under which we may live. (Charles W. Penrose, *Conference Report,* April 1901, pp. 42-43.)

## Chapter 4

# THE BOOK OF REVELATION

## (Section 77)

One of the Bible books little understood is the Book of Revelation in the New Testament. Great numbers of books have been written attempting to explain its symbols. While the Prophet was revising the Bible with the aid of Sidney Rigdon as scribe, the Lord revealed the meaning of some difficult passages in that book. Although on one occasion Joseph Smith said the Book of Revelation was one of the plainest that God caused to be written (*DHC* 5:324), he included some comments in Section 77 of the Doctrine and Covenants on certain passages in eight of the twenty-two chapters of that book.

### General Information

The Book of Revelation is also known as the Apocalypse, a Greek word meaning "to reveal the future." The author, John the apostle, describes this revelation as telling of "things which must shortly come to pass." (Rev. 1:1; see also Rev. 1:19; 4:1.) The revelation is addressed to seven churches of the Roman province of Asia: Ephesus, Smyrna, Pergamum, Thyatira, Sardis, Philadelphia, and Laodicea. (Rev. 1:4, 11.) John relates that the visions of the book were received when he was on the island of Patmos, which lies off the southwest coast of Asia Minor. At this time the apostle had been banished during a period of Roman persecution against the Christians.

Latter-day Saint writers have generally interpreted the seven churches, to whom the Revelation is specifically addressed because of their spiritual condition, as the remaining branches of the Church which were worthy of revelation; for the Church at large had gone into a state of apostasy. Elder James E. Talmage writes on this point, as follows:

During the banishment of John the Revelator on the isle of Patmos, when nearly all the apostles had been taken from the earth, many of them having suffered martyrdom, the apostasy was so wide-spread that only seven "churches," i.e. branches of the Church, remained in such condition as to be considered deserving of the special communication John was instructed to give. In a marvelous vision he beheld the seven churches typified by seven golden candlesticks, with the stars in his hand, stood "one like unto the Son of Man."

The church at Ephesus was approved for its good works, specifically for its rejection of the Nicolaitan heresies; nevertheless reproof was administered for disaffection and neglect, thus: —"thou hast left thy first love. Remember therefore from whence thou art fallen, and repent and do the first works; or else I will come unto thee quickly, and will remove thy candlestick out of his place, except thou repent." [Rev. 2:4, 5.]

To the church at Pergamos John was commanded to write, denouncing the false doctrines of certain sects and teachers, "which thing I hate" said the Lord. The church of the Laodiceans was denounced as "lukewarm," "neither hot nor cold," and as priding itself as rich and not in need, whereas it was in reality "wretched, and miserable, and poor, and blind, and naked." (Rev. 3:17.)

The foregoing scriptures are ample as proof that even before the ancient apostles had finished their earthly ministry, apostasy was growing apace. (*The Great Apostasy,* 1953 edition, pp. 44-45.)

## Section 77—A Key to Interpretation

The great confusion existing in the Christian world regarding the Book of Revelation is due to the loss of the key to interpret it. In an informative observation on this point, the *Doctrine and Covenants Commentary* (page 478) brings out that it will never be understood if one assumes that there has not been an apostasy and a restoration of the true church. This authoritative source continues:

But this Revelation (Section 77) is not a complete interpretation of the book. It is a key. A key is a very small part of the house. It unlocks the door through which an entrance may be gained, but after the key has been turned the searcher for treasure must find it for himself. It is like entering a museum in which the students must find out for themselves what they desire to know. The sources of information are there. (*Ibid.*)

## Purpose

The subject matter which follows is designed to point out many significant truths from Section 77 which are not known to the world. It is not the purpose of this discussion to attempt an analysis of the entire Book of Revelation. Obviously, the most important lessons to be learned are those which are founded upon the words of the prophets of this dispensation.

Repeatedly, the elders of the Church have been warned against delving into what are known as scriptural mysteries, meaning those things which the Lord has not clearly made known. Upon this point the Prophet Joseph Smith has said:

I make this broad declaration, that whenever God gives a vision of an image, or beast, or figure of any kind, He always holds Himself responsible to give a revelation or interpretation of the meaning thereof, otherwise we are not responsible or accountable for our belief in it. Don't be afraid of being damned for not knowing the meaning of a vision or figure, if God has not given a revelation or the interpretation of the subject. (*DHC* 5:343.)

Again from the Prophet:

Oh, ye elders of Israel, harken to my voice; and when you are sent into the world to preach, tell those things you are sent to tell; preach and cry aloud, "Repent ye, for the kingdom of heaven is at hand; repent and believe the Gospel." Declare the first principles, and let mysteries alone, lest ye be overthrown. Never meddle with the visions of beasts and subjects you do not understand. (*Ibid.*, p. 344.)

It is declared "The Book of Revelation is one of the grandest books in sacred literature, and the Lord clearly designs that the Saints should become familiar with it. Else, why this Revelation in the Doctrine and Covenants?" (*Doctrine and Covenants Commentary*, p. 478.)

## The Earth

Latter-day Saints believe that the creation of the earth was purposeful in that it was to be the home for man. In an earlier revelation, the Lord made known that marriage is designed to bring the spirit sons and daughters of God to earth where they may continue their eternal advancement. By doing so "the earth might answer the end of its creation." (D&C 49:16.)

In answer to the question: "What is the sea of glass?" of Revelation 4:6, the Prophet answered that: "It is the earth, in its sanctified, immortal and eternal state." (D&C 77:1.) This will be the condition of the earth when final judgment has been rendered to its inhabitants, and it becomes the abiding place of celestial beings. In this condition another revelation declares that it will be as a Urim and Thummim to enable its occupants to know of kingdoms inferior to the celestial state. (D&C 130:9.) Before this time, however, the earth will die and undergo a change equivalent to the resurrection. (D&C 88:25-26.) These thoughts suggest a belief of the Latter-day Saint that the earth is a living organism. (Moses 7:48-49.)

There are three conditions of the earth spoken of in the inspired writings,—the present, in which everything pertaining to it must go through a change which we call death; the millennial condition, in which it will be sanctified for the residence of purer intelligences, some mortal and some immortal; and the celestial condition, spoken of in the twenty-first and twenty-second chapters of Revelation, which will be one of immortality and eternal life. (James E. Talmage, *Articles of Faith,* p. 517.)

### Man and Animal

In the second verse of Section 77 a question is raised relative to the four beasts spoken of in Revelation 4:6. (See *Doctrine and Covenants Commentary*, p. 472 for further information.) After saying that these are figurative expressions to describe heaven and the happiness of man, beasts, and the fowls of the air, the Prophet gives some light on the spirit of man and animal. A salient thought is expressed in the observation that the temporal has its spiritual counterpart. This gives background for the truth that "the spirit of man [is] in the likeness of his person, as also the spirit of the beast, and every other creature which God has created." As stated in an earlier chapter, Chapter 2, the truth is that not only spirit-man existed before mortal birth, but also the rest of God's creation, including vegetation, was spirit. (Moses 3:5.) As the First Presidency, composed of Presidents Joseph F. Smith, John R. Winder, and Anthon H. Lund wrote:

> By His almighty power He organized the earth, and all that it contains from spirit and element, which exist co-eternally with Himself. He formed every plant that grows, and every animal that breathes, each after its own kind, spiritually and temporally —"that which is spiritual being in the likeness of that which is temporal and that which is temporal in the likeness of that which is spiritual." (D&C 77:2.) He made the tadpole and the ape, and the lion and the elephant; but He did not make them in His own image, nor endow them with Godlike reason and intelligence. (*Improvement Era,* 13:81, November 1909.)

This official statement denounces the theory that man has ascended from the lower forms of animals as a doctrine that Latter-day Saints cannot accept.

We are informed that "the whole animal creation will be perfected and perpetuated in the Hereafter, each class in its 'distinct order or sphere,' and will enjoy 'eternal felicity.' That fact has been made plain in this dispensation." (First Presidency, *Improvement Era,*

13:81; D&C 77:3-4.) This statement clearly affirms that animal and plant creation will be resurrected. (D&C 29:23-25.)

## Key to History

It is plain that in verses 6 and 7 of Section 77, concerning the book with its seven seals, which John saw, there is revealed the period of the earth's temporal existence since the fall of Adam. (*Doctrine and Covenants Commentary*, p. 474.)

If one determined the meaning of each of the figures symbolizing these seals as the various horses, the martyrs, etc., mentioned in chapter 6 of the Book of Revelation, he would recognize the general secular history of the earth. The prophetic history is revealed in chapters 12 through 14, with miscellaneous information in the remaining part of the book.

## Saturday Night of Time

Four angels are spoken of in Revelation 7:1 (D&C 77:8) that have power to save and to destroy life. President Joseph Fielding Smith observes that these four angels seem to fit the description of those mentioned in the parable of the wheat and the tares, and he quotes President Wilford Woodruff as saying that these powers are already being manifest on the earth. Furthermore, these messengers are some who have the power of committing the gospel to the earth. (Joseph Fielding Smith: *Church History and Modern Revelation*, 1:300-301.)

In the twelfth verse of Section 77, the seven thousand years as time periods of the earth's mortality are again mentioned. Elder Orson F. Whitney has emphasized what many other Latter-day prophets have said concerning the period in which we live—these are the last days that are drawing near to the second coming of Christ.

The symbolism of the Sabbath, and the symbolism of other days as well, is plainly indicated in the writings of Joseph Smith. In one place he says—or the Lord says through him: "All things have their likeness and are made to bear record of me." We need not be surprised, therefore, to find among the Prophet's teaching this—I quote from his Key to the Apocalypse. (77:6, 12.)

"What are we to understand by the book which John saw, which was sealed on the back with seven seals?

"We are to understand that it contains the revealed will, mysteries, and the works of God; the hidden things of his economy concerning this earth during the seven thousand years of its continuance, or its temporal existence.

"What are we to understand by the sounding of the trumpets, mentioned in the 8th chapter of Revelation?

"We are to understand that as God made the world in six days, and on the seventh day he finished his work, and sanctified it, and also formed man out of the dust of the earth, even so, in the beginning of the seventh thousand years will the Lord God sanctify the earth, and complete the salvation of man, and judge all things, and shall redeem all things, except that which he hath not put into his power, when he shall have sealed all things, unto the end of all things; and the sounding of the trumpets of the seven angels are the preparing and finishing of his work, in the beginning of the seventh thousand years—the preparing of the way before the time of his coming."

The "days" here referred to were not ordinary days of twenty-four hours each, based upon earth's diurnal revolutions. He who "made the world" before placing man upon it, had not then appointed unto Adam His reckoning. (Abraham 5:13.) They were not man's days, but God's days, each having a duration of a thousand years.

"The book which John saw" represented the real history of the world—what the eye of God has seen, what the recording angel has written; and the seven thousand years, corresponding to the seven seals of the Apocalyptic volume, are as seven great days during which Mother Earth will fulfill her mortal mission, laboring six days and resting upon the seventh, her period of sanctification. These seven days do not include the period of our planet's creation and preparation as a dwelling place for man. They are limited to Earth's "temporal existence," that is, to Time, considered as distinct from Eternity.

The Prophet's translation of the Book of Abraham explains that those greater days are "after the time" or according to the reckoning of Kolob, a mighty governing planet nearest the Celestial Throne, a planet revolving once in a thousand years. (Abraham 3:4.) This period, then, is a day upon Kolob. . . .

According to received chronology—admittedly imperfect, yet approximately correct—four thousand years, or four of the seven great days given to this planet as the period of its "temporal existence," had passed before Christ was crucified; while nearly two thousand years have gone by since. Consequently, Earth's long week is now drawing to a close, and we stand at the present moment in the Saturday Evening of Time, or near the end of the sixth day of human history. Is it not a time for thought, a season for solemn meditation? Morning will break upon the Millennium, the thousand years of peace, the Sabbath of the World! (*Saturday Night Thoughts,* pp. 10-12.)

## Special Missionaries

In verse 11 of Section 77, we are told there will be 144,000 high priests selected from the various tribes of Israel to administer the everlasting gospel for those who will come into the Church of the Firstborn. The Prophet Joseph Smith, in speaking of the salvation of the dead, said:

I am going on in my progress for eternal life. It is not only necessary that you should be baptized for your dead, but you will have to go through all the ordinances for them, the same as you have gone through to save yourselves. There will be 144,000 saviors on Mount Zion, and with them an innumerable host that no man can number. Oh! I beseech you to go forward, go forward and make your calling and your election sure. (*DHC* 6:365.)

## Cleansing of the Earth

That the Lord has on many occasions inspired his prophets to speak of our times and the future in connection with the cleansing of the earth is very well known. (D&C 5:16-20; 43:18-29; 63:32-37.) The ninth chapter of the Book of Revelation (D&C 77:13) reveals some instruments of destruction that will cleanse the earth. Of these events President Joseph Fielding Smith has written:

These terrible events pictured in the ninth chapter of Revelation are now being fulfilled. Part of this we have witnessed, the rest will shortly come to pass. This is, and will be, in the nature of the cleansing process to prepare the earth and its inhabitants, those who will be fortunate enough to remain, for the coming of our Savior when he shall commence his reign for a thousand years upon the earth. The reading of this chapter with the knowledge that the time of its fulfillment is at hand, should cause all men some thoughtful sober thinking. (*Church History and Modern Revelation,* Vol. I, p. 303.)

## John's Mission

In Section 77, verse 14, we are told that the little book which was eaten by John, found in Revelation 10:8-11, is interpreted to be a mission for him to gather the tribes of Israel. This was the beginning of the new dispensation of the gospel after the period of apostasy. (*Doctrine and Covenants Commentary*, pp. 476-477.) John the Revelator is presently engaged in this mission. In the conference of the Church of June 1831, it is related that:

. . . The Spirit of the Lord fell upon Joseph in an unusual manner, and he prophesied that John the Revelator was then among the Ten Tribes of Israel who had been led away by Shalmaneser, king of Assyria, to prepare them for their return from their long dispersion, to again possess the land of their father. (*DHC* 1:176, footnote.)

## Two Witnesses

The final verse in Section 77 refers to Revelation, chapter 11, where the two prophets raised up to the Jewish nation in the last days will have power to prevent the destruction of the Jewish people by nations against Jerusalem. In the process, however, these prophets will have been overcome themselves and then by the power of God restored to life. This episode yet to be enacted in the land of Jerusalem will be mentioned again in a subsequent chapter.

## Chapter 5

# THE CHURCH INDEPENDENT

### (Sections 78, 83)

It will be remembered that the Prophet Joseph Smith, aided by Sidney Rigdon as scribe, was engaged in the revision of the Bible when he received the revelation known as the "Vision." After this glorious revelation was received, the Prophet continued his work on the Bible while residing in Hiram, Ohio. The interest of the saints concerning the building of Zion upon the American Continent continued unabated. Although the first revelation concerning the laws that would apply in the building up of Zion was received about thirteen months before this time, it was necessary to reemphasize and implement the instructions concerning the fundamental law of consecration, one of the major laws to bring Zion to fruition. Section 78 was received in response to the need to point up further the importance of this law in the establishing of Zion. Closely associated with this objective was the corollary objective of independence of the Church in this world.

In the first two verses of Section 78, the assembled members of the Melchizedek Priesthood, because of their inquiry about the law of consecration (sometimes called the "United Order"), were told that they should receive words of wisdom for their salvation in this order.

Beginning with this revelation and in a number of Sections which follow, persons, places, and objects are given unusual names. The superscription of Section 78 informs us that it was undesirable at that time that this information be known. Later, as in our present edition of the Doctrine and Covenants, both names are given.

## Background

In February 1831, the revelation known as the "Law" (Section 42) was given that the saints might know how to build Zion upon the earth. In this revelation and subsequent instruction, the Lord said that the saint should consecrate his belongings for the common good of all the members of the Church in that order. In surrendering his possessions by legal title, it was said that each person should receive a stewardship to be worked by the individual for himself, his family, his circumstances, wants, and needs. The residues or surpluses from the stewardship were to be set aside for many purposes.

> And again, if there shall be properties in the hands of the church or any individuals of it, more than is necessary for their support after this first consecration, which is a residue to be consecrated unto the bishop, it shall be kept to administer to those who have not, from time to time, that every man who has need may be amply supplied and receive according to his wants.
>
> Therefore, the residue shall be kept in my storehouse, to administer to the poor and the needy, as shall be appointed by the high council of the church, and the bishop and his council;
>
> And for the purpose of purchasing lands for the public benefit of the church, and building houses of worship, and building up of the New Jerusalem which is hereafter to be revealed. (D&C 42:33-35.)

On April 30, 1832, while the Prophet was in council with some of the brethren in Missouri, he received a revelation which answered the questions of some concerning widows and orphans under the law of consecration. (Section 83.) Basic principles of responsibility are laid down in Section 83. The husband is to provide for his wife and children. With the loss of one parent the other parent is responsible for the care of the children. (Verses 2, 4.) In the event that the husband and father is dead, the Church provides for the widow and children out of the storehouse. (Verse 6.) It was also provided that the poor could receive inheritances from the storehouse. Another principle of importance which is clarified in this revelation is that when children reach a time when they need an inheritance and the parents are unable to provide it from their own inheritance, the Church may provide an inheritance for the children. (Verse 5.) Worthiness is a standard that also determines who should receive from the Church.

### Equality

With the foregoing purposes and principles of the law of consecration set forth, the Lord said that when these purposes were put into operation, a wonderful blessing would come to the individual and to the Church. Equality in temporal things would serve to enhance the glory of God through man's salvation.

> That you may be equal in the bonds of heavenly things, yea, and earthly things also, for the obtaining of heavenly things.
>
> For if ye are not equal in earthly things ye cannot be equal in obtaining heavenly things;
>
> For if you will that I give unto you a place in the celestial world, you must prepare yourselves by doing the things which I have commanded you and required of you.
>
> And now, verily thus saith the Lord, it is expedient that all things be done unto my glory, by you who are joined together in this order. (D&C 78:5-8.)

The equality of temporal goods here does not mean that everyone has exactly the same possessions, but sufficient for his purpose according to his wants and needs. Concerning this President J. Reuben Clark, Jr., said:

> . . . Obviously, this is not a case of "dead-level" equality. It is "equality" that will vary as much as the man's circumstances, his family, his wants and needs, may vary. (*Conference Report*, October 4, 1942, p. 55.)

President Brigham Young said the plan of the gospel envisions a oneness consisting of the temporal as well as the spiritual. (*Journal of Discourses* 17:40.)

The Lord had said that the world was in sin because some possessed that which was above others. (D&C 49:20.) Fundamental to the law of consecration is the principle that everything belongs to the Lord; therefore, whatever one possesses may be surrendered if called for to build up Zion. (*Ibid.*, 104:14-17, 54-57.) With this and other principles in mind, Elder John A. Widtsoe has given us some basic principles of the United Order:

Its objective was to provide every man who is willing to work with the necessities and the comforts of life, thus abolishing poverty from the earth. It was to be a cooperative plan but directly opposed to modern communism, since it recognized man as a free agent, respected the rights of private property, and preserved and encouraged individual initiative. The United Order thus established rests upon four basic principles.

First, the earth is the Lord's. Men are only stewards of their possessions. All that man has should be used therefore in accordance with the Lord's expressed will.

Second, all men are children of God—of a divine family. Therefore, the Lord requires that they must help one another as needs arise, provided that he who will not work shall have no claim upon his brother.

Third, every man must be respected as a free agent. He may enter the order at his pleasure. Once in the order, he must be allowed to use, fully, and as he pleases, any properties placed in his hands. He may leave the order at his pleasure.

Fourth, the government of the order is vested in a central agency, sustained by the members of the order, presided over by the bishop, his counselors, and such helpers as may be needed. This central agency would have power to adjust the disputes normally arising among strongly individualized human beings. (*Joseph Smith,* pp. 192-93.)

## For My Glory

When men work out their own salvation it redounds to the glory of God. (Moses 1:39.) The elders named in verse 9 of Section 78 were to follow the instruction to visit the brethren in Zion (Missouri) and sit in council with them on matters relating to the United Order. They were reminded of Satan's efforts to blind the eyes of those who are under covenant to follow the commandments. When a person enters into an agreement with the Lord under the new and everlasting covenant (the gospel or any of its covenants, such as the law of consecration), he is expected to comply with all aspects of that covenant. Rewards or blessings for observance of the law may be expected by those who observe the full requirements. On the other hand, as in the case of these brethren, disobedience brings loss of calling, as well as being turned over to the buffetings of Satan. (Verse 12.)

## The Church Independent

All blessings and promises of the Lord are fulfilled upon obedience to the principles upon which they are predicated. In 1832, the Lord promised the saints that by obedience to the law of consecration the Church would become independent above all other creatures of the earth. (D&C 78:13-14.) Although the members of that early period did not obey the covenant of consecration, the promise is still in effect. The Church is today a light unto the world, and it will continue to be a standard for the nations. (*Ibid.*, 115:4-6.) When the Lord's organization becomes the power in the world it is destined to be, it will then be independent from all other organizations, whether political, financial, or industrial. (*Doctrine and Covenants Commentary*, p. 482.) In connection with these ideas and, particularly, the place of the Church as a light for the world, Elder John A. Widtsoe said:

> Some day the world under stern necessity will adopt and practice the economic program known to the Church as the United Order—but in a manner wholly different from Socialism or Communism. (*Joseph Smith*, p. 197.)

One should remember that the Lord has commanded us to be united as a people that salvation may be ours and that his work may make the necessary progress for the betterment of mankind. Such unified action would contribute to the prophesied independence of the Church.

The member of the Church has covenanted to work for the advancement of the Church members individually and the Church as an organization. Agreeable to this truth, Elder Harold B. Lee, of the Council of the Twelve, has given us some ways in which the Latter-day Saint may fulfill this responsibility:

> . . . If we would be united in paying our fasting offerings and observing the law of the fast as fully as the Lord has taught it, and if we were united in carrying out the principles of the welfare program as they have been given to us by our leaders today, we would be free from want and distress and would be able fully to care for our own. . . .
>
> If we were fully united as a people in our missionary work, we would rapidly hasten the day when the gospel would be preached to all people without and within the boundaries of the organized stakes of Zion. . . .
>
> If we were fully united in keeping the law of sacrifice and paying our tithes as we have been schooled today, we would have sufficient to build our temples, our chapels, our schools of learning. . . .
>
> If we were united as a people in electing honorable men to high places in our civil government, regardless of the political party with which we have affiliation, we would be able to safeguard our communities and to preserve law and order among us. . . .
>
> If we were united in safeguarding our youth from promiscuous associations that foster marriages out of the Church and out of the temples, by having socials and recreations as a united people, as has been the practice from our pioneer days, we would be building all Latter-day Saint homes on a sure and happy foundation. . . .
>
> If we were united in safeguarding the Church from false doctrines and error and in standing as watchmen upon the tower as teachers and leaders in watching over the Church, then we would be free from these things that cause many to stumble and fall and lose their faith. . . .
>
> If we were united in our temple work and in our genealogical research work, we would not be satisfied with the present temples only, but we would have sufficient work for temples yet

to come, to the unlocking of the doors of opportunity to those beyond who are our own kin, and thus ourselves become saviors on Mount Zion. . . . (*Conference Report,* April 1950, pp. 96-97.)

To the degree that the saints are a united people, the general purposes of the Lord will be fulfilled. But, as far as the individual is concerned, there cannot be salvation in its highest sense if he is not united with the onward, progressive movement of the Church as an organization.

## Tribulation

In the 1830's the Saints were warned of coming tribulation before the day of complete fulfillment of the promises. (D&C 58:1-5; 78:14.) The world has yet many tribulations to endure because, in the main, it will not give heed to the words of the living prophets. (D&C 45:25-33.) Preparation for the future in terms of economic welfare has been the counsel of the General Authorities for many years. In the 1941 general conference Elder Harold B. Lee of the Council of the Twelve said:

. . . A brief review of the past instruction of our leaders should only serve to warn the disobedient and to encourage the obedient to continue faithful. Today listen to the words of President Wilford Woodruff that he spoke more than forty years ago:

"So far as temporal matters are concerned, we have got to go to work and provide for ourselves. The day will come when you will see the necessity for making your own shoes and clothing, raising your own food, and uniting together to carry out the purposes of the Lord. We will be preserved in the mountains of Israel in the day of God's judgment."

I therefore say to you, my brethren and sisters, prepare for that which is to come. (*Conference Report,* October 1941, p. 114.)

## Adam, Our Prince

When the Church becomes independent from all other creatures in the world through the providence of God, then those who have endeavored by preparation for that event shall be made rulers over many kingdoms. Exaltation in the celestial kingdom gives rulership over kingdoms and posterity. (D&C 78:14-15.) This message serves as an introduction to some information regarding Adam, the progenitor of the human race. This is the first time in the modern revelations where Adam-ondi-Ahman is mentioned. (*Doctrine and Covenants Commentary*, pp. 482-83.) This is the place where Adam met with his posterity and gave them a patriarchal blessing. (D&C 107:53-57.) Adam-ondi-Ahman is located north of Jackson County in Daviess County, Missouri.

> . . . the Holy One of Zion, who hath established the foundations of Adam-ondi-Ahman;
>
> Who hath appointed Michael your prince, and established his feet, and set him upon high, and given unto him the keys of salvation under the counsel and direction of the Holy One, who is without beginning of days or end of life. (D&C 78:15-16.)

These verses give us an understanding of the position that Adam holds in Latter-day Saint belief. Adam is the prince over all of his posterity and as such will preside over them, under the direction of the Holy One who is Jesus Christ, when the earth becomes celestialized. (D&C 107:54-55.)

## Conclusion

The saints at that day, and today, are little children in an understanding of the great blessings in store for the faithful. Though one might know that many kingdoms may be ruled (D&C 78:15, 17) and all things inherited (Verse 22), few understand what this means. We can understand present blessings, and we may thrill in the contemplation of great blessings to come if we are wise stewards; consequently, the Lord reminds us that what is now received should be accepted in thankfulness. If this is done, then the riches of eternity are ours.

## Chapter 6

# INDIVIDUAL RESPONSIBILITY AS A MEMBER AND MISSIONARY

## (Sections 79, 80, 81, and 82)

During the month of March 1832, revelations were received calling three elders into missionary service. (Sections 79 and 80.) Sometimes missionary calls were to specific localities, as in the case of Jared Carter who was called to serve in the eastern countries (States), while others were given a more general area of proselyting. Brothers Stephen Burnett and Eden Smith were told to go to any of the directions of the compass and labor. (D&C 80:1-3.)

There are few callings in the Church that can compare with the missionary call. It provides opportunities to fulfill one's obligation to represent the Lord before the world; to build up Zion by increasing her citizens; to gain a better understanding of gospel fundamentals; and, at the same time, provides a foundation for a life of service at home.

The missionary who tries to honor his missionary call finds that the Lord will sustain him in his labors if he will do his part. The obtaining of the spirit of one's calling will bring the powers of the Holy Ghost to one's assistance. President John Taylor calls our attention to the missionary's calling in the following passage:

> . . . It is for us to magnify our calling and honor our God in any and every position that we may be called upon to fill. . . . I would say that this Priesthood is not for the honor of man, not for his exaltation alone; but it is imparted to man in order that he may be made the medium of salvation to others. . . . Talking of the Elder, why he is a herald of salvation; he is a legate of the skies; he is commissioned of the great Jehovah to bear a message

to the nations of the earth, and God has promised to sustain him. He has always sustained His faithful Elders, and He always will. (*Journal of Discourses* 24:35.)

## Sustaining Power for Missionaries

While on his mission to the Eastern States, Elder Jared Carter was joined by his brother Simeon. These two missionaries labored for a period in Bolton, New York, on the shore of Lake George. While conducting meetings in that place, they met John Tanner, a wealthy resident of the community, who had invented a wheel chair to carry himself because of an infected leg which doctors had despaired of ever healing. He had been told that he would never again be able to walk. Mr. Tanner's presence at the meeting was prompted by his desire to confound the Mormon missionaries because of their belief in the ministry of angels and the Book of Mormon. Impressed by their message, however, he invited them to his home that he might learn more about their beliefs. Mr. Tanner confessed that he was converted to their teachings, but, because of his physical condition, he could not be baptized. Whereupon, the following conversation ensued:

> Elder Jared Carter said to him, "You believe in the power of the Lord to heal your leg, do you not?" Tanner said he did most assuredly.
>
> Then Elder Carter said in a loud voice, placing his hand heavily on the shoulder of the sick man: "John Tanner, in the name of Jesus Christ I command you to rise and walk!"
>
> The ailing man got out of his chair, but hesitated to set his lame foot on the floor.
>
> "In the name of the Lord," said the Elder, "set down your other foot, and do not be afraid!"
>
> Tanner set it down. It was healed! He could walk without any difficulty—as well, in fact as he had ever done. He strode up and down the room, praising God for the miracle. (*Juvenile Instructor,* Vol. 75, 1940, page 291.)

The three men walked to the lake and Mr. Tanner was baptized. Two years later he sold his possessions in

New York, and moved to Kirtland, Ohio, to join the saints. Subsequently, Brother Tanner used much of his wealth to build up Zion.

One of the well-known experiences of missionary success was the record made by Elder Wilford Woodruff in the British Mission in the year 1840. While laboring in Staffordshire on his birthday, he was directed by the Holy Ghost to go south. Obedient to this inspiration, Elder Woodruff traveled to Herefordshire where he met Mr. John Benbow, a wealthy farmer, who told him that over 600 people of the "United Brethren" faith might be taught. Elder Woodruff, with the material aid of Mr. Benbow, preached to these people and, in a short time, all but one of them accepted the true Church of Jesus Christ. A further example of the sustaining power of the Holy Ghost in his ministry came about in an interesting manner. At the request of a minister, the local constable attended a meeting to arrest Brother Woodruff for preaching the gospel. While the peace officer waited, at the request of the missionary, for the end of the meeting, he became convinced of the truth delivered there and requested baptism. Two clerks of the Church of England were also sent to one of the meetings, and both of them were baptized. (Joseph Fielding Smith, *Essentials in Church History*, pp. 282-283.) In eight months' time, mainly through the efforts of Elder Woodruff in Herefordshire, Worcestershire, and Gloucestershire, 1800 people were brought into the Church.

## Preparation for Missionary Service

Section 80 provides us with some ideas about preparation for missionary service. The two missionaries called by this revelation were told to "declare the things which ye have heard, and verily believe, and know to be true." (Verse 4.) The successful missionary is possessed of sufficient knowledge to impart the fundamentals of the gospel to his listener. Careful preparation for the calling and function of the service to be rendered is a key to success. A necessary preparation is to live worthy to receive the inspiration of the Holy Ghost. If one has learned the gospel, the Lord will bring the necessary knowledge forth when the time is appropriate. Above everything else, the missionary should have a testimony of the restoration of the gospel and thus be able to bear record that Jesus is the Savior. In the words of Elder John A. Widtsoe:

> These, then, are the steps on the way to truth: Desire, prayer, study, and practice. They form the eternal price which must be paid for truth.
>
> This way must be found by each person for himself. Another cannot desire, pray, study, or practice in our stead and for us. Truth must be won individually. (*Evidences and Reconciliations,* 3:84-85.)

When one knows the truth of the gospel, he will not teach something that will confuse or destroy faith. He will seek to learn the truth and teach only the truths that will advance the salvation of his fellow men.

The guide to success in missionary work, in other Church teaching positions, or other callings where counsel is required, is the word given in the standard works of the Church and the instructions of the living prophets. (D&C 10:62-63.)

## Organization of the First Presidency

It was during March 1832, that Joseph Smith received Section 81 revealing that the First Presidency should be organized. Frederick G. Williams, by this revelation, was called to be a counselor to President Smith. One year later, March 18, 1833, the First Presidency was organized with Sidney Rigdon also serving as a counselor. During that interim, however, these brethren assisted the Prophet. The following reason for the gradual development of the Church organization was given by President Anthon H. Lund:

> . . . When the Church was organized on the 6th day of April, 1830, as far as we can learn there were but nine persons in the Church. Of course, with nine persons it was impossible to establish this perfect organization of the Priesthood. Joseph Smith and Oliver Cowdery were called and ordained Apostles; but there could not be Twelve Apostles, there could not be (a quorum of) Seventy, for at that time the Church was too small. It took time for the work to grow; but the Lord had given revelation upon the subject, and when the proper time came the Presidency of the Church was organized, with the Prophet Joseph as President and Sidney Rigdon and Frederick G. Williams as his counselors. Afterwards the Twelve Apostles were chosen, and then the Seventies. But in the beginning, when there were not enough to form these different quorums, the Elders presided, because they held the Melchizedek Priesthood. The Lord, however, had a perfect organization for His Church, and He gave it unto them when they were ready to receive it. (*Conference Report,* November, 1901, p. 75.)

### Keys of the Kingdom

An important truth is given in verse 2 of Section 81 regarding the Presidency of the Church. Brother Williams was told that Joseph Smith, the President, had received the keys of the Kingdom of God and that these powers would reside in the Presidency of the Melchizedek Priesthood. In August, 1830, the Lord referred to the time, when, in June of the preceding year, Peter, James, and John, had conferred these keys and a dispensation of the gospel for the last time. (D&C 27:12-13.) Briefly, the keys thus restored, together with those later conferred, gave the rights, privileges, and powers necessary to carry out all of the functions of the priesthood upon the earth. In Section 81, Brother Williams was informed that he was to counsel with the Prophet. The counselors were not to receive revelation for the Church, but they were entitled to inspiration that they might act in unison with the President on all matters which came before them.

Emphasis is given in the revelation of the need for prayer to receive the full blessings of leadership. (Verse 3.) In addition to his Presidency duties, which would also involve helping the weak and those in need (Verse 5), Brother Williams was told that he would proclaim the gospel, and then he would be able to do the greatest good for his fellow men and also for the glory of God. (Verse 4.) Faithful performance of Brother Williams' calling, as is true of all Latter-day Saints, would give him a crown of eternal life in the Father's mansions. (Verse 6.)

Regardless of the office held in the kingdom, there is need for each member of the Church to do missionary work.

### Background—Section 82

The month before Section 82 was received, the Prophet Joseph Smith was counseled to organize the saints in Zion for their temporal benefit. (D&C 78:3-4.) Shortly after arriving at Independence, Missouri, a general council of the Church was convened, at which time the Prophet was sustained as the President of the High Priesthood, to which office he was ordained on the 24th of January, 1832. During an intermission of the council, a difference between Bishop Edward Partridge and Sidney Rigdon was settled, and then the revelation recorded in Section 82 was received. The Lord recognized the settlement of this difference between the brethren and said that as they had forgiven each other, so also he would forgive them. (D&C 82:1.)

### Degrees of Responsibility

Since all mankind will be judged by the law to which they are responsible on the earth, men will vary in their responsibility to account for the deeds done in the body.

> For of him unto whom much is given much is required; and he who sins against the greater light shall receive the greater condemnation. (D&C 82:3.)

The principle that greater light and understanding bring greater responsibility, should appeal to everyone as a just principle. For example, if a person does not have an opportunity to hear the fulness of the gospel, then he should not be held to that law. It is also true that if one does have the opportunity to know the commandments of that law, and does not live them, then he should lose the blessings of living that law. Although one may learn the letter of the law, some may claim that they do not understand the necessity of complying with the commandment. What of them? Elder James E. Talmage has this informative answer:

> . . . Such may ask: Are men to suffer penalty in the hereafter because they cannot understand what is required of them in mortality? The degree of the culpability is to be determined by the fundamental cause of their ineptitude in matters spiritual. Failure to comprehend may be due to bias or to lack of desire to know. . . .
>
> Are you unable to realize that baptism is essential to salvation? Perhaps the cause lies in the fact that you have never developed the essential condition of faith in the Lord Jesus Christ; or, perchance, you have never repented of your sins. Faith and repentance, as the Scriptures aver, are prerequisites to effective baptism; and it is as unreasonable to expect a faithless unrepentant sinner to comprehend the essentiality of baptism as to expect one untrained in the rudiments of arithmetic to understand algebra.
>
> Willful ignorance of Gospel requirements is sin. Man is untrue to his Divine lineage and birthright of reason when he turns away from the truth, or deliberately chooses to walk in darkness while the illumined path is open to his tread. Positive rejection of the truth is even graver than passive inattention or neglect. Yet to every one is given the right of choice and the power of agency, with the certainty of his meeting the natural and inevitable consequence. (*Vitality of Mormonism,* pp. 280-281.)

Latter-day Saints are more responsible before the Lord because they are under covenant by baptism, by temple ordinances, as well as by the enlightenment of the

Holy Ghost. "What I say unto one I say unto all" is a truth which has application many times in these revelations. Although a truth may be spoken to one or several people, usually it is applicable to the many.

It is just as true today as in 1832 that the adversary is gaining ground and his darkness reigneth to a great degree upon the earth. (D&C 82:5.) This condition brings about this warning to the world:

> And the anger of God kindleth against the inhabitants of the earth; and none doeth good, for all have gone out of the way. (Verse 6.)

## Sin No More

To the brethren in Missouri (and to all members of the Church) the Lord counseled them to sin no more. And "unto that soul who sinneth shall the former sins return." (D&C 82:7.) After quoting Ezekiel, chapter 18, verse 24, the *Doctrine and Covenants Commentary* gives this explanation:

> . . . God forgives the repentant sinner so completely that "his transgressions shall not be mentioned unto him"; on the other hand, the righteous, who turn away from righteousness, cannot hope that his former life will save him. The principle works both ways, and is, therefore, eminently just. (Page 490.)

## Temporal Commandment

As a preface to instructions regarding the brethren's mission to Missouri to manage the affairs of the poor under the order of Enoch in Kirtland, as well as Zion, the Lord set forth this truth which is similar to another oft-quoted one. (See D&C 130:20-21.)

> I, the Lord, am bound when ye do what I say; but when ye do not what I say, ye have no promise. (D&C 82:10.)

The meaning of this passage is well known. The Lord operates the universe, his Church, and the plan of salvation, by law. When the law is observed, the blessing of that law follows.

In the operation of the law of consecration, it was intended that each person should manage his stewardship so that not only his family would profit but that the Lord's storehouse would be filled to meet every need, "Every man seeking the interest of his neighbor, and doing all things with an eye single to the glory of God." (Verse 19.)

If the brethren privileged to live this law of stewardship were to break their covenants, they "shall be dealt with according to the laws of my Church and shall be delivered over to the buffeting of Satan until the day of redemption." (Verse 21.)

The brethren were also advised "and this is wisdom, make unto yourselves friends with the mammon of unrighteousness and they will not destroy you. Leave judgment alone with me for it is mine and I will repay." (Verses 22-23.) The Saints were to treat their nonmember friends with kindness, to live at peace with them, but never take to their bosoms principles of unrighteousness. The gospel teaches that one should refrain from sinning, and a way to accomplish this is to keep from the areas of temptation. Tolerance does not mean acceptance of principles that are contrary to the Lord's way of happiness. One can be friendly with those who do not accept Latter-day Saint standards of conduct, but tolerance is not indulgence.

## Summary

Four sections of the Doctrine and Covenants have made up this chapter. We have learned that the Lord gave instructions on missionary work that are applicable today; that the faithful missionary is promised the Holy Ghost to direct him in his labors; and that the powers of the Priesthood are available to the diligent. Regardless of position in the Church, no one is exempt from missionary responsibility. Finally, we learned that the powers of darkness are present on the earth, and diligence in keeping the commandments is necessary. Tolerance for people not of our faith was enjoined, but tolerance does not mean acceptance of their ideas and practices which are incompatible with the covenants which the Latter-day Saint has made with God.

## Chapter 7

# THE REVELATION ON PRIESTHOOD

## (Section 84:1-42)

From the spring until the fall of 1832, the Prophet Joseph Smith continued the revision of the Bible. In July the first copy of the *Evening and Morning Star* was received by him. This brought joy to the Prophet and the saints because they now had a publication in which to present the message of the restoration of the gospel to the world. This publication also served as the printed depository of many revelations since bound copies of the revelations did not come off the press in quantity until 1835. It will be remembered that of the 1833 edition all save a few copies of some of the forms of the unfinished book were destroyed when a Missouri mob destroyed the press upon which it was being printed. This new periodical was also a means through which the saints could answer the false charges which their enemies made against them.

During the month of September the elders came in from their missions to report their stewardships. While thus engaged on the 22nd and 23rd of that month, the Lord opened the mind of the Prophet and gave him a remarkable revelation on priesthood.

### New Jerusalem Temple

Section 84 begins with the assertion that the Church is to gather the Lord's people as predicted by the prophets. Moreover, the gathering place at that time, and also in the future, is the city of New Jerusalem where the saints will stand in the last days. (Verses 1-2.) A prophecy is made concerning the temple which will be erected in that city located in the western boundaries of the State of Missouri, the place already dedicated by the Prophet. In this prediction, the Lord says that the temple upon which his glory would rest would be reared in this generation. (Verses 3-5.)

Inasmuch as that temple has not been built within an hundred years of 1832, some members of the Church have wondered about the length of a generation. Although a generation, under certain conditions, is mentioned in the Book of Mormon as an hundred years (Helaman 13:8-11), the term, under some conditions, refers to an indefinite period. For example, Jesus said that it was an evil and adulterous generation that sought after a sign (Matt. 12:39), and in our dispensation the Lord said that "this generation shall have my word through you [Joseph Smith]." (D&C 5:10.) From these examples, it is clear that the dispensation of the fulness of times is considered a generation, for the people of our time are still receiving the word of the Lord in the revelation received through Joseph Smith. There is no way of determining the number of years meant in Section 84, verses 4 and 5. There are two things to be known, however. First, that the Lord has said through his Prophet that the temple will be built in this generation, and second, that from the time this announcement was made the leaders of the Church have never departed from the Lord's intention.

## Priesthood Genealogy

This revelation dealing with the priesthood appropriately begins with information about the building of the temple. The temple is the sanctuary where the highest ordinances and blessings of the priesthood are received. (D&C 124:25-42.) Next, we find the genealogy of the priesthood as held by Moses. (D&C 84:6-16.) The priesthood is eternal and continues in the true Church. (Verse 17.)

## The Knowledge of God

After referring to the lesser or Aaronic Priesthood as a part of the Melchizedek Priesthood, the powers of the higher priesthood are stated in this way:

> And this greater priesthood administereth the gospel and holdeth the key of the mysteries of the kingdom, even the key of the knowledge of God.
>
> Therefore, in the ordinances thereof, the power of godliness is manifest.
>
> And without the ordinances thereof, and the authority of the priesthood, the power of godliness is not manifest unto man in the flesh;
>
> For without this no man can see the face of God, even the Father, and live. (D&C 84:19-22.)

The Melchizedek Priesthood holds the key to all the spiritual blessings of the gospel. The knowledge of God and the true plan of salvation is possible only through the divine means that the Lord has established. Life eternal is unavailable without the ordinances of the gospel administered by the authority to seal those ordinances on the earth as they are sealed in the heavens. The mysteries of the kingdom of God, as administered in the temple of God, are reserved for those who desire exaltation. These ordinances are for the faithful and not for the world. (Matt. 13:10-13; Alma 12:9-11.) In Section 84, verses 21 and 22, it is said that in order for one to see the face of God, and, therefore, to know him, the Priesthood is necessary.

## Ancient Israel

In Section 84, attention is directed to the experience of the children of Israel in the days of Moses. (Verses 23-27.) Moses endeavored to teach the principles of exaltation to Israel, but they hardened their hearts and thus denied themselves the opportunity to enter into the Lord's presence. Moses held the higher priesthood and, while on Mount Horeb, the Lord gave him the fulness of the gospel with its principles and ordinances of exaltation. When Moses saw the idolatrous condition of the Israelites, he broke the tablet of writings. Another tablet containing the law of carnal commandments, as mentioned in Section 84, verses 26 and 27, was given him and the Melchizedek Priesthood was taken away from Israel. In the revision of the Bible by Joseph Smith, we find the following, which is in harmony with Section 84:

> And the Lord said unto Moses, Hew thee two other tables of stone, like unto the first, and I will write upon them also, the words of the law, according as they were written at the first on the tables which thou brakest; but it shall not be according to the first, for I will take away the priesthood out of their midst; therefore my holy order, and the ordinances thereof, shall not go before them; for my presence shall not go up in their midst, lest I destroy them.
>
> But I will give unto them the law as at the first, but it shall be after the law of a carnal commandment; for I have sworn in my wrath, that they shall not enter into my presence, into my rest, in the days of their pilgrimage. (Exodus 34:1, 2.)

Thus ancient Israel lost its opportunity to receive the ordinances of godliness to receive the knowledge of God. With the loss of the higher priesthood, the Aaronic Priesthood administered a preparatory gospel, or law of carnal commandments, until the coming of Christ in the meridian dispensation. There were times from Moses to Christ when the prophets held the higher priesthood, but it was not conferred upon others as it is today. (*Teachings of the Prophet Joseph Smith*, p. 181.)

## John the Baptist

John the Baptist, the forerunner of Christ, was raised up by God to make straight the way of the Lord. We are informed that he was baptized while yet in his childhood and the priesthood was conferred upon him by an angel of the Lord. (D&C 84:28.) The New Testament says that he was called of God. (Luke 3:2.)

## Sons of Moses

After mentioning that the priesthood—Melchizedek and Aaronic—has offices as appendages (D&C 84:29-30), reference is again made to the temple to be constructed in Jackson County, Missouri. These few verses are highly interesting because they point out a service to be performing by present-day priesthood bearers and the functioning of the temple in the New Jerusalem. It is said that the sons of Moses and the sons of Aaron shall offer an acceptable offering in that temple, and that these brethren will be filled with the glory of the Lord in that house. (Verses 31-32.)

But who are they today that have the promise of officiating in the temple when it is built in Independence, Missouri? The Lord answers in this manner:

> For whoso is faithful unto the obtaining these two priesthoods of which I have spoken, and the magnifying their calling, are sanctified by the Spirit unto the renewing of their bodies.
>
> They become the sons of Moses and of Aaron and the seed of Abraham, and the church and kingdom, and the elect of God. (Verses 33-34.)

These are Latter-day Saint priesthood holders who honor and magnify their callings—in other words, those who keep the commandments and answer to the calls made upon them to function in the priesthood.

## Importance of Priesthood

Two important aspects of priesthood are made known in verses 35 to 42 of Section 84. First, the acceptance of the priesthood by the priesthood bearer:

And also all they who receive this priesthood receive me, saith the Lord;

For he that receiveth my servants receiveth me;
And he that receiveth me receiveth my Father;
And he that receiveth my Father receiveth my Father's kingdom; therefore all that my Father hath shall be given unto him.
And this is according to the oath and covenant which belongeth to the priesthood. (Verses 35-39.)

In these verses one is promised the highest blessing available to the child of God—eternal life. This is expressed in verse 38 in the most complete way possible. *All that the Father hath* shall be given to him who accepts the Lord through his servants. Acceptance of the Lord's servant means completely obeying the will of the Lord as given by his ancient and modern prophets. That one may understand the binding force of this promise, the revelation refers to the oath and covenant of the priesthood.

The second important responsibility pertaining to the priesthood is found in these words:

Therefore, all those who receive the priesthood, receive this oath and covenant of my Father, which he cannot break, neither can it be moved.
But whoso breaketh this covenant after he hath received it, and altogether turneth therefrom, shall not have forgiveness of sins in this world nor in the world to come. (Verses 40-41.)

Attention is directed in the foregoing words to those who possess the priesthood. The authority to bind and seal which God gives to his faithful sons is of such importance that a covenant (agreement or contract) is made between the recipient and the Lord. In essence it is: if you abide by the law of the priesthood, every blessing within my power to give will be granted you, even to become as I am.

Every man who has received the Melchizedek Priesthood has received the oath and covenant of that priesthood. This agreement pertains to the higher priesthood and not the Aaronic. (*DHC* 5:555.)

### First Requirement of the Oath and Covenant

From the foregoing scriptures regarding the responsibility of the priesthood member and the priesthood, Elder Delbert L. Stapley of the Council of the Twelve suggested the necessity of faithfulness or obedience to gospel standards. He then asked the following questions that the elder might evaluate his faithfulness: (These questions are also applicable to every member of the Church.)

1. Can a man be faithful who does not abide by the first two great commandments, to love the Lord God with all his heart, soul, strength, and mind, and his neighbor as himself?
2. Can a man be faithful who is not honest and truthful in all dealings and relationships with his fellow men?
3. Can a man be faithful who does not honor the Sabbath day and keep it holy, attend the Sacrament and priesthood meetings; also worthily fulfill all other duties in keeping with his callings and obligations that day?
4. Can a man be faithful who does not plan and arrange for daily family prayer in the home?
5. Can a man be faithful who does not teach his children the true principles of the gospel of Christ and then set them a worthy example by living according to those truths?
6. Can a man be faithful who does not observe and keep the Word of Wisdom?
7. Can a man be faithful who does not pay an honest tithing and fast offering?
8. Can a man be faithful who does not obey the law of chastity and is not morally clean in his life and habits?
9. Can a man be faithful who does not, through obedience and sacrifice, prepare himself worthily for the holy temples of God where he can receive his endowments and sealings in the higher ordinances of the gospel and thus bind his family happily and eternally together in love and understanding?
10. Can a man be faithful who does not honor and obey the laws of the land? (*Conference Report* April 1957, p. 76.)

The foregoing questions only point up some areas of responsibility. Other measures of faithfulness might also be suggested, but each one of those mentioned is highly important in keeping the oath and covenant of the priesthood.

## Second Requirement of Oath and Covenant

In order to give further guidelines of responsibility, Elder Stapley reminded the general conference that the second requirement of the oath and covenant of the priesthood is to magnify one's calling (D&C 84:33), and then he proceeded to ask the following questions:

1. Can a man magnify his office and calling without honoring and abiding in the priesthood faithfully and worthily as a devoted and true servant of God?
2. Can a man magnify his calling without giving spiritual and humble dignity to his office?
3. Can a man magnify his calling who refuses to accept positions and responsibilities of trust when called upon to serve by his stake president, bishop, or other constituted authority?
4. Can a man magnify his calling if he is not obedient to gospel standards and requirements, and if he also fails to be amenable to the counsel and direction of righteous men who are properly called and approved by the people as their authorized leaders?
5. Can a man magnify his calling who refuses to sustain by his faith, prayers, and works those whom God has called and ordained to preside over him?
6. Can a man magnify his calling who does not use his priesthood in righteousness for the blessing and benefit of his fellow men?
7. Can a man magnify his calling who does not banish all iniquity from his soul, that he may gain favor with God and thus enjoy power in the use of the priesthood to bless people?

Again, may I summarize by asking, "Can a man magnify his calling who is not willing to sacrifice and consecrate all for the building of God's kingdom in righteousness, truth, and power in the earth?" (*Conference Report,* April 1957, pp. 76-77.)

## The Penalty

The letter and the spirit of this revelation on the oath and covenant of the priesthood give emphasis to the binding force of this covenant. The Lord says that he will hold inviolate the agreement as long as man honors and magnifies the priesthood. (D&C 84:40.) The responsibility for maintaining the contract is upon man. Man is on trial, not God. The seriousness of this oath is also pointed up by the fact that he who altogether turns away from the priesthood shall not have forgiveness. (Verse 41.) Because this expression "shall not have forgiveness of sins in this world nor in the world to come," is associated with the penalty received by the son of perdition, it should be known that all men who so turn away from the priesthood may not, as a necessary result, become sons of perdition. It is possible for the unfaithful priesthood bearer to become indifferent to keeping the commandments and to fail to magnify his calling, yet never to receive the light and understanding nor fall to such depths of wickedness as to become a son of perdition. It is apparent, therefore, that the loss of forgiveness entails the great punishment of being denied the priesthood in the future life. Without the priesthood no man may enter into the exaltation. This truth should point out the importance of the priesthood to all members of the Church. No one in the Church should take lightly any responsibility assigned him by the servants of God.

## Chapter 8

# THE REVELATION ON PRIESTHOOD (continued)

## (Section 84:43-120)

### Hearken to the Spirit

The call is sent forth in Section 84 that all people should give careful heed to the words of eternal life, and to live by every word that comes from God. (Verses 43-44.) They are reminded that the word of the Lord is light and truth and that this enlightenment comes from the Spirit of Jesus Christ. (Verse 45.) Those who hearken to this Spirit come unto the Father, and then the Father teaches them of the covenant and gives them a testimony of the truth. (Verses 47-48.) But the Spirit of Christ prepares the person for acceptance of the fulness of truth. Every man that comes into the world receives light from that Spirit. (D&C 84:46; 88-11-13.)

With the understanding that everyone is a child of God in the spirit, we recognize why the Lord gives to all of his children a guide to lead them unto all truth. The function of this Spirit and its universality are enumerated by President George Q. Cannon as follows:

> . . . it is a Spirit that pleads with men to do right. The heathen have it. There is no degraded Indian in these mountains or valleys who does not have a portion of that Spirit pleading with him to do that which is right. It pleads with all the heathen, the Pagan as well as the Christian; the Methodist and Baptist as well as the Latter-day Saints. Everywhere throughout the earth where man dwells this Spirit rests upon him. It comes from God. It pleads with man to do right. It pleads with man to resist the blandishments of Satan. No man ever did a wrong but that Spirit warned him of it to a greater or less extent. (*Journal of Discourses* 26:191.)

This Spirit should not be confused with the Holy Ghost which is given to those who obey the principles of the gospel and have hands laid upon their heads for that gift. (Acts 5:32; John 14:16-17.)

## The Righteous and the Wicked

In connection with the important truth that all men have to a greater or lesser extent the Spirit of the Lord which enlightens them and gives them power to discern between right and wrong, it must be known that, through succumbing to the enticings of Satan, sin is perpetuated. Each individual, to some degree, is in the bondage of sin, and therefore, in need of repentance. The Lord desires that his children understand the need for their acceptance of the fulness of truth. It is only by the atonement of Jesus Christ that sin is forgiven by obedience to the principles and ordinances of the gospel. That person who does not come unto Jesus Christ in the manner he has prescribed, continues to remain under the bondage of sin or spiritual death. On the other hand, the person who has accepted Jesus Christ through his priesthood has come into spiritual life, which is the state of the righteous. President Joseph F. Smith has set this forth in these words:

> . . . Now, all the world today, I am sorry to say, with the exception of a handful of people who have obeyed the new and everlasting covenant, are suffering this spiritual death. They are cast out from the presence of God. They are without God, without gospel truth, and without the power of redemption; for they know not God nor His Gospel. In order that they may be redeemed and saved from the spiritual death which has spread over the world like a pall, they must repent of their sins, and be baptized by one having authority, for the remission of their sins, that they may be born of God. (*Conference Report,* October 1899, p. 72.)

## Unbelief Among the Saints

Notwithstanding the saint has come into spiritual life, he may lose the influence of the Holy Ghost due to sin. When Section 84 was received, the inhabitants of Zion had not paid necessary attention to the revelation and the inspired writings in the Book of Mormon. The consequence of this neglect and unbelief was darkness of mind. (Verses 54-56.) Escape from this condemnation was open to Zion on condition that she abide by the teachings of the revelations and not talk about them only. (Verse 57.) Repentance would bring forth results beneficial to them, but slothfulness would bring a scourge and judgment. (Verse 58.)

## Signs Follow the Believer

The elders addressed in this revelation were to go into the world testifying unto all that, as they accepted the first principles and came into the kingdom of God, the Holy Ghost would be received. (D&C 84:62-64.) The Lord then indicated that various signs—wonderful works, casting out of devils, healing the sick, etc.—would follow the believer. (Verses 65-72.)

A very important admonition was given the elder and member who participated in or received such a blessing.

> But a commandment I give unto them, that they shall not boast themselves of these things, neither speak them before the world; for these things are given unto you for your profit and for salvation. (Verse 73.)

Miracles have been in the Church of Jesus Christ in all dispensations. The spiritual gifts of the Holy Ghost, one of which is miracles, are a part of the fulness of the gospel. (D&C 46:21.) That signs follow the believer is well known to the Latter-day Saint, for thousands of saints can testify that these blessings have been received.

We may correctly say that miracles (signs) are a characteristic of the true church. Miracles in and of themselves, however, are not evidences of the truth. Men are not saved in the kingdom of God by miracles. As stated by President Brigham Young:

> The latter-day Saints and every other person who is entitled to salvation, and all except those who have sinned against the Holy Ghost, may know that Jesus is the Christ in the same way that Peter knew it. Miracles do not give this knowledge to mankind, though they may serve as collateral evidence to strengthen the believer. The miracles of Jesus were known to the Jews, yet they suffered him to be put to death as a deceiver of mankind and one possessed of a devil. (*Journal of Discourses* 10:193.)

What means are at the disposal of the saint that he may tell his friends how to distinguish between the genuine and the spurious representative of God? Healing is only one of the many parts of the gospel of Jesus Christ. To say that any one of the principles or ordinances *is* the gospel would be erroneous, and to believe that because an organization has an ordinance, such as baptism, that it is the true church would be equally false. The key to discerning which is the true church may be stated thus: When all of the principles and ordinances, as taught by Christ, are combined in the one organization, there the true church exists. For our present purpose, if a healing is effected in an organization where all of the truths of the gospel are not taught, then that organization does not have the power of salvation in it. The purpose of the gospel of Christ is to make exaltation in the celestial kingdom possible. If the authority to administer the saving principles and ordinances of the gospel is not present, then there is no exaltation possible.

### The Laborer is Worthy of His Hire

With the command that the entire world should have the message of salvation taught to them (D&C 84:75-76), the Lord counseled his servants that they become as his "friends" of old, to preach the gospel with power. (Verse 77.) As of old, they were to travel without purse or scrip (baggage) to prove the world, for the laborer was worthy of his hire. All of those who would take this commission, if faithful in the discharge of their duties, would neither be weary in mind nor in body, and they would not go hungry or without water. They were not to be concerned for the material things of life.

> For, consider the lilies of the field, how they grow, they toil not, neither do they spin; and the kingdoms of the world, in all their glory, are not arrayed like one of these.
>
> For your Father, who is in heaven, knoweth that you have need of all these things.
>
> Therefore, let the morrow take thought for the things of itself. (Verses 82-84.)

When Jesus delivered the Sermon on the Mount during his mortal ministry, similar counsel was given to his disciples. (Matt. 6:25-34.) Some writers have criticized this sermon, saying that if this advice were taken by the world, all initiative and progress would be stopped. Clarification of this point is made in the Book of Mormon when the Sermon on the Mount was given on this continent. The resurrected Lord turned to the twelve disciples and gave to them this admonition: it was not for the world. Again, in this dispensation, the counsel is not for the world but for those who are called into his ministry, and if they are faithful, the promises will be fulfilled. The following testimony from President John Taylor summarizes the fulfillment of this promise to the faithful:

> . . . I see men around me in every direction who have traveled thousands and thousands of miles without purse or scrip, to preach the Gospel to the nations of the earth. They have traversed plains, mountains, deserts, seas, oceans and rivers; they have gone forth trusting in the living God, bearing the precious seed of eternal life. It is true they have not been comprehended or understood by the nations, but that does not alter the fact.

Many who went forth in their weaknesses have returned rejoicing, bringing their sheaves with them, as trophies of the victory of the principles of eternal life that they themselves had communicated. I say there is not another instance on record today of like disinterested, affectionate regard for the welfare of the human family as has been manifested by the Elders of this Church. I have traveled thousands and hundreds of thousands of miles to preach the Gospel among the nations of the earth, and my brethren around me have done the same thing. Did we ever lack anything necessary to eat, drink and wear? I never did. God went with his Elders, and they have gathered together his people as they are here today. They have been seeking to carry out the desire of the Lord and the wish of the Almighty in regard to the human family. They were told to go trusting in the name of the Lord, and he would take care of them and go before them, and that the Spirit should go with them and his angels accompany them. (*Journal of Discourses* 14:189.)

But what of the present? For many years Latter-day Saint missionaries have taken purse and scrip. With the speed-up of missionary work and with existing laws against this practice, the Lord has ruled otherwise, as he did in the meridian dispensation. (Luke 22:36.) In reference to this change, President Charles W. Penrose has said:

. . . Indeed, all my ministry among the people of the world was literally "without purse or scrip." Now I do not say that this should be done now. I believe that as circumstances change, the Lord changes his commandments, to correspond therewith. As Jesus taught, a great many of you who went out in the world took "neither brass nor gold nor silver in your purses nor scrip for your journey, nor two coats, for the laborer is worthy of his hire," but afterwards he said: "When I sent you out without purse or scrip, did you lack anything?" And they said, "Nay, Lord," but now he said, "He that has no purse let him get one and he that hath no sword let him buy one." Circumstances had changed and so the word was changed. He didn't change, but the circumstances being changed the word of the Lord was different. So in these times conditions have changed very much from those times. (*Conference Report,* October 1921, p. 17.)

## Take No Thought Beforehand

The Lord also counseled the missionaries of this dispensation to treasure up in their minds the words of life that when the appropriate hour came, the words of life could be called forth. Although they were instructed to take no thought beforehand what they should say, they were to study diligently the revelations necessary to teach the gospel. (D&C 84:85.) The missionary was to "reprove the world of all their unrighteous deeds, and to teach them of a judgment which is to come." (Verse 87.)

## Rewards and Punishment

All who assist the Lord's servants will in no wise lose their reward. On the other hand, those who reject his missionaries or who fail to provide for them when required, will find that they have brought themselves under condemnation. (D&C 84:88-91.) It has been decreed, also, that those places that reject the word of the Lord will be condemned, but diligent search should be made in the cities and villages for those who will hearken to the message. (Verse 92-95.)

When, in the judgment of the Lord, the world has had its opportunity to accept him through his servants, and, as predicted, the world at large will have rejected the message, plagues shall go forth in judgment upon the nations. (D&C 84:96-97; 63:32-37; 45:26-44.) The earth will be cleansed from wickedness, and in that day all shall know the Lord as the King of kings. With knowledge of him as their lawgiver, they that remain will lift up their voices in singing the new song given in verses 99 through 102 in Section 84.

These verses speak of millennial conditions. Zion is now being built upon the earth in preparation for the Lord's second advent. In time, the city of Zion (New Jerusalem) will be erected to the glory of God. When the Savior comes to establish his kingdom upon the earth, great shall be the joy of the redeemed, who have looked for that glorious day from the beginning. Satan, the arch-enemy of man, no longer will have influence for he will be bound. The promised restitution of all things (Acts 3:19-21) will have been accomplished in the gathering together into one of all promises and activities planned for the benefit of man. The Zion of Enoch and the Zion of the latter days will meet joyously. (Moses 7:62-64.) In that day the Lord shall stand on the earth in the midst of his people who have been redeemed by his power. The redeemed shall then send forth their songs of praise to the Most High.

### Conclusion

In order that the persons to whom Section 84 was addressed might understand, there is repeated the instruction that the families of the missionaries should be cared for, and the Lesser Priesthood members in that day were to prepare the way for the preaching of the gospel. (Verses 103-108.)

The important counsel was given that each man should stand in his own office and none should say unto the other there was no need of him. (Verses 109-110.) In this priesthood revelation, it is appropriate to observe that the priesthood, which gives life to the Church organization, marks the difference between the true Church of Jesus Christ and the dead forms of religion. Section 84 ends with a command that the bishop of the Church carry the message of warning to certain large cities of the United States. In time, when the cup of iniquity is full, the Lord's power will be manifest, and he shall come to reign with his people. (Verses 111-120.)

## Chapter 9

# THE ONE MIGHTY AND STRONG

## (Section 85)

By commandment, William W. Phelps was promised certain blessings after his baptism. (Section 55.) At this early period (June 1831), he was given the assignment to travel with the Prophet Joseph Smith and Sidney Rigdon to Independence, Missouri, where he was to engage in the printing business. (Verses 4-5.) At the time the Prophet wrote to him (November 27, 1832) about conditions in Missouri, he was editor and printer of the *Evening and Morning Star*, the first periodical published by the Church. Brother Phelps was also an assistant to Bishop Edward Partridge. In reply to a letter from him, the Prophet, already concerned about the welfare of the saints in Missouri, gave instructions regarding the allotting of inheritances to the saints. Matters of great weight rested upon the Prophet's mind, and by inspiration he sensed the feelings of Brother Phelps in these words:

> . . . My God, great and mighty art Thou, therefore show unto Thy servant what shall become of those who are essaying to come up unto Zion, in order to keep the commandments of God, and yet receive not their inheritance by consecrations, by order of deed from the Bishop, the man that God has appointed in a legal way, agreeably to the law given to organize and regulate the Church, and all the affairs of the same. (*DHC* 1:298.)

Then, revealing the source of his own feelings toward Brother Phelps, the Prophet wrote:

> Brother William, in the love of God, having the most implicit confidence in you as a man of God, having obtained this confidence by a vision of heaven, therefore I will proceed to unfold

to you some of the feelings of my heart, and to answer the question. (*Ibid.*)

## Letters As Revelations

From this letter of November 27, 1832, we have received Section 85 of the Doctrine and Covenants. (*DHC* 1:298-299.) Historically, there are many examples of letters becoming scripture as the writer was inspired to pen words of admonition, encouragement, and commandment. The apostle Paul indicated that his knowledge of the gospel of Jesus Christ was received not from men but from the Lord, the Giver of revelation. (Galatians 1:11-12.) Christian scripture consists of many letters written to branches of the Church and to individuals during the New Testament period. (Romans, Corinthians, Galatians, Colossians, Timothy, etc.) The apostles Peter and John have also contributed scripture in the form of letters. In the Book of Mormon we have the letter of Mormon to his son Moroni that explains the doctrine of the atonement as it relates to little children. (Moroni 8.) Subsequent sections in the Doctrine and Covenants also come from letters. (Section 121, 122, 123, 127, 128.)

## Church Record to Be Kept

Important instructions were given to the Lord's clerk in Zion (Missouri) regarding the keeping of a faithful record. Under the law of consecration, the steward was required to manage his inheritance (stewardship) not only for his own welfare but also for the general purposes of the Church. Records were to be kept of those who consecrated their property and of the stewardships received. (D&C 85:1.) The following verse of the revelation describes somewhat the nature of some of our records of today: "And also their manner of life, their faith and works. . . ." In that day those who came to Zion and did not consecrate, and, consequently, did not receive an inheritance, were considered unfaithful to their covenants. A penalty for these and also those who had apostatized after receiving their inheritance was not to have their names enrolled with the faithful. (Verses 2-3.)

### Book of Life

An accurate record of acts is maintained in the heavens comparable with recordings made in the "book of the law of God" (D&C 85:1-5) kept by the Lord's clerk on the earth. In a later revelation, the Lord emphasized the necessity for keeping accurate records that there might be agreement with the "book of life" which is kept in heaven. (D&C 128:7.) In the New Testament period, John the Revelator explained that all things shall be inherited by the faithful, while the disobedient shall not enter into the abode of God.

> And there shall in no wise enter into it any thing that defileth, neither whatsoever worketh abomination, or maketh a lie: but they which are written in the Lamb's book of life. (Rev. 21:27.)

The Lamb's book of life is the book of life kept in the heavens.

### Present Application

In 1832, and as long as the law of consecration was in force, the Lord intended that his saints would prepare themselves against the day of burning when the Savior would come in flaming fire taking vengeance upon those who were not keeping his commandments. (D&C 85:3; II Thessalonians 1:7-8.) This message is similar to the promise that the same judgment would come to those who would not tithe:

> Behold, now it is called today until the coming of the Son of Man, and verily it is a day of sacrifice, and a day for the tithing of my people; for he that is tithed shall not be burned at his coming.

For after today cometh the burning—this is speaking after the manner of the Lord—for verily I say, tomorrow all the proud and they that do wickedly shall be as stubble; and I will burn them up, for I am the Lord of Hosts; and I will not spare any that remain in Babylon.

Wherefore, if ye believe me, ye will labor while it is called today. (D&C 64:23-25.)

It is apparent from the discussion about the book of life and its purpose, that the inheritances of the saints in the future life will be determined by their faithfulness. In the annual conference of 1900, speakers mentioned this subject and also applied Section 85 to conditions as they are now. The law of consecration in force in 1832 is not required of the saints today, but every member of the Church is under obligation to keep the commandments, among which is the law of tithing. By commandment, a faithful record is kept of the non-tithe payers as well as of those who pay tithing. In the language of Elder Rudger Clawson:

. . . The lines are being drawn. It must be known to the authorities of this Church and to the people who are faithful and who are not faithful. God requires it and it must be recorded, for the reason plainly set forth in the revelation, that those whose names are not found recorded in the book of the law of God shall have no inheritance in Zion in that day when our eternal inheritances shall be divided out to us. (*Conference Report,* April 1900, p. 44.)

## "The Still Small Voice"

There are various means by which the Lord communicates with his children and, especially, the prophets. In the Doctrine and Covenants there are many forms of revelation noted: for example, the visitation of heavenly beings, Section 27; by vision, as Section 76; the use of the Urim and Thummim, as Sections 3, 6, 7, 11; inspiration, Sections 8, 20 and 21; and other ways.

We come now to another method of revelation—the Lord speaking into the mind. An example is Enos, who, after struggling in the spirit said: "behold, the voice of the Lord came into my mind again. . . ." (Book of Mormon; Enos 10.) Jeremiah experienced revelation in this same way. (Jeremiah 1:4, 11, 13.)

One of the notable experiences of the Prophet Joseph Smith in receiving revelation is found in Section 85, as follows:

> Yea, thus saith the still small voice, which whispereth through and pierceth all things, and often times it maketh my bones to quake while it maketh manifest. . . . (Verse 6.)

Nephi, in calling his wayward brothers to repentance, reminded them of the times when an angel "hath spoken unto you in a still small voice, but ye were past feeling, that ye could not feel his words." (1 Nephi 17:45.) Every member of the Church is entitled to receive divine guidance in the daily affairs of his life, as well as in his Church positions. President Heber J. Grant once said:

> The Lord gives to many of us the still, small voice of revelation. It comes as vividly and strongly as though it were with a great sound. It comes to each man, according to his needs and faithfulness, for guidance in matters that pertain to his own life. For the Church as a whole it comes to those who have been ordained to speak for the Church as a whole. . . . (*Conference Report*, April 1945, p. 9.)

Very early in the dispensation, the Lord revealed that there was only one person at a time who has the right and power to receive revelation for the Church. (D&C 28:2-7; 43:2-4; *The Doctrine and Covenants Speaks*, Vol. 1, Chapter 18.)

### Interpretation

Verses 7 and 8 of Section 85 were given by the Lord about Bishop Edward Partridge and his calling in regulating the Church in Missouri, with special reference to the law of consecration. Because of a misundertanding of this revelation, President Joseph F. Smith and his counselors, John R. Winder and Anthon H. Lund, wrote upon this subject for the benefit of the believer. In their preface to their interpretation, they wrote:

> Perhaps no other passage in the revelations of the Lord, in this dispensation, has given greater rise to so much speculation as this one. [D&C 85:6-8.] Also, it has been used by vain and foolish men to bolster up their vagaries of speculation, and in some cases their pretensions to great power and high positions they were to attain in the Church. . . .
>
> One would think in such a matter as this that sufficient native modesty would assert itself to restrain a man from announcing himself as the one upon whom such high honors are to be conferred, and who is to exercise such great powers in establishing the Saints in their inheritances; and that even if one suspected, for any reason, that such a position, and such exceptional powers were to be conferred upon him, he would wait until the Lord would clearly indicate to the Church, as well as to himself, that he has been indeed sent of God to the work of so noble a ministry, as is described in the passage under question. Those, however, who have so far proclaimed themselves as being the "one mighty and strong," have manifested the utmost ignorance of the things of God and the order of the Church. Indeed their insufferable ignorance and egotism have been at the bottom of all their pretensions, and the cause of all the trouble into which they have fallen. They seem not to have been aware of the fact that the Church of Christ and of the Saints is completely organized, and that when the man who shall be called upon to divide unto the Saints their inheritances comes, he will be designated by the inspiration of the Lord to the proper authorities of the Church, appointed and sustained according to the order provided for the government of the Chuch. (*Improvement Era* 10:929-930, October 1907.)

These are the verses that concern us in this chapter:

> And it shall come to pass that I, the Lord God, will send one mighty and strong, holding the scepter of power in his hand, clothed with light for a covering, whose mouth shall utter words,

eternal words; while his bowels shall be a fountain of truth, to set in order the house of God, and to arrange by lot the inheritances of the saints whose names are found, and the names of their fathers, and of their children, enrolled in the book of the law of God;

While that man, who was called of God and appointed, that putteth forth his hand to steady the ark of God, shall fall by the shaft of death, like as a tree that is smitten by the vivid shaft of lightning. (D&C 85:7-8.)

In their explanation of these verses, the First Presidency set forth these ideas:

1. Conditions of jealousy, pride, unbelief, and hardness of heart prevailed among the brethren in Missouri. (D&C 84:54-58, 76.) Bishop Edward Partridge was a party to this condition, resulting in the foregoing revelation being received.

2. Bishop Partridge and most of the saints in Missouri partially repented, although in March 1833, the Lord declared that he was not well pleased with the bishop. Eight years later the bishop died due to persecution in Missouri, forgiven of the Lord. "Who shall say that his repentance, his sacrifices, his sufferings and faithfulness did not procure for him a mitigation of the severe judgment decreed against him in the revelation contained in the eighty-fifth section of the Doctrine and Covenants? At any rate, the Lord said, some three years later, that he was well pleased with Bishop Partridge." (*Improvement Era* 10:938-939; see also *DHC* 2:302-303.)

3. Bishop Partridge was the man referred to in the revelation who should fall by the shaft of death, if he did not repent. (D&C 85:8.)

4. If Bishop Partridge had not repented, the Lord would have appointed "one mighty and strong" to take his place; therefore, the First Presidency considered "the whole incident of the prophecy closed." (*Improvement Era* 10:940.)

## Bishop Edward Partridge

Bishop Edward Partridge was called to the bishopric February 4, 1831 (D&C 41:9), and at that time the Lord referred to him as "like unto Nathanael of old." Before this, he was a member of the Campbellites and joined the Church in December 1830. During the severe persecution of the saints in Missouri (due partly to their failure to keep the commandments the Lord), he "acted a most noble, and self-sacrificing part, and bore many indignities with the greatest patience." Partly stripped of his clothing, the bishop was taken to the public square in Independence, Missouri, because he would not denounce the Book of Mormon, and he was tarred and feathered as the mob jeered. Later, he, with five others, offered himselves as ransom for the Church, even to be scourged and put to death, if that would stop the inhuman cruelties heaped upon the saints by the Missourians. Later, he assisted the saints in their flight from Missouri and assisted in their location in Illinois. On May 27, 1840, Bishop Partridge died in Nauvoo, accepted of the Lord.

## An Alternative

From this revelation it can be seen there is no escape from the definite word of the Lord on how his servants are to be appointed. President Joseph F. Smith and his counselors drew attention to the important truth that if there was ever a need for the "one mighty and strong," he would have to occupy the same position as Bishop Partridge—the Presiding Bishop. It would be that bishop's duty in the future, under the law of consecration, to "arrange by lot the inheritances of the Saints." (D&C 57:7, 15; 58:14, 17; 85:7.) Furthermore, that bishop would have to be called in the Lord's way, and not as men might wish to make their own rules. The order of calling priesthood officers was established early in the dispensation. With the restoration of the priesthood, it was stated that authority is necessary to call men into the Lord's service. Before this, Hyrum Smith was told that he was not to preach the gospel until he had been called. (D&C 11:15.) In the revelation on organizing the Church, it was stated that priesthood officers were to be appointed and ordained. (*Ibid.*, 20:2-3, 38-39, 60.) Moreover, they were to be approved by a vote of the Church in appointed meetings. (D&C 20: 61-65.)

These steps are necessary to receive the approval of the Lord: (1) a call by revelation or authority; (2) approval of the members of the Church; and (3) an ordination by one who has the authority. These steps were indicated later, as noted above, to validate the call of the president of the Church. (*Ibid.*, 28:2-7; 43:2-4.) The presiding bishop, as all officers in the Church, is no exception, as witness the instruction concerning the appointment of Bishop Edward Partridge:

> And again, *I have called* my servant Edward Partridge; and I give a commandment, that he should be *appointed by the voice of the church,* and *ordained* a bishop unto the church, to leave his merchandise and to spend all his time in the labors of the church;
>
> To see to all things as it shall be appointed unto him in my laws in the day that I shall give them. (*Ibid.*, 41:9-10.) [Italics by the author.]

Future bishops unto the Church will receive their appointment in the same manner. The Lord declares that there can be no exception.

Pretenders to Church office or to the rights and privileges of the Church have arisen and will probably continue to arise occasionally; therefore, it behooves Latter-day Saints to be aware of the foregoing keys against deception. In concluding their message on this revelation (Section 85), President Joseph F. Smith and his counselors wrote in 1907:

. . . we would say that the Latter-day Saints by this time, should be so well settled in the conviction that God has established his Church in the earth for the last time, to remain, and no more to be thrown down, or destroyed; and that God's house is a house of order, of law, of regularity, that erratic disturbers of that order of men . . . ought not to have any influence with them, nor ought the Saints to be disturbed in their spirit by such characters and their theories. The Church of Christ is with the Saints. It has committed to it the law of God for its own government and perpetuation. It possesses every means for the correction of every wrong or abuse or error which may from time to time arise, and that without anarchy, or even revolution; it can do it by process of evolution—by development, by an increase of knowledge, wisdom, patience and charity. (*Improvement Era* 10:942.)

## No Inheritances for Some

The remaining verses of Section 85 reaffirm, with emphasis, that the unfaithful members of the Church not having their names recorded in the book of the law will not obtain an inheritance, but their lot will be found among the unbelievers where there are wailing and gnashing of teeth. (Verses 9-11.) The consequences of disobedience are serious indeed when one considers the penalty imposed upon the children of the priests mentioned in Ezra 2:61-63. They shall be cut off from the ordinances of the house of the Lord, and from their fathers who are dead and who were faithful. The separation of fathers, mothers, and children in eternity, with the loss of eternal life, is far more serious than some members of the Church are prone to consider. President Joseph F. Smith in discussing this matter was emphatic, as brought out in this chapter, that Section 85 not only has reference to the law of consecration, but also to the law of tithing because it took the place of the former law. (*Conference Report*, October 1899, p. 42.)

## Chapter 10

# THE PROPHECY ON WARS

## (Sections 86 and 87)

The two revelations for study in this chapter were received in the month of December 1832. Many times before this date the Lord revealed that troublous times were ahead for the people of this dispensation if they did not repent. (D&C 1:11-17, 35; 5:15-20; 29:14-21; 45:26-44.)

### Section 86

Early in December of 1832, Joseph Smith received a revelation explaining the parable of the wheat and tares. This revelation clarified, in some respects, the New Testament recording of this parable. (Matt. 13:24-30, 37-43.) The New Testament says that the Lord is the sower of the wheat, while the revelation refers to the apostles as the sowers. Because this parable is to have its fulfillment in the present generation, it is probable that the latter fact is mentioned because it is the apostles who direct the work of taking the gospel to the nations of the earth. Since the apostles are the direct representatives of the Savior, their acts are the same as the Lord's. (D&C 1:38.) In the parable the wheat is sown by the Lord's apostles while, in opposition, the tares are sown by Satan and represent his followers. (Matt. 13:38; D&C 86:3.)

Both accounts of the parable refer to the eventual triumph of the Lord in saving the wheat and burning the tares. (Matt. 13:39-43; D&C 86:7.) Significant in the revelation is the truth that these are the last days when the parable is to be fulfilled. (D&C 86:4.) With the restoration of the gospel, the seed is again sown, but the

Lord will not permit the tender blade of wheat to be destroyed by pulling up the tares until the harvest is ripe, and this notwithstanding the angels "are ready and waiting to be sent forth to reap down the fields." (*Ibid.*, Verse 5.)

## A Modern Prophet Speaks

At a testimony meeting of Salt Lake Temple workers in Brigham City, Utah, June 24, 1894, President Wilford Woodruff related some events of the last days which he had received by vision. The allusion to the "angels of destruction" and "the wheat and the tares" emphasized the message of Section 86.

. . . I want to ask this congregation a question: When I have the vision of the night opened continually before my eyes, and can see the mighty judgments that are about to be poured out upon this world, when I know these things are true, and are at the door of Jew and Gentile; while I know they are true and while I am holding this position before God and this world, can I withhold my voice from lifting up a warning to this people, and to the nations of the earth? I may never meet with this people again; I cannot tell how that may be. But while I live and see these things continually before my eyes I shall raise my warning voice. Now, the question I wanted to ask you is this: We have fourteen [hundred] million people on this earth, and over them all there hangs a cloud of darkness almost entirely upon their shoulders. Can you tell me where the people are who will be shielded and protected from these calamities and judgments which are even now at our doors? I'll tell you. The Priesthood of God who honor their priesthood, and who are worthy of their blessings are the only ones who shall have this safety and protection. No other people have the right to be shielded from these judgments. They are at our very doors; not even this people will escape them entirely. They will come down like the judgments of Sodom and Gomorrah. And none but the priesthood will be safe from their fury. God has held the angels of destruction for many years, lest they should reap down the wheat with the tares. But I want to tell you now, that those angels have left the portals of heaven, and they stand over the earth waiting to pour out the judgments. And from this very day they shall be poured out. Calamities and troubles are increasing in the earth, and there is a meaning to these things. Remember this, and reflect upon these matters. If you do your duty, and I do my duty, we'll have the protection, and shall pass through the afflictions in peace and in safety. Read the scriptures and the revelations. They will tell you about these things. Great changes are at our doors. The next twenty years will see mighty changes among the nations of the earth. You will live to see these things, whether I do or not. I have felt oppressed with the weight of these matters and I felt I must speak of them here. It's by the power of the Gospel that we shall escape. (*The Young Woman's Journal,* Vol. V, 1894, pp. 512-513.)

Mighty changes have occurred on the earth beginning with World War I, which began twenty years after President Woodruff's vision. Governments have changed, and unrest among the nations has increased. Conflicts and warfare have taken their toll among peoples. Advances in technology and better means of destroying men have been devised. Natural calamities have also been evident since that time.

## Great Promises

Several important truths are given in the closing verses (8 to 11) of Section 86. These truths emphasize the need for Latter-day Saints to live in accordance with their lineage and the promises that the Lord has made to them. The saints have the privilege of being saviors to the house of Israel through the ministrations of the priesthood, of which they are lawful heirs through their fathers. Sometimes one might think that the Israelite lineage of the Latter-day Saints is only figurative, but this revelation says that we are lawful heirs to the priesthood "according to the flesh" (Verse 9)—literal descendants of the patriarchs to whom the promises were made that their descendants would be custodians of the gospel and the priesthood through the ages. (Abraham 2:8-11.) The Lord assures us that these promises are to remain with his chosen people in the last days, in order that the restitution of all things spoken of by the prophets may be fulfilled for the benefit of the world. No other people upon this earth have such a great destiny. There will probably be some who will not fulfill their part of that destiny, but this latter-day work will not be stopped.

## Prophecy on War

Ever mindful of world events, due, in part, to the Angel Moroni's prophecy that the words of the prophets concerning the last days were about to be fulfilled (Joseph Smith 2:36-41), the Prophet recorded some events which to him indicated that these were the last days. Among these writings is this introduction to Section 87:

> Appearances of troubles among the nations became more visible this season than they had previously been since the Church began her journey out of the wilderness. The ravages of the cholera were frightful in almost all the large cities on the globe. The plague broke out in India, while the United States, amid all her pomp and greatness, was threatened with immediate dissolution. The people of South Carolina, in convention assembled (in November), passed ordinances, declaring their state a free and independent nation; and appointed Thursday, the 31st day of January, 1833, as the day of humiliation and prayer, to implore Almighty God to vouchsafe His blessings, and restore liberty and happiness within their borders. President Jackson issued his proclamation against this rebellion, called out a force sufficient to quell it, and implored the blessings of God to assist the nation to extricate itself from the horrors of the approaching and solemn crisis.
>
> On Christmas day (1832), I received the following revelation and prophecy on war. (*DHC* 1:301 [Section 87 follows].)

With the foregoing prophecies before him, and conditions shaping up in the world that gave promise to the fulfillment of the Lord's word to this generation, the Prophet was deeply concerned about the conditions in the United States. One year before receiving this revelation on war (Section 87), these two significant prophecies heralded the great American Civil War:

> Ye hear of wars in far countries, and you say that there will soon be wars in far countries, but ye know not the hearts of men in your own land. (D&C 38:29.)

The second prophecy is more specific relative to conditions in the United States.

> Ye hear of wars in foreign lands; but, behold I say unto you, they are nigh, even at your doors, and not many years hence ye shall hear of wars in your own lands. (*Ibid.*, 45:63.)

Among the numerous prophecies given by Joseph Smith, the one on war in the last days stands out as strong evidence that he possessed the prophetic gift. Called to give the Lord's word to this generation (*Ibid.*, 5:10), he spoke fearlessly of the judgments of the last days.

The following main essentials of Section 87 about the American Civil War support the Prophet's calling: (1) The wars of the last days would commence with the rebellion of South Carolina. (2) This war would terminate in the death and misery of many souls. (3) The Southern States would be divided against the Northern States. (4) Slaves would rise up against their masters and be disciplined for war. Other elements of the prophecy relating to subsequent events will be considered also.

In addition to the foregoing and also the two warnings given before December 25, 1832 (*Ibid.*, 38:29; 45:63), the Prophet wrote to N. C. Seaton, Esq., editor of a paper in Rochester, New York, on January 4, 1833:

> And now I am prepared to say by the authority of Jesus Christ, that not many years shall pass away before the United States shall present such a scene of bloodshed as has not a parallel in the history of our nation. . . . (*DHC* 1:315.)

### Dates and Conditions

In the preceding section the Prophet's journal is quoted as an introduction to Section 87. In that statement of conditions in the United States and in other parts of the world, he noted that South Carolina had declared itself independent and that President Andrew Jackson had taken steps to quell that rebellion.

What brought about that situation in South Carolina? Several years before 1832, discontent was manifest in the South over federal tariff laws that protected the industrialists of the North while the Southern planters suffered. The tariff act of 1828 was called a tariff of abomination in the South, and the one of 1832 was also considered with equal or great abhorrence. This discontent led South Carolina to favor the nullification of the federal tariff laws, and, if necessary, to withdraw from the Union. President Jackson issued his Proclamation on Nullification on December 10, 1832, which denied to any state the power to secede from the Union. Although South Carolina appealed to the other states for support, it was not forthcoming. Virginia and Georgia were sympathetic to the cause, but would do nothing for South Carolina. (See William B. Hesseltine, *The South in American History*, p. 198.) Although a crisis had developed in the nation, the ingredients to bring about an armed conflict between the states were not there. New tariff legislation in 1833 indicated a conciliatory attitude on the part of the South and the North.

In another section of the Doctrine and Covenants, dated the same day as Section 87, the Prophet recorded:

> I prophesy, in the name of the Lord God, that the commencement of the difficulties which will cause much bloodshed previous to the coming of the Son of Man will be in South Carolina.
>
> It may probably arise through the slave question. This is a voice declared to me, while I was praying earnestly on the subject, December 25th, 1832. (D&C 130:12-13.)

It is important to note that the Prophet prophesied that the American Civil War would probably begin through the slave question, not because of it, but that slavery would be a contributing cause. Much has been written on the cause of the Civil War. While some have advocated the single cause of slavery, others have denied this and some have suggested that slavery was only the surface issue, while deeper causes lay at its origin. (See Edwin C. Rozwenec, ed.: *Slavery as a Cause of the Civil War*, 1949.)

Although received in 1832, the prophecy was not published until 1851, in the first edition of the Pearl of Great Price. The revelation, however, was well known among the members of the Church and, according to some of the apostles, it was used in missionary work. Elder Wilford Woodruff said that he and many others had a copy of the revelation twenty-five years before the rebellion. (*Journal of Discourses* 14:2.) There were few Americans, in 1851, who believed that the Civil War was imminent, and in 1832 it was even farther from their minds.

### History is Prophecy Reversed

South Carolina rebelled against the Federal Government and that actual war commenced on April 12, 1861, with the firing upon federal-held Fort Sumter in Charleston harbor. The war pitted twenty-two Northern States against eleven Southern States. (D&C 87:1-3.) Misery and death stalked the land in that ferocious war. No human being, except the Lord's Prophet, knew the tremendous toll of lives and destruction of property that would result. The estimated cost of that war was eight billion dollars, a huge sum in that day.

The Southern States did call upon Great Britain for aid, but that nation did not enter the conflict. However, she did permit Southern cruisers to be fitted out in her shipyards, resulting in the payment of a $15 million damage claim to the Union after the war. The South also called for aid from France and Spain, but none was granted.

## Beginning of Modern Wars

The prophecy on war is about wars. (D&C 87:1.) The Civil War began a train of wars and calamities on the earth.

> And the time will come that war will be poured out upon all nations, beginning at this place. . . .
>
> And thus, with the sword and by bloodshed the inhabitants of the earth shall mourn; and with famine, and plague and earthquake, and the thunder of heaven, and the fierce and vivid lightning also, shall the inhabitants of the earth be made to feel the wrath, and indignation, and chastening hand of an Almighty God, until the consumption decreed hath made a full end of all nations. (Verses 2, 6.)

Since the Civil War, the nations of the earth have suffered famine, plague, earthquakes, and wars. The remarkable fulfillment of this prophecy is the fact that scarcely a year has passed since 1861 when the nations have been free of internal or external wars. The geographic impact of war was felt in World War I in the answer to the call upon other nations by Great Britain to defend herself and her allies. (Verse 3.)

Following verse 3 of Section 87, it seems that the order of events of the remaining part of the prophecy is about the post-Civil War period, which would culminate in the "end of all nations."

## Conclusion

Joseph Smith was ordained to give the Lord's word to this dispensation. (D&C 5:10.) He predicted many details concerning the American Civil War. History has proved him a foreteller of these events. War and other calamities were to be poured out upon all nations after the Civil War. In fact, peace was to be taken from the earth in our dispensation. (*Ibid.*, 1:35.) Do the wars and calamities since that time attest to the fact that peace has been taken from the earth? Is the world ready or near-ready for the wheat to be gathered and the tares to be burned as predicted?

## Chapter 11

# GOD'S POWER IN THE WORLD

## (Section 88:1-14)

After the Prophet Joseph Smith had visited Jackson County, Missouri, in the spring of 1832, a number of problems arose among the saints in that area. In the chapter on the "one mighty and strong" (Chapter 9), we learned of a problem in connection with Edward Partridge, the Bishop in Zion. Because of the failure of the authorities and saints in Missouri to carry out the plans for their temporal welfare under the law of consecration, the Prophet became concerned. On January 14, 1833, he wrote a letter to W. W. Phelps, editor of the *Evening and Morning Star*, in which he enclosed the revelation dated December 27, 1832, known as Section 88 in the Doctrine and Covenants. This revelation is named the "Olive Leaf" by the Prophet. He explains that it is "the Lord's message of peace to us." Here are the Prophet's words:

> I send you the "olive leaf" which we have plucked from the Tree of Paradise, the Lord's message of peace to us; for though our brethren in Zion indulge in feelings towards us, which are not according to the requirements of the new covenant, yet, we have the satisfaction of knowing that the Lord approves of us, and has accepted us, and established His name in Kirtland for the salvation of the nations; for the Lord will have a place whence His word will go forth, in these last days, in purity; for if Zion will not purify herself, so as to be approved of in all things, in His sight, He will seek another people; for His work will go on until Israel is gathered, and they who will not hear His voice, must expect to feel His wrath. Let me say unto you, seek to purify yourselves, and also all the inhabitants of Zion, lest the Lord's anger be kindled to fierceness. (*DHC* 1:316.)

Section 88 gives doctrines and great principles of salvation that are outstanding in their scope and sublimity of thought.

In the opening verses of the revelation, several ideas are given that should be known to all. The Lord says that angels rejoice over the brethren, for their prayers have come up to the Lord of Sabaoth and are recorded in the book of the sanctified in the celestial world. (D&C 88:1-2.) Contrary to some ideas, the word *Sabaoth* does not mean "Sabbath," but "hosts"; consequently, the Lord is the master of many. President Joseph Fielding Smith reminded those attending a general conference of the Church that to have one's name on the membership records does not save one in the eternal world. Our names must be found in the records maintained in the heavens as a result of our having kept the commandments. (*Conference Report*, September 1950, p. 10.) The good deeds that we do here in placing the kingdom of God first will redound to our everlasting benefit.

## The Comforters

When Jesus was in mortality, he taught his disciples that there were two Comforters. (John 14:16-26.) In Section 88 the Lord speaks of only one Comforter, but since the expression "another Comforter" is used in verse 3, it is well for us to recall the discussion of the Savior with his ancient disciples. In the fourteenth chapter of John he tells his hearers that by keeping the commandments they show their love of the Father and that they will be blessed in having the Comforter to be with them. The world does not receive this blessing because they have not accepted him, but the disciples may have the influence of the Holy Ghost through their obedience. Further on, the Lord points out that the Comforter referred to is the Holy Ghost. This Spirit will teach the convert and bring all things necessary to his remembrance. (John 14:16-17, 26.)

During the discourse on the Comforter as the Holy Ghost, Jesus spoke of a second Comforter that would abide with the disciples:

> He that hath my commandments, and keepeth them, he it is that loveth me: and he that loveth me shall be loved of my Father, and I will love him, and will manifest myself to him. . . .
>
> Jesus answered and said unto him, If a man love me, he will keep my words: and my Father will love him, and we will come unto him, and make our abode with him. (John 14:21, 23.)

In commenting upon this subject, Joseph Smith said that after a person has become a member of the Church and has received the first Comforter, or the Holy Ghost, if he will continue to humble himself in living every word of God and after the trial of his faith, the Lord Jesus Christ will then visit him and make his abode with him from time to time. The Prophet also said that this blessing was received by the ancient saints when they had the heavens opened to them in vision and had communion with God. (*DHC* 3:380-381.)

In Section 88, the Comforter known as the Holy Ghost is spoken of as "the Holy Spirit of promise," (verse 3) which will "abide in your hearts." The second Comforter, the Savior, cannot abide in one's heart. (D&C 130:22-23.) In the next verse, we learn that this Comforter "is the promise . . . of eternal life, even the glory of the celestial kingdom." (Verse 4.) Eternal life as used here is the same as the attainment of godhood, or exaltation, in the celestial kingdom, or to become a member of the church of the Firstborn after the resurrection. (*Ibid.*, verse 5; 76:54-60.)

### The Light of Christ

The members of the Church were promised the wonderful blessing of enjoying the gift of the Holy Ghost to give them guidance to eternal life. (D&C 88:3-5.) Having addressed this comforting message to those who had made covenant with him in baptism, the Lord instructs us concerning his power and the means by which God's children throughout the world receive his blessings. We are informed that there is a light which proceeds "forth from the presence of God to fill the immensity of space." (*Ibid.*, verse 12.) This Spirit, influence, and force is felt by all men, and it is throughout all parts of man's environment. Although the scripture states that it comes from the presence of God, this Spirit is the light of Christ. Jesus, in the pre-earth life, was creator of this earth, and he is man's Atoner. For these and other reasons, one may say that although this "light" emanates from God, it comes also from those who have attained all power in the exaltation. Four distinct functions performed by the light of Christ are mentioned. These are: (1) creative power; (2) life-giving force; (3) governing or sustaining force; and (4) enlightening or inspiring power.

## Creative and Life-sustaining Powers

In the following verses we learn that the "light of Christ" is the power by which the sun, moon, stars, and "even the earth upon which you stand" were created. (*Ibid.*, verses 6-10.)

> And the light which shineth, which giveth you light, is through him who enlighteneth your eyes, which is the same light that quickeneth your understandings;
>
> Which light proceedeth forth from the presence of God to fill the immensity of space—
>
> The light which is in all things, which giveth life to all things, which is the law by which all things are governed. (*Ibid.*, verses 11-13.)

Here is stated the power of God manifest in all creation—in all things. Men have looked into the heavens and have marvelled at the greatness of the universe and the orderliness of these creations. Many thoughtful men have recognized in God's creations the evidence to support the belief that there exists a power greater than themselves. After Korihor, the anti-Christ, had asked Alma for a sign to support his belief in God, the prophet reminded him that he had seen many evidences of God's existence. In addition to the testimony of the prophets, Alma said:

> . . . The scriptures are laid before thee, yea, and all things denote there is a God; yea, even the earth, and all things that are upon the face of it, yea, and its motion, yea, and also the planets which move in their regular form do witness that there is a Supreme Creator. (Alma 30:44.)

When one considers the marvels of nature, there is found convincing testimony to support belief in God.

### Intelligence-Inspiring Power

In addition to the powers already mentioned as functions of the "light of Christ," the one most important in terms of its personal blessing to each individual is that of imparting enlightenment, inspiration, and guidance.

> And the light which shineth, which giveth you light, is through him who enlighteneth your eyes, which is the same light that quickeneth your understandings;
>
> Which light proceedeth forth from the presence of God to fill the immensity of space— (D&C 88:11-12.)

Job's statement "there is a spirit in man: and the inspiration of the Almighty giveth them understanding" (Job 32:8), reminds one of this "light." Also important in understanding additional information about this Spirit are these ideas found in modern revelation: (1) man should live by God's word; (2) what the Lord gives is truth, light, and Spirit, even the "light of Christ"; (3) every man in the world receives this light; (4) to the degree that man seeks for and abides by that Spirit, so is he enlightened until he comes unto the Father. (D&C 88:44-47.)

These truths are not only for the Latter-day Saint, but for *all* men. When one understands the functions of the "light of Christ," his eyes are opened to the ways in which God governs his universe, and he also sees the application of God's attributes of justice and mercy.

Who are the inhabitants of the earth? They are all spirit sons and daughters of God. "For we are also his offspring." (Acts 17:28.) Is the Father concerned about the welfare of his children? The earth and the things of the earth were created that man might receive the resurrection and, if faithful, eternal life; this is God's work and glory. (Moses 1:39.) The Lord has given to every man sufficient light and understanding that, if acted upon, will lead him back into the presence of the Father. Notice how the Book of Mormon prophet Mormon expressed this truth:

> For behold, the Spirit of Christ is given to every man, that he may know good from evil. . . .
>
> And now, my brethren, seeing that ye know the light by which ye may judge, which light is the light of Christ, see that ye do not judge wrongfully; for with that same judgment which ye judge ye shall also be judged.
>
> Wherefore, I beseech of you, brethren, that ye should search diligently in the light of Christ that ye may know good from evil; and if ye will lay hold upon every good thing, and condemn it not, ye certainly will be a child of Christ. (Moroni 7:16, 18, 19.)

In the words of President Joseph Fielding Smith, we learn:

> The Lord has not left us to grope in darkness, but has given to every man that is born with understanding the power to discern between good and evil, truth and falsehood, through the power of the intelligence, light of truth, or light of Christ, born with him. However, as man departs from the truth, the power of intelligence forsakes him and for that cause he does not come unto God. (*The Way to Perfection*, p. 230.)

The great truth which governs the degree to which men receive the "light of Christ" is given in Section 88, verse 63, that when men draw unto God, he draws unto them by his Spirit. Therefore, the instruction is: seek diligently and he shall be found, and his treasures will be opened unto you.

## Revelation—the Book of Mormon

In discoursing on his desires to preach the gospel to all people, Alma taught the doctrine that men of all nations may receive God's light.

> For behold, the Lord doth grant unto all nations, of their own nation and tongue, to teach his word, yea, in wisdom, all that he seeth fit that they should have; therefore we see that the Lord doth counsel in wisdom, according to that which is just and true. (Alma 29:8.)

One way in which the Lord has given his "word" to *all* people is through the inspiration received by the "light of Christ." We can see in this principle the important fact again, that the Father gives to all of his children sufficient to guide and direct them regardless of race or place on the earth. To each is given according to his needs as he can assimilate truth for his advancement in the earth life. The final judgment will be made on the great principle of the light and knowledge possessed by the individual. (D&C 76:110-111.) In reference to this principle, Joseph Smith taught:

> . . . He holds the reins of judgment in His hands; he is a wise Lawgiver, and will judge all men, not according to the narrow, contracted notions of men, but, "according to the deeds done in the body whether they be good or evil," or whether these deeds were done in England, America, Spain, Turkey, or India. He will judge them, "not according to what they have not, but according to what they have," those who have lived without law, will be judged without law, and those who have a law, will be judged by that law. We need not doubt the wisdom and intelligence of the Great Jehovah; He will award judgment or mercy

to all nations according to their several deserts, their means of obtaining intelligence, the laws by which they are governed, the facilities afforded them of obtaining correct information, and His inscrutable designs in relation to the human family; and when the designs of God shall be made manifest, and the curtain of futurity be withdrawn, we shall all of us eventually have to confess that the Judge of all the earth has done right. (*DHC* 4:595-596.)

## God Knows and Rules

One may think of the "light of Christ" as a great communication system. An important lesson to be learned by all men, and especially Latter-day Saints who believe that God does know the thoughts of men and that he rules among the nations, is this expression from Elder B. H. Roberts:

> . . . *He knows,* not only "what's done," but also "what's resisted"; that He knows of the struggle for the attainment of virtue—the hungering and the thirsting after righteousness; that He knows the strength of the temptation, and the weakness of the tempted; that He knows the heart . . . and He will judge, not after the sight of the eyes, neither reprove after the hearing of the ears, but with righteousness shall He judge, and reprove with equity [Isa. 11:3, 4]; judging, "not according to the appearance, but judge righteous judgment." [John 7:24.] Men can be assured of a correct registration and truthful report of their deeds, and a judgment upon them neither partial nor prejudiced; which, while it may cause the wicked to tremble, to men conscious of the uprightness of their intentions, and of honest effort in right directions, as God gives them vision to see the right—what encouragement to earnest striving this conception of living in the very presence of God must bring! (*The Seventy's Course in Theology,* Fifth Year, 1912, p. 13.)

## God's Omnipresence

In the great discourse on Mars' Hill in Athens, Paul spoke of the principle that all men live, and move, and have their being in God. (Acts 17:28.) The erroneous concept that God is everywhere and therefore he is a spirit only is held in the apostate Christian world. The teaching of God's omnipresence is true, but that he is not personal is declared false by the Lord in the revelations received in our dispensation. Men have mistaken a manifestation of God, the "light of Christ," as being God himself. God is everywhere present by his Spirit, the "light of Christ," but God and the Christ are personal beings of flesh and bone and individually present in only one place at a time. (D&C 130:22.)

### The Holy Ghost and the Light of Christ

There is a difference between the "light of Christ" and the Holy Ghost. Sometimes in scripture the terms denoting one or the other are used interchangeably, but the distinction is evident in each specific case by the use of the term in its context.

The "light of Christ" is given to all men, regardless of race or color. (John 1:9.) On the other hand, the Holy Ghost is received by those who are obedient. (Acts 5:32.) The latter is a special gift received by the laying on of hands. (Acts 8:14-17; D&C 33:15.) Also, there is a power from the Holy Ghost which is "temporary"; that is, if the person having been led to the truth of the gospel by the "light of Christ" receives a testimony by the power of the Holy Ghost (Moroni 10:4-5), and then he does not accept baptism and the laying on of hands by authority, the testimony is lost to him. The case of Cornelius in the New Testament is a case where the power was known and baptism accepted. (Acts 10.) The Prophet Joseph Smith, in commenting upon this case, said that if Cornelius had not accepted the gospel the Holy Ghost would not have remained with him. (*DHC* 4:555.)

President Joseph F. Smith said the following about the difference between the "light of Christ" and the Holy Ghost:

> The question is often asked, Is there any difference between the Spirit of the Lord and the Holy Ghost? The terms are fre-

quently used synonymously. We often say the Spirit of God when we mean the Holy Ghost; we likewise say the Holy Ghost when we mean the Spirit of God. The Holy Ghost is a personage in the Godhead, and is not that which lighteth every man that cometh into the world. It is the Spirit of God which proceeds through Christ to the world, that enlightens every man that comes into the world, and that strives with the children of men, and will continue to strive with them, until it brings them to a knowledge of the truth and the possession of the greater light and testimony of the Holy Ghost. If, however, he receive that greater light, and then sin against it, the Spirit of God will cease to strive with him, and the Holy Ghost will wholly depart from him. (*Gospel Doctrine,* pp. 67-68.)

## Chapter 12

# THE EARTH AND MAN

## (Section 88:14-35, 97-104)

In the revelation known as the "Olive Leaf," the Lord gave instructions to his servants regarding the Holy Ghost, also known as the Holy Spirit, with the promise of eternal life. (D&C 88:3-4.)

From a discussion on the Comforter, the Holy Ghost, given only to the obedient who receive the baptism of water and the Spirit by one having authority, to a consideration of the "light of Christ" given to all men because they are spirit sons and daughters of God, the revelation proceeds to speak "peace" to the hearts of the saints in revealing what man should know about the glories of the eternal worlds following the resurrection.

### The Soul of Man

The eternal truth is revealed that man had a pre-earth life as a spirit entity. In this second estate, the earth period, man becomes a living soul. (Genesis 2:7.) We learn in Section 88 that "the spirit and the body are the soul of man." (Verse 15.) This concept is immediately followed with the truth that both the body and the spirit are to be resurrected. (Verse 16.) It is the soul that will be redeemed; therefore, we should be mindful of how we care for the body, for it is an essential part of man's eternal make-up. (Verse 28.) With this understanding of the value of the body in the eternal plan, man's body becomes precious, but as Elder James E. Talmage said:

> . . . Be not afraid of soiling its hands; be not afraid of scars that may come to it if won in earnest effort, or in honest fight, but

beware of scars that disfigure, that have come to you in places where you ought not have gone, that have befallen you in unworthy undertakings; beware of the wounds of battle in which you have been fighting on the wrong side. (*Conference Report,* October 1913, p. 117.)

## The Earth

The revelation continues in pointing out that the earth has an eternal destiny as well as does man. It is decreed that the faithful will inherit the earth. (Matt. 5:5.) The inheritance of the earth as an eternal home will come to those who have lived the law of the celestial kingdom. The earth was created that it would be the habitation of the mortal tabernacles for the spirit sons and daughters of God. (D&C 49:16-17.) But this was not to be the end of the earth's usefulness, for in fulfilling the measure of its creation it would also become a celestial kingdom. (*Ibid.*, 88:18-20.)

In order that we may fully understand that our position in the eternal worlds following the resurrection, is to be determined by the law we obey, we are instructed as follows:

> That bodies who are of the celestial kingdom may possess it [the earth] forever and ever; for, for this intent was it made and created, and for this intent are they sanctified.
>
> And they who are not sanctified through the law which I have given unto you, even the law of Christ, must inherit another kingdom, even that of a terrestrial kingdom, or that of a telestial kingdom.
>
> For he who is not able to abide the law of a celestial kingdom cannot abide a celestial glory. (Verses 20-22.)

They who cannot abide the terrestrial law must abide a telestial kingdom. There will be some who will be unable to abide the telestial glory. These are the sons of perdition. (Verses 23-24.) Perdition is also known as a kingdom, but of "no glory." (Verse 24.)

## Spiritual Bodies

It requires modern revelation to interpret and understand passages in the Bible which have given rise to erroneous doctrines. An example comes from Section 88 where we find the following words:

> For notwithstanding they die, they also shall rise again, a spiritual body. (D&C 88:27.)

The term spiritual body is found in the writings of Paul in a discussion of the resurrection. He said that the body is sown a natural body, but it is raised a spiritual body. (1 Cor. 15:44.) Because Paul in this same letter said that "flesh and blood cannot inherit the kingdom of God" (verse 50), it is believed by some not of our faith that the body is not actually raised from the grave, but that it is the spirit of man that is revived or resurrected. It is true that "flesh and blood" (mortals) cannot inherit the kingdoms assigned resurrected beings. The resurrection of which we shall partake will be the raising of the body as flesh and bones—tangible, material substance. (Philippians 3:20-31; Alma 11:43-45; D&C 129:1-2.) This body will not contain blood, but, as Joseph Smith said: "All will be raised by the power of God, having spirit in their bodies, and not blood." (*DHC* 4:555.) President Brigham Young declared:

> . . . the blood will not be resurrected with the body, being designed only to sustain the life of the present organization. When that is dissolved, and we again obtain our bodies by the power of the resurrection, that which we now call the life of the body, and which is formed from the food we eat and the water we drink will be supplanted by another element. (*Discourses of Brigham Young*, p. 374.)

This explains why the scriptures refer to the resurrected body as "a spiritual body" or as Amulek put it, "the whole becoming spiritual and immortal." (Alma 11:45.) In this condition man will not be subject to decay or dissolution, but will remain free from disease and the ills of earth life or mortality. (1 Cor. 15:52; 2 Nephi 9:13.)

### "Ye Shall Receive Your Body"

The Prophet Joseph Smith was emphatic in maintaining that in the resurrection we do not lose the fundamental parts of the body which were ours in mortality.

> . . . There is no fundamental principle belonging to a human system that ever goes into another in this world or in the world to come: I care not what the theories of men are. We have the testimony that God will raise us up, and he has the power to do it. If anyone supposes that any part of our bodies, that is, the fundamental parts thereof, ever goes into another body, he is mistaken. (*DHC* 5:339.)

President John Taylor taught that even though the body may be destroyed or blown to the four winds of heaven, yet the particles out of which the body was created cannot be destroyed because they are eternal. (*Journal of Discourses*, 18:333.)

### Perfect Bodies

As resurrected beings we shall have perfect bodies. The disfigurements of the flesh will be removed. A question is sometimes raised as to whether or not there will be a difference in the resurrection between the person who dies in young adulthood and the one who leaves mortality at an advanced age. The scriptures do not speak expressly to this question, but only of the perfected body. (Alma 11:42-45; 40:23; D&C 88:28.) However, President Joseph F. Smith said:

> In the resurrection of the dead the child that was buried in its infancy will come up in the form of the child that it was when it was laid down; then it will begin to develop. From the day of the resurrection, the body will develop until it reaches the full measure of the stature of its spirit, whether it be male or female. (*Improvement Era,* June 1909, p. 594.)

The body will come forth as it is laid to rest, for there is no growth or development in the grave. As it is laid down, so will it arise, and changes to perfection will come by the law of restitution. But the spirit will continue to expand and develop, and the body after the resurrection will develop to the full stature of man. (*Ibid.*, June 1904, pp. 623-624.)

The Prophet Joseph Smith taught:

As concerning the resurrection, I will merely say that all men will come from the grave as they lie down, whether old or young; there will not be "added unto their stature one cubit," neither taken from it; all will be raised by the power of God, having spirit in their bodies, and not blood. (*DHC* 4:555.)

## Kingdoms of the Resurrection

As discussed in earlier chapters, each person will receive the reward that he has earned in the earth life. (Chapter 3.) In summary, we may quote President George Q. Cannon:

. . . The Lord has shown to us that there are differences of rewards. Some of his children will attain to what is called celestial glory. Others of his children will not have faith enough nor exercise their agency in the direction to gain that glory; but they will gain terrestrial glory. There are others that will not progress that far; they will feel reluctant to obey the laws that pertain to the terrestrial, and they will obtain telestial glory. There are still others that will not attain even to the telestial glory. Why is it that there are these differences? Is it because God has chosen some of us for the telestial glory, some of us for the terrestrial glory and some of us for the celestial glory? No, there is no such predestination as this. We are all born with our free agency; with the power within ourselves, aided by the blessing of God, to attain unto the highest glory. How shall we attain unto the highest glory? There is only one way, and that is by observing the highest laws. The highest laws, when obeyed, bring as a reward the highest glory; and the man or woman who expects to attain to the highest glory without obeying these laws, deceives himself or herself. It cannot be done. If I rise above the telestial glory, I must obey a law that will lift me above that. If I rise to the terrestrial glory, it will be by obeying terrestrial law. If I do not obey laws higher than that, I cannot attain to a higher glory.

I want to impress upon you . . . that our exaltation, our future glory, depends entirely upon our obedience to law. We should not lose sight of this. (*Conference Report,* April 1900, p. 54.)

The foregoing discussion is in harmony with the "Olive Leaf" revelation where it is also indicated that those who become sons of perdition will be resurrected and return to that place for which they prepared themselves by disobedience. (D&C 88:29-32.)

It is by obedience to God's law—eternal law—that blessings come; and also by disobedience, a loss of one's potential blessing.

And again, verily I say unto you, that which is governed by law is also preserved by law and perfected and sanctified by the same.

That which breaketh a law, and abideth not by law, but seeketh to become a law unto itself, and willeth to abide in sin, and altogether abideth in sin, cannot be sanctified by law, neither by mercy, justice, nor judgment. Therefore, they must remain filthy still. (Verses 34-35.)

### The Resurrection, When?

The Lord has revealed that every person who has lived upon the earth will receive a resurrection. This means both the "just and unjust." (Acts 24:15; see also Rev. 20:13, 1 Cor. 15:21-22.) By reason of the transgression of Adam, death entered the world, and through the atonement of Jesus Christ all mankind will be redeemed from this temporal death. There is no exception. (2 Nephi 9:6-7, 12-13; Alma 12:16-18.)

The general scriptural pronouncement is that there is a time for the righteous and a time for the unrighteous to be raised from the grave. (Rev. 20:5, 12-13; D&C 29:22-26.) There will be two general resurrections—the first, which is known as the "just," and the second, which is named the "unjust." A modern revelation, however, teaches us that these general classifications should be separated into two parts each. (D&C 88:97-102.) This revelation states that each of these resurrections, four in number, will be heralded by the sounding of an angel's trump. The first trump is at the Savior's second coming.

> And they who have slept in their graves shall come forth, for their graves shall be opened; and they also shall be caught up to meet him in the midst of the pillar of heaven—
>
> They are Christ's, the first fruits, they who shall descend with him first, and they who are on the earth and in their graves, who are first caught up to meet him; and all this by the voice of the sounding of the trump of the angel of God. (D&C 88:97-98.)

It is recorded in scripture (Matt. 27:51-53 and 3 Nephi 23:9-10) that many souls arose from the dead at the time of the Savior's resurrection. This, however, did not commence what is known to us as the first resurrection. This is clarified by Joseph Fielding Smith in the following quotations:

> While there was a general resurrection of the righteous at the time Christ arose from the dead, it is customary for us to speak of the resurrection of the righteous at the Second Coming of Christ as the first resurrection. (*Doctrines of Salvation,* 2:295.)
>
> It is the opinion of some that the resurrection is going on all the time now, but this is purely *speculation without warrant in the scriptures.* It is true that the Lord has power to call forth any person or persons from the dead, as he may desire, especially if they have a mission to perform which would require their resurrection. For example, we have the case of Peter, James, and Moroni.
>
> We are given to understand that the *first* resurrection yet future, which means the coming forth of the righteous, will take place at *one particular time,* which is when our Savior shall appear in the clouds of heaven, when he shall return to reign. (*Ibid.,* p. 299.)

The second trump is sounded after the resurrection of the saints. The length of time between these two events is not revealed. Jesus' coming marks the beginning of the millennium, therefore, the resurrection of terrestrial beings occurs after the millennium begins:

> And after this another angel shall sound, which is the second trump; and then cometh the redemption of those who are Christ's at his coming; who have received their part in that prison which is prepared for them, that they might receive the gospel, and be judged according to men in the flesh. (D&C 88:99.)

Thus ends the first general resurrection, except as that resurrection will continue into the millennium until all the worthy or honorable dead have received this blessing. At the end of the thousand years of peace and righteousness, the second general resurrection will begin with the telestial beings rising from their graves. Before this, however, they shall be judged to return to the spirit world not to be resurrected until the thousand years are ended.

> And again, another trump shall sound, which is the third trump; and then come the spirits of men who are to be judged, and are found under condemnation;
>
> And these are the rest of the dead; and they live not again until the thousand years are ended, neither again, until the end of the earth. (Verses 100-101.)

Without the time interval being indicated, the last part of the last, or second resurrection, that of the sons of perdition, is described as follows:

> And another trump shall sound, which is the fourth trump, saying: There are found among those who are to remain until that great and last day, even the end, who shall remain filthy still. (Verse 102.)

## Visions of the Resurrection

We have the testimonies of Latter-day prophets concerning the resurrection. These testimonies bring to the saint an awareness, born of the Spirit, that the resurrection is a reality, and that men will come forth from their graves as they were laid down. The Prophet Joseph Smith stated:

> Would you think it strange if I relate what I have seen in vision in relation to this interesting theme? Those who have died in Jesus Christ may expect to enter into all that fruition of joy when they come forth, which they possessed or anticipated here.
>
> So plain was the vision, that I actually saw men, before they had ascended from the tomb, as though they were getting up slowly. They took each other by the hand and said to each other, "My father, my son, my mother, my daughter, my brother, my sister." And when the voice calls for the dead to arise, suppose I am laid by the side of my father, what would be the first joy of my heart? To meet my father, my mother, my brother, my sister; and when they are by my side, I embrace them and they me. . . .
>
> All your losses will be made up to you in the resurrection, provided you continue faithful. By the vision of the Almighty I have seen it.
>
> More painful to me are the thoughts of annihilation than death. If I have no expectation of seeing my father, mother, brothers, sisters and friends again, my heart would burst in a moment, and I should go down to my grave.
>
> The expectation of seeing my friends in the morning of the resurrection cheers my soul and makes me bear up against the evils of life. It is like their taking a long journey, and on their return we meet them with increased joy.
>
> God has revealed His Son from the heavens and the doctrine of the resurrection also; and we have a knowledge that those we bury here God will bring up again, clothed upon and quickened by the Spirit of the great God; and what mattereth it whether we lay them down, or we lay down with them when we can keep them no longer? Let these truths sink down in our hearts, that we may even here begin to enjoy that which shall be in full hereafter. (*Teachings of the Prophet Joseph Smith*, pp. 295-296.)

As President of the Church, Wilford Woodruff related a vision of the resurrection given to him while laboring as a missionary in the State of Tennessee during the lifetime of Joseph Smith.

After laboring in that part (Memphis, Tennessee) for a length of time, I received a letter from Joseph Smith and Oliver Cowdery, in which they requested me to stay in that country and take charge of the churches that we had built up there. The Prophet promised me many things, and said I would lose no blessings by tarrying in that country and doing as he wished me, and letting the other brethren go and get their endowments. I was then at the house of Brother Abraham O. Smoot's mother. I received this about sundown. I went into a little room where there was a sofa, to pray alone. I felt full of joy and rejoicing at the promises God had made to me through the Prophet. While I was upon my knees praying, my room was filled with light. I looked and a messenger stood by my side. I arose, and this personage told me he had come to instruct me. He presented before me a panorama. He told me he wanted me to see with my eye and understand with my mind what was coming to pass in the earth before the coming of the Son of Man. He commenced with what the revelations say about the sun being turned to darkness, the moon to blood, and these stars falling from heaven. Those things were all presented to me one after another, as they will be, I suppose, when they are manifest before the coming of the Son of Man. Then he showed me the resurrection of the dead—what is termed the first and second resurrection. In the first resurrection I saw no graves nor anyone raised from the grave. I saw legions of celestial beings, men and women who had received the gospel all clothed in white robes. In the form they were presented to me, they had already been raised from the grave. After this he showed me what is termed the second resurrection. Vast fields of graves were before me, and the Spirit of God rested upon the earth like a shower of gentle rain, and when that fell upon the graves, they were opened, and an immense host of human being came forth. They were just as diversified in their dress as we are here, or as they were laid down. This personage taught me with regard to these things. . . . (*The Deseret Weekly*, Vol. 53, No. 21, November 7, 1896, p. 642.)

## Chapter 13

# THE LAW, MAN, AND THE UNIVERSE

### (Section 88:36-75)

The last two chapters have come from Section 88, known as the "Olive Leaf." The revelation began with a discussion of the Holy Ghost and the "light of Christ." Following this information, the Church is instructed in matters relating to the resurrection of man and the earth being the eventual habitat of celestialized beings.

### All Kingdoms Have a Law

Law and order exist in all of God's creations. In this revelation, the Lord informs the reader that "All kingdoms have a law given." (D&C 88:36.) This truth pertains to the universe "and there is no space in the which there is no kingdom." These kingdoms have their laws in which there are bounds and conditions. (Verses 37-38.)

These thoughts led President Anthon H. Lund to indicate the value of this reign of law in the universe:

> We believe that everything is ruled by law. We are thankful that it is so, for otherwise we would live in a world of chance, in a fearful uncertainty of what would happen next. I believe that the material laws that can be traced in the creation had an intelligent will behind them, that the laws themselves were never superior to the will of God. He made those laws, and by His power they became effective to accomplish His purposes. (*Conference Report,* April 1916, p. 12.)

These ideas help us to understand that in a world-system comprised of worlds or even in a minute particle of matter, there is order. If the conditions under which we exist were to be less than orderly, then confusion, uncertainty, doubt, and even despair, would be found. On the other hand, as the Lord has said, "all kingdoms have a law" and the laws govern; consequently, when man lives a law, the blessings or benefits of that law are his. Therefore, the Lord declares that all beings who abide in the law are justified because they cleave unto principles (laws) that bring them nearer to God. (Verse 39.) Man discovers that violation of eternal law brings greater influences to bear upon him in continuing to do wrong. No greater truth was spoken than found in verse 40 of Section 88, upon which President Charles W. Penrose had this to say about the attraction of evil to evil and virtue to virtue:

> . . . If we do evil, evil impressions come naturally, and if we love to do good a good influence, a good spirit, is with us, and round about us, and in our being and we are sustained and supported thereby; and if we are corrupt and wicked and abominable and rebellious, the effects of our acts are right in our nature, and these things will be disclosed just as naturally as the opening of books made of paper and written upon with ink. (*Conference Report,* April 1917, p. 18.)

## God Is in All Things

In Chapter 11 consideration was given to the manner by which God, though personal, having form and of tangible substance, is able to be in constant communication with his creations and is everywhere, as the scriptures aver. (Psalms 139:7-12; Acts 17:27-28.) God is everywhere by the "light of Christ." (D&C 88:6-13; 84:44-47.) Because of God's omnipresence through this spirit, the Lord said that he is through all things, all things are round about him, he is in all things, and all things are before him. (*Ibid.*, 88:41.)

Not only is God omnipresent, but he is also omniscient. He knows all things. (*Ibid.*, verse 41:38:2.) The present is before his eyes, as the past may be, as well as the future. Latter-day Saints have a statement in the

*Lectures on Faith* given in Kirtland to the School of the Prophets concerning the necessity of understanding that God possesses all of his attributes in perfection.

> . . . God is the only supreme governor and independent being in whom all fulness and perfection dwell; who is omnipotent [all-powerful], omnipresent [everywhere present] and omniscient [all-knowing]; without beginning of days or end of life; and that in him every good gift and every good principle dwell . . . (Lecture Second, p. 13.)
>
> . . . without the knowledge of all things, God would not be able to save any portion of his creatures; for it is by reason of the knowledge which he has of all things, from the beginning to the end, that enables him to give that understanding to his creatures by which they are made partakers of eternal life; and if it were not for the idea existing in the minds of men that God had all knowledge, it would be impossible for them to exercise faith in him. (Lecture Fourth, p. 43.)

## Joseph Smith Inspired

Elder Orson Pratt called attention to verses 42 through 68 of Section 88 as evidence that Joseph Smith, who had little formal schoolroom education, and was but a youth, was inspired to give information concerning the reign of law in the universe, that other worlds are inhabited, and that it is man's opportunity to be in harmony with eternal law. Brother Pratt said:

> . . . Yet these words were given to him, and they contain information and knowledge far beyond that which you will find recorded in the writings of the learned, information expressed so simply that a common mind can, in some degree, grasp it, and yet so sublime and so great that when we come to investigate its depths, it requires greater powers and greater understanding than what man naturally possesses. . . .
>
> . . . We are also told that God is in the stars, those worlds so distant from ours, those great centers around which, no doubt, millions on millions of opaque bodies revolve as our planets revolve around our central body,the sun; that he is in those stars, that he is their light, and the power by which they are governed;

or to come home directly to our earth, he is in the earth, and is the power and light and glory that is attached to the elements of our globe.

This would seem to exhibit before us the nature of that Being whom we worship. We worship him because of his glory, greatness, goodness, justice, mercy, knowledge, and wisdom. We worship him, because he has the power to govern and control the universe, and because he has commanded us to do. He is a personage. . . . (*Journal of Discourses,* 17:324.)

The Lord likened the various kingdoms (worlds) to a parable in which the owner of a field sent his servants into the field at a different hour, even to the twelfth servant, and then the Lord visited each one of his servants at an appointed time. Each servant received the light of the Lord's countenance in the hour in which he was visited. (D&C 88:42-60.) Then the revelation represents the parable as applying to other worlds and their inhabitants:

Therefore, unto this parable I will liken all these kingdoms, and the inhabitants thereof—every kingdom in its hour, and in its time, and in its season, even according to the decree which God hath made. (D&C 88:61.)

We know by revelation that the Lord's creations are numerous. (Moses 1:33-35; 7:30.) In their time each is to be visited by the Lord, that the inhabitants thereof will find the joy and blessing of the light which only he can give to them. In the sermon quoted above from Elder Pratt, we learn that our own earth will be visited by the Lord during the time prophesied as the millennium. As pointed out in the revelations, he shall reign upon the earth for the thousand years. (*Ibid.,* 7:64-65; D&C 43:29-30.) Thus, from world to world will the Lord visit the pure in heart, who make up Zion. (*Ibid.,* 97:21.) Elder Pratt discourses further concerning subsequent events relative to these creations.

But there is another thing I want you to understand. This will not be kept up to all eternity, it is merely a preparation for something still greater. And What is that? By and by, when each of these creations has fulfilled the measure and bounds set and the times given for its continuance in a temporal state, it and its inhabitants who are worthy will be made celestial and glorified together. Then, from that time henceforth and for ever, there will be no intervening veil between God and his people who are sanctified and glorified, and he will not be under the necessity of withdrawing from one to go and visit another, because they will all be in his presence. It matters not how far in space these creations may be located from any special celestial kingdom where the Lord our God shall dwell, they will be able to see him at all times. Why? Because it is only the fall, and the vail that has been shut down over this creation, that keep us from the presence of God. Let the vail be removed, which now hinders us from beholding the glory of God and the celestial kingdom; let this creation be once perfected, after having passed through its various ordeals, after having enjoyed the light of the countenance of our Lord, in our hour and in our season, and let all things be perfected and glorified, and there will be no necessity for this vail being shut down. (*Journal of Discourses,* 17:332.)

Who are these inhabitants of other worlds? The revelations are clear in this regard. These inhabitants "are begotten sons and daughters unto God." (D&C 76:24.)

## Prayers Are Answered

As indicated in last chapter's lesson, through the "light of Christ" men are endowed with conscience, and their ability to come to the fulness of the gospel is determined largely by their response to the light they have received. If a person will seek the Lord earnestly, the Lord has promised to draw close to him. (D&C 88:63.) If he asks for things that are not expedient for him, it shall turn to his condemnation. (Verses 64-65.) Consequently, the Lord has admonished his children to call upon him in sincere prayer that they may know his will concerning them. Prayer is not intended, said President Joseph

Fielding Smith, to gratify some desire which may not be the best for you. Actually, we should not be too insistent or demanding of the Father for our own wishes, but seek for light to know the will of the Lord. (*Church History and Modern Revelation* 1:371.)

The Lord knows our needs better than we do. His vantage point is vastly different from ours. If Latter-day Saints would seek to learn the Lord's will concerning themselves and live by that knowledge, then the scripture would be fulfilled promising that their prayers would be answered (D&C 88:64.)

## Truth Is Eternal

Among the many great truths in the Doctrine and Covenants are those expressed in the following verse:

> Behold, that which you hear is as the voice of one crying in the wilderness—in the wilderness, because you cannot see him—my voice, because my voice is Spirit; my Spirit is truth; truth abideth and hath no end; and if it be in you it shall abound. (D&C 88:66.)

We are shut out of the immediate presence of God, therefore, we are in a "wilderness." We can, however, hear the voice of the Lord through his Spirit, which is truth. There follows in the revelation a statement that truth is absolute. Truth is eternal—it has no end! It does not change. Man's conception of a truth may change, but this does not affect the truth.

The fundamental principles of the gospel remain the same. They do not change. The principles that will sanctify people in the past will sanctify the people of our dispensation. Elder James E. Talmage asked the following question and then answered it:

> . . . Have you ever found a single passage in Holy Writ that indicates in the least degree any revision or alteration of the fundamental laws and principles of the gospel? Have you ever

found it necessary for God to amend Himself and His words? Men make constitutions and enact laws, and then have to repeal and alter them, but the fundamental laws of truth are eternal; they will never be amended, they will never be changed. As declared to Adam, so is it declared unto the world today: Except ye have faith in God and in His Son Jesus Christ, as the one and only Savior and Redeemer of mankind; except ye repent of your sins with a real and genuine repentance; except ye be baptized by immersion in water, at the hands of one having authority, and receive the gift of the Holy Ghost by the authorized laying on of hands, there is no possibility of your finding place in the kingdom of God. . . . You have never learned of any revision, amendment to or alteration in the law of the gospel of Jesus Christ, and in the form of the Church. Like the gospel itself, the Church adapts itself to the necessities of the times, to the conditions of life, but without the alteration of a single vital principle revealed of God. (*Conference Report,* October 1918, pp. 60-61.)

## Keep Your Minds Single To God

"If your eye is single to my glory," and "sanctify yourselves that your minds become single to God," are keys to successful Latter-day Saint living as indicated in these verses:

> And if your eye be single to my glory, your whole bodies shall be filled with light, and there shall be no darkness in you; and that body which is filled with light comprehendeth all things.
>
> Therefore, sanctify yourselves that your minds become single to God, and the days will come that you shall see him; for he will unveil his face unto you, and it shall be in his own time, and in his own way, and according to his own will. (D&C 88:67-68.)

Does the instruction to keep one's mind single to God mean that all of one's thoughts should be about God? This does not seem reasonable, in view of one's responsibility to care for children, earn a livelihood, and the multitudinous other things that require concentration and attention during a day. But do we as a people think enough about real issues in life, or is our attention on less important things? President Joseph F. Smith decried the many hours spent by Latter-day Saints on matters which are wasteful when more important matters might be considered:

> ... Think of it, how many hours, how many days and months we spend, as the children of God, in the pursuit of the temporalities of life, in devoting our thoughts to those things which pertain to the present temporal life or existence, not the spiritual existence, or that portion or particular part of the temporal existence which pertains to, and is part of, the spiritual existence of man. Men and women talk, they use their tongues and their lips very much in conversation and in the expressions of their views and thoughts which pertain only to worldly things, to trivial matters, of no value, to the groveling things, so to speak, of the world, and devote very few moments to useful and uplifting thought and very few words comparatively, are spoken by them which pertain to the eternal, everlasting growth, development and happiness of mankind. We think of the world, of the present, more in regard to the temporalities of life, than we think about the principles of eternal truth that make for the salvation, happiness and well-being, temporally and spiritually, of our souls. (*Conference Report,* October 1913, p. 3.)

How can one keep his mind single to God? Two suggestions follow as helps: (1) Undertake the daily practice of studying the scriptures, alone, or with your family. A regular, systematic practice of study will be of great worth in accomplishing this objective and in bringing a spiritual influence into the home. (2) To bring one to a realization of basic truth concerning himself and his relationship to God, every Latter-day Saint might often ask himself these three fundamental questions: Where did I come from? Why am I here? What shall be my place in the future life?

### Let Your Eye Be Single to My Glory

It is the will of the Lord that the Latter-day Saints apply their minds faithfully to understand his will. President Lorenzo Snow, after reminding the saints that Jesus was dependent upon the Father and he sought "but the will of the Father" (John 5:30), applied this principle in the following way:

> . . . Our eye should be single to the glory of God. That is what we have left the other life for and come into this. We should seek to promote the interests of the Most High God, and to feel as Jesus felt, "I can of mine own self do nothing." Inasmuch as we act today and tomorrow, this week and next week, in the interest of God, and have our eye single to His glory, there can be no failure. . . . A man's mind should be single to the glory of God in everything that he starts to accomplish. (*Millennial Star* 56:451-452.)

If each member of the Church were to follow this counsel, truly, the heavens would be opened to him, for all mysteries would be unveiled, even the wonders of heaven. (D&C 76:5-10.) Then the promise of the Lord would be fulfilled, wherein he said that by continuing in God, more light is received, "and that light groweth brighter and brighter until the perfect day." (*Ibid.*, 50:24.)

## Idle Thoughts and Loud Laughter

Twice in Section 88 association of laughter, idle thoughts, and light-mindedness is made.

> Remember the great and last promise which I have made unto you; cast away your idle thoughts and your excess of laughter far from you.
>
> Therefore, cease from all your light speeches, from all laughter, from all your lustful desires, from all your pride and light-mindedness, and from all your wicked doings. (D&C 88:69, 121.)

Does the Lord condemn laughter and expect his saints to be sober and serious all of the time? Upon other occasions, he has counseled that one should have a "glad heart and a cheerful countenance" (*Ibid.*, 59:15) and receive merriment in the dance, song and music. (*Ibid.*, 136:28.) If one reads carefully the scriptures quoted above, he will be impressed with the ideas that are associated with "loud" or "excess" of laughter—idle thoughts, lustful desires, pride, light-mindedness, and wicked doings. Unseemly and boisterous conduct at any time is out of harmony with the Spirit of the Lord. Laughter motivated by impure thoughts, light-mindedness toward sacred things, and unseemly conduct are condemned by the Lord; yet, happiness, joy, and cheerfulness are earmarks of the Saint.

## Purify Your Hearts

The elders who had been called to testify and warn this generation were to return to Kirtland to receive instructions and to be endowed that they might go forth with greater zeal to build up the Church upon the earth. (D&C 88:70-73.)

Consistent with this charge these "first laborers" were to purify their hearts, and, by their delivering their message to this people, they were to be clean from the blood of this generation. (Verses 74-75.)

President J. Reuben Clark, Jr. has given some thoughts to sober our thinking in the realization that we should purify our hearts:

> . . . Clean hands—clean of defilement of our fellow men, clean from the goods of our fellow men, clean from the blood of our fellow men; that must be the cleanliness which must be ours. Pure hearts—pure before the Lord; greed and lust and covetousness banished from our hearts, standing pure before God, that he may look therein and see there nothing which would cause him pain, and nothing which would make us blush.
>
> I have often said: "I wonder how we would all stand, and individually how I would stand, if I were told that God was yonder in the mountain and I could go to him if I wished." I wonder if my life has been such that I could go and stand before the Being who could look me through and see my secret thoughts and hopes and ambitions. Unless and until my brothers and sisters, we could stand that test, we are not living as the Lord would have us live. (*Conference Report,* October, 1935, pp. 90-91.)

## Chapter 14

# KNOWLEDGE AND EVENTS OF THE FUTURE

## (Section 88:76-116)

Among the many great truths revealed in Section 88, known as the "Olive Leaf," is the promise of seeing the Savior in his own time and in his own way, provided that the Church member will keep his mind single to God that light may dissipate darkness from mind and body. (D&C 88:67-68.)

With this counsel before the elders, they were admonished to assemble themselves together that they might purify their hearts in preparation for their ministry assignments. (Verses 70-75.)

### Prayer and Fasting

Immediately following these admonitions, the Lord commands that his people fast and pray. Prayer and fasting have often been counseled, with many beneficial results promised. Elder James E. Talmage points out that faith is developed with the power to do good when one follows this counsel. (*Jesus the Christ*, p. 395; see also Mark 9:14-29.) Alma received a testimony of the truth by fasting and praying over a long period of time. (Alma 5:46.) In order to qualify in missionary service there is a need to seek the Lord humbly through this method. Alma records that the sons of Mosiah through diligent study and because "they had given themselves to much prayer and fasting" had the spirit of prophecy "and the spirit of revelation, and when they taught, they taught with power and authority of God." (Alma 17:2-3.) One of the many benefits of fasting is to prepare one for sincere and humble prayer.

The Lord, through his prophets, has instituted the fast day, with its opportunity for devout prayer, that the membership of his Church might realize, at least monthly, the benefits of this kind of devotion. (D&C 88:76; Alma 6:6; 3 Nephi 27:1; Moroni 6:5.)

President David O. McKay indicated that fasting from two meals once each month and giving the value of these meals for the relief of those in need is the application of Jesus' teachings. (*Conference Report*, April 1932, p. 65.)

The Prophet Joseph Smith emphasized the need for all to know God through prayer and to pray over one's temporal possessions. (*DHC* 5:31.) This counsel joins prayer to keeping the commandments in bringing forth the blessings of the Father. Real intent is the measure of success in prayer and in all of one's devotions. (Moroni 7:6-8.)

## Teach One Another

In one of the better known admonitions from Section 88 is the counsel to teach one another the doctrine of the kingdom. (D&C 88:77.) Following this counsel to the early Church, the Lord pointed out the need to become schooled in all things that pertain to the kingdom of God. (Verses 78-79.)

The foregoing advice was given to brethren who had been and would yet proclaim the gospel, as is evident from the verses which follow:

> That ye may be prepared in all things when I shall send you again to magnify the calling whereunto I have called you, and the mission with which I have commissioned you.
>
> Behold, I sent you out to testify and warn the people, and it becometh every man who hath been warned to warn his neighbor. (Verses 80-81.)

In terms of missionary preparation, with what should the missionary become acquainted in following this instruction to be prepared by study? It is evident from the foregoing verses that the Lord wanted his servants, who were to warn and to testify of the restoration of the gospel, to learn those things which would be of greatest value in discharging this responsibility. Here are the essentials from verses 78 and 79, above:

First and foremost, to learn of the law of the gospel that pertains to the kingdom of God, insofar as it was expedient for them to know. This is the study of the principles and ordinances of salvation, which, of course, includes those great moral precepts that should ever guide the Latter-day Saint. President Brigham Young said:

> There are a great many branches of education: some go to college to learn languages, some to study law, some to study physic, and some to study astronomy, and various other branches of science. We want every branch of science taught in this place that is taught in the world. But our favorite study is that branch which particularly belongs to the Elders of Israel—namely, theology. Every Elder should become a profound theologian—should understand this branch better than all the world. There is no Elder who has the power of God upon him but understands more of the principles of theology than all the world put together. (*Journal of Discourses,* 6:317.)

Second, subjects which further prepare the missionary to testify and warn; that is, specific topics within the framework of the gospel of Jesus Christ and related fields of study. What are they?

(a) "Things both in heaven and in the earth and under the earth."

(b) "Things which have been."

(c) "Things which are."

(d) "Things which must shortly come to pass."

(e) "Things which are at home."

(f) "Things which are abroad."

(g) "The wars and the perplexities of the nations, and the judgments which are on the land."

(h) "A knowledge also of countries."

To the elders abroad in 1833, this counsel was given:

> ... Apply yourselves diligently to study, that your minds may be stored with all necessary information. (*DHC* 1:469.)

## Another Application

It is true that verses 77 through 79, and especially the latter, when disassociated from their context—addressed to missionaries—set forth the basic Latter-day Saint philosophy of education. The sciences and social studies may be found in this counsel, such as astronomy, agronomy, geology, history, political science, languages, geography, and current events. (*Doctrine and Covenants Commentary*, p. 556.) From the beginning of this dispensation the leaders of the Church have encouraged the membership to become educated in the things of God and also in secular subjects. President Brigham Young said this in these words:

> Not only does the religion of Jesus Christ make the people acquainted with the things of God, and develop within them moral excellence and purity, but it holds out every encouragement and inducement possible, for them to increase in knowledge and intelligence, in every branch of mechanism, or in the arts and sciences, for all wisdom, and all the arts and sciences in the world are from God, and are designed for the good of His people. (*Journal of Discourses*, 13:147.)

President John Taylor indicated his feelings regarding the eventual place of the Latter-day Saints in the world of education, in prophesying that Zion will be ahead of the world even in secular learning. (*Ibid.*, 21:100.)

The following remarks of two later presidents of the Church emphasize the purpose of education:

President David O. McKay: But gaining knowledge is one thing and applying it, quite another. Wisdom is the right application of knowledge; and true education—the education for which the Church stands—is the application of knowledge to the development of a noble and Godlike character.

A man may possess a profound knowledge of history and of mathematics; he may be an authority in psychology, biology, or astronomy; he may know all the discovered truths pertaining to geology and natural science; but if he has not with this knowledge that nobility of soul which prompts him to deal justly with his fellow men, to practice virtue and holiness in personal life, he is not a truly educated man. (*Gospel Ideals,* p. 440.)

President Joseph Smith: Educate yourself not only for time, but also for eternity. The latter of the two is the more important. Therefore, when we shall have completed the studies of time, and enter upon the commencement ceremonies of the great hereafter, we will find our work is not finished, but just begun. . . . (*Gospel Doctrine,* p. 269.)

Because Latter-day Saints believe that the temporal affairs of life have their spiritual meaning, the incentive to become educated is given greater stimulus. (D&C 29:34-35.)

It seems necessary, always, to keep in mind that the saving principles of the gospel of Jesus Christ save in this life and in the life to come and should never be neglected in preference to secular learning as such.

## Missionary Responsibility

The missionary prepared to teach the principles of salvation and to learn the essentials of his environment is told that he should testify and warn the people. Today, as in 1832, all are to make known the principles of the gospel. This responsibility, so discharged, would free the missionary from the blood of his generation and leave the world without excuse. (*Ibid.*, 88:81-82.) Those people who would come to the Lord early would never be forsaken by him. (Verse 83; Roy W. Doxey, *The Doctrine and Covenants Speaks*, Vol. 1, Chapter 37.)

### Be Free

To be a true disciple of the Lord is to be free. (John 8:31-32.) The elders of the Church were to continue in the freedom which they had received through the gospel of Jesus Christ. The converts of 1832 had come out of the world to become citizens of the kingdom of God. To them the Lord addressed these words:

> Abide ye in the liberty wherewith ye are made free; entangle not yourselves in sin, but let your hands be clean, until the Lord comes. (D&C 88:86.)

In terms of a person's purpose in life, true freedom is to be free from those practices which hinder one from advancing on to the goal of eternal perfection. When the Prophet Joseph Smith defined salvation, he said: "Salvation is nothing more nor less than to triumph over all our enemies and put them under our feet." (*DHC* 5:387.) Examples of man's enemies are the antonyms of the virtues such as those found in Section 4—skepticism, ignorance, hate, intolerance, fear, selfishness, and so forth. Members of the Church have found a new life in Jesus Christ through the benefits of release from the bondage of sin into freedom, a freedom which must be continually maintained through prayer, activity in the Church, and obedience to the other commandments. Habits and practices that bring one into bondage are contrary to the freedom which the gospel teaches one should seek.

"Entangle not yourselves in sin." (D&C 88:86.) The words of Elder James E. Talmage suggest to one that the person who lives close to sin in printed material, television, movies, etc., may soon find himself in bondage.

> Hosts of capable souls have heedlessly put themselves into the enemy's power by yielding to the treacherous invitation to frater-

nize with sin. Such a one is made welcome in the camp of the foe, and, at first a visitor, he sooner or later awakens to the fact that he is a prisoner, and withal a deserter from the ranks of patriotism and honor. . . . (*The Vitality of Mormonism,* 1948 ed., p. 335.)

## Until the Lord Comes

From the beginning of this dispensation, the warning voice of the Lord has been uttered in revelation and the fulfillment of the prophecies by disturbances on the earth. (D&C 1:35; 29:14-21; 43:18-27; 45:26-42.)

Similar warnings of judgments to come were given in 1832, and the Lord's prophets since then have called upon all to repent lest these judgments come upon them. The First Presidency of 1949 (President George Albert Smith, J. Reuben Clark, Jr., David O. McKay) indicated that 5,000 missionaries were proclaiming the gospel in the world, and their purpose was stated as:

> . . . The mission of these ambassadors is to cry repentance unto this generation as well as to teach the Gospel of Jesus Christ in its fulness. Should this message be rejected, the Lord has warned the people as follows . . . [D&C 88:89-91 quoted]
>
> As the representatives of our Heavenly Father, we admonish people everywhere to turn unto the Lord and forsake evil, lest His judgments overtake them. Only through a return to the teachings of the Master can peace come to the world and the kingdom of God be made ready for the return of the Prince of Peace to reign as King of Kings and Lord of Lords. (*The Deseret News,* December 14, 1949.)

Following the predicted earthquakes, war, floods, and commotion among the inhabitants of the earth, angels are to fly through the heavens crying "prepare ye for the Bridegroom cometh." (D&C 88:92.)

## The Sign of the Son of Man

When the Savior was asked concerning the signs of his coming in the last days, he replied by mentioning several of these signs, one of which was "the sign of the Son of Man." (Matt. 24:30.) In our generation, he has revealed that during the tribulations of the last days, this sign shall be seen by all people. (D&C 88:93.) What is this sign? The Prophet discoursed upon the signs of Jesus' second coming and said that the Lord would reveal his intent to his servants the prophets concerning the judgments.

> . . . There will be wars and rumors of wars, signs in the heavens above and on the earth beneath, the sun turned into darkness and the moon to blood, earthquakes in divers places, the seas heaving beyond their bounds; then will appear one grand sign of the Son of Man in heaven. But what will the world do? They will say it is a planet, a comet, etc. But the Son of Man will come as the sign of the coming of the Son of Man, which will be as the light of the morning cometh out of the east. (*DHC* 5:337.)

## The Seven Trumps

Seven angels are to sound their trumps, each trump marking an event, beginning with the binding of the apostate church. Then silence will reign for an half an hour, preparatory to the second coming of the Lord. At his advent, the resurrection of celestial beings will occur, followed by the resurrection of the terrestrial beings. The millennium will come when the Savior and men shall live in peace and righteousness for a thousand years. At the end of that period, telestial persons will come from their graves, and, finally, after the millennium, the sons of perdition will be resurrected. (D&C 88:94-102; chapter 7.)

The revelation continues with the remaining three trumps, announcing that all shall worship God their Maker "for the hour of his judgment is come." (D&C 88:103-104.) Announcement of the fall of Babylon, or wickedness, will follow with the triumphant cry by the seventh angel:

> . . . It is finished; it is finished! The Lamb of God hath overcome and trodden the wine-press alone, even the wine-press of the fierceness of the wrath of Almighty God. (Verse 106.)

## All Things to Be Known

During the millennium the solution of many vexing problems concerning the earth and its inhabitants will be given. (D&C 101:32-34.) The Lord has revealed that for each of the seven thousand years of earth's temporal existence since Adam's fall, men's acts have been recorded. The revealing of the secret acts of men and "the thoughts and intents of their hearts" and the mighty works of God in each one of these seven periods, will occur during the millennial period of peace and brotherhood upon the earth. (*Ibid.*, 88:108-110; 77:6-7, 12; chapter 56.)

## Post-Millennial Events

The last great effort of Satan to ascend to the throne of God will come when he is loosed at the end of the millennium. A great division among the people will result when Satan reigns for a little season. He will gather together his forces, comprising the spirits who followed him in the pre-mortal world and those mortals who apostatized from the truth at the end of the millennium, for the final conflict. Michael, or Adam, the seventh angel, even the archangel, shall gather together his armies, even the hosts of heaven to battle against Satan and his armies. (D&C 88:111-113.)

> And then cometh the battle of the great God; and the devil and his armies shall be cast away into their own place, that they shall not have power over the saints any more at all.
>
> For Michael shall fight their battles, and shall overcome him who seeketh the throne of him who sitteth upon the throne, even the Lamb. (*Ibid.,* verses 114-115.)

With the final defeat of the devil and his followers, they will be cast into the hell which was prepared for them from the beginning. (*Ibid.*, 29:38; 76:44.) Then follows the sounding of the last three angels' trumps already mentioned, announcing the judgment, the fall of wickedness, and the triumph of God's work for the salvation of men. (*Ibid.*, 88:103-107.)

## Chapter 15

# GREAT TRUTHS; THE SCHOOL OF THE PROPHETS

### (Section 88:117-141)

Through this revelation (Section 88) given to the Propht Joseph Smith, we have learned that peace is spoken to all men. The section begins with an exposition on the Holy Ghost and the functions and blessings of the "light of Christ." A message of peace to all who read Section 88 is that earth-life—mortality—is of extreme importance in the great plan of life and salvation, for each of us will be resurrected with a tangible, immortal body that, together with our spirit, will endure throughout the eternities in the kingdom which we have merited through our obedience to laws. The physical infirmities of mortality will be corrected, for in the resurrection men will be physically perfect. (Alma 11:42-45; 40:23.)

The Lord further spoke peace to his saints in certifying to the reality of the life beyond the grave, and that the faithful Latter-day Saint will find blessed association with loved ones with the joy of coming forth in the first resurrection to advance onward to the perfection of eternal life. (D&C 88:97-98; 76:50-70.) This revelation also assures man that the universe is governed by law and, thus, man can have a sense of security and faith in himself and in the Creator. The Latter-day Saint realizes that God is omnipotent, omnipresent, and omniscient; that he knows the end from the beginning and is in control of all his kingdoms. He may thus have his prophets foretell the present conditions and also the future, that the saints may enjoy this peace. (James E. Talmage, *Articles of Faith*, p. 491.)

There is peace in the knowledge that prayers are answered and that God's truth is unchanging—it abideth forever, having no end! We are taught, also, in this revelation of the need for prayer and fasting, and of the application of knowledge—both secular and gospel—that prepares one to be a more effective servant. One of the important segments of knowledge in the 88th Section is the information about world conditions before the coming of the Savior, and also events which will culminate in the final victory of the Eternal Father through His Son Jesus Christ. (Chapter 14.)

## Organized Study

The verses which follow in Section 88 (verses 117-141) instruct the elders to organize study activities that they may effectively present their message to the world. In the process of giving directions on how this organized study may be accomplished, great truths are enunciated to guide them in their study.

In this revelation, the Lord calls upon his servants, those who are the first laborers in this last kingdom, to organize themselves and to purify their hearts that they may be accepted by the Father. (Verses 74-75.) They are also instructed to come together in a solemn assembly where the Priesthood members may prepare themselves by study and by faith. (Verse 117.)

## "As All Have Not Faith"

The Lord placed emphasis upon the necessity of his people to seek learning from the best books. The following passage is found not only in the "Olive Leaf" but also in the dedicatory prayer of the Kirtland Temple. (D&C 109:7.)

> And as all have not faith, seek ye diligently and teach one another words of wisdom; yea, seek ye out of the best books words of wisdom; seek learning, even by study and also by faith. (D&C 88:118.)

Faith is a gift of God through Jesus Christ. The Savior made it possible to have faith in him through his sacrificial death in "bringing about means unto men that they may have faith unto repentance." (Alma 34:15.) The spark of faith with which men are born, engendered by the "light of Christ," is increased in many ways. Although faith is a gift, it must be accepted and developed to bring men back into God's presence. One way in which faith is enlarged is through study. When men learn what the Lord Jesus Christ has done for them, there is quickened in their hearts a love which grows and deepens as they realize the meaning of the atonement. In the Book of Mormon, Jacob, son of Lehi, reveals that only through the atonement of Jesus would mankind receive a resurrection from the dead. Without the atonement, all mortals would go into the spirit world to remain forever and ever, "to rise no more." Realizing the wisdom, goodness, mercy, and greatness of the great plan, the Nephite prophet continues:

> O the wisdom of God, his mercy and grace! For behold, if the flesh should rise no more our spirits must become subject to that angel who fell from before the presence of the Eternal God, and became the devil, to rise no more.
>
> And our spirits must have become like him, and we become devils, angels to a devil, to be shut out from the presence of our God, and to remain with the father of lies, in misery, like unto himself. . . .
>
> O how great the goodness of our God, who prepareth a way for our escape from the grasp of this awful monster; yea, that monster, death and hell. . . . (2 Nephi 9:8-10.)

When an honest man realizes what might have been had there been no atonement, his love for the Eternal Father and his Atoner, Jesus Christ, is quickened and faith grows in his heart. Alma explained that when the soul is touched by desire through understanding of the Lord's plan, "it beginneth to enlarge" and enlighten the understanding and, as this seed is nurtured by good works of diligence and patience, the rewards of faith come. (Alma 32:21-43.)

In 1832, the brethren were counseled that, since all did not have faith, a way to develop this gift was to study words of wisdom from the best books. Viewed from the purpose of life which can only be considered from the eternity of the past as well as the future, the "best books" are those which give man knowledge and faith in God's eternal purposes. To the Latter-day Saint, these are the standard works of the Church—the Bible, the Book of Mormon, the Doctrine and Covenants, and the Pearl of Great Price—and the sermons and writings of God's prophets. Brigham Young, Jr., an apostle, expressed this necessity in these words:

> . . . I say unto you fathers, let the Bible, the Book of Mormon and the Doctrine and Coventants be upon your tables, and have them read in your households. Elders of Israel, read them, especially the Book of Mormon, which is a pure translation from the original. He who reigns above has said that it is true. There is more contained in the Book of Mormon pertaining to this great work of the latter days than can be found in all the rest of the books put together, save only the Book of Doctrine and Covenants. It delineates and foreshadows the destiny of the Latter-day Saints. . . . (*Conference Report,* October 1901, p. 67.)

It was indicated in the last chapter that all useful knowledge should be sought after, but it remains true that the knowledge that brings exaltation comes by revelation. Elder John A. Widtsoe said:

> There are of course many kinds of knowledge; some of lesser, some of higher value. When Joseph Smith said that a man cannot be saved in ignorance, [D&C 131:6] he meant naturally ignorance of the laws which altogether lead to salvation. Such knowledge is of the highest value. It should be sought after first. Then other kinds of knowledge may be added to support and amplify the more direct knowledge of spiritual law. . . . (*Evidences and Reconciliations* 3:71.)

## "By Study and Also by Faith"

In the obtaining of the knowledge that saves here and in the hereafter, effort and faith must be used. The trusting and believing soul, who, in his humility, seeks the Lord's will through the scriptures and the living prophets, finds his reward. The doubter, lacking teachableness and submissiveness, finds himself receiving the lesser portion of revealed truth. Alma gave these ideas in a way that impresses one with the strength of his conviction:

> And therefore, he that will harden his heart, the same receiveth the lesser portion of the word; and he that will not harden his heart, to him is given the greater portion of the word, until it is given unto him to know the mysteries of God until he know them in full. (Alma 12:10.)

How shall we receive knowledge by faith? Elder B. H. Roberts has given us an insight into this tremendous thought in these words:

> Knowledge by faith! What a thought—knowledge by faith! But let no one suppose that knowledge by faith is to be obtained by an easy road or method. It will demand effort and strenuous life and the exaltation of life itself to obtain knowledge by faith. . . .
>
> You perhaps remember in our Word of Wisdom, that it is said if the saints will observe that Word of Wisdom, and keep the commandments of God, that they shall have access to hidden treasures of knowledge by reason of faith. Knowledge by faith requires exalted living. . . .
>
> But it is no lazy man's task—this getting knowledge by faith. It requires the bending of the whole soul, the calling up of the depths of the human mind, and linking them with God—the right connection must be formed. Then comes knowledge by faith. (*Discourses of B. H. Roberts,* pp. 25-26.)

## Seriousness of Purpose

There is nothing in this life that requires more serious study than to learn the purpose of existence and then to determine how that purpose can be accomplished. In order that the Lord's servants might be prepared to undertake their positions as missionaries to testify and warn the world, it was necessary that a house be prepared where they might study, pray, fast, and grow in faith. (D&C 88:119.) Later, the people were reprimanded for not following the counsel to build the Kirtland Temple, which served this purpose. (*Ibid.*, 95:11-17.)

Light speeches, wicked doings, light-mindedness, and loud laughter arising out of boisterous conduct should not be permitted when men come together to be enlightened by the Spirit. (*Ibid.*, 88:121; Chapter 13.)

The following advice, based upon this passage, was given by President Joseph F. Smith:

> . . . The Lord has called upon us to be a sober-minded people, not given to much laughter, frivolity and light-mindedness, but to consider thoughtfully and thoroughly the things of His kingdom that we may be prepared in all things to understand the glorious truths of the gospel, and be prepared for blessings to come. Let me read a verse from the Doctrine and Covenants. This is the command of the Lord to the Latter-day Saints.
>
> "Remember the great and last promise which I have made unto you. Cast away your idle thoughts and your excess of laughter far from you." And then again, in the same section, I have read from Section 88:69; I now read from verse 121: "Therefore, cease from all your light speeches, from all laughter, from all your lustful desires, from all your wicked doings." This is the word of the Lord to the Latter-day Saints. I believe that it is necessary for the Saints to have amusement, but it must be of the proper kind. I do not believe the Lord intends and desires that we should pull a long face and look sanctimonious and hypocritical. I think he expects us to be happy and of a cheerful countenance, but he does not expect of us the indulgence in boisterous and unseemly conduct and the seeking after the vain and foolish things which amuse and entertain the world. He has commanded us to the contrary for our own good and eternal welfare. (*Conference Report,* October 1916, p. 70.)

## Cease to Be Covetous

The last of the ten commandments concerns covetousness. Covetousness is to long inordinately for something that is another's. (Exodus 20:17.) Richard L. Evans of the Council of the Twelve, has pointed out that all of the ten commandments are inter-related and the last one—"thou shalt not covet"—is related to the others in this way:

> He who covets the mere material "things" of life may have "other" gods before him, and may "bow down before them," in thought and in spirit, if not in physical fact.
>
> He who covets may become coarse and careless in other things also, such as taking "the name of the Lord God in vain."
>
> He who covets may desecrate the Sabbath day to get gain.
>
> He who covets may fail to sustain his father and his mother in their need.
>
> Some who have coveted have killed to get gain.
>
> Many who have coveted a "neighbour's wife" have committed the grievous sin of adultery.
>
> He who covets is more likely to steal (or to swindle or embezzle or engage in sharp practices).
>
> He who covets may bear false witness to get gain. (*The Ten Commandments Today,* p. 142.)

There is another phase of covetousness implied in the same passage from which this discussion is taken; namely, that one should not be stingy with his knowledge of the gospel. "Learn to impart one to another as the gospel requires." Those who have the ability and the information to enlighten the lives of others should bring forth the words of salvation to their fellow men. As members of the Church we should bear our testimonies—impart one to another as the gospel requires. The words of eternal life are to be spoken appropriately, however, and without giving offense.

## Other Truths

Counsel is given the elders to cease from idleness, uncleanliness, finding fault with one another, sleeping longer than is needful. And, then, as if to climax a series of great truths with one truth that, if lived, would comprehend all others—love—the Lord revealed:

> And above all things, clothe yourselves with the bond of charity, as with a mantle, which is the bond of perfectness and peace.
>
> Pray always, that ye may not faint, until I come. Behold, and lo, I will come quickly, and receive you unto myself. Amen. (D&C 88:125-126.)

As said elsewhere in this lesson, it is only through what Jesus has done for us that we may receive joy unbounded instead of misery. "Clothe yourselves with the bond of charity." Charity is the pure love of Christ. (Moroni 7:47.) Without this love, no man can inherit the kingdom of heaven. (Ether 12:34; 2 Nephi 26:30.) One can understand the emphasis put upon the need for charity by Paul in view of the Book of Mormon teaching on this great virtue. (1 Cor. 13.) Peace is promised the Church in the truths given in this lesson and ending with the counsel to become clothed with the love of Christ.

## School of the Prophets

In order that the holders of the priesthood might learn their duties and receive instruction in the gospel and other subjects which would prepare them for the ministry, the Lord commanded that there be organized a School of the Prophets. (D&C 88:119-120, 122, 127-141.) The manner in which this school was to be conducted is given in this revelation. (Verses 122, 128-136.) Only those, however, who were clean from the blood of this generation were to participate. (Verse 138.) Preaching the gospel and keeping the covenants were the means by which these elders could be made clean.

In the winter of 1832-33, the School of the Prophets was organized in Kirtland, where meetings were conducted. The ordinance of washing of feet was attended to as commanded. (Verses 139-141; *Essentials in Church History*, p. 151.)

The brethren (many of whom had not had the opportunity for formal school education) were thirsting for knowledge. The Lord made provision through this plan that they might learn of the doctrine of the kingdom and secular subjects. These men were different from others in that they had the Holy Ghost to enlighten them in their learning. President John Taylor said:

> Now, then, if men, without much of the advantage of what is termed education in this world, are filled with the Spirit of God, the revelations of the Holy Ghost, and can comprehend the relationship of man to God, can know their duties, and can teach a people, a nation, or a world how they may be saved and obtain thrones, principalities, powers and dominions in the eternal worlds,—if men can understand these principles by the gift of the Holy Ghost and the revelations of the Most High, and are enabled to place them before the people so that they can comprehend them, then, I say, these are the men of education—the men of intellect—the men who are calculated to bless and ennoble the human family. This is the kind of education that we want; and the more simple those principles can be conveyed the better: they are more adapted to the wants and intelligence of the human family. . . .
>
> This is the difference between the system that we have embraced and the systems of the world—they are of men, this is of God. . . .
>
> What did any of us know as rational, eternal beings, until we were educated in this Church? (*Journal of Discourses* 5:260-261.)

## Chapter 16

# AN INTRODUCTION TO THE WORD OF WISDOM

## (Section 89:1-3)

On the 27th day of February 1833, the Prophet Joseph Smith received the revelation known as the Word of Wisdom. Latter-day Saints know this section in the Doctrine and Covenants as the one that emphasizes certain temporal benefits to be received by the members of the Church who live by its teachings. To think of this revelation as benefiting the observer physically only is erroneous because there are rich spiritual blessings to be derived from its observance.

### Background

As far as we know, most of the revelations in the Doctrine and Covenants came in answer to inquiry by the Prophet Joseph Smith of the Lord. President Brigham Young gives us the following information.

. . . I think I am as well acquainted with the circumstances which led to the giving of the Word of Wisdom as any man in the Church, although I was not present at the time to witness them. The first school of the prophets was held in a small room situated over the Prophet Joseph's kitchen, in a house which belonged to Bishop Whitney, and which was attached to his store, which store probably might be about fifteen feet square . . . The brethren came to that place for hundreds of miles to attend school in a little room probably no larger than eleven by fourteen. When they assembled together in this room after breakfast, the first they did was to light their pipes, and, while smoking, talk about the great things of the kingdom, and spit all over the room, and as soon as the pipe was out of their mouths a large chew of tobacco would then be taken. Often when the Prophet entered the room to give the school instructions he would find himself in a cloud of tobacco smoke. This, and the complaints of his wife at having to clean so filthy a floor, made the Prophet think upon the matter, and he inquired of the Lord relating to the conduct of the Elders in using tobacco, and the revelation known as the Word of Wisdom was the result of his inquiry. (*Journal of Discourses* 12:158.)

## For the Saints in Zion

Section 89 is a revelation whose title was given by the Lord. As pointed out above by Brigham Young, the Word of Wisdom was given for the benefit of the council of high priests assembled in Kirtland. Notwithstanding the revelation was given to these persons, it was to go also to the saints in Zion, and to the Church.

> A Word of Wisdom, for the benefit of the council of high priests, assembled in Kirtland, and the church, and also the saints in Zion—
>
> To be sent greeting; not by commandment or constraint, but by revelation and the word of wisdom, showing forth the order and will of God in the temporal salvation of all saints in the last days. (D&C 89:1-2.)

## Not by Commandment

To help the saints realize the need to observe this law, many of the living prophets have emphasized that the words in verse two establish that this revelation is to be lived by all Latter-day Saints. Elder George F. Richards said the following on this subject:

> . . . I would call your attention to a part of the second paragraph in the 89th section, which reads as follows, referring to this revelation; it "was given by revelation, and the word of wisdom, showing forth the *order* and *will* of God in the temporal salvation of all Saints in the last days." We have accepted Joseph Smith as the prophet, seer, and revelator of this last dispensation, and in doing so we accept those revelations as being the word of the Lord to us. Here the Lord expresses His *will,* in very plain terms, that this revelation is given "showing forth the *order* and *will* of God." If for no other reason, this should be sufficient for any consistent Latter-day Saint to induce him to yield implicit

obedience unto this word. I can think of no gospel subject that will apply directly to more people among us as Latter-day Saints than this Word of Wisdom, unless it may be the principle of obedience, which includes yielding obedience unto this word; or repentance, which also includes turning away from these things which are forbidden, and obeying the will of the Lord (*Conference Report,* October 1908, pp. 87-88.)

Elder John A. Widtsoe comments upon this subject by asking this question:

> . . . But if a law is given by revelation showing the order and will of God should it not be more binding than a command because it calls for man's understanding cooperation? (*Joseph Smith,* p. 199.)

If a Latter-day Saint believes that his non-observance of the Word of Wisdom is justified because of the words "not by commandment or constraint," it would seem to put him in a category of the slothful who will lose his reward. Here is what the Lord said in 1831:

> For the power is in them, wherein they are agents unto themselves. And inasmuch as men do good they shall in nowise lose their reward.
>
> But he that doeth not anything until he is commanded, and receiveth a commandment with doubtful heart, and keepeth it with slothfulness, the same is damned. (D&C 58:28-29.)

In view of the foregoing scriptures, is there a real difference between the "will" of God to his children and "commandment?" The same Being who gave Section 89 said this in the Sermon on the Mount:

> Not every one that saith unto me, Lord, Lord, shall enter into the kingdom of heaven; but he that doeth the will of my Father which is in heaven. (Matt. 7:21.)

Perfection is the goal of the Latter-day Saint. (3 Nephi 12:48.) Sometimes it is maintained that one cannot be perfect in this life, but, as we have been told many times, there are areas of gospel living in which one can be perfect. (Roy W. Doxey, *The Doctrine and Covenants Speaks*, pp. 397-399.) Elder George F. Richards continued his remarks quoted previously in this manner:

. . . In our onward march towards perfection we will not leave the first principles of the Gospel of the Master, but will continue to observe them. In the Church, we, the teachers, are placed for the express purpose of bringing the people up to a knowledge of the Son of God, showing them the way unto perfection. I desire to say here that we never can reach perfection until we yield obedience unto this simple word of the Lord. We are required to do the will of God, at any sacrifice. I have in mind the word of the Lord upon this subject, contained in the revelations: "Let no man be afraid to lay down his life for my sake; for whoso layeth down his life for my sake, shall find it again, and whoso is not willing to lay down his life for my sake is not my disciple." [D&C 103:27-28.] We are not asked now, my brethren and sisters, to lay down our lives to show our obedience to the Lord, and our worthiness to be His disciples, but we are asked by the Lord to abstain from the use of strong drinks and tobacco, in every form, also to abstain from the use of meats to excess. This is a simple requirement. How can we hope to have faith to lay down our lives, how can we claim to be willing to do so, while our lives and actions, every day, show to our neighbors and to the Lord that we are not willing to rid ourselves of the use of strong drink or tobacco—those things which are forbidden of the Lord? Let us be consistent with ourselves and our professions of faith. (*Conference Report* October 1908, p. 88.)

Is it possible to love the Lord with all of our hearts, with all of our might, mind, and strength, as commanded, and not follow him as a true disciple? (D&C 59:5.) Elder Mark E. Petersen of the Council of the Twelve, in a commentary on this first great commandment, wrote:

We have our decisions to make each day. We may be half-hearted Latter-day Saints; we may be part tithepayers, part observers of the Word of Wisdom, part keepers of the Sabbath day, part supporters of the leaders and programs of the Church. But that is not the way the Lord would like it. The decision we must make in our own best interest is that we do our best—for ourselves, and for him. But in doing our best for him, we must forget our selfish interests, "for he that loseth his life for my sake, shall find it." (*Your Faith and You,* p. 260.)

The true disciple of the Master is known as one who follows him by obediently keeping his law. (D&C 41:5-6.)

## Temporal Salvation

Salvation in this life and in the life to come is dependent upon what one does in observing the will of the Lord, as we have already learned. President Brigham Young emphasized this truth in the following way:

> . . . Salvation is an individual operation. I am the only person that can possibly save myself. When salvation is sent to me, I can reject or receive it. In receiving it, I yield implicit obedience and submission to its great Author throughout my life, and to those whom He shall appoint to instruct me; in rejecting it, I follow the dictates of my own will in preference to the will of my Creator. (*Journal of Discourses* 1:312.)

In order that none might say that he or she is excluded from the necessity of doing the will of the Lord, the Word of Wisdom was given for the "temporal salvation of all saints in the last days. . . ." (D&C 89:2.)

The leadership of the Church has counseled the members in all kinds of activities relating to their daily lives. The gospel is not to be lived only one day of the week. (*Ibid.*, 59:11.) The Word of Wisdom, tithing, fast offerings, the Welfare Plan—all of these may be considered as directly affecting our temporal welfare because they pertain to activities which are a part of our earth-labors or which relate to physical salvation. The true significance of temporal salvation was made known early in this dispensation. In essence it is: The temporal welfare of the saint is vital to his spiritual salvation. Actually, there is no difference between the temporal and spiritual laws of God. (*Ibid.*, 34-35.)

This sublime truth led President Joseph F. Smith to say:

> You must continue to bear in mind that the temporal and the spiritual are blended. They are not separate. One cannot be carried on without the other, so long as we are here in mortality.

## Word of Wisdom and Spirituality

In harmony with the foregoing information, other "prophets, seers, and revelators" of this dispensation have voiced the truth that the Word of Wisdom is spiritual. Some ways in which obedience is good and disobedience to this spiritual law brings harmful effects were given by President Stephen L Richards, as follows:

> Every commandment of God is spiritual in nature. There are no carnal commandments. We have learned this from modern revelation. While the commandments have effect upon the body and temporal things they are all in essence spiritual. The Word of Wisdom is spiritual. It is true that it enjoins the use of deleterious substances and makes provision for the health of the body. But the largest measure of good derived from its observance is in increased faith and the development of more spiritual power and wisdom. Likewise, the most regrettable and damaging effects of its infractions are spiritual, also. Injury to the body may be comparatively trivial to the damage to the soul in the destruction of faith and the retardation of spiritual growth. So I say, every commandment involves a spiritual principle. (*Conference Report,* April 1949, p. 141.)

For those who think of the Word of Wisdom as being a dietary law that promotes good health, and that its spiritual effects do not count as a requisite to eternal life, the foregoing thoughts certainly suggest otherwise. In addition, President Heber J. Grant pointed out that the observer of this law will find increased knowledge, as promised in verse 19 of Section 89.

> No man who breaks the Word of Wisdom can gain the same amount of knowledge and intelligence in this world as the man

who obeys that law. I don't care who he is or where he comes from, his mind will not be as clear, and he cannot advance as far and as rapidly and retain his power as much as he would if he obeyed the Word of Wisdom. (*Conference Report,* April 1925, p. 10.)

## Word of Wisdom a Commandment

As early as September 9, 1851, President Brigham Young, before a conference of the Church, put a motion to the congregation that they discontinue the use of tea, coffee, tobacco, and whiskey. The motion was carried unanimously. (*Millennial Star* 14:35.) In the August 1867 conference, President Young referred to the last conference when the Lord told him by the Holy Spirit to call upon the saints to observe the Word of Wisdom, and that they who did not observe it would increase in the spirit of the world and become darkened in mind. (*Journal of Discourses* 12:117.)

President George A. Smith, in 1871, said that a person loses the Spirit and grows cold in his religion when he does not keep the Word of Wisdom. (*Ibid.,* 14:212.) In the October 1880 general conference the membership unanimously voted to accept the revelations in the Doctrine and Covenants as binding upon the Church. The First Presidency composed of President Heber J. Grant, J. Reuben Clark, Jr., and David O. McKay, in the October conference 1942, said:

> . . . we reinvoke obedience to God's law of health given us by God Himself.
>
> . . . We urge the Saints to quit trifling with this law and so to live it that we may claim its promises. (*Improvement Era,* November 1942, p. 687.)

The Word of Wisdom is a commandment!

## What of the Future?

"Who's on the Lord's Side Who?" The answer to this question is left with the individual. As pointed out earlier, the disciple of the Lord will keep His commandments and ever work for the cause of Zion. As to the individual, the Lord has held out eternal life for the faithful. But what of the Church, which is composed of individuals? Definite objectives or goals have been presented by the Lord.

> Arise and shine forth, that thy light may be a standard for the nations. (D&C 115:5.)
>
> . . . that the church may stand independent above all other creatures beneath the celestial world. (*Ibid.*, 78:14.)

When the Saints were driven from Jackson County, Missouri, the Lord declared that this was due, in part, to the transgression of the people—speaking of the Church and not of individuals—and they were not united as required by the law of the celestial kingdom. In order to realize the grand objective of establishing Zion on the American continent as commanded, it was necessary that this be done through living the law. (*Ibid.*, 105:1-5.)

The keeping of the commandments, including the Word of Wisdom, will bring sanctification to the Church and exaltation to the individual.

## Chapter 17

# THE WORD OF WISDOM—A LIFE-GIVING REVELATION

## (Section 89:4-21)

Section 89, known as the Word of Wisdom, was received in 1833 as a revelation from God. The Lord gave his people counsel in this revelation that they might not be deceived by the adversary. It has been demonstrated by science that alcohol, tobacco, tea, and coffee are not good for man, as stated by the Lord. The Word of Wisdom is prophetic in revealing that "conspiring men" will seek to deceive mankind. The literal fulfillment of this prophecy further confirms Joseph Smith as a prophet of the Lord.

### A Notable Prophecy

In order to prevent the Latter-day Saints from being deceived, the Lord forewarned them against the wiles of men. Specifically given in the revelation on the Word of Wisdom is the following prophecy of the last days:

> Behold, verily, thus saith the Lord unto you: In consequence of evils and designs which do and will exist in the hearts of conspiring men in the last days, I have warned you, and forewarn you, by giving unto you this word of wisdom by revelation. (D&C 89:4.)

President David O. McKay describes some of the methods that are used to deceived mankind:

> "Evils and designs which do and will exist in the hearts of conspiring men. . . ." The purpose of that impressed me in the twenties and the thirties of this century. I just ask you men tonight to recall the method employed by certain tobacco interests to induce women to smoke cigarettes.

You remember how insidiously they launched their plan. First, by saying that it would reduce weight. They had a slogan: "Take a cigarette instead of a sweet."

Later, some of us who like the theatre, noticed that they would have a young lady light the gentleman's cigarette. Following this a woman's hand would be shown on billboards lighting or taking a cigarette. A year or two passed and soon they were brazen enough to show the lady on the screen or on the billboard smoking a cigarette.

I find here a clipping which I set aside in the early thirties, which corroborates this idea. This is 1931:

"It is well known that the cigarette manufacturers are after the young women and girls, now. They say there are twenty-five million of these in the United States, and if they can popularize smoking among them, they will be able to increase their sales from three billion, six hundred dollars annually to six billion dollars. This is their claim and their aim."

Now, it is common to see beautiful young women depicted on billboards, and in the popular journals advertising certain brands of cigarettes. "Last year three of the large cigarette manufacturers, we are informed, spent fifty-four million dollars in advertising their wares. This is probably a greater outlay than has ever before been spent to popularize any kind of merchandise. . . ."

I may be wrong, but I thought I saw an indication recently that conspiring men now have evil designs upon our youth. Keep your eyes and ears open, to observe if they are not taking the same steps now to get our young men as they did to entice women to use that vile weed. (*Conference Report,* September 1949, pp. 185-186.)

## Tobacco—Its Effects

In the Word of Wisdom the Lord said this about tobacco:

> And again, tobacco is not for the body, neither for the belly, and is not good for man, but is an herb for bruises and all sick cattle, to be used with judgment and skill. (D&C 89:8.)

That tobacco is not good for man has been demonstrated in many ways both in the laboratory and in the lives of individuals.

Since much publicity has been given to the high incidence of lung cancer to cigarette smoking, a controversy has raged between the tobacco industry and public agencies over the cause of lung cancer. Studies, however, have disclosed that the risk of lung cancer is greatly increased by cigarette smoking.

## Wine or Strong Drink

In the Word of Wisdom the Lord condemns the use of alcohol, as follows:

> That inasmuch as any man drinketh wine or strong drink among you, behold it is not good, neither meet in the sight of your Father, only in assembling yourselves together to offer up your sacraments before him.
>
> And, behold, this should be wine, yea, pure wine of the grape of the vine, of your own make. (D&C 89:5-6.)

In an earlier revelation, the Lord instructed the Prophet Joseph Smith by an angel that wine was unnecessary in the sacrament, but any liquid could be used as long as it was done with an eye single to the glory of God. (*Ibid.*, 27:2-4.) Water is used as a sacramental emblem today in the Church.

From the beginning of this dispensation to the present, drunkenness and the use of alcohol, except for medicinal purposes, has been condemned by the prophets.

An impressive thought in connection with the Word of wisdom and moderate drinking is given by President McKay in these words:

> . . . I am glad when I study this passage to find that the Lord did not say, "Strong drink *to excess* is not good;" nor "Drunkenness is not good." Suppose he had weakened that expression by modifying it and saying, "Strong drink in excess, or when taken in large quantities, is not good," how soon we should have justified ourselves that a little drink is good. But like other eternal truths it stands unqualified; *strong drink is not* good." (*Conference Report,* April 1911, p. 62.)

Parents who, even though observing the Word of Wisdom themselves, serve alcoholic beverages to guests in their homes, are subjecting their children to influences which adversely affect their attitudes. We are reminded of the counsel of President George Albert Smith not to step over into the devil's territory.

## Hot Drinks

The Word of Wisdom does not use the words *tea* and and *coffee*, yet Latter-day Saints have been instructed that the phrase "hot drinks," used in verse 9 of Section 89, refers to these beverages. Hyrum Smith, the brother of the Prophet, in a sermon of May 29, 1842, made such a definition.

> . . . And again, "hot drinks are not for the body, or belly;" there are many who wonder what this can mean; whether it refers to tea or coffee, or not. I say it does refer to tea, and coffee. (*Times and Seasons,* Vol. III, p. 800.)

President Brigham Young on October 30, 1870 said:

> . . . I have heard it argued that tea and coffee are not mentioned therein; that is very true; but what were the people in the habit of taking as hot drinks when that revelation was given? Tea and coffee. We were not in the habit of drinking water very hot, but tea and coffee—the beverages in common use. (*Journal of Discourses* 13:277.)

## "Wholesome Herbs"

In addition to specifying certain harmful products that man should not partake of, the revelation advises the use of grains, vegetables, fruits, and meat sparingly. It also mentions certain grains for the use of animals. These are known as the positive aspects of the Word of Wisdom. In these words, we find counsel:

> And again, verily I say unto you, all wholesome herbs God hath ordained for the constitution, nature, and use of man—

Every herb in the season thereof, and every fruit in the season thereof; all these to be used with prudence and thanksgiving. (D&C 89:10-11.)

It has been pointed out that "wholesome herbs" as used in Joseph Smith's day meant all plants and vegetables.

### "In the Season Thereof"

Some few readers of the Word of Wisdom assume that because herbs and fruits should be eaten "in the season thereof" modern methods of food preservation are disapproved. It is true that fruits should be eaten when ripe and vegetables when mature to obtain the most nutrition from them, but it is neither logical nor scientific to maintain that they should not be used at a time when they are not available in the fresh state if they are properly preserved.

### Meat Is Ordained for Man

Yea, flesh also of beasts and of the fowls of the air, I, the Lord, have ordained for the use of man with thanksgiving; nevertheless they are to be used sparingly;

And it is pleasing unto me that they should not be used, only in times of winter, or of cold, or famine.

All grain is ordained for the use of man and of beasts, to be the staff of life, not only for man but for the beasts of the field, and the fowls of heaven, and all wild animals that run or creep on the earth;

And these hath God made for the use of man only in times of famine and excess of hunger. (D&C 89:12-15.)

Two years before this revelation was received, the Lord said that to forbid meat on religious grounds was not of him. Moreover, the beasts and fowls were provided for man's food and raiment, but man was not to waste animal life by wanton killing. (*Ibid.*, 49:18-21.)

### Wheat for Man

Wheat is not the only grain for man, but it is the best, according to the Word of Wisdom.

> All grain is good for the food of man; as also the fruit of the vine; that which yieldeth fruit, whether in the ground or above the ground—
>
> Nevertheless, wheat for man. . . . (D&C 16-17.)

Wheat has long been recognized by man as a good food, and nutritional science has found that this grain promotes bodily strength, greater resistance against infections, freedom from deficiency and degenerative disease, and endurance.

### Animal Foods

Section 89 recommends that certain grains are of greater value to some animals than to others.

> . . . and corn for the ox, and oats for the horse, and rye for the fowls and for swine, and for all beasts of the field, and barley for all useful animals, and for mild drinks, as also other grain. (D&C 89:17.)

### "And All Saints Who Remember . . ."

The saints who remember to keep the commandments, including the Word of Wisdom, are promised that they will receive health in their navel, and marrow to their bones. (D&C 89:18.)

The two expressions, "health in their navel and marrow to their bones," are meaningful in the light of present-day knowledge. The unborn baby is nourished and may also be poisoned through the navel or umbilicus. Bone marrow manufactures the various blood cells needed for health.

## Walking Obediently

There have been some who have thought that by obediently living the Word of Wisdom the blessings promised in that revelation would come. It is true that if one lives a law, such as a health law, the benefits of fulfilling that law will be realized. On the other hand, the Latter-day Saint who lives the Word of Wisdom cannot expect to receive all of the promised blessings—hidden treasures of knowledge, wisdom, spirituality, and the destroying angel to pass them by—if he does not abide the other commandments. (D&C 89:18.)

The Prophet Joseph Smith taught that though an individual fulfill one commandment and neglect others he will not receive salvation.

> I . . . spoke to the people, showing them that to get salvation we must not only do some things, but everything which God has commanded. . . . It mattereth not whether the principle is popular or unpopular, I will always maintain a true principle, even if I stand alone in it. (*DHC* 6:223.)

One of the distressing facts about breaking the Word of Wisdom by smoking and drinking alcoholic beverages, is the effect it has on the individual, the home, and society. The First Presidency (President Heber J. Grant, J. Reuben Clark, Jr., David O. McKay) in their message of October 1942, made the following accusations against liquor:

> Drink brings cruelty into the home; it walks arm in arm with poverty; its companions are disease and plague; it puts chastity to flight; and it knows neither honesty nor fair dealing; it is a total stranger to truth; it drowns conscience; it is the bodyguard of evil; it curses all who touch it.
>
> Drink has brought more woe and misery, broken more hearts, wrecked more homes, committed more crimes, filled more coffins, than all the wars the world has suffered. (*Conference Report*, October 1942, p. 8.)

President Grant drew attention to the consequences of young people breaking the Word of Wisdom and showed how, frequently, this disobedience leads to far more serious sin.

> . . . I want it understood—that the use of liquor and tobacco is one of the chief means in the hands of the adversary whereby he is enabled to lead boys and girls from virtue.
>
> Nearly always those who lose their virtue, first partake of those things that excite passions within them or lower their resistance and becloud their minds. Partaking of tobacco and liquor is calculated to make them a prey to those things which, if indulged in, are worse than death itself. (*Gospel Standards*, p. 55.)

Elder Mark E. Petersen of the Council of the Twelve also pointed out the destructive influence of the cigarette in the life of the member of the Church. He declared that there is the feeling of discomfort in being with people who don't smoke, so the smoker finds other people than those at Church with whom to associate. Since smoking is against one of the commandments and the smoker doesn't like to hear about the Word of Wisdom, he begins staying away from his Church meetings. These things lead to forgetting about praying and paying tithing. When the time comes to choose a life's companion the chances are that it will be someone in the smoking crowd. In other words, the cigarette has helped select the marriage partner. When the children arrive in the home, it is not likely they will be taught to pray, go to Church, pay tithing, etc., because the parents are indifferent to these opportunities. (*Conference Report*, April 1948, pp. 152-56.)

Disobedience to the commandents brings loss of the Holy Ghost, and the living of the commandments gives one that Spirit with all of its blessings against being deceived.

### "Hidden Treasures"

The Holy Ghost and the gifts that come from that Spirit will enlighten and give knowledge, protection, wisdom, peace, and joy. These are some of the promised blessings of keeping the commandments. Here is what the Lord said:

> And shall find wisdom and great treasures of knowledge, even hidden treasures; and shall run and not be weary, and shall walk and not faint. (D&C 89:19-20.)

What is the greatest treasure that one may have in this life to assist him on the road to exaltation? Knowledge that saves! (*Ibid.*, 131:6; 130:18-19.) In addition to knowing the principles of salvation, there is the important "hidden treasure" of knowing by the Holy Ghost that God lives, Jesus Christ is the Savior, that Joseph Smith is God's Prophet, and his successors are also holders of the keys of the priesthood.

Finally, the Lord promises that the destroying angel shall pass by the saints and not slay them, as he promised ancient Israel. (D&C 89:21; Exodus 12:12-13, 29-30.) This promise does not mean that death will not come to the obedient. It is in the eternal plan that death comes to all. However, death may be bitter or sweet. (D&C 42:45-47.) He who has walked in obedience to the commandments shall receive the blessings of the angel of life—peace, mercy, hope, love, and to open the door of light and eternal life with its everlasting joys. (*Conference Report*, April 1925, pp. 61-62.)

The First Presidency in 1943 with the reference to the Word of Wisdom, wrote:

> This declares the divine wisdom. It is God's law of health, and is binding upon each and every one of us. We cannot escape its operation for it is based upon eternal truth. Men may agree or disagree about this word of the Lord; if they agree, it adds nothing; if they disagree, it means nothing. Beyond His word we cannot reach, and it is enough for every Latter-day Saint, willing and trying to follow divine guidance. ("Message of the First Presidency," October 3, 1943.)

## Chapter 18

# THE FIRST PRESIDENCY—KEYS OF THE KINGDOM

## (Sections 90, 91, 92)

In December 1832, the Lord instructed the Prophet Joseph Smith that all who should become members of the School of the Prophets should, by ordinance, be clean from the blood of this generation. (D&C 88:138-141.)

They were told that wilful sinning would bring the penalty of being turned over to the buffetings of Satan until the day of redemption. (*DHC* 1:323-324.)

### Knowledge and Sin

On March 8, 1833, the Lord gave Section 90, in which confirmation is made of blessings wherein forgiveness of sins was granted by the Lord. The Prophet Joseph Smith was informed that his sins were forgiven (verse 1), and Sidney Rigdon and Frederick G. Williams were also given the same assurance. The *Doctrine and Covenants Commentary* brings our attention to the fact that the sins of these brethren were not serious, but as men learn more of their responsibilities in the Church and also advance in understanding of the need for closer observance to the commandments, they recognize wherein they may improve their lives. (Pages 576-577.) Is it not true that more knowledge of gospel principles brings the conviction by the Spirit that further efforts must be made to perfect one's life?

### The Keys of the Priesthood

What are the "keys" of the priesthood? Joseph Smith and Oliver Cowdery received these keys at the hands of John the Baptist, Peter, James, and John and the heavenly visitants mentioned in Section 110. Without these powers the Lord's Church would not be a kingdom of order. With the prophet holding these powers throughout the world, he may direct the use of the priesthood by every person who has received an ordination to the priesthood. The "keys" constitute the power to direct the use of the priesthood. An important principle that every person should know is derived from an understanding of the functioning of these keys. No male ordained to the priesthood may exercise this authority in performing ordinances unless he is given permission to do so. The priesthood ordination bestows the power to act for the Lord, but the person's acts in using the priesthood are not valid if the Church officer over him has not authorized him to use the priesthood. For example, in the ordinance of baptism, even though one may be an ordained high priest, he cannot baptize unless the bishop of his ward or the presiding officer where he resides gives him permission to baptize. The bishop, in this case, holds the keys of authority in his ward. Similarly, a stake president holds keys for his stake. But, in both of these cases, neither bishop nor stake president has authority to function outside of the ward or stake over which he is set apart to preside. Thus, the powers of presiding, under the keys of the priesthood, are limited to the jurisdiction given to the officer by the authority of the president of the Church. The prophet sees that the Lord's work is carried on throughout the world by conferring local jurisdiction to the many officers who function under him.

### Joseph Smith and the Keys

Six months after the Church was organized, the Lord gave a revelation in which he instructed the Church that there is only one man at a time who holds all the keys of the priesthood. At that time it was the First Elder of the Church—Joseph Smith. It was indicated in that revelation that the Prophet was to hold these powers "until I shall appoint unto them another in his stead." (D&C 28:7.) Even the appointment of the Prophet to preside over the Church was to be done by the common consent of the Church, by the prayer of faith. (*Ibid.*, verses 12-13.) One-half year passed, and a situation arose in the Church that demanded a reiteration of the principle of one revelator for the Church. Another person claimed such a right, but the Lord's kingdom is one of order.

In the course of this reaffirmation of this most important principle, the Lord said concerning Joseph Smith:

> And this ye shall know assuredly—that there is none other appointed unto you to receive commandments and revelations until he be taken, if he abide in me. (*Ibid.*, 43:3.)

What process continued the existence of the keys of the priesthood following the martyrdom of the Prophet? At the time of the ordination of each apostle he is given all of the priesthood authority received by the Prophet Joseph Smith. The conferring of the keys of the Priesthood does not diminish the priesthood of the person performing the ordination. There are thousands of elders holding the same authority. Similarly, there may be many who hold the keys of the priesthood, as the twelve apostles, but there is only one person at a time who holds these keys *actively;* that is, to receive revelation *for* the Church and to direct its activities. The twelve apostles hold these keys *inactively;* that is, they use these latter authorities when called upon by the president of the Church. And when the president dies, they use these powers to appoint the new president of the Church by revelation.

## The Keys and Worthiness

President Joseph F. Smith discussed these powers and the need for worthiness on the part of him who holds them, as indicated in verse 5 of Section 90.

. . . If any man in that position should become unfaithful, God would remove him out of his place. I testify in the name of Israel's God that He will not suffer the head of the Church, him whom He has chosen to stand at the head, to transgress His laws and apostatize; the moment he should take a course that would in time lead to it, God would take him away. Why? Because to suffer a wicked man to occupy that position, would be to allow, as it were, the fountain to become corrupted, which is something He will never permit. And why will he not suffer it? Because it is not the work of Joseph Smith; it is not the work of Brigham Young or of John Taylor. It is is not the work of man but of God Almighty; and it is His business to see that the men who occupy this position are men after His own heart, men that will receive instructions from Him, and that will carry out the same according to the counsels of His will. (*Journal of Discourses* 24:192.)

## The First Presidency Organized

On March 18, 1833, ten days after Section 90 was received, the First Presidency was organized with Joseph Smith as president, Sidney Rigdon, first counselor, and Frederick G. Williams, second counselor.

Before the Quorum of the Twelve was appointed, the Lord made known that the Prophet would hold the keys of the kingdom throughout time and eternity.

Verily I say unto you, the keys of the kingdom shall never be taken from you, while thou art in the world, neither in the world to come;

Nevertheless, through you shall the oracles be given to another, yea, even unto the church. (*Ibid.*, 90:3-4.)

## The Twelve and the Keys

The expressions "oracles" and "even to the church" are explained in this authoritative passage:

. . . In the plural it [oracles] means the Revelations given by God. . . . (Rom. 3:2; 1 Peter 4:11.)

. . . Yet when the Prophet should be taken the "oracles" would be given to another, "even to the Church." Therefore after the martyrdom the keys remained and were in possession of the Church and exercised through the presiding council, which at that time was the council of the Twelve Apostles, and in the Church the oracles are found and will continue unto the end of time. (*Doctrine and Covenants Commentary,* p. 577.)

When the Prophet Joseph Smith was martyred, the president of the Quorum of the Twelve and the other members of the Twelve presided over the Church. What powers do the apostles possess that would give them authority to preside over the Church upon the death of the Prophet? Among others, President Wilford Woodruff has left his testimony of the conferring of the keys of the Priesthood by Joseph Smith upon the Twelve.

The last speech that Joseph Smith ever made to the Quorum of the Apostles was in a building in Nauvoo, and it was such a speech as I never heard from mortal man before nor since. He was clothed upon with the Spirit and power of God. His face was clear as amber. The room was filled as with consuming fire. He stood three hours upon his feet. Said he: "You Apostles of the Lamb of God have been chosen to carry out the purposes of the Lord on the earth. Now, I have received, as the Prophet, seer and revelator, standing at the head of this dispensation, every key, every ordinance, every principle and every Priesthood that belongs to the last dispensation and fulness of times. And I have sealed all these things upon your heads. Now, you Apostles, if you do not rise up and bear off this kingdom, as I have given it to you, you will be damned."

I am the only witness left on earth that can bear record of this, and I am thankful that I have lived to see the day in which I stand. (*Conference Report,* April 1898, p. 89.)

. . . I laid my hands on Brothers Sidney and Frederick, and ordained them to take part with me in holding the keys of this last kingdom, and to assist in the Presidency of the High Priesthood, as my Counselors; after which I exhorted the brethren to faithfulness and diligence in keeping the commandments of God. (*DHC* 1:334.)

## Keys and Presidency

When the First Presidency meets as a quorum these brethren act by reason of the keys of the kingdom. The

Lord has revealed wherin this quorum's decision would be valid—and also the Council of the Twelve and the First Council of the Seventy—only by the unanimous voice of each member of the quorum. The virtues that should influence righteous decisions were also enumerated, such as meekness, patience, godliness, and so forth. (*Ibid.*, 107:27-31.) When the President dies, the Quorum of the First Presidency no longer exists. This is what the Prophet Joseph Smith said in a meeting with the twelve apostles on January 26, 1835:

> . . . the Twelve are not subject to any other than the first Presidency. . . . and where I am not, there is no First Presidency over the Twelve. (*DHC* 2:374.)

From the foregoing, it is clear that the counselors act under the direction of the president, and their authority exists only as long as there is a president. Otherwise, they, if apostles in the Quorum of the Twelve, return to their places of seniority in that quorum. The twelve apostles, holding the keys of the priesthood, become the active leaders of the Church with the president of the twelve being in charge of the Church and the other members of the Twelve as counselors until the Quorum of the First Presidency is organized.

In all matters the president of the Church presides; his counselors assist him. In the following verse the Lord sets forth clearly the powers of the president.

> And this shall be your business and mission in all your lives, to preside in council, and set in order all the affairs of this church and kingdom. (D&C 90:16.)

At this time (March 1833) the First Presidency was to hold not only the keys of the Church but also the keys to the School of the Prophets. (D&C 90:7.) But in both of these administrations Joseph Smith was to preside. (*Ibid.*, Verses 12-13.)

## The Past and the Future

Through the work of the First Presidency, preparation for giving the gospel of salvation to the inhabitants of Zion (Jackson County, Missouri) and to the nations was to go forth.

Other nations were to hear the message through the missionaries who were to present the gospel to the Gentiles first, and then to the Jews. (D&C 90:8-9.) This instruction is in fulfillment of prophecy.

With the complete fulfillment of this prophecy, yet future, the Lord's power will be demonstrated in the bringing about of a paradisiacal environment, which will characterize the millennial reign of the Savior. The gospel shall be taught in that day in the various languages. verses 12-13.)

## Other Duties of the Prophet

At an earlier date the Prophet and Sidney Rigdon were engaged in the "translation" (revision) of the Bible. The Prophet's present responsibility was to work on this revision and then to attend to his other duties.

Only some of the responsibilities of the Prophet are mentioned in this revelation to indicate ways in which he was to preside over the affairs of the Church. The president of the Church is to receive revelation and thus to make known the mysteries of the kingdom. (D&C 90:13-14.) Here again is repeated the important principle that the Prophet is to receive revelation *for* the Church and to "set in order all the affairs of this church and kingdom." (Verse 16.)

Significant among the Prophet's duties was this counsel, which would be applicable to all members of the Church:

> . . . and study and learn, and become acquainted with all good books, and with languages, tongues, and people. (Verse 15.)

Applicable to the Latter-day Saint is the admonition to beware of pride. To set one's house in order means to overcome the weaknesses which prevent close communion with the Holy Ghost. A part of this endeavor is to be clean in body and mind and to be industrious. (Verses 17-18.)

## Temporal Instructions

Verses 19 through 33 contain several instructions concerning temporal matters. For example, Frederick G. Williams was to have a home for his family; the debts of the Lord's storehouse were to be paid; and counsel was given on the number who should be accommodated in the home of Joseph Smith, Sr. In verse 25 the meaning of "let your families be small" pertains to those not of his immediate family who were receiving lodging in his home.

Reference is made to Vienna Jaques, the only woman other than the Prophet's wife, Emma, who is mentioned by name in the Doctrine and Covenants. (*Ibid.*, 90:28-31.) She was to go to Jackson County, Missouri, and receive a stewardship from the bishop.

## Importance of Covenants

An outstanding message in Section 90 is the following:

> Search diligently, pray always, and be believing, and all things shall work together for your good, if ye walk uprightly and remember the covenant wherewith ye have covenanted one with another. (Verse 24.)

The expression "the covenant wherewith ye have covenanted one with another" has at least two meanings. First, when one enters the Church by baptism he covenants to keep the commandments of the Lord. The member of the Church who does not continue in this agreement no longer represents the Lord and, thus, his actions cast reflection upon all members who are endeavoring to demonstrate their true citizenship in the kingdom. Secondly, the agreement to work for the salvation of the living and the dead was also made in the pre-earth life. "Joseph Smith, by revelation, instructed the Saints and said that the Lord 'ordained and prepared' the means, 'before the foundation of the world, for the salvation of the dead who should die without a knowledge of the Gospel.'" (Joseph Fielding Smith: *The Way to Perfection*, p. 176.)

## Zion Warned

In the concluding verses of this revelation, a warning was given to Zion that if she did not repent, she would be chastened until she was clean (*Ibid.*, verses 34-37.)

The literal fulfillment of this prophecy is history. The saints were literally driven from Missouri because of their transgressions. (*Ibid.*, 101:1-8; 105:1-10.)

Many of the prophets, subsequent to the expulsion of the members of the Church from Missouri, have applied this warning to us of a later period. Among these was President Wilford Woodruff, who said:

> We have been favored, as no other people have, with wise counsels. Their extent and variety are immeasurable. They cover every department of human life. So far as we have observed them, prosperity and happiness have been the results. Whatever difficulties we may have to contend with to-day are due, if not wholly, at least in great part, to our disregard of them. (*An Epistle of the Council of the Twelve Apostles of the Church of Jesus Christ of Latter-day Saints,* Semi-annual Conference, October 10, 1887, p. 9.)

## Section 91

While the Prophet was revising the scriptures, he inquired of the Lord concerning the Apocrypha of the Old Testament. These books, being of uncertain origin, were once a part of the Protestant Bible, and they continue to be in the Douay version (Catholic). Section 91 informs us that although the books in the main were translated correctly there were many additions by the hands of men. It was unnecessary for the Apocrypha to be revised, the Prophet was advised, but by the Spirit the reader could distinguish between the truth and the spurious.

## Section 92

This revelation is a commandment that Frederick G. Williams be received as a member of the United Order. The expression "you shall be a lively member" is a first principle with Latter-day Saints. They know that the active member receives the manifold blessings of participation, one of which is to know that a commandment is being lived. (D&C 42:40.)

## Chapter 19

# JOHN'S TESTIMONY OF JESUS

## (Section 93:1-20)

The material for study in this chapter comes from one of the most important revelations received by Joseph Smith. Probably better than any other revelation in the Doctrine and Covenants, Section 93 provides us with information concerning the Savior that is intended to enable us to worship him better. (D&C 93:19.)

The Lord mentioned in the first verse is Jesus Christ. Unmistakably the reader is told that the only way by which a person may come unto Him is by forsaking his sins. This truth, stated differently, is that the atonement of Christ remits sins only if the person repents and accepts the Savior by baptism. (D&C 29:17; 42:1.)

### To Know Him

The promised blessing of those who keep the commandments is to know God. (John 17:30.) To know God means more than the usual meaning that one may, by the Holy Ghost, know of his existence and of his plan of salvation. (This means of knowledge is known to thousands of Latter-day Saints. Keeping the commandments is an essential to meet the requirements.)

Men may also literally "see his face" in this life. (*Ibid.*, 67:10-14; 93:1.) The Prophet Joseph Smith, in commenting upon the word of Jesus to his disciples in John 14:12-27, said:

> The other Comforter spoken of is a subject of great interest, and perhaps understood by few of this generation. After a person has faith in Christ, repents of his sins, and is baptized for the remission of his sins and receives the Holy Ghost, (by the

laying on of hands), which is the first Comforter, then let him continue to humble himself before God, hungering and thirsting after righteousness, and living by every word of God, and the Lord will soon say unto him, Son, thou shalt be exalted. When the Lord has thoroughly proved him, and finds that the man is determined to serve Him at all hazards, then the man will find his calling and his election made sure, then it will be his privilege to receive the other Comforter, which the Lord hath promised the Saints, as is recorded in the testimony of St. John, in the 14th chapter, from the 12th to the 27th verses . . . [Especially verses 16, 17, 18, 21 and 23.]

Now what is this other Comforter? It is no more nor less than the Lord Jesus Christ Himself; and this is the sum and substance of the whole matter; that when any man obtains this last Comforter, he will have the personage of Jesus Christ to attend him, or appear unto him from time to time, and even He will manifest the Father unto him, and they will take up their abode with him, and the Lord will teach him face to face, and he may have a perfect knowledge of the mysteries of the Kingdom of God; and this is the state and place the ancient Saints arrived at when they had such glorious visions—Isaiah, Ezekiel, John upon the Isle of Patmos, St. Paul in the three heavens, and all the Saints who held communion with the general assembly and Church of the First Born. (*Teachings of the Prophet Joseph Smith,* pp. 150-151.)

Many names might be furnished of those who have literally seen the Lord other than those who are named by the Prophet Joseph Smith. The brother of Jared (Ether 3:13-20); Nephi and his brother Jacob (2 Nephi 11:2-3); Moroni (Ether 12:38-41); Stephen, the first Christian martyr (Acts 7:54-56); Sidney Rigdon (D&C 76:22-24); Oliver Cowdery (*Ibid.*, 110:1-10); and many others of this dispensation have seen the resurrected Lord.

To know God is in the ultimate sense to become like him. For this purpose the Melchizedek Priesthood is available to man that the ordinances of the House of the Lord might prepare him for this greatest measure of salvation. (*Ibid.*, 88:19-23; 124:27-28, 41-42.)

Elder Marion G. Romney of the Council of the Twelve, counsels us as follows in the way to eternal life:

With complete surrender to the spirit of the gospel let us, honestly and without guile, search our own souls and find the weakness which presently impedes our upward climb to eternal life. If that weakness be faultfinding, evil speaking of the Lord's anointed, or profaning the name of Deity, let us desist. If it be neglecting our prayers, let us pause night and morning in our mad rush and kneel with our families and in our secret chambers while we pour out our souls in thanksgiving and petition, until hungering and thirsting after righteousness we are filled with the Holy Ghost. If it be failure to obtain the sealing ordinances of the temple for ourselves and families, let us straightway prepare to enter that holy place and obtain them before it is too late. If it be the giving way to anger, of appetite for the things forbidden in the Word of Wisdom, or surrendering to baser lusts; if it be desecration of the Sabbath day or refusing to contribute of our time and means according to the laws of the Church for the building of the kingdom; whatever it be, let us find it, recognize it, and do something about it daily. (*Conference Report,* October 1965, p. 17.)

## The True Light

He who comes to the Savior may not only see his face, and know that he is, but he will also understand some other basic truths about Him. First, that he is the light which lighteth every man that comes into the world. (D&C 93:2.) About this principle, known as the "light of Christ," we have already learned several other facts: (1) it proceeds from the presence of God to fill the immensity of space (*Ibid.*, 88:12); (2) it performs the following functions: (a) creative, (b) life-giving, (c) governing, (d) enlightening or inspiring (*Ibid.*, verses 6-13); (3) it is a great communication system by which God's power is everywhere in the world; (4) as men draw closer to God, his light is received more abundantly, even to bringing them to the Father. (Chapter 11.)

Jesus Christ is the true light. This truth is related to the property of the light of Christ that inspires and gives enlightenment to men. It is this influence in the world that ennobles man, raises him to greater heights of accomplishments, and teaches him that there is joy in right doing; whereas, regret and sorrow follow when man does not live up to the light he possesses. (D&C 84:45-47; Moroni 7:10-19.)

In other revelations the Lord speaks of himself as the light which shineth in darkness but the darkness comprehends it not. (D&C 6:21; 39:1-2; 45:7.) In this sense the revelations from the Lord are light, as opposed to darkness. (*Doctrine and Covenants Commentary*, pp. 36-37.)

## The Oneness of the Father and the Son

In Section 93 and other scriptures, the doctrine that the Eternal Father and his Son Jesus Christ are one is known. (D&C 93:3; John 10:30; 1 John 5:7.) As a part of this concept, further emphasis is given in this language: the Son is in the Father, and the Father is in the Son. (John 14:10.) This truth should not confuse a Latter-day Saint in his belief that the Eternal Father and the Son are separate and distinct as to their individuality. (D&C 130:22; John 17:11, 20-24.) Of what does this oneness consist? Elder James E. Talmage wrote:

> This unity is a type of completeness; the mind of any one member of the Trinity is the mind of the others: seeing as each of them does with the eye of perfection, they see and understand alike. Under any given conditions each would act in the same way, guided by the same principles of unerring justice and equity. The one-ness of the Godhead, to which the scriptures so abundantly testify, implies no mystical union of substance, nor any unnatural and therefore impossible blending of personality. Father, Son, and Holy Ghost are as distinct in their persons and individualities as are any three personages in mortality. Yet their unity of purpose and operation is such as to make their edicts one, and their will the will of God. (*The Articles of Faith,* p. 41.)

## The Father and the Son

Jesus speaks of himself as having received a fulness from the Father, and he is therefore known as the Father. He, of course, was the Son because he was tabernacled in the flesh as the offspring of the Father. (D&C 93:4.) That Christ is known in the scriptures as the Father is well known. (Isa. 9:6; Ether 3:14; 2 Nephi 19:6; Mosiah 16:15; Alma 11:38-40.)

According to an exposition on the doctrine of the Father and the Son by the First Presidency and the Twelve Apostles, issued on June 30, 1916, there are three different meanings of the title "Father" as applied to Jesus Christ. These are: (1) "Father" as Creator (Ether 4:7; Mosiah 16:15); (2) "Father" of those who abide in His Gospel (D&C 50:41; 25:1; 34:3; 39:1-4); (3) "Father" because he represents the Father who gave him the right to use the title (John 5:43; 3 Nephi 20:35; 28:10; D&C 50:43).

## The Works of the Father Manifest

Jesus came into the world to perform the works of his Father and that men might know of the Father. (D&C 93:5; John 5:19.) In this latter sense he became the revelation of God to the world, and therefore, he was known as the "Word." (John 1:1, 14; D&C 93:8; *Teachings of the Prophet Joseph Smith*, p. 346.) Jesus was also the "Word" because "the word of God came through Him and was embodied in Him. (Charles W. Penrose, *Conference Report*, April 1915, p. 37.)

## John's Record

The introduction to Section 93 in the Doctrine and Covenants and also the *Doctrine and Covenants Commentary* (p. 590) identify the testator of the Savior in this revelation to be John the Beloved, the apostle of the

Lord. Of him it is recorded that he saw and bore record of the Lord's glory, but his complete record is yet to be revealed. (D&C 93:6.) The author of the Book of John reveals the incompleteness of the record by saying that "the world itself could not contain the books that should be written about the Savior." (John 21:25.)

The promise is given, however, that the fulness of John's record will be revealed if faithfulness is present. (D&C 93:18.)

### Jesus As Creator

Jesus was in the beginning before the world was created. (D&C 93:7.) As the messenger of salvation he brought the words of the Father to men, and he also revealed the character of God in his life. Only the being who was truth, who taught only the truth, could redeem men and the world. Jesus paid for the transgression in Eden that brought spiritual and physical death into the world, by sacrificing his life, the life of a being who was sinless and capable of rescuing men from these deaths. (*Ibid.*, verses 8-9; 2 Nephi 9:6-12; D&C 45:3-4.) The Savior redeemed us, as the Apostle Paul said: "he hath purchased [us] with his own blood." (Acts 20:28.)

John testifies that men were made by him; in fact, all things were his creation. This earth was created by him through the "light of Christ"; consequently, all men and animals were created through him for all are made of the dust of the earth. (D&C 88:10.) The fulness with which Christ is the creator is expressed in this authoritative source:

> Christ was the actual Maker of the worlds, as an architect is the actual maker of the houses he builds. They were made *by* Him. But they were also made *through* Him; for He was as stated before, the Executive of the Father in the work of creation. They were also made *of* Him; for He is the very source of the light and life that permeate creation. (*Doctrine and Covenants Commentary,* p. 591.)

It should also be noted that not only was Christ the creator of this earth but of "worlds." (D&C 93:10; 88:6-10.)

## The Only Begotten of the Father

The references to Jesus in the scriptures as the "Only Begotten of the Father" are many. (John 3:16, 18; 2 Nephi 25:12; Alma 9:26; D&C 20:21; Moses 6:52.) The First Presidency in 1916 affirmed the literalness of Jesus' birth by his mortal mother, Mary, and the Eternal Father, and Elder James E. Talmage has written about this doctrine. (*The Articles of Faith*, p. 466; *Jesus The Christ*, p. 81.) Because he was the Begotten Son of the Father in the flesh, it was possible for him to offer the infinite atonement for men.

## From Grace to Grace

John's testimony is that Jesus grew from grace to grace, that all things were not his at first.

> And I, John, saw that he received not of the fulness at the first, but received grace for grace;
>
> And he received not of the fulness at first, but continued from grace to grace, until he received a fulness;
>
> And thus he was called the Son of God, because he received not of the fulness at the first. (D&C 93:12-14.)

Born as a babe, reared from boyhood to manhood, the Child Jesus developed as other children. As with us, the memory of his former life in the spirit world was withheld that his growth might be an experience of mortality. Elder Talmage points out that this growth was "from good to greater good, not from evil to good." (*Jesus The Christ*, p. 112.)

In the temple, at the age of twelve, Jesus knew of his divine parentage through the Eternal Father. He was about his Father's business, not the business of Joseph, his legal father. (*Jesus the Christ*, pp. 113-116.)

The Bible is silent on Jesus' boyhood and the years up to the time of his ministry at thirty years, except for the event of the temple at the age of twelve. (Luke 2:41-52.) Additional information regarding his formative years to the time of his ministry is given us by the Prophet Joseph Smith.

> And it came to pass that Jesus grew up with his brethren, and waxed strong, and waited upon the Lord for the time of his ministry to come. And he served under his father, and he spake not as other men, neither could he be taught; for he needed not that any man should teach him. And after many years, the hour of his ministry drew nigh. (*Inspired Version,* Matt. 3:22-25.)

"For he needed not that any man should teach him" suggests that the normal difficulties of teaching and disciplining were not present in his life, except for the period of infancy.

Ultimately, as an exalted man, Jesus declared that he had received all power from the Father. (Matt. 28:16-18; D&C 93:16-17.) Even as Jesus received a fulness after the resurrection, so also may the faithful in their exalted state. (Romans 8:17; D&C 84:38.)

## The Heavens Were Opened

In testifying of Christ's divinity as the Only Begotten Son of God, John refers to the time when Jesus was baptized. (D&C 93:15.) Several times the Father testified from the heavens of his relationship to his Only Begotten Son; the occasion of Jesus' baptism is one of these. (Matt. 17:5; John 12:27-28.)

At Jesus' baptism the heavens were opened and John the Baptist saw the Spirit of God descending like a dove, with the voice of the Father saying, "This is my beloved Son, in whom I am well pleased." (Matt. 3:16; c.f. Mark 1:9-11; Luke 3:21-22.)

Does the Holy Ghost come in the form of a dove? No, said the Prophet Joseph Smith, but the dove is the sign of the Holy Ghost. (*DHC* 5:260-261.)

## Summary

The intent of John's testimony given by the Savior to the Prophet Joseph Smith in the first 19 verses of Section 93 is to show wherein Jesus Christ is divine. What truths about Christ are pointed to in establishing this greatest of truths?

First, the Savior is the true light, which gives understanding to all men through what is known as the "light of Christ." This "light" is life-giving and sustains man's environment as a place where he can work out his salvation.

Second, he is the "Word," the giver of the revelations, and also he was the revelation of God to the world while in his mortal ministry.

Third, so completely does he represent the Father that he and the Father are one in will, mind, purpose, etc. Because this is so, he is known as the "Father" in the scriptures.

Fourth, by giving his life in atonement for sin, he became man's Redeemer and Savior.

Fifth, he is the creator of worlds, including our earth, and therefore, since man is created of the earth, he is man's creator.

Sixth, he is literally the Only Begotten Son of the Father in the flesh. Thus, Jesus had power over death and yet he was capable of dying that he might become man's Redeemer.

Seventh, notwithstanding his divine birth, he like all men, developed as a babe to manhood, but he grew faster and understood early in life his mission. Through this process, he received a fulness from the Father.

Eighth, from the heavens the Father acknowledged Jesus Christ as his Son and also that he was pleased with his ministry while in mortality.

## Conclusion

What do these truths mean to the Latter-day Saints? The Savior says that they were given,

> . . . that you may understand and know how to worship, and know what you worship, that you may come unto the Father in my name, and in due time receive of his fulness.
>
> For if you keep my commandments you shall receive of his fulness, and be glorified in me as I am in the Father; therefore, I say unto you, you shall receive grace for grace. (D&C 93:19-20.)

To accept the foregoing truths about Jesus Christ indicates that the way to godhood is possible. The application of this truth was well expressed by Elder B. H. Roberts as he contrasted common beliefs of the world about Jesus Christ and the truth as revealed in the scriptures:

> Jesus Christ is God manifested in the flesh, proved to be so from the scripture; the character of God is revealed in the wonderful life that Jesus, the Son of God, lived on earth; in it we see God in action; and from it we see the gentleness, the compassion, the love, and also the justice and severity of God. Jesus Christ is God; and He is also man; but I deplore those sectarian refinements which try to tell us about the humanity of Jesus being separate from the divinity of Jesus. He Himself made no such distinctions. He was divine, spirit and body, and spirit and body was exalted to the throne of His Father, and sits there now with all the powers of the Godhead residing in Him bodily, an immortal, glorified, exalted man! The express image and likeness of God the Father; for as the Son is, so is the Father. Yet when the Latter-day Saints announce to the world that we believe God to be an exalted man, we are told that we are blasphemers. But as long as the throne of Jesus Christ stands sure, so long as His spirit remains in His immortal body of flesh and bones, glorified and everlasting, shall keep His

place by the side of the Father, so long will the doctrine that God is an exalted man hold its place against the idle sophistries of the learned world. The doctrine is true. It cannot be unthroned. A truth is a solemn thing. Not the mockery of ages, not the lampooning of the schoolmen, not the derision of the multitude, not the blasphemy of the world, can affect it; it will always remain true. And this doctrine, announced by Joseph Smith to the world, that God is an exalted man, that Jesus Christ is the revelation of God to the world and that He is just like his Father, and that those who are His brethren may become as He is, when they have walked in His footsteps—that is a doctrine that will stand sure and fast as the throne of God itself. For Jesus Christ was God manifested in the flesh. He was the revelation of God to the world. He was and is and ever will remain an exalted man. He is, and always will remain, God. ("The Doctrine of Deity," *The Seventy's Course in Theology*, p. 188-189.)

## Chapter 20

# PRE-MORTAL EXISTENCE

## (Section 93:21-23, 27-29, 33-34)

In the last chapter we learned of Jesus' pre-mortal existence. John bore record that Jesus was in the beginning, before the world was. (D&C 93:7.) In fact, in that existence, Jesus created "worlds"; he was the creator of men and of all things. (*Ibid.*, verse 10.) And then, he was made flesh and dwelt among men. (*Ibid.*, verse 4.)

### Faith in Christ

In the Christian world many theologians teach that Jesus Christ was not literally the son of God, that he was only mortal—not divine; that his excellence was only in his teachings and not that he died for man's sins and that man might live as a resurrected being. An indication of the beliefs of some "religious liberals" regarding this understanding of Jesus is found in the following excerpts:

> For traditional Christianity maintains that Jesus was the literal Son of God, of the same substance as the Father, an immortal and divine creature who, as part of an involved plan for the salvations of men's souls, assumed mortal form and came to earth for a brief period nineteen hundred years ago. On this arbitrary assumption as to the divinity of Christ rests the whole imposing structure of orthodox Christianity . . . For him, Jesus was a man, not a superman; a Jew thoroughly versed in the customs and religious ideas of his people; a teacher and preacher in the grand traditions of the Hebrew prophets . . . but withal, gloriously, a man, even as you and I. . . .
>
> The religious liberal is committed . . . to a belief as "not God who made himself a man, but a man who made himself a god." (Waldemar Argow, *What Do Religious Liberals Believe?* pp. 49, 50, 54.)

These thoughts regarding Jesus seem to be increasing in a Christian world committed by the Bible to the acceptance of Jesus as the Son of God.

In a comprehensive survey conducted a few years ago, it was indicated that despite the acknowledged belief in God by over 96 per cent of Americans, there was little real vitality in their belief. When the leadership is steeped in false teachings that do not give real, genuine faith, then it can be expected that the followers will not have a vital faith. In this survey, the following was revealed by three leading theologians of the Jewish, Protestant, and Catholic faiths:

> Most Americans regard religion as a private, painless pathway to heaven.
>
> Nearly three-quarters of them do not think of God as having any intimate relation to their daily life.
>
> Nearly three-quarters do not consciously connect their religion with their judgments of right and wrong.
>
> Religious education in America ends in the elementary stage. College students get adult education in the secular field, but only infant education in the religious field. (Henry C. Link, *The Way to Security,* p. 213.)

In the Lord's Preface to the Doctrine and Covenants, purposes for the restoration of the true church and gospel are given. Among these is the intent of the Lord that faith shall increase in the hearts of men. (D&C 1:21.) Fundamentally, this was to be accomplished through an awakening of the spirit within one to a recognition of the truth as taught in the gospel of Jesus Christ. Without the true knowledge of the Godhead, consisting of the Father, his Son Jesus Christ, and the Holy Ghost, it would be impossible to come to the faith that saves. The Spirit which converts accompanies truth as people are prepared for it. (John 17:3; 1 Cor. 2:14.) Has the true knowledge of the members of the Godhead, and especially of the being and mission of the Savior, kindled faith in the breasts of Latter-day Saints? Elder Orson F. Whitney eloquently expresses an answer to this question, using Latter-day Saint pioneers as an example:

There is no more eloquent preaching than when men and women will forsake their native land, their homes, their parents, their children, their material possessions—every earthly thing, and cross the stormy ocean, the heated plains, the frosty mountains, many of them laying down their lives, to be buried in a lonely grave by the wayside, pulling handcarts, wading rivers, crossing deserts, climbing mountains, and settling in a barren waste—all for what? Was it for gold and silver, houses and lands, flocks and herds, and the betterment of their temporal condition? Was it for the honors of men and the applause of the world that they did these things? No, it was because they loved God and wanted to build up his kingdom. They had heard the voice of the Shepherd; they were his sheep, and a stranger they would not follow. (John 10:1-5.) . . . There is no more eloquent preaching of the Gospel than is found in the toils and privations, in their struggles and achievements. (*Conference Report,* April 1915, p. 101.)

## Jesus the Firstborn

Jesus Christ is proclaimed by the prophets, ancient and modern, as the literal son of God in the spirit and also in the flesh. Jesus is the Firstborn of all the spirit sons and daughters of God.

And now, verily I say unto you, I was in the beginning with the Father, and am the Firstborn. (D&C 93:21; c.f. Rom. 3:14; Col. 1:15.)

Because he is the Firstborn, we know the Savior as our Elder Brother. The First Presidency and the Council of the Twelve Apostles, on June 30, 1916, expressed a word of caution to the members of the Church concerning the status of the Redeemer and our relationship to him as our Brother. It is as follows:

There is no impropriety, therefore, in speaking of Jesus Christ as the Elder Brother of the rest of human kind. That He is by spiritual birth Brother to the rest of us is indicated in

Hebrew: "Wherefore in all things it behooved him to be made like unto his brethren, that he might be a merciful and faithful high priest in things pertaining to God, to make reconciliation for the sins of the people." (Hebrews 2:17.) Let it not be forgotten, however, that He is essentially greater than any and all others, by reason (1) of His seniority as the oldest or firstborn; (2) of His unique status in the flesh as the offspring of a mortal mother and of an immortal, or resurrected and glorified Father; (3) of His selection and foreordination as the one and only Redeemer and Savior of the race; and (4) of His transcendent sinlessness.

In order that none might be mistaken in their understanding of the relationship of Jesus to us mortals, the First Presidency continued:

> Jesus Christ is not the Father of the spirits who have taken or yet shall take bodies upon this earth, for He is one of them. He is the Son, as they are sons or daughters of Elohim. (James E. Talmage, *Articles of Faith,* pp. 472-473.)

## Church of the Firstborn

The important truth is given that only through Jesus Christ may one be a partaker of the glories of the eternities. The expression "through Jesus Christ" is significant in its meaning, for to understand this is the key to eternal life. One must be begotten through him. (D&C 93:22.) To be born of Christ, in this sense of begetting, is to accept him literally as the Savior who bought us with his blood. (Acts 20:28.) This acceptance must be total, unqualified, as stated in the following by President J. Reuben Clark, Jr.:

> Jesus is the Messiah, he is the Savior of the world. Through his atoning blood, his suffering, his death and his resurrection, we may become perfect beings, and in no other way and by no other means. That is the great truth which permeates every thing which God has said to his children on this earth. Without that we would be as dead bodies and dead spirits, shut off from true salvation, from exaltation, from eternal progression, the

great new truth of modern revelation. We must never forget that Jesus is the Christ, the Redeemer of the world. There is no escape from this . . . Turn, twist, philosophize, mass sophistries as we will, this truth remains. (*Conference Report,* April 1934, p. 93.)

The "by no other means" in addition to faith, are repentance of sins, baptism by immersion for the remission of sins, and the receiving of the Holy Ghost by one having authority. To follow this path leads to exaltation in the celestial kingdom. But the path must be one of faith in Christ. All those who follow him, walking in obedience to the commandments, including marriage for eternity, will become members of the "church of the Firstborn." (D&C 76:53-62.) Entrance into the celestial kingdom, following the resurrection, will not insure exaltation or godhood. Some in that kingdom will not have observed all of the commandments, especially temple marriage and its obligations, so they must become ministering servants—though saved in the celestial kingdom—to those who become members of the church of the Firstborn. (*Ibid.,* 132:15-17.)

The church of the Firstborn will consist of those,

> . . . into whose hands the Father has given all things—
>
> They are they who are priests and kings, who have received of his fulness, and of his glory . . .
>
> Wherefore, as it is written, they are gods, even the sons of God—
>
> These are they who are just men made perfect through Jesus the mediator of the new covenant, who wrought out this perfect atonement through the shedding of his own blood. (*Ibid.,* 55-56, 58, 69.)

## Ye Were in the Beginning

In Section 93 there are two verses that reveal a doctrine that has tremendous meaning for Latter-day Saints and all who desire to receive knowledge that gives meaning to the earth-life. The verses are:

> Ye were also in the beginning with the Father.
> Man was also in the beginning with God . . . (Verses 23, 29.)

In this message about man, including other modern scriptures, an entire vista of information is opened up. It is not the Doctrine and Covenants that gives much information about man's pre-earth life, but the Pearl of Great Price. (Abraham 3:22-23; Moses 3:5.) Upon the basis of the modern scriptures the prophets of this dispensation have provided sufficient about that life to make a clear picture of its principles and implications for the earth-life.

Basic to an understanding of the plan of salvation is man's relationship to God. Concerning man, we learn that he is a dual being consisting of a physical body and a spirit entity. The most important truth regarding man's spirit is to be understood as literally having parents in the life before this. The word "begotten" is to be understood as literally as the begetting of Jesus Christ in the spirit and also in the flesh by our Heavenly Father. Paul the Apostle taught that we are the offspring of God. (Acts 17:27, 28.) Old Testament prophets referred to the relationship of man and God by saying he is "the God of the spirits of all flesh." (Numbers 16:22; 27:16.) The writer of Hebrews speaks of the "Father of Spirits." (Heb. 12:9.)

The importance of the doctrine of the Fatherhood of God is known in many ways: (1) the highest measure of salvation, exaltation or godhood, is possible because of the divine birth that man received as the Father's child—the child may attain the heights of the Father; (2) the concern for the well-being of the child by earthly parents is many times magnified with our Heavenly Father; (3) greater meaning is attached to prayer and the assurance of its being answered; (4) security is found in knowing that whatever happens in life, there is meaning in those events.

## Man's Creation

Man's origin is clarified by the First Presidency composed of Joseph F. Smith, John R. Winder, and Anthon H. Lund:

> Adam, our great progenitor "the first man" was, like Christ, a pre-existent spirit, and like Christ he took upon him an appropriate body, the body of a man, and so became a "living soul." The doctrine of pre-existence—revealed so plainly, particularly in the latter days, pours a wonderful flood of light upon the otherwise mysterious problem of man's origin. It shows that man, as a spirit, was begotten and born of heavenly parents, and reared to maturity in the eternal mansions of the Father, prior to coming upon the earth in a temporal body to undergo an experience in mortality. It teaches that all men existed in the spirit before any man existed in the flesh, and that all who have inhabited the earth since Adam have taken bodies and become souls in like manner . . . The Church of Jesus Christ of Latter-day Saints, basing its belief on divine revelation, ancient and modern, proclaims man to be the direct and lineal offspring of Deity. ("The Origin of Man," *Improvement Era,* XIII, pp. 75-81.)

## Man's Spirit

The spirit of man is in the form of his earthly body. In an explanation concerning a passage of scripture, the Lord revealed to the Prophet that "the spirit of man [is] in the likeness of his person." (D&C 77:2.) This divine truth, stated catagorically, should be understood to mean that certain disfigurements of the flesh in mortality would not be inherited from the shape of the spirit. The fact that the body conforms to the pre-existent spirit is also made known in the Book of Mormon. In a wonderful revelation to the brother of Jared, whose faith permitted him to behold the pre-existent Jesus Christ, the Son of God said:

> Behold, I am he who was prepared from the foundation of the world to redeem my people. Behold, I am Jesus Christ—Seest thou that ye are created after mine own image? Yea, even

all men were created in the beginning after mine own image. Behold, this body, which ye now behold, is the body of my spirit; and man have I created after the body of my spirit; and even as I appear unto thee to be in the spirit will I appear unto my people in the flesh. (Ether 3:14-16.)

## Man Is Eternal

We have learned that man was in the beginning with God. Latter-day Saint theology teaches, however, that man is eternal. If there was a beginning to man as a spirit, and man is eternal, without beginning or end, then, how is this possible? As to form, spirit, man had a beginning, but not as to conscious existence. The Prophet Joseph Smith taught, in this manner, the wonderful truth that man is eternal:

I have another subject to dwell upon, which is calculated to exalt man . . . the soul—the mind of man—the mortal spirit. Where did it come from? All learned men and doctors of divinity say that God created it in the beginning; but it is not so; the very idea lessens man in my estimation. I do not believe the doctrine; I know better. Hear it, all ye ends of the world; for God has told me so; and if you don't believe me it will not make the truth without effect . . . We say that God himself is a self-existent being . . . Man does exist upon the same principles . . . The mind or the intelligence which man possesses is co-equal [co-eternal] with God himself . . . I am dwelling on the immortality of the spirit of man. Is it logical to say that the intelligence of spirits is immortal, had no beginning, neither will it have an end. There never was a time when there were not spirits; for they are co-equal [co-eternal] with our Father in Heaven. (*DHC* 6:310.)

From what source did the Prophet receive his information on the eternal nature of man? From the same source—revelation—that Abraham received the following:

. . . there is nothing that the Lord thy God shall take in his heart to do but what he will do it. Howbeit that he made the greater star; as, also if there be two spirits and one shall be more intelligent than the other, yet these two spirits, notwithstanding one is more intelligent than the other, have no beginning; they existed before, they shall have no end, they shall exist after for they are gnolaum, or eternal. (Abraham 3:17-18.)

Section 93 points out that:

Intelligence, or the light of truth, was not created or made, neither indeed can be . . . For man is spirit. The elements are eternal, and spirit and element, inseparably connected, receive a fulness of joy; and when separated, man cannot receive a fulness of joy. (Verses 29, 33, 34.)

These passages suggest the same idea expressed by the Prophet when he used the expression, "the intelligence of spirits" in the above quotation—the spirit of man consists of intelligence, the uncreatable substance. Eternal matter—spirit—combined with intelligence constitutes the eternal man.

President Joseph Fielding Smith of the Council of the Twelve once wrote this observation concerning intelligence and spirit:

Some of our writers have endeavored to explain what an intelligence is, but to do so is futile, for we have never been given any insight into this matter beyond what the Lord has fragmentarily revealed. We know, however, that there is something called intelligence which always existed. It is the real eternal part of man, which was not created or made. This intelligence combined with the spirit constitutes a spiritual identity or individual. The spirit of man, then is a combination of the intelligence and the spirit which is an entity begotten of God. (*The Progress of Man,* p. 11.)

## Summary

We have learned that in a "Christian" world that has generally departed from faith in the Lord Jesus Christ, modern revelation affords Latter-day Saints a concept of Christ as the literal Son of God in the spirit and in the flesh; that he was the Firstborn of all the spirit sons of

God. Furthermore, we learned that all men lived before birth into this life. In fact, man is eternal in his nature because of the uncreatable intelligence which is a part of his spirit entity. Many benefits are received by man in this life by his knowing of his relationship to God. The knowledge of this relationship provides the Latter-day Saint with the motivation to become a member of the church of the Firstborn after the resurrection, or to be exalted in the celestial kingdom. To reach this blessing demands full obedience.

> And no man receiveth a fulness unless he keepeth his commandments.
>
> He that keepeth his commandments receiveth truth and light, until he is glorified in truth and knoweth all things. (D&C 93:27-28.)

## Some Values

Without the knowledge of the pre-earth life, Latter-day Saints would be unable to understand many phases of this life. One's place in the eternal plan is better known. We believe that chance in our coming to this life is ruled out. All of us are here because of planning made in the councils in the heavens before the foundation of the earth was laid. To realize that, while in this life, one is fulfilling a purpose holds tremendous value in shaping one's life.

The life in the pre-mortal world has conditioned us in this life. Elder James E. Talmage expressed his belief that the pre-mortal life has a definite influence upon this life.

> In the antemortal eternities we developed with individual differences and varied capacities. So far as we can peer into the past by the aid of revealed light we see that there was gradation of intelligence, and consequently of ability, among the spirits, precisely as such differences exist amongst us mortals . . . Every spirit born in the flesh is an individual character, and brings to the body prepared for its tenancy a nature all its own. The tendencies, likes and dislikes, in short the whole disposition of

the spirit may be intensified or changed by the course of mortal life, and the spirit may advance or retrograde while allied with its mortal tabernacle. . . . The spirit lived as an organized intelligence before it became the embodied child of human parents; and its pre-existent individualism will be of effect in its period of earth life. Even though the manifestations of primeval personality be largely smothered under the tendencies due to bodily and prenatal influence, it is there, and makes its mark. This is an analogy with the recognized laws of physical operation—every force acting upon a body produces its definite effect whether it acts alone or with others and even opposing forces. (*The Vitality of Mormonism,* pp. 240-241.)

## Foreordination

There were among the spirit children of our Father many who had excelled in that world. Among those who were recognized as his "rulers" was Abraham. (Abraham 3:23.) Others who were foreordained to positions of responsibility in this life were: Adam (2 Nephi 2:22-26); Jeremiah (Jer. 1:4, 5); and Joseph Smith (2 Nephi 3:14-15; D&C 124:1.) Our Father's knowledge about these servants and all of his children was such that he could "see the end of their earthly career even from the first." (*Articles of Faith,* p. 191.) Elder James E. Talmage also believed that, "Everyone of us was known by name and character to the Father, who is 'the God of the spirits of all flesh' (Numbers 16:22; 27:16), in our antemortal or primeval childhood; and from among the hosts of His unembodied children God chose for special service on earth such as were best suited to the accomplishment of His purpose." (*The Vitality of Mormonism,* p. 237.) The foreknowledge of God does not hold that people are designated for glory or condemnation or demerit. Elder Talmage believed that "God's knowledge of spiritual and human nature enables Him to conclude with certainty as to the actions of any of his children under given conditions; yet that knowledge is not of compelling force upon the creature." (*Articles of Faith,* p. 119.)

## Other Values

We are thus able to see that the Lord is directing the affairs of men not only in religious events but also in other areas of earth-life. The Prophet Joseph Smith once said:

> Every man who has a calling to minister to the inhabitants of the world was ordained to that very purpose in the Grand Council of heaven before the world was. (*DHC* 6:364.)

The mission of Columbus was foreknown. (1 Nephi 13:12.) The Lord also raised up men to write the Constitution of the United States. (D&C 101:79-80.)

The doctrine of premortality also gives us light upon the question of the different races in the world. President Joseph Fielding Smith wrote that assignments were made to the tribes and nations before the earth was created; that the more choice spirits would come through better grades of nations and that this distribution was in accordance with the laws of mercy and justice. (*The Way To Perfection*, pp. 46-48.)

Unto Abraham, Isaac, and Jacob (Israel) the promise was given that their posterity would have special privileges in holding the priesthood and would be custodians of the gospel through the ages. It is from these ancient patriarchs that the Latter-day Saints are descended. Why these special privileges to a certain lineage? Because they were entitled to these blessings due to their valiancy in the pre-earth life. These values and others afford Latter-day Saints considerable advantage in understanding not only their own place in this life but also the Lord's purposes for all men.

The doctrine of premortality sheds a flood of light upon many questions that confront us in life.

## Chapter 21

# MAN AND TRUTH

## (Section 93:24-26, 30-53)

### Introduction

The last two chapters, written from Section 93, have given information about the Savior and also man. Jesus Christ is the literal Son of God in the spirit and in the flesh. Man is also a child of God in the spirit. Man is eternal. His spirit, in the likeness of his mortal body, consists of intelligence and spirit element, which are uncreatable. Since man was in the pre-earth life with God, that life influences his present existence. This doctrine also answers many questions about this life that otherwise would be mysteries.

### Great Truths

The revelation for study in this chapter carries some teachings of power worthy of new revelation. In connection with man's premortality, the Lord also revealed:

> Ye were also in the beginning with the Father; that which is Spirit even the Spirit of truth;
>
> And truth is knowledge of things as they are, and as they were, and as they are to come;
>
> And whatsoever is more or less than this is the spirit of that wicked one who was a liar from the beginning. . . .
>
> Man was also in the beginning with God. Intelligence, or the light of truth, was not created or made, neither indeed can be.
>
> All truth is independent in that sphere in which God has placed it, to act for itself, as all intelligence also; otherwise there is no existence.
>
> Behold, here is the agency of man, and here is the condemnation of man; because that which was from the beginning is plainly manifest unto them, and they receive not the light.

And every man whose spirit receiveth not the light is under condemnation.

For man is spirit. . . .

The glory of God is intelligence, or, in other words, light and truth.

Light and truth forsake that evil one. (D&C 93:23-25, 29-33, 36-37.)

In verse 23 our Father in Heaven and men are declared to have the same quality—spirit of truth. Then there follows a definition of truth. Also, intelligence, the uncreatable material that gives eternalness to man, is called the "light of truth." What man does in accordance with this divine quality depends upon what he shall be.

### Truth—Absolute

Truth is knowledge! Truth is constant—absolute! Truth never changes; men may change as to their concepts of truth, but truth, never! It is that which was, is, and will continue to be. Expressed in another revelation—"truth abideth and hath no end." (*Ibid.*, 88:66.)

Men of science consider truth to be relative; that is, it changes. What is "true" today may change tomorrow. This belief concerning men's research is necessary in order that man's investigations may continue. The scientist builds upon the findings of others and thus advancement is made in discovering additional fragments of truth.

But what about religious truth, as contained in the gospel of Jesus Christ, restored through the Prophet Joseph Smith and his successors? Latter-day Saints may not accept the belief that the truths revealed in this dispensation are merely the result of an evolutionary change from the distant past through man's experience. Such a belief omits the important fact of revelation from a personal God to his Prophet. Bear in mind that as far as the gospel is concerned, its truths have come from revelation. Ultimately, the standard by which men may know about God and their relationship to him comes from revelation. Man by reason, searching, cannot find out God. Man's environment will not provide the answers; it must be revealed! The acceptance of this truth will bring this understanding:

> We take the sacred writings into our hands, and admit that they were given by direct inspiration for the good of man. We believe that God condescended to speak from the heavens and declare His will concerning the human family, to give them just and holy laws, to regulate their conduct, and guide them in a direct way, that in due time He might take them to Himself, and make them joint heirs with His Son. But when this fact is admitted, that the immediate will of heaven is contained in the Scriptures, are we not bound as rational creatures to live in accordance to all its precepts? Will the mere admission, that this is the will of heaven ever benefit us if we do not comply with all its teachings? Do we not offer violence to the Supreme Intelligence of heaven, when we admit the truth of its teachings, and do not obey them? Do we not descend below our own knowledge, and the better wisdom which heaven has endowed us with, by such a course of conduct? For these reasons, if we have direct revelations given us from heaven, surely those revelations were never given to be trifled with, without the trifler's incurring displeasure and vengeance upon his head, if there is any justice in heaven. . . . (Joseph Smith, *DHC* 2:11.)

All truth has not been revealed. Some truths are withheld because men lack faith. (Alma 12:9-11.) Our ninth Article of Faith declares that God "will yet reveal many great and important things pertaining to the kingdom of God." We have, however, all that is necessary for the attainment of exaltation in the celestial kingdom. If there should be more for this purpose, he who has faithfully done all that is required of him will find opportunity and ability to do whatever else may be necessary. The further acquisition of knowledge to exalt will be available in the spirit world for the dead; in the Millennium for the living. (D&C 101:32-34.)

## Truth-Differentiation

Is all truth of equal value?

Elder James E. Talmage said:

Not all knowledge is of equal worth. The knowledge that constitutes the wisdom of the heavens is all embraced in the Gospel as taught by Jesus Christ; and willful ignorance of this, the highest type of knowledge, will regulate its victim to the inferior order of intelligences. (*The Vitality of Mormonism*, p. 277.)

Elder John A. Widtsoe:

While Latter-day Saints understand that all truth is from God, and is desirable, and will be ours in time, yet we also know that all truth is not of equal value to humanity . . . Latter-day Saints understand that the truth of the greatest worth to humanity is that which controls and shapes human actions, that which interprets to us our relationship to God, our Maker, and to our fellowman; that which lays before us the great plan of salvation and explains why I am here, whence I came, where I am going and what I must do to conform to the greater laws of life. Such knowledge becomes the greater truth. (*Conference Report*, October 1926, pp. 81-82.)

Does all truth have the same validity? Elder Widtsoe says:

Not only do Latter-day Saints distinguish carefully between the greater and lesser truths, but they also recognize that not all truth has the same validity. We cannot accept all knowledge as being of equal certainty. Some knowledge I know to be absolutely certain, some appears to be true, and some I hope may be true . . . Latter-day Saints are careful to examine the validity of the truth set before them. We make the satisfying claim that the truth of greatest validity, that of greatest certainty, is the truth that has come from the mouth of God by revelation to his children in this and in every age through the history of the world. (*Ibid.*, p. 82.)

Why is the foregoing true? Because of what has already been learned from Section 93. We lived with

God before we were born upon this earth. We are here for a purpose, primarily to advance through faith toward godhood. If we learn all of the information about secular things in a given field of endeavor important for this life, and yet we do not measure up to the purpose of our existence, we have lost our grand opportunity.

## Truth Is of God

"The Spirit of truth is of God." (D&C 93:26.) How may one receive truth? President Stephen L Richards answers as follows:

> . . . we must, of necessity, have God's aid in the acquisition of truth. His aid comes through faith and prayer. Faith contemplates the acceptance of the spiritual reality of a world outside the domain of science. It postulates humility and dependence on divine power, the antipathies of egotism and self-sufficiency. A contrite heart is a fertile field for planting the seeds of truth. In such a field they come to fruition in a knowledge, understanding, and conviction of the great concepts of life which defy the reason and philosophy of the arrogant, and self-sufficient who will not stoop to the methods of the humble.

## The Power of Truth

There is a quality about truth—the power to testify of itself. The Prophet Joseph Smith said:

> In relation to the power over the minds of mankind which I hold I would say, it is in consequence of the power of truth in the doctrines which I have been an instrument in the hands of God of presenting unto them, and not because of any compulsion on my part. (*DHC* 6:273.)

There is a spirit about truth that captures the attention and allegiance of those who are prepared for it. Elder Orson F. Whitney told the following experiences with a minister who had written against the Book of Abraham in *The Pearl of Great Price*:

. . . I met (minister), with whom I was quite well-acquainted and he said to me: "Why have you not answered me?" "I have," was my reply; "I have been answering you all over the country, but it hasn't gotten into the papers." "Oh indeed, and what have you been saying?" he inquired. "I have been saying this:

Truth is truth, where'er 'tis found
On Christian or on heathen ground.

And whether it be taken from an ancient hill in North America, as was the Book of Mormon, or from the catacombs of Egypt, as was the Book of Abraham, if it's true, no matter who translated it, or how many supposed flaws appear in the translation. The character of the content and spirit that goes along with it, determines better than all else its truth, its authenticity. We know Shakespeare's writings by the very sound of them, they have the Shakespearean ring. Literary experts can tell the difference between those writings and all others. We recognize Milton's poetry by the Miltonic ring; the poetry of Byron and Tennyson. Then, if God speaks, why should it not have a God-like ring, something that no man can counterfeit, not any but a spiritual expert fully appreciate."

(He) agreed with me. Not as to the Book of Abraham, but as to the best way of testing any book. "I am one with you," he said, "in the belief that the highest evidence of the truth of any work is the spirit that it breathes and the wisdom that it inculcates. "Then," said I, "this Book of Abraham needs no defense from men or from anyone else. It speaks for itself; it defends itself. By the majesty of its language, by the sublimity of its teachings and by the Spirit that permeates them, it proclaims itself divine." (*Conference Report,* April 1926, pp. 34-35.)

## Light and Truth

The glory of God is intelligence, or in other words, light and truth.

Light and truth forsake that evil one. (D&C 93:36-37.)

The divine essence in man, intelligence, is light and truth. In discussing faith and knowledge, Alma mentions faith that,

. . . it hath sprouted up, that your understanding doth begin to be enlightened, and your mind doth begin to expand.

O then, is not this real? I say unto you, Yea, because it is light; and whatsoever is light, is good, because it is discernible, therefore ye must know that it is good . . . (Alma 32:34-35.)

After defining truth in the absolute sense, the Lord reveals that "whatsoever is more or less than this is the spirit of that wicked one who was a liar from the beginning." (D&C 93:25.) Light, then, "is the wisdom and ability to forsake everything 'more or less' than truth." (Marion G. Romney, *BYU Bulletin*, May 31, 1957.)

Because man is intelligence (light and truth) he is capable by reason of his nature to recognize truth and by his free agency reject error. Men may cloud their ability to discern light and truth because of sin. The greater the sin and the continuance in sin, the more is negated the power to distinguish between truth and falsehood. It is probable, however, that men do not lose all of this power, except the sons of perdition.

## The Way of Truth

Jesus saith unto him, I am the way, the truth, and the life: no man cometh unto the Father, but by me. (John 14:6.)

The Spirit of truth is of God. I am the Spirit of truth, and John bore record of me, saying: He received a fulness of truth, yea, even of all truth; (D&C 93:26.)

But when the Comforter is come, whom I will send unto you from the Father, even the Spirit of truth, which proceedeth from the Father, he shall testify of me: (John 15:26.)

Verily I say unto you, he that is ordained of me and sent forth to preach the word of truth by the Comforter, in the Spirit of truth, doth he preach it by the Spirit of truth or some other way? (D&C 50:17.)

For the word of the Lord is truth, and whatsoever is truth is light, and whatsoever is light is Spirit, even the Spirit of Jesus Christ.

And the Spirit giveth light to every man that cometh into the world; and the Spirit enlighteneth every man through the world, that hearkeneth to the voice of the Spirit. (D&C 84:45-46.)

In the foregoing scriptures we learn several things about the Spirit of truth: (1) Jesus is the Spirit of truth; (2) the Comforter—the Holy Ghost—is the spirit of truth; (3) there is a spirit which imparts truth known as the spirit of Jesus Christ, called elsewhere the "light of Christ" (D&C 88:6-13; Moroni 7:14-19), and which light gives understanding to all men. We have learned of the functions and place of this Spirit in our world. (Chapter 20.) Briefly, the words of the Savior—the Scriptures—are revelation. All revelation received since the creation has come through Jesus Christ. (D&C 76:12-13.) There are different ways in which truth is revealed—by dreams, visions, pure intelligence into the mind, etc.—but always through Jesus Christ. To the obedient to the teachings of Christ—faith, repentance, baptism, the receiving of the gift of the Holy Ghost, and the keeping of the commandments—the Holy Ghost may be the constant companion culminating in an everlasting dominion. (*Ibid.*, 121:46.) On the pathway to exaltation, revelation is received to enlighten, comfort, guide against error, and testify of the truth—of the Father, the Son Jesus Christ, and gospel teachings. In addition to the Comforter, there is the "light of Christ" which gives inspiration to all men. It is the spirit by which men discern truth from error.

All of these powers and influences guide men into "light and truth." All of them come from Jesus Christ to bless men that they might succeed in the journey back to the Father's presence to receive a fulness of joy after the resurrection. (*Ibid.*, 93:33-34.)

## Standard of Judgment

After quoting Moroni the Book of Mormon prophet as follows, Elder Marion G. Romney of the Council of the Twelve interprets this test by which one may know truth from falsehood:

Take heed, my beloved brethren, (he said), that ye do not judge that which is evil to be of God, or that which is good and of God to be of the devil. . . .

For behold, the Spirit of Christ is given to every man, that he may know good from evil; wherefore, I show unto you the way to judge; for every thing which inviteth to do good, and to persuade to believe in Christ, is sent forth by the power and gift of Christ; wherefore ye may know with a perfect knowledge it is of God. (In other words that it is truth.)

But whatsoever thing persuadeth men to do evil, (he continued), and believe not in Christ, and deny Him, and serve not God, then ye may know with a perfect knowledge it is of the devil; for after this manner doth the devil work. . . .

And now, my brethren, seeing that ye know the light by which ye may judge, which light is the light of Christ, see that ye do not judge wrongfully; for with that same judgment which ye judge ye shall also be judged. (Moroni 7:14-19.)

Here is Elder Romney's interpretation:

In applying this test, that everything which persuadest to believe in Christ is of God and that everything which persuadeth not to believe in Christ is of the devil, we start with the assurance that whatever the Lord has revealed is truth, "diamond truth" to borrow a phrase from the Prophet, that it is consistent with all that is, all that was, and all that is to come. This is and must be so because God's wisdom is infinite, being founded upon complete knowledge. "All things," said the Prophet Lehi speaking of things of the works of God, "have been done in the wisdom of him who knoweth all things." (2 Nephi 2:24.)

Implicit in this text is the assumption that wisdom is dependent upon knowledge and that God's wisdom is infinite because He is omniscient. "He knoweth all things, and there is not anything save he knows it." (2 Nephi 9:20.) He possesses with respect to all matters that knowledge which is truth, the object of our search, "knowledge of things as they are . . . as they were, and as they are to come. . . ."

Does what you have learned persuade you "to do good" and "to believe in Christ?" If so, it is "of God," and being of God it is truth. It will never have to be repudiated.

To elucidate upon this standard of judgment, Elder Romney provides this example:

That you may understand more clearly what I have in mind, let me give you an illustration or two. One of the fundamental doctrines of revealed truth is that in the garden of Eden, God endowed man with free agency. (Moses 7:32.) The preservation of this free agency is more important than the preservation of life itself, for without it, "there is no existence." (D&C 93:30.) It is, therefore, clear that everything which militates against man's enjoyment of this endowment persuades not to believe in Christ, for He is the author of free agency. . . .

Do they [programs and ideas affecting our daily lives] facilitate or restrict the exercise of man's divine endowment of free agency? Tested by this standard, most of them will fall quickly into their proper category as between good and evil.

In giving another example, Elder Romney reminds us that when men exercise their free agency they will be held accountable for their choices. (Alma 42:27.) Then, he gives this example:

Recently I heard a sociologist explain to a gathering of young people that society and not the individual is responsible for his misconduct. How does this concept stand up when tested by the revealed principle of accountability "that men will be punished for their own sins, and not for Adam's transgression," (*The Articles of Faith*) and that every man in the day of judgment, will "be accountable for his own sins." (D&C 101:78.)

Truth and error cannot be reconciled. All you need to do is distinguish between them, accept truth and forsake the error. That is what the Lord has always done. In fact, His ability to do so is, as we have seen, inherent in the intelligence which is His glory. The error of Lucifer and the truth of Jesus could not be reconciled even in heaven. Error had to be cast out. (*Brigham Young University Bulletin,* May 30, 1957.)

## Why Men Are Accountable

As indicated above, man is a free agent with the right to choose. Because he enjoys this right, aided by the "light of Christ," he is responsible for his acts. The additional truth is given in Section 93 that since man is intelligence, this divine essence, "light and truth," makes man responsible.

All truth is independent in that sphere in which God has placed it, to act for itself, as all intelligence also; otherwise there is no existence.

Behold, here is the agency of man, and here is the condemnation of man; because that which was from the beginning is plainly manifest unto them, and they receive not the light.

And every man whose spirit receiveth not the light is under condemnation. (D&C 93:30-32.)

Because of the power in truth, man should be able to recognize it; for part of his being is "light and truth."

In the beginning every spirit was innocent, but in the war in heaven Lucifer rebelled, taking many with him. These spirits lost their innocence, but those who kept their first estate come to earth in mortal bodies and are innocent. (*Ibid.*, 93:38.) This innocence continues until the age of eight is reached and then each person becomes accountable for his sins. (*Ibid.*, 68:25-27.)

## The Voice of the Good Shepherd

Satan takes light and truth from men as they disobey the commandments. Some of man's disobedience to the commandments is due to the tradition in which he was reared. (*Ibid.*, 93:39.)

When it comes to accepting the truths of the Gospel, men may not understand them because they have lost the ability to comprehend due to the traditions of their fathers and of individual sin which has darkened their susceptibility to truth. (*Ibid.*, 76:75; James E. Talmage, *The Vitality of Mormonism*, pp. 279-282.) The voice of the Good Shepherd becomes too dim to be understood.

Latter-day Saints may know the voice of the master as they observe the commandments. (John 10:1-14; D&C 50:17-22.) President Brigham Young asks and then answers the question "How are we to know the voice of the Good Shepherd from the voice of a stranger?" He proceeds to say that when the Spirit of God reveals and testifies, it cannot be mistaken.

When an individual, filled with the Spirit of God, declares the truth of heaven, the sheep hear that, the Spirit of the Lord pierces their inmost souls and sinks deep into their hearts; by the testimony of the Holy Ghost light springs up within them, and they see and understand for themselves . . . I have said to the Latter-day Saints, many and many a time, and I would say to them now, live your religion, that the Spirit of God may be within you like a well of water springing up to everlasting life . . . Be prepared that you may know the voice when it comes through the servants of God, then you can declare for yourselves. "This is the word of the Lord." My caution and counsel to the Latter-day Saints, and to all the inhabitants of the earth is—"Live so that you will know truth from error." (*Journal of Discourses* 16:74-75.)

## Children—Light and Truth

The Lord has commanded Latter-day Saints to rear their children in light and truth. (D&C 93:40, 49.) There is none in the Church who is beyond this commandment. Even members of the First Presidency in 1833 were told they had not kept this commandment. This was said of President Frederick G. Williams and Sidney Rigdon, counselors to President Joseph Smith. Unless they were obedient in setting their houses in order Satan would continue to have power over them. (*Ibid.*, 93:41-44.) Even the Prophet lacked in this matter also. An important truth was also taught regarding children.

Your family must needs repent and forsake some things, and give more earnest heed unto your sayings, or be removed out of their place. (*Ibid.*, 93:48.)

In other words, responsibility is not only the parent's but also the child's. But the major obligation is with the parents who are to teach their children principles of righteousness. (*Ibid.*, 68:25-31.) The home evening program in use throughout the Church is one of the best means by which this commandment can be lived by parents and children. No other people have the opportunity to rear their children in light and truth as do the Latter-day Saints. It is also true that no other people are under the same responsibility as they are. When one considers the truth that the children who come into a Latter-day Saint family are known to have come from our Father and that what we do or do not do for them here, determines, in a large measure, their eternal future, the weight of this responsibility is better appreciated.

Latter-day Saint families are intended to be eternal. The association of parents and children throughout the eternities is the desired goal of every faithful member of the Church. Eternal marriage is the qualifying ordinance, together with keeping the commandments and obligations received in the House of the Lord. The words of President Joseph F. Smith are especially pertinent to these thoughts:

> We are living for eternity and not merely for the moment. Death does not part us from one another, if we have entered into sacred relationships with each other by virtue of the authority that God has revealed to the children of men. Our relationships are formed for eternity. We are immortal beings, and we are looking forward to the growth that is to be attained in an exalted life after we have proved ourselves faithful and true to the covenants that we have entered into here, and then we shall receive a fulness of joy. (*Gospel Doctrine,* 6th edition, pp. 277-278.)

## Chapter 22

# TWO TEMPLES AND PERSECUTION

## (Sections 94, 95, and 96)

### Background

Six months after the Church was organized in 1830 a revelation appointed Oliver Cowdery to preach the gospel to the Lamanites. (D&C 28:8.) Subsequently, others were appointed to accompany him, including Elder Parley P. Pratt, a recent convert to the Church from the Campbellites, whose headquarters were in Ohio. (*Ibid.*, 30:5-6.) Although the mission to the Lamanites did not bring many of them into the Church, the mission was highly successful among the people in the Ohio Valley. Especially in and around Kirtland was the harvest bounteous. The opening of this area brought increased strength to the fast-growing kingdom of God. Only a few months later, the Lord commanded the members of the Church in other places to assemble to Ohio. (*Ibid.*, 37:3.) Less than a month later, the Prophet Joseph Smith was told by revelation that he should go to Ohio where further instruction would be received to guide the Church. (*Ibid.*, 38:32, 42.) In this same revelation the land of Ohio was designated as a "land of promise, a land flowing with milk and honey . . . a land of your inheritance." (*Ibid.*, verses 18-20.)

Upon the Prophet's arrival in Ohio in February, 1831, a movement was instituted to make of Kirtland the headquarters of the Church. By commandment in July of that year the Prophet arrived in Jackson County, Missouri, where that area was appointed the place of the city of Zion, or New Jerusalem, long prophesied as the city of glory where the Lord would rule the nations of the earth during the Millennium. (*Ibid.*, 57; 45:66-75.) Returning to Kirtland the Prophet continued to receive revelation for the building up of the Lord's kingdom.

### Build a Stake

On May 6, 1833, the Lord commanded that preparations be made for laying the foundation of "a city of the stake of Zion" in the land of Kirtland. (*Ibid.*, 94:1.) Once before in the revelations we find reference to a stake. In order that all might know their responsibility to their children the Lord said in 1831, that parents "in any of her stakes" were to teach their children correct principles and to see that they were baptized. (*Ibid.*, 68:25-31.) At that time a stake of the Church had not been organized. The first, as commanded was organized in Kirtland, Ohio.

The term "stake of Zion" indicates that these places are a part of the Zion which consists of North and South America, according to the Prophet Joseph Smith. (*Teachings of the Prophet Joseph Smith*, p. 362.) Stakes are territorial divisions within the Church, presided over by a president and his two counselors; while wards are divisions within the stake, with a bishopric consisting of the bishop and two counselors. Stakes may be, and have been, organized outside the confines of North and South America since they are divisions of the Church. President Brigham Young said that eventually Zion will be everywhere on the earth. (*Journal of Discourses* 9:138.) The city of New Jerusalem is the center place of Zion. Elder Joseph Fielding Smith informs us that,

> The term "Stake of Zion" . . . is a comparison to the stakes which bind a tent. Isaiah says: "Look upon Zion, the city of our solemnities: thine eyes shall see Jerusalem a quiet habitation, a tabernacle that shall not be taken down; not one of the stakes thereof shall ever be removed, neither shall any of the cords thereof be broken." (Ch. 33:20.) Again: "Enlarge the place of thy tent and let them stretch forth the curtains of thine in-

habitations: spare not, lengthen thy cords, and strengthen thy stakes." (Ch. 54:2.)

Zion is the tent, the settlements surrounding her, are the cords and stakes. (*Essentials in Church History,* pp. 146-147.)

A further command was given to organize a stake in Kirtland in January 1832, while the Prophet was in Jackson County, as follows:

For I have consecrated the land of Shinehah (Kirtland) in mine own due time for the benefit of the saints of the Most High, and for a stake of Zion.

For Zion must increase in beauty, and in holiness; her borders must be enlarged; her stakes must be strengthened; yea, verily I say unto you, Zion must arise and put on her beautiful garments. (D&C 82:13-14.)

A committee was appointed on March 23, 1833, to purchase lands in Kirtland in order that the stake of Zion must be established. This committee reported that several farms were available for purchase. Contributions were made by members of the Church to purchase property, one of whom was Sister Vienna Jaques who was commanded to consecrate her means for this purpose. (*Ibid.*, 90:28-29.) On September 4, 1833, the Prophet addressed a letter to this good sister in Jackson County, Missouri, in which he said that the Spirit prompted him to always remember her for what she had done for the kingdom. (*DHC* 1:407-409.) In order to remove the mortgage from one farm, the Lord commanded Brother John Johnson to pay off this mortgage. (D&C 96:6-9.) By these arrangements, the Church obtained property upon which the Kirtland Temple was eventually built.

## Section 94

By revelation the Church was instructed to build two houses in Kirtland. One of these was for the First Presidency that they might have a place in which to perform their work and obtain revelations. (*Ibid.*, 94:3.) The size of the building and a general pattern was supplied. The second building was for the printing and translation of the scriptures and for other purposes. Specific instructions were also given concerning this house. (*Ibid.*, verses 10-12.) Other brethren were to receive an inheritance on the property also. (*Ibid.*, Verses 13-17.)

### Buildings and Revelation

Many times as in Section 94, the Lord instructs his Prophet concerning matters which some might not consider proper subject matter for a revelation. Why should the Lord reveal that a printing plant, or a house for the First Presidency, or some other purely temporal project be commanded?

These questions with others of a similar nature are important because the answer is based upon a fundamental principle upon which the Lord has spoken. The Lord said that at no time has he given a commandment which was solely temporal, but all of his commandments are spiritual. (*Ibid.*, 29:34-35.) This principle makes of the gospel a practical, every-day religion. Because Latter-day Saints know that they are to contribute their time, means and skills to the building of Zion on the earth, this principle means very much in their lives. Elder Albert E. Bowen, member of the Quorum of the Twelve (1937-1953), said:

> We have a very practical religion. It pertains to our lives now. And the reward of observance of the law is not altogether postponed to a future on the other side of the grave. Building up the kingdom involves some very practical things. It is not altogether concerned with the non-material lying out in the ethereal realm. The building of meetinghouses, places of worship, schools, temples, for example, clearly is for spiritual purposes. But they involve a large element of the material. They are essential to the building up of the Kingdom of God. And where would you classify the beautifying of your home; the

making of refined surroundings? It is necessary to provide the things that sustain life, to master the arts and crafts and trades that meet the needs of progress and improvement. I do not think I can find the line that divides the spiritual from the temporal. (*Conference Report,* April 1951, p. 124.)

Elder John A. Widtsoe said:

The all-important thing in life, after all, is to find a place in the universal scheme of things, for all the acts of our lives. There is a spiritual meaning of all human acts and earthly events. . . . It is the business of man to find the spiritual meaning of earthly things. (*Ibid.,* April 1922, pp. 96-97.)

This principle answers the questions, "why work on a welfare project? a work meeting project in Relief Society? a chapel under construction, etc.? Also, why contribute money in tithing, fast offerings, and other donations?"

### Introduction—Section 95

With the commandment before the brethren that two houses were to be built, the Lord informs them in Section 95, given one month later, that they were under condemnation because they had failed to observe another commandment given December 27, 1832, six months before. Section 94 said that they were not to begin construction until commanded; so the construction of these two houses was postponed. (D&C 94:16.) The earlier commandment was to build a House of the Lord, to:

Organize yourselves; prepare every needful thing; and establish a house, even a house of prayer, a house of fasting, a house of faith, a house of learning, a house of glory, a house of order, a house of God;

That your incomings may be in the name of the Lord; that your outgoings may be in the name of the Lord; that all your salutations may be in the name of the Lord; with uplifted hands unto the Most High. (*Ibid.,* 88:119-120.)

This is the commandment to build the Kirtland Temple; the neglect of which brought forth the following:

> Verily, thus saith the Lord unto you whom I love, and whom I love I also chasten that their sins may be forgiven, for with the chastisement I prepare a way for their deliverance in all things out of temptation, and I have loved you—
>
> Wherefore, ye must needs be chastened and stand rebuked before my face;
>
> For ye have sinned against me a very grievous sin, in that ye have not considered the great commandment in all things, that I have given unto you concerning the building of mine house; (*Ibid.,* 96:1-3.)

## Chastisement

People sometimes wonder wherein chastisement is beneficial. The ideas mentioned above provide an answer. Through chastening repentance often comes, resulting in forgiveness of sins. Thus Latter-day Saints find deliverance even from temptation; for, humility born of chastisement strengthens one against temptation.

Chastisement may come in many forms. Suffering is one of these. The partial answer to the question, "why suffering?" is found in these ideas: Pain brings humility in the recognition that men are dependent upon God. It also teaches obedience. Our awareness of God's suffering for us is brought closer to us through our own suffering. As Elder Mark E. Petersen said:

> Suffering sometimes comes in the form of loving chastisement. "As many as I love, I rebuke and chasten." (Rev. 3:19.) The Lord said at one time "Whom the Lord loveth he chasteneth." (Heb. 12:6.) At another time the writer of the Proverbs said under the inspiration of the Lord, "My son, despise not the chastening of the Lord; neither be weary of his correction; for whom the Lord loveth he correcteth; even as a father the son in whom he delighteth." (Prov. 3:11.) (*Your Faith and You,* p. 257.)

Through chastisement we learn our lessons sometimes better than in any other way. This provides an opportunity to know wherein we erred and also the means of making necessary corrections.

### A Grievous Sin

In failing to begin the building of the temple commanded for Kirtland, the brethren were chastized. This was a grievous sin. The members of the Church were in poverty. Despite this the commandment had been given, and it was expected that they comply with it. The implications of this fact are very important for each member of the Church. Throughout Nephi's life he saw barriers and obstacles surmounted as he learned this truth:

> . . . I will go and do the things which the Lord hath commanded for I know that the Lord giveth no commandments unto the children of men, save he shall prepare a way for them that they may accomplish the thing which he commandeth them. (1 Nephi 3:7.)

Poverty is not a reason for not observing the commandments. All too often some members of the Church feel that they cannot pay a full tithing because they have other financial obligations which should be paid first. If there is a time when full obedience to this law, as well as others, should be made, it is when one needs the Lord's blessings to bring oneself out of financial bondage. On these occasions, it would seem that the member who rejects the tithing principle feels that he doesn't need the Lord's help to find deliverance. It is the faithful, dedicated Latter-day Saint who, through his obedience, despite the circumstance, finds the rich blessings.

### Purpose of the Temple

Immediately the brethren met to begin the preparations for the temple as commanded. The committee, consisting of Hyrum Smith, Reynolds Cahoon, and Jared Carter, issued a plea for support in building this edifice.

The revelation stated that the purpose of this building was that the Lord's disciples might go forth to prune the vineyard for the last time. In the circular sent out by the committee, it was said that this house would be the place where the Elders might call a solemn assembly, treasure up words of wisdom, that they might go to the Gentiles for the last time. (*DHC* 1:349.)

Before the Saints had established Kirtland as a gathering place, the Lord promised that when his servants were endowed there would be a gathering to the bosom of the Church. (D&C 38:38.) This endowment would be such that they would be taught from on high to accomplish this purpose. (*Ibid.*, 43:16.) Although missionary work had been performed, yet the great missionary program would be inaugurated when the temple would be built in which his servants would be endowed. But only those who walked in the light would be chosen in that day. (*Ibid.*, 95:5-9.)

### Power to Build

The brethren were motivated by the promise that the commandment given to build a temple could be accomplished provided they kept the commandments. (*Ibid.*, verses 11-12.)

Specific directions were given as to the interior size—fifty-five feet wide, sixty-five feet long—and the purpose of each floor of the building (a place of sacrament and preaching services, and a school for the apostles). (*Ibid.*, verses 13-17.)

### Two Months' History

Between June and August 1833, the spirit of persecution increased against the Saints in Jackson County. Also, work commenced immediately on the Kirtland Temple. On July 23rd the Prophet records that the cornerstones of the temple were laid after the order of the priesthood. (*DHC* 1:400.) Although the "order of the Priesthood" in laying the cornerstones of a temple were not at that time recorded by the Prophet, he gave specific directions about the service performed at the Nauvoo Temple, as follows:

> If the strict order of the Priesthood were carried out in the building of Temples, the first stone would be laid at the south-east corner, by the First Presidency of the Church. The south-west corner should be laid next, the third, or north-west corner next; and the fourth, or north-east corner last. The First Presidency should lay the south-east stone and dictate who are the proper persons to lay the other cornerstones.
>
> If a Temple is built at a distance, and the First Presidency are not present, then the Quorum of the Twelve Apostles are the persons to dictate the order for that Temple; and in the absence of the Twelve Apostles, then the Presidency of the Stake will lay the south-east cornerstone; the Melchizedek Priesthood laying the cornerstones on the east side of the Temple, and the Lesser Priesthood those on the west side. (*DHC* 4:331.)

Later, this edifice was completed and the keys of the priesthood restored that the servants of the Lord might go forth with power to teach the nations. (D&C 110.)

It will be remembered that in July 1831, the site of the New Jerusalem was revealed and that in August the temple site was dedicated in Independence, Jackson County, Missouri. (D&C 57; *DHC* 1:199.) This was the beginning of an event that had been predicted by the ancients. (Ether 13:4-6.)

Toward the end of June 1833, the First Presidency sent instructions to the brethren in Zion on the future plans for the building of the city and also the temple. Actually this temple will consist of 24 compartments, the details of which are found in the history of the Church. (*DHC* 1:359-362.)

July 1833, was a fateful month in the lives of the members of the Church in Jackson County. A manifesto of the mobocrats in that county charged the Saints with certain evils that they believed were sufficient to deny them residence in the county. A summary of these reasons are provided by President Joseph Fielding Smith, as follows:

Some of the "evils" of the "Mormons" were stated to be as follows: The declaration that miracles have been performed and supernatural cures achieved among the sick; a belief in heavenly manifestations and that they have held converse with God and his angels; possession and exercise of the gifts of divination and unknown tongues; and "fixed with the prospect of obtaining inheritance without money and without price." Yet they were well aware that the "Mormons" had never made the attempt to obtain lands except by purchase, as the Lord had commanded them. Nevertheless all these "crimes" must be punished; for against such evils "self preservation, good society and public morals," made demands that the "Mormons" should be expelled. The following articles were drawn up and unanimously approved, to be submitted to the elders of the Church.

(1) "That no Mormon shall in future move and settle in this county.

(2) "That those now here, who shall give a definite pledge of their intention within reasonable time to remove out of the county, shall be allowed to remain unmolested until they have sufficient time to sell their property, and close their business, without any material sacrifice.

(3) "That the editor of the *Star* be required forthwith to close his office and discontinue the business of printing in this county; and as to all other stores and shops belonging to the sect, their owners must in every case strictly comply with the terms of the second article of this declaration; and upon failure, prompt and efficient measures will be taken to close the same.

(4) "That the Mormon leaders here are required to use their influence in preventing any further emigration of their distant brethren to this county, and to counsel and advise their brethren here to comply with the above requisitions.

(5) "That those who fail to comply with these requisitions be referred to those of their brethren who have the gifts of divination, and of unknown tongues, to inform them of the lot that awaits them." (*Essentials of Church History,* pp. 158-159; also, *DHC* 1:374-376.)

With these demands before them the Saints were denied time to communicate with their Prophet. The Lord had commanded them to come to the land of their inheritance where the New Jerusalem would be built, a fact seized upon by the Missourians as having their lands taken from them. Finally, they were given only fifteen minutes to comply. The mob then determined that the Church's printing plant be destroyed where the *Evening and Morning Star* was published. Missouri was a slave state and the mob had interpreted an editorial in the *Star* as favoring the bringing of free negroes and free mulattoes into the state. Brother William W. Phelps, the Church printer, lost his personal belongings and the printing equipment was also destroyed. Bishop Edward Partridge and Brother Charles Allen were taken to the public square and tarred because they would not renounce their belief in the Church.

On the same day the cornerstone of the Kirtland Temple was laid, the mob threatened the members of the Church in Jackson County with beatings and the destruction of their homes. Several of the leaders of the Church —John Corrill, John Whitmer, William W. Phelps, Algernon S. Gilbert, Edward Partridge and Isaac Morley, offered themselves to beaten to death, if necessary, that the other members of the Church might not be harmed. The mobbers demanded, however, that every member of the Church leave the county or be beaten to death. The leaders then agreed to the demands of the Missouri mob to begin moving by January, with the exodus to be completed by April 1834.

Jackson County, Missouri, was the promised land for the saints. It was there that the rich blessings of the earth were to be found. The laying of the foundation of the city of Zion, the New Jerusalem, was their privilege, but the Lord had said that their permanence in that land was not intended at that time. Two years earlier, the Lord said that the saints could not understand the glory which would follow after much tribulation, but the hour was not yet. (D&C 58:1-5.)

## Chapter 23

# HOW TO ACT AMID PERSECUTION

### (Sections 97; 98:23-48)

In the month of July the persecution of the Saints in Jackson County, Missouri commenced. At the beginning of the following month, the Prophet Joseph Smith received a revelation that concerned primarily the saints in Missouri. (D&C 97.) He did not know what had happened to the saints in Jackson County, although he knew that trouble was possible. Many of the members were endeavoring to learn the truth, and upon them the Lord would be merciful at the judgment. (D&C 97:1-2.)

Special commendation was given to Elder Parley P. Pratt who was conducting the School of Elders in Missouri. (*Ibid.*, verses 3-5.) He labored diligently to succeed in this calling. He walked barefoot about six miles to attend this school held in the outdoors. (*Autobiography of Parley P. Pratt*, pp. 93-94.)

Not all of the saints were acceptable to the Lord, for he said:

> The axe is laid at the root of the trees; and every tree that bringeth not forth good fruit shall be hewn down and cast into the fire. I, the Lord, have spoken it.
>
> Verily I say unto you, all among them who know their hearts are honest, and are broken, and their spirits contrite, and are willing to observe their covenants by sacrifice—yea, every sacrifice which I, the Lord, shall command—they are accepted of me. (D&C 97:7-8.)

As a preliminary to some strong admonitions concerning the need for greater diligence upon the part of some members of the Church, the Lord probably had reference to the fact that already the deadwood in the Church was hewn down and cast into the fire.

## Sacrifice

There are several meanings of the word sacrifice but it seems that the one most pertinent to the language of Section 97 is: the giving up of some cherished or desired object. The sacrifice required of the saint is the giving up of everything, if necessary, even life itself. (*Ibid.*, 98:13-15; 101:35-38.) To be accepted of the Lord means that the Lord approves of one's actions, but to remain in this condition, requires continued faithfulness to commandments.

President Brigham Young points out in the following how trivial some of the sacrifices we make on this earth compared with the greatness of the blessings to be received:

> Now, you Elders who understand the principles of the kingdom of God, what would you not give, do, or sacrifice, to assist in building up His kingdom upon the earth? Says one, "I would do anything in my power." Says another, "I would sacrifice all my property." Wonderful indeed! Do you not know that the possession of your property is like a shadow, or the dew of the morning before the noonday sun, that you cannot have any assurance of its control for a single moment! It is the unseen hand of Providence that controls it. In short, what would you not sacrifice? The Saints sacrifice everything; but, strictly speaking, there is no sacrifice about it. If you give a penny for a million of gold! a handful of earth for a planet! a temporary worn out tenement for one glorified, that will exist, abide, and continue to increase throughout a never ending eternity, what a sacrifice to be sure! (*Journal of Discourses* 1:114.)

The reward of sacrifice, as required, will bring forth precious fruit. (D&C 97:9.) "Precious fruit" may refer to the fruit of the tree of life mentioned in Lehi's dream—"the greatest of all the gifts of God." (1 Nephi 15:36; D&C 14:7.)

## Jackson County Temple

Instructions had been given that a temple should be built in Jackson County, Missouri, and the site had been dedicated August 3, 1831, by the Prophet Joseph Smith. (D&C 57:3.) Section 97 contains a command to build this temple, and this was the sacrifice required of the people. Above all, its purpose was for the salvation of the members of the Church, a place of thanksgiving, a place of instruction where the Church might be perfected in all things pertaining to the kingdom of God. This perfection would come by reason of understanding the principles and doctrines of the gospel through the keys which had already been conferred. (*Ibid.*, 97:10-14.) With the fulfillment of this commandment, and the sanctity of that edifice being preserved, the promise of the Lord's presence was given. In that temple the pure in heart would see God. The seeing of God should not be considered figurative. In all dispensations the pure in heart have known him. Elder Orson Pratt in a commentary on Section 97 said:

> No natural man hath seen God at any time. A natural man could not behold the face of the Lord in his glory, for he could not endure it; but when a mortal man or woman here on the earth has put away the natural or carnal mind; when he or she has put away all sin and iniquity, and has complied with the laws and commandments of God, then, like Jacob of old, he or she may see God face to face, and, like Moses, talk with the Lord as one man talks with another. It is written here in this book which you and I have received as a part and portion of our rule of faith and practice, "The Doctrine and Covenants," as follows: [quoted Section 93:1-3.] Again it is written in another revelation: [quoted 97:15-17.] (*Journal of Discourses* 14:272-273.)

## If Zion Do These Things

If the saints would faithfully discharge their responsibilities as given in Section 97, great blessings would come to the Church in Zion. She would become very great and very glorious in her prosperity. Zion would be honored by the nations, never to be moved out of her place, for it was to be the abode of God. The temple was to allow the faithful to be endowed with powers. As pointed out in an authoritative place, temples bring assistance against the powers of the Adversary.

> The history of Temples teaches us that the people of God have been strong, or weak, in proportion to the faithfulness with which they have attended to their sanctuaries. The history of the Temple of Jerusalem is, as Dr. Joseph Angus, in his *Bible Handbook,* notes, "an index to the history of the Jews. When it fell, they were scattered; as it rose from its ruins, they gathered round it again; and history dates the captivity, with equal accuracy, from the destruction of the Temple, or from the first capture of Jerusalem." Speaking of the Temples in his dispensation, someone has declared that the completion of the Nauvoo Temple was the salvation of the Church from annihilation, although the Saints were forced to flee into the desert. Since the completion of the Salt Lake Temple, the adversary has had less power to injure the Church than he had before. If we remember that the Temples are the palaces of God, where His Presence is manifested, we can understand why, when the adversary was marshalling his forces against the Church, our Lord urged the Saints to build the Temple speedily. We can also understand why the evil one planned to have them scattered before they could rear that sacred edifice. (*Doctrine and Covenants Commentary,* p. 612.)

All of this was dependent upon how well Zion—the pure in heart—kept the commandments.

> And, now, behold, if Zion do these things she shall prosper . . .
>
> Therefore, verily, thus saith the Lord, let Zion rejoice, for this is Zion—THE PURE IN HEART . . . (D&C 97:18, 21.)

The saints were already being persecuted in Jackson County, and the order to move or to be killed had been given by the mob. Despite this situation, fully known to the Lord, he promised that if they would do as commanded, Zion could be redeemed. The challenge to be pure in heart was complied with by many, but apparently not in sufficient strength to warrant the blessings of

Zion's redemption at that time. How many must keep the commandments in order to forestall the judgments predicted? In reference to the judgments to be poured out upon the world in the last days, President Brigham Young said if the judgments of God come upon the Latter-day Saints it will be because the majority have turned from the Lord. If six-tenths or three-fourths will keep the commandments the judgments will not come upon them. (*Journal of Discourses* 10:335-336.)

Zion as the "pure in heart" is a condition rather than a place. Ordinarily, we think of Zion as a place, such as North and South America, the center place in Jackson County, or the western part of the United States, but as true as these geographical places are Zion, the most important factor is the condition. Appropriate to the meaning of Zion and its application to what has already been written, President Young said:

> We can make Zion, or we can make Babylon, just as we please. We can make just what we please of this place. The people can make Zion: they can make a heaven within themselves. When people gather here, they should come with a determination to make Zion within themselves, with the resolution that "I will carry myself full of the Spirit of Zion wherever I go; and this is the way in which I will control evil spirits; for I mean that my spirit shall have control over evil," and do you not see that such a course will make Zion? (*Ibid.,* 5:4.)

## Covenanted Zion

The saints in Jackson County in 1833, as also the saints throughout the world today, were under covenant to build Zion, but this could be done only by having the spirit of Zion in their hearts. (D&C 6:6.) To accomplish this goal one must always be on guard against the Adversary of righteousness. President Stephen L Richards categorized the present world as "self-sufficient, egotistical, materialistic, and skeptical," whereas, "the philosophy of Zion is humility, not servility, but a willing recognition of the sovereignty of God and dependence on his providence." Zion is being attacked from all sides today, he continued. The attack is on our concept of personal moral purity, and in the home it is the curtailment of the size of the family. A serious aspect of our times is that of indifference and neglect among the membership. Zion, however, will survive, notwithstanding some will succumb to these attacks of Satan. Those, however, who feel themselves self-sufficient do not enjoy the one great blessing for aid and comfort—the Spirit of God. (*Conference Report*, October 1951, pp. 110-117; quoted in Roy W. Doxey, *The Latter-day Prophets and the Doctrine and Covenants*, 3:333-335.)

## Saints Did Not Heed

Elder Parley P. Pratt recorded in his *Autobiography* that the revelation numbered Section 97 was not complied with by the Church leaders in Jackson County, although there were many faithful there. Because Zion did not then consist of sufficient to bring to pass the fulfillment of Zion's destiny, "the threatened judgment was poured out to the uttermost, as the history of the five following years will show." (p. 96.) Within that period the saints were expelled from the State of Missouri.

## Judgments of the Last Days

These following verses concerning the judgments to come upon the wicked apply to the time before the second coming of Christ (*Conference Report*, October 1917, pp. 44-45; *Progress of Man*, p. 478):

> For behold, and lo, vengeance cometh speedily upon the ungodly as the whirlwind; and who shall escape it?
>
> The Lord's scourge shall pass over by night and by day, and the report thereof shall vex all people; yea, it shall not be stayed until the Lord come;

For the indignation of the Lord is kindled against their abominations and all their wicked works. (D&C 97:22-24.)

In the "Lord's Preface" to the Doctrine and Covenants, given in 1831, it is said that the time will come when peace shall be taken from the earth. (*Ibid.*, 1:35.) The American Civil War was the beginning war of modern times. (*Ibid.*, 87:1.) As said in the *Doctrine and Covenants Commentary*:

The American Civil War was only the beginning of a series of conflicts, each leading up to the world-war of 1914. This is all the more remarkable, because since the middle of the 19th century, the peace movement in the world assumed so definite proportions as to warrant the hope that there would be no war in the 20th century. (p. 536.)

During the Civil War the area of Jackson County was invaded and the land laid to waste. (B. H. Roberts, *New Witnesses for God*, Vol. 1, pp. 298-299.) Because of wickedness the people of the earth are to feel the wrath and indignation of the Lord. These judgments—the "Lord's scourge"—will continue until the second coming of Christ.

## Zion Shall Escape If . . .

In a context of promised destruction upon Jackson County in particular, and the world in general, because of wickedness, the revelation then turns to the members of the Church, who are known as "Zion."

Nevertheless, Zion shall escape if she observes to do all things whatsoever I have commanded her.

But if she observe not to do whatsoever I have commanded her, I will visit her according to all her works, with sore affliction, with pestilence, with plague, with sword, with vengeance, with devouring fire. (D&C 97:25-26.)

The only way of safety is through keeping the commandments. In the words of Elder Melvin J. Ballard of the Council of the Twelve:

Why should we hope to escape, who have been baptized into this Church, yet ignore the commandments of the Lord? For there are among us those who do not keep the Word of Wisdom, some of us do not pay our tithing; we do not sanctify ourselves by adding unto our faith, virtue; to virtue, knowledge, temperance, and patience, and godliness, and brotherly kindness. Why should we claim exemption—we who will testify that we believe God has spoken—why should we escape if we do not keep the commandments of the Lord? (*Conference Report,* June 1919, pp. 88-89.)

On the other hand, if Zion keeps the commandments, the Lord has promised to multiply blessings upon her and upon her generations forever. (D&C 97:27-28.)

## Background Section 98

Only a few days after Section 97 was received and seventeen days after the Missouri mob began their work of destruction among the saints, the Lord revealed further information regarding the manner in which they should conduct themselves.

The saints are enjoined to be patient in tribulation. Their prayers had been heard and their fulfillment would be realized. We also learn of the important principle that afflictions work to one's good and for the glory of God. (*Ibid.*, 98:1-3.)

Three laws are explained in this revelation that the saints might know what the Lord commanded of the ancients and what should be expected of us today.

## The Law of Retaliation

The first of these laws is the law of retaliation discussed in verses 23 through 32. It requires that families in the Church bear patiently the abuse and smiting of others the first, second, and third time, but if the offense is committed the fourth time, then a warning should be given and, if necessary, the offender should be rewarded according to his works. However, if one patiently endures after the fourth time, his reward will be even greater. The doctrine of patience under persecution is the teaching of the Sermon on the Mount. (Matt. 5:21-22, 43-44.) An example of not striking back at an enemy is that of the converted Lamanites who were attacked by the Lamanites. They would not retaliate though many of them were killed. Their example was the means of bringing many to repentance. (Alma 24:17-25; 27:3.)

### The Law of War

The next law is the law of war. First, we should understand that anciently the Lord told his people when they could go to war. Then they would be justified. War in itself was not the object of life, and if a nation would come against his people they should sue for peace. If, after this, the enemy did not accept this offer of peace the second or third time the Lord would fight their battles. This promise extended to their children's children to the third and fourth generations. (D&C 98:33-38.) Ancient Israel was not to go to war until their peace offer was refused. (Deut. 20:10 c.f. Deut. 2:26-29.)

The Book of Mormon provides us with a concept of war that is consistent with the counsel given in Section 98. Moroni, who lived in the first century before Christ, is described as a man of perfect understanding, a true believer in liberty, and one who did not delight in bloodshed. The Nephites at that time followed this instruction:

> Now the Nephites were taught to defend themselves against their enemies, even to the shedding of blood if it were necessary; yea, and they were also taught never to give an offense, yea, and never to raise the sword except it were against an enemy, except it were to preserve their lives.
>
> And this was their faith, that by so doing God would prosper them in the land, or in other words, if they were faithful in keeping the commandments of God that he would prosper them in

the land; yea, warn them to flee, or to prepare for war, according to their danger;

And also, that God would make it known unto them whither they should go to defend themselves against their enemies, and by so doing, the Lord would deliver them; and this was the faith of Moroni, and his heart did glory in it; not in the shedding of blood but in doing good, in preserving his people, yea, in keeping the commandments of God, yea, and resisting iniquity. (Alma 48:14-16.)

The Nephites looked to their prophets for help in defeating their enemies once they were called upon to defend their families, homes, country, and religion. On one occasion this help came from the Lord through the Prophet Alma's giving vital information that brought victory over the Lamanites. (Alma 16:1-8.)

The Nephites believed that notwithstanding the Lord would fight their battles if they kept his commandments, it was necessary that they do everything possible to bring about victory in war. In charging Pahoran the Governor of the land with withholding men and supplies with which to fight the Lamanites, Moroni wrote him as follows:

Or do you suppose that the Lord will still deliver us, while we sit upon our thrones and do not make use of the means which the Lord has provided for us? (Alma 60:21.)

An official statement adopted in 1831 gives the position of the Church regarding this principle:

We believe that all men are bound to sustain and uphold the respective governments in which they reside, while protected in their inherent and inalienable rights by the laws of such governments; and that sedition and rebellion are unbecoming every citizen thus protected, and should be punished accordingly; and that all governments have a right to enact such laws as in their own judgments are best calculated to secure the public interest; at the same time, however, holding sacred the freedom of conscience. (D&C 134:5.)

## The Law of Forgiveness

In closing Section 98 the law of forgiveness is given. This law contains the elements of the other two laws in this revelation. Repeated transgressions by one people or nation against another should be forgiven. This practice of forgiveness should be continued as long as they repent; however, if they do not repent then the nation should bear it patiently, even unto the third time. If it happens the fourth time, they should not be forgiven and these testimonies should be brought before the Lord. Repentance should include four-fold restitution. If, however, repentance is not done then their children unto the third and fourth generation should receive the Lord's vengeance. If the children or their children should repent, no judgment would fall upon them. (D&C 98:39-48.)

As pointed out above, a nation should not engage in an offensive war, but it has the right to defend itself against those who come against her. President Charles W. Penrose counseled the Latter-day Saints against the desire to shed blood or to destroy. (*Conference Report*, April 1917, pp. 20-22; quoted in *The Latter-day Prophets and the Doctrine and Covenants*, 3:362-364.) Effort should be made to avert war. But if a country is drawn into a war after having tried to keep out of the conflict, every effort should be made to win the victory, as indicated in this chapter.

## Chapter 24

# THE CONSTITUTION OF THE UNITED STATES

### (Sections 98:1-22; 101:76-80)

Not long before receiving Section 98, the saints in Missouri had undergone persecution. Threats were made against their lives and some property had been destroyed. In that revelation, laws concerning war and forgiveness were given in order that the saints might understand the manner in which they should conduct themselves in a period of persecution.

The Prophet at this time did not know of the serious events that had happened in Jackson County although he did know that trouble was brewing. The Lord referred to the saints' afflictions and informed them that they "shall work together for your good, and to my name's glory." (D&C 98:3.)

In view of the difficulties in Jackson County, it is a testimony to the inspiration of this revelation, that it should contain information relative to the fundamental law of the land whose purpose is to give certain rights and privileges to those who live in America.

### America—a Choice Land

Latter-day Saints have a deep appreciation of the Lord's words concerning the land of America. The Book of Mormon tells of the city of Zion to be built upon the American continent in the last days. (Ether 12:4-6.) In 1831, it was revealed that this city would be built in Jackson County, Missouri. (D&C 57:1-3.) Later the Prophet Joseph Smith said that all of North and South America was the land of Zion in which the gathering would be in this dispensation. (*DHC* 6:318-319.)

Elder Ezra Taft Benson of the Council of the Twelve, before a general conference of the Church, specified the manner in which the Lord raised up "the first free people in modern times":

First: Prophecy is abundant that God deliberately kept the American continent hidden until after the Holy Roman Empire had been broken up and the various nations had established themselves as independent kingdoms. Keeping America hidden until after this time was no accident. (2 Nephi 1:6, 8.)

Second: At the proper time, God inspired Columbus to overcome almost insurmountable odds to discover America and bring this rich new land to the attention of the gentiles in Europe. (1 Nephi 13:12; Dr. Samuel Eliot Morison, *Admiral of the Ocean Sea,* pp. 46-47.)

Third: God revealed to his ancient American prophets that shortly after the discovery of America there would be peoples in Europe who would desire to escape the persecution and tyranny of the Old World and flee to America. (1 Nephi 13:13-16.)

Fourth: God told his prophets that the kingdoms in Europe would try to exercise dominion over the people who had fled to America, but that in the wars of independence the American settlers would win. (This is a remarkable prophecy in that 2300 years before the Revolutionary War was fought, God through his prophets predicted who would win it.) (*Ibid.,* 13:16-19.)

Fifth: The prophets were told that in the latter days when the gentiles came to America they would establish it as a land of liberty on which there would be no kings. The Lord declared that he would protect the land and whosoever would try to establish kings either from within or without would perish. (2 Nephi 10:8-14.)

Sixth: Having declared America to be a land of liberty, God undertook to raise up a band of inspired and intelligent leaders who could write a constitution of liberty and establish the first free people in modern times. The hand of God in this undertaking is clearly indicated by the Lord himself in a revelation to the Prophet Joseph Smith in these words: . . . "I established the Constitution of this land by the hands of wise men whom I raised up unto this very purpose . . ." (D&C 101:80.)

Seventh: God declared that the United States Constitution was divinely inspired for the specific purpose of eliminating bondage and the violation of the rights and protection which belongs to "all flesh." (*Ibid.*, 101:77-80.)

Eighth: God placed a mandate upon his people to befriend and defend the constitutional laws of the land and see that the rights and privileges of all mankind are protected. He verified the declaration of the founding fathers, that God created all men free. He also warned against those who would enact laws encroaching upon the sacred rights and privileges of free men. He urged the election of honest and wise leaders and said that evil men and laws were of Satan. (*Ibid.*, 98:5-10.)

Ninth: God predicted through his prophets that this great gentile nation, raised up on the American continent in the last days, would become the richest, most powerful nation on the face of the earth: even "above all other nations." (See 1 Nephi 13:15, 30; Ether 2:12.) (*Conference Report,* October 1961, p. 69.)

The foregoing steps in the development of America establish the truth that God's hand had been over this land in order that the restoration of the gospel might be possible and that the work of the Lord in the last days might come to fruition. This chapter is about the divinely inspired constitution of the United States mentioned in items six and seven above. A review of some of the history which brought this great document into existence follows.

### The Beginning of a Nation

Thirteen colonies flourished along the eastern seaboard of the country under the rule of England. By 1763 England had fought and won the French and Indian wars to protect these colonies, and in order to pay part of the cost heavy taxes were levied upon the colonies. There went up the cry "no taxation without representation." In 1774 colonial delegates to a convention met and drew up a "Declaration of Rights and Grievances" to be submitted to King George III. To make their protest heard, the colonists agreed that they would not import any goods from England until satisfaction was met. Ten thousand English troops were sent to America to enforce the law.

On April 19, 1775, the Lexington militiamen died in defense of their claims against England. In July, 1775, the Continental Congress appointed General George Washington commander-in-chief of the Continental Army. The Revolutionary War was a fact with continued fighting between England and the colonies. Only July 4, 1776, in Philadelphia, the Declaration of Independence was adopted. Thus the nation was born. As expressed in the words of President J. Reuben Clark, Jr.:

> The reason for this new birth into the family of nations, was not for the division of a great empire (this was not the division of a Roman empire); it was not that some royal son needed a throne (this was not placing a Louis of Holland, or a Joseph of Naples); it was not that an emperor wished to make secure a tributary state (this was not setting up an Herodian tetrarch in Roman Palestine); it was not that some noble house might set up its mastery over a kingdom (this was no War of Roses); it was not a group, lustful for power, warring to gain dominion over their fellows (this was not a rebellion of a Praetorian Guard). This birth was the result of none of the motives that to that time had given birth to new States. The reason for this birth was new, and it was that there should come into the world and take a guiding place among the family of nations, a government and a people dedicated to the principles that certain great fundamental truths were self-evident; "that all men are created equal, that they are endowed by their Creator with certain inalienable rights, that among these are Life, Liberty, and the Pursuit of Happiness. That to secure these rights, governments are instituted among men, deriving their just powers from the consent of the governed."
>
> . . . I say that in establishing this government, God moved forward according to His promise and declared purpose, as set out in Holy Writ to make this land "a land choice above all lands." This is the great motif which runs through our whole history. (*The Deseret News* [Church Section] March 4, 1939, p. 1.)

In 1777 the colonies drew up the Articles of Confederation in order to win the war with England and also to establish a lasting union. This form of government, which continued from 1781 to 1789, was one where the

States retained their sovereignty, freedom and independence. This league of States lacked a central power by which the Confederation could function as a nation.

Because of the inadequacy of the Articles, a convention was called to amend them. This convention in 1787, under the leadership of George Washington, set the Articles aside and drafted a new document, known as the Constitution. Washington's words were: "Let us raise a standard to which the wise and honest can repair, the event is in the hand of God."

Earlier, in the writing of the Declaration of Independence, which declared the birth of a new government, divine assistance was implored by the body responsible for that great document. Was the hand of God in the writing of the Constitution of the United States? Latter-day Saints know that prophetically the land of America is a choice land, free from captivity, and it will continue to be if the people serve the God of the land, who is Jesus Christ. As we have learned, this land, set aside by God, for the bringing forth of the fulness of the Gospel of Jesus Christ and the bringing to pass of God's purposes for man in the last days, was shielded through the ages.

During the Constitutional Convention, and after four or five weeks of discussion and argument, the progress being very slow, Benjamin Franklin addressed himself to the presiding officer, George Washington, and asked the following:

> In this situation of the Assembly, groping as it were in the dark to find political truth, and scarce able to distinguish it when presented to us, how has it happened, Sir, that we have not hitherto once thought of humbly applying to the Father of lights to illuminate our understanding?

He then reminded the convention that divine assistance had been sought during the struggle with Great Britain and that their prayers were answered. Then he said:

> I have lived, Sir, a long time, and the longer I live, the more convincing proofs I see of this truth—*that God governs in the affairs of men.*

His resolution to the Assembly was that they henceforth implore the assistance of Heaven in their deliberations.

Following this plea, the motion was seconded and several offered their opinions on the resolution, with the following ideas expressed:

> To begin prayers now, so late in the session, might cause talk, and lead the public to suspect that there was trouble behind the closed doors. It was not the Quaker custom to have prayers at political gatherings, and this was Philadelphia. Among the delegates were members of various Protestant denominations—Quaker, Episcopalian, Presbyterian, Methodist, Baptist—and Roman Catholics. Williamson of North Carolina pointed out that the Convention had no great money to pay a chaplain or chaplains. (Carl Van Doren, *The Great Rehearsal,* pp. 101-102.)

The motion was never put to a vote and the meeting adjourned. Despite this decision, the great Benjamin Franklin, senior statesman, set forth this important truth accepted by god-fearing people everywhere: God governs in the affairs of men! The men who formulated the Constitution were foreordained for this very purpose:

> . . . I established the Constitution of this land, by the hands of wise men whom I raised up unto this very purpose, and redeemed the land by the shedding of blood. (D&C 101:80.)

The opportunity to receive the fulness of the gospel at the hands of the priesthood of God was not possible to these "wise men," but through the principle of salvation for the dead the Lord revealed that this was possible. President Wilford Woodruff said about the signers of the Declaration of Independence, some of whom were in the Constitutional Convention:

I am going to bear my testimony to this assembly, if I never do it again in my life, that those men who laid the foundation of the American government and signed the Declaration of Independence were the best spirits the God of heaven could find on the face of the earth. They were choice spirits, not wicked men. General Washington and all the men that labored for the purpose were inspired of the Lord.

Another thing I am going to say here, because I have a right to say it. Every one of those men that signed the Declaration of Independence, with General Washington, called upon me, as an Apostle of the Lord Jesus Christ, in the temple at St. George, two consecutive nights and demanded at my hands that I should go forth and attend to the ordinances of the House of God for them. Men are here, I believe, that know of this, Brother J. D. T. McAllister, David H. Cannon and James G. Bleak. Brother McAllister baptized me for all those men and then I told those brethren that it was their duty to go into the Temple and labor until they had got endowments for all of them. They did it. Would those spirits have called upon me, as an Elder in Israel, to perform that work if they had not been noble spirits before God? They would not.

I bear this testimony, because it is true. The Spirit of God bore record to myself and the brethren while we were laboring in that way. (*Conference Report,* April 1898, pp. 89-90.)

Among the members of the General Authorities of the Church who have spoken often about the Constitution of the United States is President J. Reuben Clark, Jr., counselor in the First Presidency to three presidents of the Church. Because the Lord had declared that he had established this document by the hands of wise men, President Clark, accepted it as a part of his religion. The genius of the Constitution, he felt, was not only in the freedoms and rights granted to the citizens of the United States, but the separation of the fusion of governmental functions—the legislative, the executive, and the judicial.

. . . the different branches were bound together, unified into an efficient, operating whole. These branches stood together, supported one another. While severally independent, they were at the same time, mutually dependent. It is this union of independence and dependence of these branches—legislative, executive, and judicial—and of the governmental functions possessed by each of them, that constitutes the marvelous genius of this unrivalled document. The Framers had no direct guide in this work, no historical governmental precedent upon which to rely. As I see it, it was here that the divine inspiration came. It was truly a miracle. (*Stand Fast by Our Constitution,* p. 148.)

## Origin of the Bill of Rights

In order to further guarantee the right of the individual, ten amendments known as the Bill of Rights went into effect in 1791. Although there were provisions in the Constitution that belonged to a Bill of Rights the states approved the Constitution with the understanding that such a bill would be a part of the Constitution.

That our forefathers were wise in not leaving such vital matters to inference, implication, or construction will be shown by an examination of the first ten amendments.

"The executive in our governments is not the sole—it is scarcely the principal—object of my jealousy," wrote Jefferson from Paris, urging upon Madison the need of amendments making a Bill of Rights; "the tyranny of the legislatures is the most formidable turn, but it will be a remote period." (*The Constitution of the United States Its Sources and Its Applications,* p. 196.)

The additional safeguards of the Bill of Rights were not new to the colonists. They were inherited from their English ancestors.

## Revelation and Rights

In 1833, when the Lord revealed that he had established the Constitution of the United States, it was fifty years old. In addition to the Bill of Rights, two amendments had been made; one in 1798 concerning the Federal judicial power, and the other in 1804 about the election of President and Vice President. It wasn't until thirty years later that the two amendments abolishing slavery and guaranteeing citizenship and its protection were enacted. The Lord in Section 101, said:

According to the laws and constitution of the people, which I have suffered to be established, and should be maintained for the rights and protection of all flesh, according to just and holy principles;

That every man may act in doctrine and principle pertaining to futurity, may be accountable for his own sins in the day of judgment.

Therefore, it is not right that any man should be in bondage one to another.

And for this purpose have I established the Constitution of this land . . . (Verses 77-80.)

## Bill of Rights Provisions

The first ten amendments are:

### Article One

Congress shall make no law respecting an establishment of religion, or prohibiting the free exercise thereof; or abridging the freedom or speech, or of the press; or the right of the people peaceably to assemble, and to petition the government for a redress of grievances.

### Article Two

A well regulated Militia, being necessary to the security of a free State, the right of the people to keep and bear Arms shall not be infringed.

### Article Three

No soldier shall, in time of peace be quartered in any house, without the consent of the Owner, nor in time of war, but in a manner to be prescribed by law.

### Article Four

The right of the people to be secure in their persons, houses, papers, and effects, against unreasonable searches and seizures, shall not be violated, and no Warrants shall issue, but upon probably cause, supported by Oath or affirmation, and particularly describing the place to be searched, and the persons or things to be seized.

## Article Five

No person shall be held to answer for a capital, or otherwise infamous crime, unless on a presentment or indictment of a Grand Jury, except in cases arising in the land or naval forces, or in the Militia, when in actual service in time of War or public danger; nor shall any person be subject for the same offence to be twice put in jeopardy of life or limb; nor shall be compelled in any criminal case to be a witness against himself, not be deprived of life, liberty, or property, without due process of law; nor shall private property be taken for public use, without just compensation.

## Article Six

In all criminal prosecutions, the accused shall enjoy the right to a speedy and public trial, by an impartial jury of the State and district wherein the crime shall have been committed, which district shall have been previously ascertained by law, and to be informed of the nature and cause of the accusation; to be confronted with the witnesses against him, to have compulsory process for obtaining witnesses in his favor, and to have the Assistance of Counsel for his defence.

## Article Seven

In suits at common law, where the value in controversy shall exceed twenty dollars, the right of trial by jury shall be preserved, and no fact tried by a jury, shall be otherwise re-examined in any Court of the United States, than according to the rules of the common law.

## Article Eight

Excessive bail shall not be required, nor excessive fines imposed, nor cruel and unusual punishments inflicted.

## Article Nine

The enumeration in the Constitution, of certain rights, shall not be construed to deny or disparage others retained by the people.

## Article Ten

The powers not delegated to the United States by the Constitution, nor prohibited by it to the States, are reserved to the States respectively, or to the people.

Regarding these amendments, President Clark counseled as follows and gave his testimony concerning the Constitution:

Now, there are others of these great political blessings that you may have taken for granted, but they are not like the air, the sunshine, and the rain. You can lose them. Read and study the Bill of Rights; you will conclude you cannot afford to lose any of those rights. . . .

I repeat, to me the Constitution of the United States is a part of my religion; it has become so because of the words of the Lord which I have read to you. So far as I know, he has never given an approval such as this to any other government in the world. So far as I can see, the Constitution of the United States, as of 1833, was his plan of government, reserving and guaranteeing these great rights which you must enjoy if you are going to remain free, if you are going to worship as you wish, if you are going to be a free people. ("Some Political Blessings," Address at Brigham Young University, May 21, 1957.)

## Conclusion

The Prophet Joseph Smith believed that the Constitution was a part of his religion for he said:

The Constitution of the United States is a glorious standard; it is founded in the wisdom of God. It is a heavenly banner; it is to all those who are privileged with the sweets of its liberty, like the cooling shades and refreshing waters of a great rock in a thirsty and weary land. It is like a great tree under whose branches men from every clime can be shielded from the burning rays of the sun. . . .

We say that God is true; that the Constitution of the United States is true; that the Bible is true; that the Book of Mormon is true; that the Book of Covenants is true; that Christ is true. . . . (*DHC* 3:304.)

In the words of the Lord given by revelation, as the dedicatory prayer of the Kirtland Temple, March 27, 1836:

Have mercy, O Lord, upon all the nations of the earth; have mercy upon the rulers of our land; may those principles, which were so honorably and nobly defended, namely, the Constitution of our land, by our fathers, be established forever. (D&C 109:54.)

In prophetic fulfillment of the Lord's statement in verses 77 and 78 of Section 101, President Clark has said:

Speaking of the destiny that the Lord has offered to mankind in his declarations regarding the scope and efficacy of the Constitution and its principles, we may note that already the Lord has moved upon many nations of the earth so to go forward. The Latin American countries have followed our lead and adopted our constitutional form of government, adapted to their legal concepts, without compulsion or restraint from us. Likewise, the people of Canada in the British North America Act have embodied great principles that are basic to our Constitution. The people of Australia have likewise followed along our governmental footpath. In Canada and Australia, the great constitutional decisions of John Marshall and his associates are quoted in their courts and followed in their adjudications. I repeat, none of this has come because of force of arms. The Constitution will never reach its destiny through force. God's principles are taken by men because they are eternal and true, and touch the divine spirit in men. This is the only true way to permanent world peace, the aspiration of men since the beginning. God never planted his Spirit, his truth in the hearts of men from the point of a bayonet. (*Conference Report,* April 1957, p. 51.)

## Chapter 25

# HOW TO PREACH THE GOSPEL

## (Sections 99 and 100:1-12)

During the lull in persecution of the saints in Missouri, the work of the Lord continued in other parts of the country. Missionaries continued to preach the gospel of peace as commanded by the Lord. Hate, envy, and bigotry were eliminated from the soul of the person who truly accepted Jesus Christ as his Savior and who sought to receive the spirit of peace—the Holy Ghost.

### John Murdock

A few days after Section 98 was received in August 1833, the Lord called Elder John Murdock to the Eastern States on a mission. (D&C 99:1.)

Elder Murdock, an early convert to the Church, actively engaged in many important responsibilities in the Church. His first contact with the Church was through the missionaries assigned to the Lamanites in 1830. After only a short time in the Ohio Valley many were baptized by these missionaries, among whom were Sidney Rigdon, Lyman Wight, Edward Partridge, and Brother Murdock. Responsibility came early, when with some of the others he was left to take care of the branches of the Church raised up in that area. He had the honor of being a member of Zion's Camp that treked the thousand miles from Ohio to Missouri to give succor to the persecuted saints. Other service in the Church included membership on the high council in Clay County, Missouri, and in Far West, and being a bishop in Nauvoo, Illinois.

## Missionary Call

Elder Murdock faithfully discharged his duties as a member of the Melchizedek Priesthood. One can imagine the thrill which came to him as he listened to the words of the Savior through the Prophet Joseph Smith about his missionary call:

> And who receiveth you receiveth me; and you shall have power to declare my word in the demonstration of my Holy Spirit.
>
> And who receiveth you as a little child, receiveth my kingdom; and blessed are they, for they shall obtain mercy.
>
> And whoso rejecteth you shall be rejected of my Father and his house; and you shall cleanse your feet in the secret places by the way for a testimony against him. (D&C 99:2-4.)

These words are as applicable to present-day missionaries as they were to Brother Murdock. (*Ibid.*, 93:49; 84:35-38, 88-91.) When men act with the authority of the priesthood, performing their duties faithfully, seeking the Spirit to assist them, their priesthood acts are binding. The Lord recognizes his servants as though he were performing the act. Elder Orson F. Whitney emphasized this truth when he wrote:

> When the Son of Man, sitting upon "the throne of his glory," shall require of all nations and of all men a final accounting, and shall put to them the crucial question: "How did you treat my servants whom I sent unto you?" happy the nation or the man who can reply: "Lord, I showed them the respect to which they were entitled—I honored them as I would have honored Thee."
>
> Grievous the sin and heavy the penalty incurred by those who mistreat the servants of the Master. (*Saturday Night Thoughts,* pp. 219, 221.)

One of Brother Murdock's missionary companions was Elder David W. Patten, the first apostolic martyr of the dispensation.

## Cleansing of Feet

On several occasions the Lord has counseled his servants to shake the dust off their feet against those who reject them (D&C 24:15; 60:15) or to cleanse the feet in testimony. (*Ibid.*, 84:92; 99:4.) Concerning the missionary obligation to testify, President Joseph Fielding Smith wrote:

> The elders were to seek out from among the people the honest in heart and leave their warning testimony with all others, thus they would become clean from their blood. The cleansing of their feet, either by washing or wiping off the dust, would be recorded in heaven as a testimony against the wicked. This act, however, was not to be performed in the presence of the offenders, "lest thou provoke them, but in secret, and wash thy feet, as a testimony against them in the day of judgment." The missionaries of the Church who faithfully perform their duty are under the obligation of leaving their testimony with all with whom they come in contact in their work. This testimony will stand as a witness against those who reject the message, at the judgment. (*Church History and Modern Revelation* 1:206.)

The purpose of the gospel of Jesus Christ is to save and not to condemn, but men are responsible for their rejection of the truth. Condemnation comes because of the wrong use of free agency in making decisions. In order to administer the principle of testimony as commanded above, it is apparent that the person must be living so well that the Spirit will dictate when and if such condemnation be uttered. The missionary and also every member of the Church should follow the counsel of President Lorenzo Snow, who said:

> There is a way by which persons can keep their consciences clear before God and man, and that is to preserve within them the Spirit of God, which is the spirit of revelation to every man and woman. It will reveal to them, even in the simplest of matters, what they shall do, by making suggestions to them. We should try to learn the nature of this spirit, that we may understand its suggestions, and then we will always be able to do right.

This is the grand privilege of every Latter-day Saint. We know that it is our right to have the manifestations of the spirit every day of our lives. (*Conference Report,* April 1899, p. 52.)

## Murdock Twins

Upon the death of the twins of the Prophet and his wife, Emma, they took into their home the twin boy and girl of Brother John Murdock when his wife had died. A mob attacked the Prophet's home, tarred and feathered him, and because of exposure, the twin boy died. In Section 99 Brother Murdock is told that before his mission, arrangements were to be made for his motherless children to be sent to Zion (Missouri). One of these, John Riggs, found a home in Jackson County and lived amid the persecutions in that county and elsewhere. Later, he came to Utah, and no one in Utah equalled his record of bringing so many saints across the plains, eleven trips being made. Later he was called to be bishop in Beaver City. He founded the Church academy at that place.

Elder John Murdock also lived in Missouri with the saints and filled many responsible Church positions there and in Illinois.

## Background Section 100

The Prophet's journal of October 1833, records that he left for the East and Canada in company with Elder Sidney Rigdon and Freeman Nickerson. (*DHC* 1:416.) Six months before this, Brother Nickerson joined the Church and, realizing his responsibility to bring the gospel to others, performed missionary work in the Kirtland, Ohio area, where the Prophet was located. With this missionary desire he felt that his sons who lived in Canada should receive the gospel and for this purpose he elicited the Prophet's help in converting them. The party, including Mrs. Nickerson, traveled to Perrysburg, New York, where they stayed at the home of Brother Nickerson. It was at this place on October 12, 1833, that Section 100 was received.

## Missionary Journey

An indication of the events that took place while on this missionary trip is found in the Prophet's account from the day the revelation was received until his return to Kirtland on November 4th, as follows:

> . . . Elder Rigdon preached to a large congregation, at Freeman Nickerson's, and I bore record while the Lord gave His Spirit in a remarkable manner.
>
> Monday, 14. Continued our journey towards Canada, and arrived at Lodi, where we had an appointment, and preached in the evening to a small assembly, and made an appointment for Tuesday, the 15th, at 10 o'clock a.m. to be in the Presbyterian meeting house. When the hour arrived, the keeper refused to open the doors, and the meeting was thus prevented. . . .
>
> Sunday, 20. At 10 o'clock we met an attentive congregation at Brantford; and the same evening a large assembly at Mount Pleasant, at Mr. Nickerson's. The people gave good heed to the things spoken.
>
> Tuesday, 22. —We went to the village of Colburn; and although it snowed severely, we held a meeting by candle-light on Wednesday evening, and were publicly opposed by a Wesleyan Methodist. He was very tumultuous, but exhibited a great lack of reason, knowledge, and wisdom, and gave us no opportunity to reply.
>
> Thursday, 24. —At the house of Mr. Beman, in Colburn, whence we left for Waterford, where we spoke to a small congregation; thence to Mount Pleasant, and preached to a large congregation the same evening, when Freeman A. Nickerson and his wife declared their belief in the work, and offered themselves for baptism. Great excitement prevailed in every place we visited.
>
> Saturday, 26 —Preached at Mount Pleasant; the people were very tender and inquiring.
>
> Sunday, 27. —Preached to a large congregation at Mount Pleasant, after which I baptized twelve, and others were deeply impressed, and desired another meeting, which I appointed for the day following.

Monday, 28. —In the evening, we broke bread, and laid on hands for the gift of the Holy Ghost, and for confirmation, having baptized two more. The Spirit was given in great power to some, and peace to others.

Tuesday, 29. —After preaching at 10 o'clock a.m., I baptized two, and confirmed them at the water's side. Last evening, we ordained F. A. Nickerson an Elder; and one of the sisters received the gift of tongues, which made the Saints rejoice exceedingly.

Tuesday, the 29th of October, also we took our departure from Mount Pleasant, on our return to Kirtland, and arrived at Buffalo, New York, on the 31st.

Friday, November. —I left Buffalo, New York, at 8 o'clock a.m., and arrived at my house in Kirtland on Monday, the 4th, 10 a.m. and found my family well, according to the promise of the Lord in the revelation of October 12th, for which I felt to thank my Heavenly Father. (*DHC* 1:421-423.)

In addition to the foregoing, Elder B. H. Roberts, author of the notes in the *Documentary History of the Church*, adds some expressions of the Prophet which show his "deeply religious and prayerful nature" as he always remembered the Lord, sought for his Spirit, and requested his protecting power, in this way:

"O God, seal our testimony to their hearts:" "I feel very well in my mind." "The Lord is with us;" "The Lord gave His Spirit in a remarkable manner to some Saints, for which I am thankful to the God of Abraham," "Lord bless my family, and preserve them." "This day we expect to start for Canada. Lord be with us on our journey. Amen." (*DHC* 1:423, footnote.)

## Promises Fulfilled

Several items in the Prophet's missionary journey should be given further consideration. One of these is the reference to the well-being of his family. The promise of the Lord that his family would be well was fulfilled, as reported by him. (D&C 100:1.) The natural concern that the missionary has for his family at home should not detract from his call to preach the gospel. Many brethren who went forth to teach the nations have shown their faith and trust in the Lord not only to provide for them but also for their families. President John Taylor remarked:

> It is true there ought to be sympathy and some care for those with whom they have been immediately associated; yet their families as well as our families, and all of us and our affairs are in the hands of God, and, inasmuch as they go forth putting their trust in the living God all will be peace, and they will find peace and contentment from this time forth until they return, inasmuch as they will magnify their callings and lean upon their God. In this is their safety, in order that they may be enabled to bear a faithful testimony to the world among whom they may travel to deliver their message of warning and of glad tidings of great joy to the honest in heart. (*Journal of Discourses* 10:37.)

Another promise in Section 100 that was fulfilled in this missionary journey was the opening of that region for teaching the gospel. The Prophet's success in baptisms performed is evidence that an "effectual door was opened up in that region" and thus the salvation of souls accomplished. (D&C 100:3-4.)

## A Wonderful Promise

In view of what happened on this mission the following promises to the Prophet and Sidney Rigdon were literally fulfilled:

> Therefore, verily I say unto you, lift up your voices unto this people; speak the thoughts that I shall put into your hearts, and you shall not be confounded before me;
>
> For it shall be given you in the very hour, yea, in the very moment, what ye shall say.
>
> But a commandment I give unto you, that ye shall declare whatsoever thing ye declare in my name, in solemnity of heart, in the spirit of meekness, in all things.
>
> And I give unto you this promise, that inasmuch as ye do this the Holy Ghost shall be shed forth in bearing record unto all things whatsoever ye shall say. (D&C 100:5-8.)

When the Prophet's party arrived in Mount Pleasant, Canada, Freeman Nickerson introduced them to his two wealthy sons, Moses and Freeman, the latter told his father: "Well father, I will welcome them for your sake, but I would just about as soon you had brought a nest of vipers and turned them loose upon us."

Through the eyes of a young girl, Lydia Bailey (later married to Newell Knight), who stayed at the Nickerson home, we learn of this description of the Prophet and Elder Rigdon:

> . . . a tall, well built form, with the carriage of an Apollo, brown hair, handsome blue eyes, which seemed to dive down to the innermost thoughts with their sharp, penetrating gaze, a striking countenance, and with manners at once majestic yet gentle, dignified yet exceedingly pleasant.
>
> Elder Rigdon was a middle-aged man of medium height, stout and quite good-looking, but without the noble grandeur that was so distinguishing a mark of the prophet. (*Lydia Knight's History,* p. 17.)

Freeman, the son, became anxious to hear something of the Prophet's religion.

> "Oh," said he, "Just let him talk; I'll silence him if he undertakes to talk about the Bible. I guess I know as much about the scriptures as he does."
>
> This was to his wife whom he directed to place the family Bible on the table in the parlor.
>
> As soon as supper was over, he invited his visitors and family to go up stairs to the parlor, where he said they would have some talk. All, accordingly repaired to the large well-furnished room, and the Mr. N. said to the Prophet:
>
> "Now, Mr. Smith, I wish you and Mr. Rigdon to speak freely. Say what you wish and tell us what you believe. We will listen."
>
> Turning to his wife, he whispered, "Now you'll see how I shall shut him up."
>
> The Prophet commenced by relating the scenes of his early life. He told how the angel visited him, of his finding the plates, the translation of them, and gave a short account of the matter contained in the Book of Mormon.

As the speaker continued his wonderful narrative, Lydia, who was listening and watching him intently, saw his face become white and a shining glow seemed to beam from every feature.

As his story progressed he would often allude to passages of scripture. Then Mr. N. would speak up and endeavor to confound him. But the attempt was soon acknowledged even by himself to be futile.

The Prophet bore a faithful testimony that the Priesthood was again restored to the earth, and that God and His Son had conferred upon him the keys of the Aaronic and Melchizedek Priesthoods. He stated that the last dispensation had come, and the words of Jesus were now in force—"Go ye into all the world and preach the gospel to every creature. He that believeth and is baptized shall be saved; but he that believeth not shall be damned."

Following this, Elder Rigdon spoke; whereupon, Mr. N. said:

And is this then the curious religion the newspapers tell so much about? Why if what you have just said is not good sound sense, then I don't know what sense is." (*Ibid.*, pp. 17-19.)

Within a few days, Lydia and Mr. N. and all of his household were baptized. In a meeting the following day, the Prophet recorded of that event that "one of the sisters received the gift of tongues." Moses Nickerson spoke up and said he wished that someone would receive the gift of tongues as the ancient saints did. The Prophet said:

"If one of you will rise up and open your mouth it shall be fulfilled, and you shall speak in tongues."

Every one then turned as by a common instinct to Lydia, and said with one voice, "Sister Lydia rise up."

And then the great glory of God was manifested to this weak but trusting girl. She was enveloped as with a flame, and, unable longer to retain her seat, she arose and her mouth was filled with the praises of God and His glory. The spirit of tongues was upon her, and she was clothed in a shining light, so bright that all present saw it with great distinctness above the light of the fire and the candles. (*Ibid.*, pp. 21-22.)

## Missionary Principles

Argument and contention is of Satan, and never converts. (3 Nephi 11:29.) In another revelation, the Lord counsels his servants to treasure up in their minds the words of life, and it will be given to them what to say. (D&C 84:85.) Study and understanding of the scriptures—the words of life—are necessary that the Lord may bring forth what is necessary for every situation. The promise is that if his servants will do this they shall not be confounded by men. The case of Mr. Nickerson is an excellent example of this truth. The power of testimony in this example, brings conviction to the hearer. When a man speaks by the power of the Holy Ghost, that Spirit carries the message into the hearts of men. (2 Nephi 33:1.) All things must be done in the spirit of humility, solemness of heart, and in the name of the Savior. If this is done, the Holy Ghost will bear witness of the truth spoken. (D&C 100:7-8.) The results of this program are expressed in these words:

> Therefore, why is it that ye cannot understand and know, that he that receiveth the word by the Spirit of truth receiveth it as it is preached by the Spirit of truth?
>
> Wherefore, he that preacheth and he that receiveth, understand one another, and both are edified and rejoice together. (*Ibid.*, 50:21-22.)

## Sidney Rigdon, Spokesman

Joseph, who was sold into Egypt and is the progenitor of most Latter-day Saints, prophesied that in the last days that prophet who would be named Joseph, as well as his father, would have a spokesman. (2 Nephi 3:18.) Section 100 informs us that Sidney Rigdon was that spokesman. (D&C 100:9.) Moses, the prophet, also had a spokesman in the person of his brother Aaron. (Exodus 4:15-16.)

Sidney Rigdon is described as a forceful speaker, eloquent, and convincing. He performed well in this calling.

### Joseph the Testator

Unto the Prophet Joseph Smith was promised the power to be "mighty in testimony." (D&C 100:10.)

Although the account of the Prophet's testimony at the Nickerson's is an example of this power, an event a few years later gives more powerfully the fulfillment of this promise. For many months the Prophet remained in a Richmond, Missouri jail under false charges, and upon one of these nights, Elder Parley P. Pratt recorded:

> In one of those tedious nights we had lain as if in sleep till the hour of midnight had passed, and our ears and hearts had been pained, while we had listened for hours to obscene jests, the horrid oaths, the dreadful blasphemies and filthy language of our guards, Colonel Price at their head, as they recounted to each other their deeds of raping, murder, robbery, etc., which they had committed among the "Mormons" while at Far West and vicinity. They even boasted of defiling by force wives, daughters and virgins, and of shooting or dashing out the brains of men, women, and children.
>
> I had listened till I became so disgusted, shocked, horrified, and so filled with the spirit of indignant justice that I could scarcely refrain from rising upon my feet and rebuking the guards; but had said nothing to Joseph, or anyone else, although I lay next to him and knew he was awake. On a sudden he arose to his feet, and spoke in a voice of thunder, or as the roaring lion, uttering, as near as I can recollect, the following words:
>
> *"SILENCE, ye fiends of the infernal pit. In the name of Jesus Christ I rebuke you, and command you to be still; I will not live another minute and hear such language. Cease such talk, or you or I die THIS INSTANT!"*
>
> He ceased to speak. He stood erect in terrible majesty. Chained, and without a weapon; calm, unruffled and dignified as an angel, he looked upon the quailing guards, whose weapons were lowered or dropped to the ground; whose knees smote together, and who, shrinking into a corner, or crouching at his

feet, begged his pardon, and remained quiet till a change of guards.

I have seen the ministers of justice, clothed in magisterial robes, and criminals arraigned before them, while life was suspended on a breath, in the Courts of England; I have witnessed a Congress in solemn session to give laws to nations; I have tried to conceive of kings, of royal courts, of thrones and crowns; and of emperors assembled to decide the fate of kingdoms; but dignity and majesty have I seen but *once,* as it stood in chains at midnight, in a dungeon in an obscure village of Missouri. (*Autobiography of Parley P. Pratt,* pp. 210-211.)

## Conclusion

Section 100 provides us with some principles and illustrations from the experiences of the Prophet Joseph Smith on how to preach the gospel. Since all members are counseled to be missionaries, the information is appropriate to all, with special reference to appointed missionaries. First, one must know what he is to teach. Second, he must seek to enjoy the guidance of the Holy Ghost by (a) living the commandments and (b) praying for the inspiration that comes from the Spirit. Third, rely, in faith, upon the Spirit to guide one in what to say. Fourth, remember the source from which the inspiration comes by acknowledging the Lord's hand in all things. Fifth, be earnest, enthusiastic, serious of heart, yet not boastful, but meek in all exhortations.

The promise is that the Holy Ghost will bear witness to the message so delivered.

## Chapter 26

# DISCIPLESHIP

### (Section 100)

The forepart of Section 100 (verses 1-12) are instructions to the Prophet Joseph Smith and Sidney Rigdon on how they should perform their missionary labors while in Canada with the Nickerson family. Sidney Rigdon, in fulfillment of a Book of Mormon prophecy, is designated as a spokesman to the people. (2 Nephi 3:18; D&C 100:9.)

### Zion Shall be Redeemed

The Zion of Jackson County, Missouri, was undergoing persecution. Because of the knowledge of Zion's greatness from the prophets and also the revelations he had received, the Prophet had a sincere concern for the success of the saints to establish Zion. (Ether 13:2-12; D&C 58:2-14.) This heartening message was received from the Lord:

> And now I give unto you a word concerning Zion. Zion shall be redeemed, although she is chastened for a little season. (D&C 100:13.)

In the due time of the Lord the center place of Zion or the New Jerusalem will yet stand upon the land of America.

### Orson Hyde and John Gould

When persecution broke out in Jackson County, the brethren sent Oliver Cowdery to Kirtland to report to the First Presidency. Soon thereafter, Orson Hyde, who later became an apostle, and John Gould were sent to Jackson County with instructions from the First Presidency. While the Prophet and his party were in Canada, the Lord revealed that these two brethren were in his hands, and if they kept the commandments they would be saved. (*Ibid.*, verse 14.) From the following we learn the experience of the servants of the Lord as they endeavor to serve him:

> During the entire history of the Latter-day Saints, the Lord has preserved His faithful servants, often miraculously, in dangers on land and sea, among enemies and false friends, until their mission was completed. (*Doctrine and Covenants Commentary,* p. 634.)

## Promises and Prophecies

The last three verses of Section 100 contain some promises and prophecies regarding the saints and the Lord's work.

> Therefore, let your hearts be comforted; for all things shall work together for good to them that walk uprightly, and to the sanctification of the Church.
>
> For I will raise up unto myself a pure people, that will serve me in righteousness;
>
> And all that call upon the name of the Lord, and keep his commandments, shall be saved. Even so. Amen. (Verses 15-17.)

It is the promises and prophecies in those verses that this chapter is about. (1) All things shall work together for the good of the sanctified, who will find rich blessings. (2) Those who keep the commandments will be saved. And (3) the Lord will raise up a people who will serve him.

## Be Comforted

In the time of worry, concern, mourning, and tribulation, the member of the Church of Jesus Christ may be blessed by the Comforter, who is the Holy Ghost. (John 14:26; 15:26.) One may receive the witness of the truth which the Lord bestows upon the sincere seeker with that Spirit.

Peace in this world, rest, and comfort are the blessings of obedience. (*Gospel Doctrine*, pp. 126-127.) Comfort comes to all those who seek for that blessing. Missionaries find comfort amid difficulties and discouragements. The sons of Mosiah rejoiced with Alma as they related their missionary experiences among the Lamanites. Because they had prepared themselves by prayer and fasting,

> . . . it came to pass that the Lord did visit them with his Spirit, and said unto them: Be comforted. And they were comforted. (Alma 17:9-10.)

It is also written that those who mourn will find comfort. (Matt. 5:4; 3 Nephi 12:4.) To those who mourn for loved ones departed this life the knowledge of conscious existence at death continues to be a bulwark of strength in time of mourning. Faithful, devoted service in this life brings its rewards. (D&C 59:2; 63:49.)

Every Latter-day Saint finds comfort in the many prophecies regarding the ultimate victory of the Lord's work. The Spirit testifies to this truth bringing joy and happiness. Moroni, the last Nephite historian was concerned as to whether or not the readers of the Book of Mormon in the last days might not heed his message because he was not mighty in writing. The Lord's answer was that if men will come unto him in faith he will make them mighty and the Lord will show the people that faith, hope, and charity will bring them to him in the last days. When Moroni heard these words his fears left, for he was comforted. (Ether 12:24-30.)

## All Things Good

In the promises to the saints of our times, the Lord makes known that "all things shall work together for good to them that walk uprightly." (D&C 100:15.) To walk uprightly is to keep the commandments. And for what purpose? The Lord has given the answer: "considering the end of your salvation." (*Ibid.*, 46:7.) If the member of the Church is salvation oriented, he will walk uprightly before the Lord and will acknowledge that this life is purposeful. His acceptance of trials, tribulations, sorrow caused by death of loved ones, and other vicissitudes through which one might pass in life, will be accepted as a part of the total experience, and therefore good. (*Ibid.*, 122:5-8.) However, only he who keeps the commandments can understand. (*Ibid.*, 59:20.) Knowledge, peace, and comfort give rest and understanding.

## Sanctification of the Church

To become sanctified is the goal of the knowledgeable Latter-day Saint. (D&C 88:67-68.) Elder Marion G. Romney has told us that through the gate of baptism and the ordinance of confirmation into the Church we have begun this process.

> Through these principles and ordinances we were cleansed and purified. Having thus washed our garments in the blood of Christ, we entered through the straight gate and stood redeemed on the narrow way which leads to life eternal. It should have then been, and it should now be, the controlling desire of every Church member, and it is the desire of every member who is on the way to eternal life always to retain this redeemed status. (*Conference Report,* October 1956, p. 17.)

To be born again by the Holy Ghost is the step to sanctification or the state of holiness, by changing from the carnal to the spiritual state. (Moroni 10:32-33; 3 Nephi 27:19-21.) Sometimes this admonition is stated in terms of seeking perfection. (3 Nephi 12:48.) Throughout the change one is to apply the principle of repentance. Elder Romney continues to explain some ways in which this goal is possible:

> With complete surrender to the spirit of the gospel let us, honestly and without guile, search our own souls and find the

weakness which presently impedes our upward climb to eternal life. If that weakness be faultfinding, evil speaking of the Lord's anointed, or profaning the name of Deity, let us desist. If it be neglecting our prayers, let us pause night and morning in our mad rush and kneel with our families and in our secret chambers while we pour out our souls in thanksgiving and petition, until hungering and thirsting after righteousness we are filled with the Holy Ghost. If it be failure to obtain the sealing ordinances of the temple for ourselves and families, let us straightway prepare to enter that holy place and obtain them before it is too late. If it be the giving way to anger or appetite for the things forbidden in the Word of Wisdom, or surrendering to baser lusts; if it be desecration of the Sabbath day or refusing to contribute of our time and means according to the laws of the Church for the building of the kingdom; whatever it be, let us find it, recognize it, and do something about it daily.

Let us resolve never to relax in our striving for that perfection in ourselves which will bring us to eternal life. (*Ibid.*)

The prophetic statement that the Church will become sanctified is a requisite to the eventual building up of Zion upon the American continent. The Lord's army in that day will constitute a large number, greater than what existed in 1834 when the saints were expelled from Jackson County, Missouri. (D&C 105:31.) Although the number of those who will be sanctified will be great, there is no assurance that this will include all who are members of the Church. Sanctification in this life and enduring to the end will warrant receiving the celestial kingdom. (*Ibid.*, 88:2, 116.) As members of the Church follow the admonition of the Lord to sanctify themselves, so much nearer is brought the day when Zion shall be redeemed. (Ibid., 43:9, 11, 16; 133:4.)

## A Pure People

Closely associated with the building of Zion is the need for the people to become pure in heart. The Lord says that his people will be pure in heart for they will serve him in righteousness. (*Ibid.*, 100:16.) Zion is the pure in heart. (*Ibid.*, 97:21.) This thought is in harmony with the definition of a saint given by the Prophet Benjamin:

> For the natural man is an enemy to God, and has been from the fall of Adam, and will be, forever and ever, unless he yields to the enticings of the Holy Spirit, and putteth off the natural man and becometh a saint through the atonement of Christ the Lord, and becometh as a child, submissive, meek, humble, patient, full of love, willing to submit to all things which the Lord seeth fit to inflict upon him, even as a child doth submit to his father. (Mosiah 3:19.)

We are to become saints in very deed, or pure in heart; that is, a change from the natural man to the spiritual man who is born again. (*Ibid.*, 5:7.)

Can it be expected that one will be eligible for the celestial kingdom and be in the presence of God unless purity of heart is one's possession? The pure in heart, Jesus said, would see God. (Matt. 5:8.) This quality of the faithful eliminates much of what today causes so much contention and evil in the world. As Elder Albert E. Bowen wrote:

> Jesus extolled the pure in heart, declaring it is they who shall see God. No one can challenge their right to that supremacy. As an ideal for a human society it is not subject to question. If men's hearts were pure we should not have the reports of bestiality which come from the battlefields respecting the treatment of helpless prisoners. Neither should we have the oppression under which the inhabitants of the world groan. Our press would not be filled with accounts of the appalling delinquencies which forebode the disintegration of personal integrity and the undermining of our very civilization itself. If men were pure in heart there would be no war at all either among nations, between classes or individuals, for there be no covetousness, or greed, or seeking of advantage or desire to destroy. Vice dens, whose noisome stenches pollute the moral atmosphere of our cities, would be cleansed and sweetened by the simple process of purification of the human heart. That one achievement would renovate the world. (*Constancy Amid Change*, pp. 37-38.)

## Steps to Discipleship

To become sanctified by purifying one's heart demands complete and full allegiance to the teachings of Jesus Christ. This idea of discipleship is that a person disciplines himself to surrender completely his life as a follower. How may one be a follower of the Master in this sense? Here are some guidelines that will, if applied, bring success: (1) cleaving to the truth by study; (2) prayer; (3) righteous conduct; (4) obedience to the prophets; (5) church service.

## Cleave to the Truth by Study

Without knowledge there is no salvation. (D&C 131:6.) Gospel knowledge, if applied, will increase faith. One of the principal reasons for lack of interest in the gospel and the resultant inactivity in church work is the lack of understanding of gospel principles. Elder John A. Widtsoe concludes that applied knowledge brings strong faith.

> Knowledge tested and tried is the beginning of faith. For that reason, "it is impossible for a man to be saved in ignorance." The extent of a person's faith depends in part on the amount of his knowledge. The more knowledge he gathers, the more intensive becomes his field of faith.
>
> The degree of faith possessed by any man depends not upon the extent of his knowledge but upon the certainty of his knowledge, which leads to the proper use of his knowledge. Thus a man of great knowledge may have weak faith, while one of limited information may have strong faith. (Alma 32:34-41; *Joseph Smith*, p. 163.)

If faith is to be enlarged to bring about salvation, it must be placed in truth. (Alma 32:21.) As the certainty of knowledge also increases, the ability to discern truth is augmented because truth is discernible to the faithful. (*Ibid.*, verse 35.)

In a world beset with false doctrines, theories, and ideologies inconsistent with the teachings of the gospel, it is increasingly necessary that Latter-day Saints be able to discern between truth and error. The Lord told his ancient disciples that in order to keep from being deceived they should treasure up his word.

> And whoso treasureth up my word, shall not be deceived, for the Son of Man shall come, and he shall send his angels before him with the great sound of a trumpet, and they shall gather together the remainder of his elect from the four winds, from one end of heaven to the other. (Joseph Smith 1:37.)

## Prayer

In Section 100, the Lord promises salvation to all who keep his commandments. The importance of prayer in the keeping of the commandments is indicated in his promise, as follows:

> And all that call upon the name of the Lord, and keep his commandments, shall be saved. Even so. Amen. (D&C 100:17.)

Only those who have enjoyed the influence of family and secret prayer can truly understand the relationship of prayer to salvation. Even in the beginning Adam was counseled to "call upon God in the name of the Son forevermore." (Moses 5:8.) From then to the present dispensation considerable emphasis has been placed upon this important principle. The place of prayer in one's life was stated by Nephi as:

> Ye must not perform any thing unto the Lord save in the first place ye shall pray unto the Father in the name of Christ, that he will consecrate thy performance unto thee, that thy performance may be for the welfare of thy soul. (2 Nephi 32:9.)

The Latter-day Saint who strives to keep the commandments, increasing in knowledge, learns an important principle of prayer given in a modern revelation, as follows:

Draw near unto me and I will draw near unto you; seek me diligently and ye shall find me; ask, and ye shall receive; knock, and it shall be opened unto you.

Whatsoever ye ask the Father in my name it shall be given unto you, that is expedient for you;

And if ye ask anything that is not expedient for you, it shall turn unto your condemnation. (D&C 88:63-65.)

In a day when many efforts are made to deceive both young and old, it is essential that families follow the injunction of the Lord of holding family prayer.

Pray in your families unto the Father, always in my name, that your wives and your children may be blessed. (3 Nephi 18:21.)

The counsel is: "Watch and pray always, lest ye enter into temptation." (Matt. 26:41; D&C 10:5.)

## Righteous Conduct

There is probably nothing that will keep a person from praying and seeking to follow the Lord's instruction more than sin will. In the following words President George Q. Cannon expressed the way in which the Lord keeps his Church from becoming corrupt:

God is cleansing this people and purging those who practise sin from their midst. Those who commit sin gradually leave the Church. They get into the dark and they become cold and indifferent, and finally leave the Church. If it were not for God's power in this respect, we would soon become corrupt, doubtless, as other people. But God in His wonderful providence has so arranged matters that impurity cannot live in this Church for any length of time. There is a cleansing process going on. God is cleansing His Church, and He is purging out the wicked and the ungodly, and He is leaving the residue. No man can be confident of standing in His Church unless he is pure in heart; for the Holy Ghost will not dwell in unholy tabernacles. Men may deceive their fellow men; women may deceive their sisters; but they cannot deceive God. They cannot commit sin and retain the Spirit of God. It will leave them sooner or later. It will decrease with them, and finally leave them, unless they repent of their sins . . . (*Millennial Star* 57:801-802.)

He who treasures his membership in the Church will repent speedily of those things that will take him away from the Lord's Spirit and communion with the saints.

It is safe to say that no one can be a successful Latter-day Saint and disregard the teachings of the prophets who live today. To court the disfavor of the Lord by rejecting his servants is to lose one's exaltation. (D&C 84:35-38, 49-53.)

And if my people will hearken unto my voice, and unto the voice of my servants whom I have appointed to lead my people, behold, verily I say unto you, they shall not be moved out of their place.

But if they will not hearken to my voice, nor unto the voice of these men whom I have appointed, they shall not be blest, because they pollute mine holy grounds, and mine holy ordinances, and charters, and my holy words which I give unto them. (D&C 124:45-46.)

## Church Service

Wherein does church activity redound to the salvation of the participant? If we serve the Lord devotedly, we must also serve our fellowmen. Participation gives communion with fellow Church members and thus the desire to keep the commandments is increased and faith is enlarged. The development of talents and gifts is possible through service to others. President George F. Richards expressed it this way:

One might ask: Why all the activity we see in the Church, in the ministry abroad, in the ministry at home, in the stakes and wards, in the genealogy and temple work, in Church school and seminary work, etc.? The answer might be briefly given thus: The salvation of man depends upon it. It is the work and glory of God to accomplish the salvation of his children, by the plan of the Gospel which he has revealed. The religious activities seen in the Church and in which we are engaged are for the purpose, and are assisting the Lord in the noblest work, the most important service in which man may be engaged. If we be not called officially into the service, there are many things we can do of our own volition which will contribute to our happiness and salvation and to the happiness and salvation of others. (*Conference Report,* April 1936, p. 79.)

It is wisdom to understand this principle, said the Prophet Benjamin.

And behold, I tell you these things that ye may learn wisdom; that ye may learn that when ye are in the service of your fellow beings ye are only in the service of your God. (Mosiah 2:17.)

## Conclusion

The Lord has made specific promises to his followers that if they walk uprightly before him, seeking to sanctify themselves and thereby to sanctify the Church, they shall be comforted. The Lord says that he will raise up a people who are pure in heart. For us the wise decision is to be one of those who shall have an opportunity to build Zion upon the earth and to be one with the sanctified to inherit the richest blessings the Lord bestows upon his faithful children.

## Chapter 27

# THE MILLENNIUM

## (Section 101:23-42)

In the first part of Section 101 the Lord said that because of the transgressions of the Saints they were persecuted in Jackson County, Missouri. Despite the fact that the Saints had been driven from the land of their inheritance, the Lord said that they would return to build up the waste places of Zion. (D&C 101:17-18.) In the meantime, the Saints were to gather together in stakes that the strength of Zion might be increased. Since 1833 when the Saints left Jackson County, the number of stakes have multiplied many times over. At this writing, there are 496 of these territorial divisions in the Church. These "holy places" are to be places of refuge against the storm of calamities which would befall the earth in the last days. (*Ibid.*, 20-23.)

### The Coming of Christ

While the Saints are established in the stakes of Zion, they are to prepare for the time when the Savior will come the second time. The covering between his abode in the heavens and the earth will be removed and "all flesh shall see me [him] together." (*Ibid.*, 101:23.)

The coming of Christ will be a literal appearance as a personage of flesh and bones. When he ascended into the heavens after his final instructions to his apostles, they were promised that he would come in like manner as they had seen him go into heaven. (Acts 1:11.) Jesus was resurrected with his physical body, which had been placed in the sepulcher following his death. (Luke 24.) He is today enthroned in the heavens, having the same body that he took into the heavens. (D&C 49:6; 130:22.) On March 7, 1831, the Lord had said that he would come with his holy angels in great power and glory, and he who would not watch for his coming would be cut off. (*Ibid.*, 45:44.)

As we take the scriptures literally in regard to his personal appearance, so also we should remember that his coming will be attendant with great destruction. The brightness of his glory will even surpass the brightness of the sun. (*Ibid.*, 133:49.) The wicked will enter the spirit world to be judged according to their works. (D&C 29:9-10; 133:64; 76:106-112.) This is what the Lord has revealed about his coming:

> And every corruptible thing, both of man, or of the beasts of the field, or of the fowls of the heavens, or of the fish of the sea, that dwells upon all the face of the earth, shall be consumed. (*Ibid.*, 101:24.)

Corrupted animal life as well as wicked men and women will be destroyed. Apparently, some animals so change their natures that they may be called "corruptible."

The destruction of the wicked at the second coming of Christ is referred to in the scriptures as the end of the world. (Joseph Smith 1:4, 31; *Teachings of the Prophet Joseph Smith*, pp. 100-101.) When that time comes, the millennial reign of Christ will commence. (D&C 29:10-11.) In some scriptures the condition of the earth is referred to as "a new heaven and a new earth." (Isa. 65:17; Richards and Little *Compendium*, pp. 185-186.) Whereas the present environment of the earth is known as telestial, during the Millennium it will be terrestrial. (Joseph Fielding Smith, *Doctrines of Salvation* 1:82.) The tenth Article of Faith describes the millennial condition of the earth as "paradisiacal." This word, given by the Prophet Joseph Smith, suggests a beautiful garden;

that is, the earth will become as it was before the fall of Adam. (*Ibid.*, pp. 84-85.)

## The Celestialized Earth

After the earth has served its purpose as the habitat for mortal man, it will undergo a further transformation known as celestialization. Then it will be like a sea of glass having the properties of the Urim and Thummim. By this means, knowledge of kingdoms lower than the celestial will be revealed. (*Ibid.*, 130:9.) This condition is not the same as during the Millennium.

## Millennial People

Sometimes members of the Church have an erroneous idea concerning the people who will dwell on the earth during the Millennium. Mortals will live during this time. Because the scriptures speak of a resurrection at the time of the second coming of Christ and that people will be caught up to meet him, it does not follow that the mortals caught up to meet him or those who are not destroyed at his coming will undergo the resurrection. (*Ibid.*, 88:97-98.) Mortals will live on the earth and follow the same pattern of life that we do now. Isaiah said that people will eat of the fruit of the vine and inhabit houses. (Isaiah 65:21-23.) Children are mentioned in the scriptures as living also. (Isaiah 11:6; 65:20; D&C 63:49-51.)

President Joseph Fielding Smith says that honorable people who presently live the terrestrial law will have the right to life then. It will not be only faithful members of the Church who will survive the destructions before and at the Lord's coming.

There will be millions of people, Catholics, Protestants, agnostics, Mohammedans, people of all classes, and of all beliefs, still permitted to remain upon the face of the earth, but they will be those who have lived clean lives, those who have been free from wickedness and corruption. All who belong, by virtue of their good lives, to the terrestrial order, as well as those who have kept the celestial law, will remain upon the face of the earth during the millennium.

Eventually, however, the knowledge of the Lord will cover the earth as waters do the sea. But there will be need for the preaching of the gospel, after the millennium is brought in, until all men are either converted or pass away. In the course of the thousand years all men will either come into the Church, or kingdom of God, or they will die and pass away. In that day there will be no death until men are old. (*Doctrines of Salvation* 1:86-87.)

Among those of "all beliefs" mentioned by President Smith will be those who "knew no law" or the heathen nations. (D&C 45:54.) These will enjoy the blessings of the Millennium. If among these nations there are those, however, who will not come up to worship, they will suffer "the judgments of God and must eventually be destroyed from the earth." (*Teachings of the Prophet Joseph Smith*, p. 269.) This is in accord with what the Prophet Zechariah said of the nations who were left of those who came up to fight against Jerusalem. (Zech. 14:16-19.)

On the other hand, it is not to be expected that all Latter-day Saints will survive the great desolations that visit the earth before and at the second coming of Christ. The Prophet Joseph Smith said:

I explained concerning the coming of the Son of Man; also that it is a false idea that the Saints will escape all the judgments, whilst the wicked suffer; for all flesh is subject to suffer, and "the righteous shall hardly escape;" still many of the Saints will escape for the just shall live by faith; yet many of the righteous shall fall prey to disease, to pestilence, etc., by reason of the weakness of the flesh, and yet be saved in the kingdom of God. So that it is an unhallowed principle to say that such and such have transgressed because they have been preyed upon by disease or death, for all flesh is subject to death; and the Savior has said, "Judge not, lest ye be judged." (*Teachings of the Prophet Joseph Smith,* pp. 162-163.)

Among the people who will live on the earth during the Millennium will be the lost tribes. They will return from the land of the north sometime near or at the second coming of Christ. The destructions of the last days will prepare the way, said the Prophet Joseph Smith, "for the return of the lost tribes from the north country." (*DHC* 1:315.) We know from the scriptures that the Savior visited them and taught them the gospel and that they have their own scriptures. (3 Nephi 15; 16.) They shall come to the Latter-day Saints and there receive their blessings. (D&C 133:26-34; 3 Nephi 21:26; Ether 13:11.)

## Death

Children will be born and live to the "age of a tree" as mortal beings, but there shall be no sorrow arising from death. (D&C 101:29.) Separation from loved ones today brings sorrow, but those who die during the Millennium "shall be changed in the twinkling of an eye, and shall be caught up, and his [their] rest shall be glorious." (*Ibid.*, 31; 63:5.) The changing of the body will be from mortality to immortality or resurrection. It is said of children that they will "grow up without sin unto salvation." (D&C 45:58.)

For how long shall people live? Isaiah said that men would live to the age of a tree which he believed to be 100 years. (Isaiah 65:20.) *The Doctrine and Covenants Commentary* gives this information on this question:

Some trees grow quite old. An authority of the Forestry Service at Washington is quoted to the effect that the pine tree may attain 700 years as a maximum length of life; the silver fir 425 years; the red beech, 245; the aspen, 210; the birch, 200; the ash, 170 years. The heart of the oak begins to decay when the tree is about 300 years old. When man lives in accordance with the laws of God, and is clean and temperate in all things, there is no reason, as far as known, why he should not live to the same age as the Patriarchs before the flood. (P. 644.)

### Animals and Man

The millennial period is known as a period of peace. "And in that day the enmity of man, and the enmity of beasts, yea, the enmity of all flesh, shall cease from before my face." (D&C 101:26; Isa. 11:6-9.) With Satan's power absent and honorable people inhabiting the earth, war shall cease. (Micah 4:4.) Men will convert their military equipment into instruments of peace and productivity. (Isa. 2:4.) With the Spirit of the Lord upon the earth in rich abundance, the present enmity existing between animals will cease, and man and animal will also be at peace.

### Increased Knowledge

One of the blessings to be received during the Millennium is the understanding of many mysteries that have perplexed man. It is promised that knowledge concerning man and the earth will be increased greatly. By revelation, men will know the truth regarding man's creation.

> Yea, verily I say unto you, in that day when the Lord shall come, he shall reveal all things—
>
> Things which have passed, and hidden things which no man knew, things of the earth, by which it was made, and the purpose and the end thereof—
>
> Things most precious, things that are above, and things that are beneath, things that are in the earth, and upon the earth, and in heaven. (D&C 101:32-34.)

As a part of the restoration of the fulness of the gospel, it was prophesied that there would be a "restitution of all things" spoken of by the mouths of the holy prophets since the world began. (Acts 3:19-21.) Among these prophecies is the restoration of the sealed portion of the Book of Mormon plates, which contain a history of the world from the beginning to the end. These plates will not be revealed during the time of wickedness and abominations, but when the Lord reveals "all things" during the Millennium. (2 Nephi 27:7, 8, 10, 11, 22.) Another prophecy about the Millennium is found in the following:

> And then shall the first angel again sound his trump, in the ears of all living, and reveal the secret acts of men, and the mighty works of God in the first thousand years.
>
> And then shall the second angel sound his trump, and reveal the secret acts of men, and the thoughts and intents of their hearts, and the mighty works of God in the second thousand years—
>
> And so on, until the seventh angel shall sound his trump; and he shall stand forth upon the land and upon the sea, and swear in the name of him who sitteth upon the throne, that there shall be time no longer; and Satan shall be bound, that old serpent, who is called the devil, and shall not be loosed for the space of a thousand years. (D&C 88:108-110.)

Greater knowledge has ever been promised those who seek sincerely, and individuals during this period will receive whatsoever they ask. (D&C 101:27; 112:10; 42:68; James 1:5.) The principle upon which this blessing is received is given in Section 88:63-65. Men today, as well as during the Millennium, should ask only for what the Spirit prompts them.

### Purpose of the Millennium

There will be a great many of the Father's children who will not have received salvation when the Millennium is begun. Men will continue to be taught the truth and be capable of exercising their free agency.

One of the principal purposes for the thousand year reign of peace is to perform temple work for those who are eligible for the fulness of the gospel. From the other side of the veil will come messengers that will provide mortals with names of those who, having accepted the gospel in the spirit world, are eligible to receive the ordinances of the temple. Expressed in the language of President Brigham Young, we read:

Before this work is finished, a great many of the Elders of Israel in Mount Zion will become pillars in the Temple of God, to go no more out: they will eat and drink and sleep there; and they will often have occasion to say—"Somebody came into the Temple last night! we did not know who he was, but he was no doubt a brother, and told us a great many things we did not before understand. He gave us the names of a great many of our forefathers that are not on record, and he gave me my true lineage and the names of my forefathers for hundreds of years back. He said to me, You and I are connected in one family: there are the names of your ancestors; take them and write them down and be baptised and confirmed, and save such and such ones, and receive of the blessings of the eternal Priesthood for such and such an individual, as you do for yourselves." This is what we are going to do for the inhabitants of the earth. (*Journal of Discourses* 6:295.)

## Resurrected Saints

Because the Millennium will be a period of the resurrection, it is improbable that these beings will continue upon the earth as do mortals. Christ will reign personally upon the earth. About this subject, the Prophet Joseph Smith said:

Christ and the resurrected Saints will reign over the earth during the thousand years. They will not probably dwell upon the earth, but will visit it when they please, or when it is necessary to govern it. (*DHC* 5:212.)

During that reign "judgment will be administered in righteousness; anarchy and confusion will be destroyed," and "nations will learn war no more!" (*DHC* 5:63.)

## Two Capitals

During the millennial period there shall be two capitals on the earth. These will be the Zion on the American

Continent and the Old Jerusalem on the eastern continent. (Isa. 2:3.)

## The Salt of the Earth

What manner of saints should we be to inherit the blessings of the Millennium, if alive when it is ushered in?

The early saints were reminded that when they accepted the everlasting gospel, they became the salt of the earth and the savor of men. (D&C 101:39.) President Brigham Young said:

> All Latter-day Saints enter the new and everlasting covenant when they enter the Church. They covenant to cease sustaining, upholding and cherishing the kingdom of the Devil and the kingdoms of this world. They enter the new and everlasting covenant to sustain the Kingdom of God and no other kingdom. They take a vow of the most solemn kind, before the heavens and earth, and that, too, upon the validity of their own salvation, that they will sustain truth and righteousness instead of wickedness and falsehood, and build up the Kingdom of God, instead of the Kingdom of this world. (*Discourses of Brigham Young*, p. 160.)

Salt was used among the Lord's people anciently as a preservative and also in animal sacrifices. (Lev. 21:13; Ezek. 43:24; Mark 9:49-50.) It was a symbol of the covenant made between God and his people. (Lev. 2:13; Num. 18:19; 2 Chron. 13:5.) When salt is used to represent a people it means that they would be an influence in carrying forward the truth of the gospel and thus become the savor of men. But if they should be as salt that loses its savor, they would be cast out of the kingdom. (D&C 101:40.) To break the commandments brings a loss of effectiveness with others and a loss of the spirit and eventual denial of the faith.

## He That Exalteth Himself

The children of Zion, though not all, had sinned against their covenants and were cast out of Jackson

County, Missouri. Transgressions bring chastisement, said the Lord. (*Ibid.*, 101:41.)

He that exalteth himself shall be abased, and he that abaseth himself shall be exalted. (*Ibid.*, 42.)

The Lord had told the saints in this revelation that they did not serve him well during their peace and prosperity, and therefore they lost their present inheritance. (*Ibid.*, 6-8.) In this way they had exalted themselves above his commandments. One of the most serious sins is to become a law unto one's self. To consider that one is beyond receiving counsel from those in authority constitutes exalting one's self. (*Ibid.*, 63:55.)

## Shall Be Abased

The person who exalts himself lacks humility. Perhaps the instruction of the Lord to Martin Harris might serve to explain what is necessary to become humble. In order for Martin Harris to see the plates of the Book of Mormon, he was told that he must no longer exalt himself but become humble.

Behold, I say unto him, he exalts himself and does not humble himself sufficiently before me; but if he will bow down before me, and humble himself in mighty prayer and faith, in the sincerity of his heart, then will I grant unto him a view of the things which he desires to see. (*Ibid.*, 5:24.)

Another requisite for greatness in the kingdom of God is to become the servant of all. (Mark 10:43-44.) Submitting to the will of the Lord is true humility. "Humble yourselves therefore under the mighty hand of God, that he may exalt you in due time," is the way of success. (1 Peter 4:6.)

## Chapter 28

# THE EVENTUAL TRIUMPH OF GOD'S WORK

## (Sections 101:43-75; 103)

Section 101 of the Doctrine and Covenants contains reasons for the persecution of the saints in Jackson County, Missouri. Also, stakes of Zion were to be places of refuge where the saints might gather, but eventually they would return to the Zion of Missouri. (Verses 17-22.)

The saints are the salt of the earth by covenant, but the unfaithful will, as salt that has lost its savor, lose their usefulness in the kingdom. The Lord said that some might be called upon to give their lives in defense of the faith, and of these he said there would come a fulness of joy in the eternal worlds. (Verses 35-40.)

### A Parable

By parable the Lord revealed wherein the saints transgressed in Zion, and a plan by which the saints in Missouri might be restored to their lands. Anciently, religious truths were given by parable, comparable to the one found in Section 101. (Isaiah 5:1-7; Matt. 21:33-46.) This form of instruction is described as follows:

> The parable conveys to the hearer religious truth exactly in proportion to his faith and intelligence; to the dull and unintelligent it is a mere story, "seeing they see not," while to the instructed and spiritual it reveals the mysteries of secrets of the kingdom of heaven. Thus it is that parable exhibits the condition of all true knowledge. Only he who seeks finds. . . .
>
> The word itself, "parable," is Greek in origin, and means a setting side by side, a comparison. In parables divine truth is explained by comparisons with material things. ("Bible Dictionary," L.D.S. Missionary Bible, p. 114.)

The parable in Section 101:43-62 interpreted in the light of Latter-day Saint Church history is as follows: A master (the Lord) sends his servants (members of the Church) into his vineyard (Jackson County, Missouri) to plant olive trees. They are to build a tower (temple) from which they would detect the movements of any enemy who would come to destroy the fruit of the vineyard. The servants did as the Lord of the vineyard required even to the building of the foundation of the tower; however, they began to question the building of the tower since it was a time of peace.

Because the servants were not united in this project an opportunity was afforded the enemy (Missouri mobs) to overrun the vineyard and cause the servants to flee. Upon hearing of this destruction, the master reminds the servants that if they had done as commanded, even to building the tower and placing watchmen (officers of the Church) upon the walls, preparation would have been made for the preservation of the vineyard.. What should be done? One of the servants (Joseph Smith, Section 103:21) was commanded to gather together other servants, the young and the middle aged, and redeem the vineyard (gather together sufficient brethren to purchase land, Section 103:23) for it was the master's, he had paid for it. But someone asks, when should the vineyard be redeemed? The answer was: "When I will," but the servant was to do as commanded in gathering the faithful to redeem in the vineyard. (D&C 101:43-60.)

The revelation continues to explain that the Prophet Joseph Smith had received a seal and blessing. He was proclaimed by the Lord as a faithful and wise steward, a ruler in the kingdom of God. (*Ibid.*, verse 61.) The Lord knew that the Prophet would do as commanded, for he revealed to Nephi that the Prophet would be a dedicated servant, "for he shall do my work." (2 Nephi 3:8.) In the parable just related, the servant did as the master commanded, "and after many days all things were fulfilled." (D&C 101:62.)

### Gather Before the Judgment

The driving from Jackson County did not dishearten the saints from continuing the work of salvation in which they were engaged. Those who could were counseled to continue to gather to places appointed—holy places. These are designated in the revelation as stakes. (*Ibid.*, verses 20-21.) In this revelation the Lord calls attention to the parable of the wheat and the tares explained earlier in Section 86. At the second coming of Christ there will be a separation of the righteous from the wicked. The wheat, his saints, will find eternal life in that day while the tares, the wicked, will be brought to judgment. Eventually all men will be judged according to their works. (*Ibid.*, verses 63-67.)

### Purchase Land

If the saints would return to the land of their inheritance it was necessary for them to purchase land in and around about Zion, a commandent which is repeated. (*Ibid.*, verses 69-71; 63:25-31.) It was intended that the various branches of the Church should contribute to the purchase of lands. (*Ibid.*, 101:71-75.)

### Seek for Redress

The saints were told to importune for redress for the crimes committed against them according to the law of the land. The constitution of the United States was prepared by men whom the Lord raised up that protection might be afforded against loss of property and liberties. (*Ibid.*, 101:76-80; Chapter 24.)

The Lord refers to the parable of the woman and the unjust judge that the saints might know how to seek for redress. (Luke 18:1-8; D&C 101:81-84.) As applied to the saints, they were to seek assistance from the judge; if he would not help then they were to go to the governor, and finally to the President of the United States. If satisfaction were not then obtained, the Lord would in his time deal with the nation. (*Ibid.*, verses 85-91.)

## Results

An informative source has summarized the attempts of the saints to follow the Lord's counsel on how to return to their lands in Jackson County, as follows:

> The Saints did importune the rulers for redress. After having knocked at the doors of judges, they addressed several communications to Governor Dunklin of Missouri. In a letter dated February 4th, 1834, this official acknowledged the duty of the authorities to reinstate the Saints in their homes and to inquire into the proceedings of Col. Pitcher in depriving them of their arms. He also admitted that the entire State was interested in the faithful execution of the laws; "for that which is the case of the *Mormons* today, may be the case of the *Catholics* tomorrow, and after them, any other sect that may become obnoxious to a majority of the people of any section of the State." He proposed to provide protection for the people while suing in the courts and returning to their homes, but he did not guarantee protection in the continued possession of the homes, and the Saints, therefore, wisely declined to return and invite the mob to commit new outrages. (*Doctrine and Covenants Commentary*, p. 652.)

Following these unsatisfactory promises, additional appeals were made of the civil authorities when the saints were driven from the state of Missouri, as this source continues:

> Petitions were sent, and, finally, the Prophet Joseph Smith appealed in person to the President of the United States, but this only elicited the famous answer, "Your cause is just, but I can do nothing for you." (*Doctrine and Covenants Commentary*, p. 652.)

## Section 103

The saints in Clay County, Missouri, held a conference and asked for volunteers to go to the Prophet in Ohio to see what could be done to restore the saints to their homes in Jackson County. Elder Parley P. Pratt wrote the following about this circumstance:

> The poverty of all, and the inclement season of the year made all hesitate. At length Lyman Wight and myself offered our services, which were readily accepted. I was at this time entirely destitute of proper clothing for the journey; and I had neither horse, saddle, bridle, money nor provisions to take with me; or to leave with my wife, who lay sick and helpless most of the time.
>
> Under these circumstances I knew not what to do. Nearly all had been robbed and plundered, and all were poor. As we had to start without delay, I almost trembled at the undertaking; it seemed to be all but an impossibility; but "to him that believeth all things are possible. . . ." (Mark 9:23.) We were soon ready, and on the first of February we mounted our horses, and started in good cheer to ride one thousand or fifteen hundred miles through a wilderness country. We had not one cent of money in our pockets on starting.
>
> We traveled every day, whether through storm or sunshine, and, rain, or snow; except when our public duties called us to tarry. We arrived in Kirtland early in the spring, all safe and sound; we had lacked for nothing on the road, and now had plenty of funds in hand. President Joseph Smith and the Church in Kirtland received us with hospitality and joy unknown except among the Saints, and much interest was felt there, as well as elsewhere, on the subject of our persecution. (*Autobiography of Parley P. Pratt,* pp. 107-109.)

The Lord revealed Section 103 which gave the answer to the most pressing questions before the saints—when shall Zion be redeemed? As the Lord had said before, it was necessary for the members of the Church in Ohio and elsewhere to gather sufficient money to help redeem Zion, and also to organize a relief expedition. If they would not follow the Lord's counsel, they would be as salt that had lost its savor. A great obligation was placed upon the Church to assist to redeem Zion. It was so important that the Prophet Joseph Smith made the following prophecy:

> If Zion is not delivered, the time is near when all of this Church, wherever they may be found, will be persecuted and destroyed in like manner. (*DHC* 2:53.)

Subsequent events proved that Zion would not be redeemed at that time. The branches of the Church were scattered from Missouri into Illinois and subsequently into the West.

### God's Work to Triumph

In a larger sense the saints were promised that if they kept the commandments they would prevail over their enemies and they would eventually inherit the earth. This prophecy is in process of fulfillment today:

> But verily I say unto you, that I have decreed a decree which my people shall realize, inasmuch as they hearken from this hour unto the counsel which I, the Lord their God, shall give unto them.
>
> Behold they shall, for I have decreed it, begin to prevail against mine enemies from this very hour.
>
> And by hearkening to observe all the words which I, the Lord their God, shall speak unto them, they shall never cease to prevail until the kingdoms of the world are subdued under my feet, and the earth is given unto the saints, to possess it forever and ever. (D&C 103:5-6.)

This remarkable prophecy has its roots in the ancient prediction made by Daniel, concerning the setting up of the kingdom of God upon the earth in the last days. (Daniel 2.) The Church of Jesus Christ of Latter-day Saints is that kingdom, and it is destined to fill the whole earth. The keys of the kingdom have already been restored and only time will see the complete fulfillment when it will cover the earth. (D&C 65:2.) The assaults of its enemies will never overcome God's work. There may appear to be times when the Church is overcome by the adversary, but these victories are only temporary. Regarding this prophecy in Section 103, President Joseph F. Smith in a general conference challenged the world to show that this prophecy was not true. Despite deadly opposition, the prophecy is in process of fulfillment, and the remainder will find complete fulfillment, he predicted. (*Journal of Discourses* 25:98.)

When the saints were driven from Illinois after being expelled from Missouri in 1839, they had founded the city of Nauvoo, which grew to some 20,000 inhabitants. At the time President Joseph F. Smith gave his testimony and assurance of the continuance of God's work, the Church membership was slightly over 160,000. Since that time, eighty years later, the Church has grown to almost three million, with an annual increase of about 100,000. Latter-day Saints do not look to the complete fulfillment of the prophecy that the Church will cover the whole earth until the Millennium. They know that when the earth is celestialized it will belong to the saints permanently, and they know that prophecy is in process of fulfillment.

That the Prophet Joseph Smith had a certain knowledge of the continuous growth of the Church very early in the dispensation is indicated in the following account reported by President Wilford Woodruff in 1898. A number of the brethren met in a priesthood meeting in 1833 and testified to the on-rolling progress of the kingdom of God on the earth, and then the Prophet made this prophecy:

"Brethren I have been very much edified and instructed in your testimonies here tonight, but I want to say to you before the Lord, that you know no more concerning the destinies of this Church and kingdom than a babe upon its mother's lap. You don't comprehend it." I was rather surprized. He said "it is only a little handful of Priesthood you see here tonight, but this Church will fill North and South America—it will fill the world."

Among other things he said, "It will fill the Rocky Mountains. There will be tens of thousands of Latter-day Saints who will be gathered in the Rocky Mountains, and there they will open the door for the establishing of the Gospel among the Lamanites, who will receive the Gospel and their endowments and the blessings of God. . . ."

I name these things because I want to bear testimony before God, angels and men that mine eyes behold the day, and have beheld for the last fifty years of my life, the fulfillment of that prophecy. . . . (*Conference Report,* April 1898, p. 57.)

No one could truthfully say that this prophecy, comparable to the one in Section 103, but more in detail, is not also in process of fulfillment.

## A Light to the World

Latter-day Saints by covenant of baptism are to be a light to the world. In this calling, they are to show the way to eternal life. If obedient to this commandment, they join with the saints to become the saviors of men. (D&C 103:9-10.) As the Savior commanded, they should not hide their talents under a bushel, but "Let your light so shine before men, that they may see your good works, and glorify your Father which is in heaven." (Matt. 12:14-16.) This sobering thought suggests that members of the Church may be saviors of men in several ways: first, to be exemplary in their lives that people will see the fruits of the gospel and seek it; second, in being exemplars of the truth people will believe their words when they are taught the gospel; and third, those who labor through genealogical research and the performance of temple work for the dead also become helpers in the salvation of others.

## Promise of Redemption

The saints shall return to the center place of Zion to build the city and temple. The Lord has so stated. (D&C

101:17-19; 103:11.) The living prophets have looked forward to the time when this will be accomplished.

The accomplishment of the purposes for which the Church has been restored is assured, but as to all members of the Church there is not the same assurance. Those who pollute their inheritances will be thrown down. (*Ibid.*, 103:14.)

## Victory Through Dedication

The way to victory and glory, said the Lord, was through three qualities: diligence, faithfulness, and prayers of faith.

Diligently performing the duties and responsibilities of one's calling and keeping the commandments bring the Lord's choicest blessings. In a priesthood revelation the Lord said:

> Wherefore, now let every man learn his duty, and to act in the office in which he is appointed, in all diligence.
>
> He that is slothful shall not be counted worthy to stand, and he that learns not his duty and shows himself not approved shall not be counted worthy to stand. Even so. Amen. (D&C 107:99-100.)

The importance of *faithfulness* in a Latter-day Saint's life and its blessing is given by Elder Delbert L. Stapley in this passage:

> Complete obedience and faithfulness obtain full fellowship in the household of faith and, more importantly, merit joint-heirship with Christ our Lord in all that the Father has committed unto him. (*Conference Report,* April 1961, p. 65.)

President J. Reuben Clark, Jr. admonished the Church to live the commandments and then the prayer of faith would be meaningful.

> Now . . . are you living so that you can go to the Lord with reasonable confidence that he will hear you? Can you go and ask him to heal your little ones? or yourself? or your wife? If you

can, when the time comes you will be happy and you will go to the Lord in faith, and the prayer of faith availeth much.

As I said . . . it has always seemed to me that in our prayer, and in our faith, we should always say to the Lord, "not our will, but thine be done." (Sec. 109:44.)

Now, brethren, do not put off putting yourselves in order, if you are not in order, yielding obedience to the commandments of the Lord, so that when the time comes, if it comes, and I pray that it will not come to any of you, but when the time comes, you will be able to go to the Lord with a pure heart, and invoke his blessings upon you. (*Conference Report,* October 1942, p. 84.)

Every person who serves the Lord diligently, faithfully, and with the prayer of faith, will find eternal life.

## Chapter 29

# THE LORD WILL PROVIDE FOR HIS SAINTS

## (Section 104)

On April 23, 1834, following the removal of the saints from Jackson County, Missouri, through persecution, the First Presidency and other high priests met in council to consider matters relating to the temporal welfare of the members of the Church. The Lord gave Section 104 of the Doctrine and Covenants at that time.

Because of the persecution of the saints in Missouri, it was impossible for them to live the law of consecration, which required that they give their property to the Church and receive a stewardship from which they would support their families and also produce a surplus to be used by the Church.

The Lord revealed that every man was accountable for his own stewardship. He reminded the saints that all things were his for he was the Creator of the heavens and the earth. Therefore, in order for the members of the Church to take care of the temporal needs of his people, they were under obligation to follow his way of making this possible. "But it must needs be done in mine own way" (D&C 104:16.) Then, the Lord declared the important truth that there is ample for the temporal needs of man, but man has the responsibility, as a free agent, to help his fellow man who is in want. (D&C 104:11-18.)

The law of consecration as described in the Doctrine and Covenants is not in force today. The Church, however, has other divinely inspired programs that are designed to give the saint an opportunity to fulfill his covenants in behalf of his fellow men. These programs are also to help him provide for himself, both temporally and spiritually. Preparations for any eventuality, whether individual, local, national, or world-wide, are a part of this over-all plan.

## The Last Days

When the Angel Moroni visited three times with Joseph Smith the night of September 21-22, 1823, important instructions were given concerning the days in which we live. Moroni referred to a number of prophecies from the Bible that would be fulfilled "soon."

In addition to the clarification of these prophecies, the important information was given that, beginning with the restoration of the gospel, the last days had begun. Judgments in the form of destructions caused by war and calamities of various kinds would be a part of these days. (D&C 43:22-27; 45:25-42; 88:87-96.)

## Facing the Future

Latter-day Saints are the most blessed people upon the earth. There are no other people who have the assurance of security that those do who are faithful to the gospel covenants they have made with the Lord. They have the promise of the Lord:

> "If thou wilt do good, yea, and hold out faithful to the end, thou shalt be saved in the kingdom of God, which is the greatest of all the gifts of God; for there is no gift greater than the gift of salvation." (D&C 6:13.)

## Trust in God; He Will Provide

The prophet Isaiah said that in the last days a marvelous work and a wonder would be wrought in that, among other things, there would come an increase in faith that would be equal to all circumstances and needs. Full and complete confidence in the word of the Lord as given anciently and today brings rewards in this life and in the world to come. Early in this dispensation, the

Lord told his people, though few in number, that they had no need to fear, but to do good, and, since they were built on his rock, the forces of evil would not overcome them. (D&C 6:36.)

The strength and power which come from the scriptures are illustrated in what Elder John A. Widtsoe said in a general conference about the above passage:

> I remember reading, when a boy, a helpful passage from the Doctrine and Covenants. Let me read it here in conclusion. As a lad I felt fear, sometimes of men, but more often of the dark outside forces. I often wondered if this persecuted people after all would be able to accomplish all that was pictured in its destiny. Then I found in my reading of the Doctrine and Covenants this passage which has been a joy and a help and a strength to me all my life, for the Lord said to his people in Harmony, Pennsylvania, before the Church was organized:
>
> "Therefore, fear not, little flock; do good; let earth and hell combine against you, for if ye are built upon my rock, they cannot prevail.
>
> "Behold, I do not condemn you; go your ways and sin no more; perform with soberness the work which I have commanded you.
>
> "Look unto me in every thought; doubt not, fear not.
>
> "Behold the wounds which pierced my side, and also the prints of the nails in my hands and feet; be faithful, keep my commandments, and ye shall inherit the kingdom of heaven. Amen." (D&C 6:34-37.)
>
> What do we care for the slanderer or the liar; what do we care for the enemy who arises to defeat our holy purposes? We have the truth, the mightiest weapon God has given to his people, and we shall win, in the end, if we do the things that God requires us to do. (*Conference Report,* October 1923, p. 27.)

The Lord has spoken consoling and comforting words to those who will believe in what he has revealed. His gospel is positive and assuring. From a revelation about the law of consecration, the Lord gave these words of assurance and admonition:

"And it is my purpose to provide for my saints, for all things are mine.

"But it must needs be done in mine own way . . ." (D&C 104:15-16.)

### In His Own Way

Have you ever fallen into the error of rejecting what the Lord has revealed by replacing his word with your own ideas about what he requires? An example may be the seemingly harmless practice of telling lies to gain advantage when the Lord has condemned this practice. (D&C 42:21; 76:103-105.)

"Strait is the gate, and narrow is the way, which leadeth unto life." (Matt. 7:14.) Such a pronouncement of the Savior as the need for baptism of water and of the Spirit to obtain salvation is an example. (John 3:5.) His counsel to the people of his dispensation was that he was the Good Shepherd and only through and by him would salvation come. (*Ibid.*, 10:7-9.) In the present dispensation he has spoken positively on this subject as follows:

"Behold, mine house is a house of order, saith the Lord God, and not a house of confusion.

"Will I accept of an offering, saith the Lord, that is not made in my name?

"Or will I receive at your hands that which I have not appointed?

"And will I appoint unto you, saith the Lord, except it be by law, even as I and my Father ordained unto you before the world was?

"I am the Lord thy God; and I give unto you this commandment— that no man shall come unto the Father but by me or by my word, which is my law, saith the Lord." (D&C 132:8-12.)

The Lord works through his children insofar as they are able to live by his commandments.

## Temporal and Spiritual

When the Lord declared that he would provide for his saints, he was referring to their everyday needs. One of the unique doctrines of the Church is that the gospel of Jesus Christ is to be lived daily. Therefore, the Latter-day Saint believes that the fulness of blessings comes through daily application of the principles of the gospel in his life. Not only is the Lord concerned with the spiritual aspects of life and the future existence, but also with one's daily affairs. He has said, "not at any time have I given unto you a law which was temporal [only] . . . for my commandments are spiritual." (D&C 29:34-35.) Consequently, when a Latter-day Saint thinks of preparing for or earning a livelihood or of the multitude of things which must be done in this life, he relates these things to his spiritual welfare. With this philosophy, he then keeps his mind single to God, as commanded. (D&C 88:67-68.)

Thus we see that, as the member of the Church makes his life a spiritual experience, though involved in some activities that seem to be quite earthly, he knows that his actions should agree daily with the Lord's own way.

## The Law of the Fast

Through his prophets the Lord has revealed that the saints should observe the law of the fast. The money saved from the meals not eaten during the fast should be given to the bishop of the ward for the use of those in need. This amount is known as the fast offering.

By this law the Lord is providing for those in his Church who are in need. Although some may be unable to fast, yet all could fulfill a fundamental purpose of the fast—to give to the Church for the poor. (Joseph F. Smith, *Gospel Doctrine*, p. 243.) President Joseph F. Smith has also told us that there may be some who are unable to fast:

Many are subject to weakness, others are delicate in health and others have nursing babies; of such it should not be required to fast. Neither should parents compel their little children to fast. I have known children to cry for something to eat on fast day. In such cases, going without food will do them no good. Instead, they dread the day to come, and in place of hailing it, dislike it; while the compulsion engenders a spirit of rebellion in them, rather than a love for the Lord and their fellows. Better teach them the principle, and let them observe it when they are old enough to choose intelligently, than to so compel them. (*Ibid.*, p. 244.)

What, then, is the obligation of the Latter-day Saints to this law? The observance of this law is mandatory upon all saints. By this means they are following the Lord's instruction that a certain number of his people are being cared for "in his own way." (D&C 88:68.)

## The Welfare Plan

The law of the fast is a part of the greater law—the Welfare Program. In 1936 it was instituted, based on earlier commandments, to take care of those in need. It is a much broader program than the law of the fast, which was established earlier in the dispensation. President J. Reuben Clark, Jr., said that:

. . . the Welfare Plan is not the United Order and was not intended to be. However, I should like to suggest to you that perhaps, after all, when the Welfare Plan gets thoroughly into operation—it is not so yet—we shall not be so very far from carrying out the great fundamentals of the United Order. (*Conference Report,* October 1942, p. 57.)

Since that day there have been many improvements in that plan, so much so that the needs of his people who are in want are being provided for "in his own way."

Recognizing that the Welfare Program has come to the Church by revelation, the Latter-day Saint is fulfilling an obligation to the Lord when he participates in welfare activities.

There are some in the Church who desire to help the poor in their own way. This practice should not be discouraged; nevertheless, every Latter-day Saint is under covenant to support the Lord's way. The bishop is the common judge in Israel by divine appointment. (D&C 107:74.) The Lord has placed upon him the mantle of discernment by which he may be able to provide for the needy as the circumstances require.

In the Welfare Program, however, the participant contributes to the common good and not to any one individual only. He places his faith in those who administer welfare orders that they will use their best judgment in taking care of the Lord's own. He is not concerned that the needy person know that he has contributed to his welfare. The Latter-day Saint knows that the Lord knows of his faithfulness.

Along these thoughts, Elder Mark E. Petersen of the Council of the Twelve, gave these instructions:

> Well, some people say: "I would like to help the poor in my own way."
>
> I think we all should help the poor in our own way, but I think likewise we should help the poor in the Lord's way, and the Lord has said so in so many words. Said He:
>
> "And it is my purpose to provide for my saints, for all things are mine. But it must needs be done in mine own way; and behold this is the way that I, the Lord, have decreed to provide for my saints, that the poor shall be exalted, in that the rich are made low." (D&C 104:15, 16.)

And then Elder Petersen asked some pertinent questions, as follows:

> How do we measure up? Are we willing to share by paying fast offerings? Are we willing to share by laboring earnestly in the Church welfare program? Or are we going to drag our feet? Are we selfish? Do we love our neighbors as ourselves?

Do we live the way we pray? Are we like the priest and the Levite in the story of the Good Samaritan? Or do we love the Lord our God with all our hearts, realizing that we cannot love God whom we have not seen if we do not love our brother whom we have seen. (*Conference Report,* April 1947, pp. 101, 102.)

## Home Food Storage

Under the Welfare Plan, there is provision for each family in the Church to provide for itself when emergencies arise. Thrift and industry are cardinal principles of the gospel plan. The idler is not acceptable to the Lord. (D&C 42:42.) His latter-day prophets have stressed the need for each Church member to provide for himself. A program to have on hand a year's supply of food, clothing, and other essential commodities is designed so that the families of the Church will have in store one year's supply of necessities to meet such circumstances as unemployment, sickness, and lack of materials when otherwise needed. This plan also envisions preparation for any calamitous event over which man does not have control, such as floods, earthquake, famine, and war.

This program is a part of the Lord's own way in providing for his saints and those who heed this counsel are blessed daily as well as during the times of crises. The application of basic principles of industry by the Church member brings satisfaction and joy as he realizes that he has accepted the Lord's "own way."

## Recapitulation

Latter-day Saints know that they are living in the last days when the Lord's word will be fulfilled. Among these calamitous happenings are war and famine. The Lord has said that the day will come when the crops of the earth will be destroyed. (D&C 29:16.) In preparation for such calamities, the saints have been warned. They have also been provided with certain laws and programs that will test their faith to see if they believe in the Lord's way. In addition, these laws are designed to fulfill specific covenant obligations that the member has to his fellow man under the general commandment to love his neighbor as himself.

> "For the earth is full, and there is enough to spare; yea, I prepared all things, and have given unto the children of men to be agents unto themselves.
>
> "Therefore, if any man shall take of the abundance which I have made, and impart not his portion, according to the law of my gospel, unto the poor and the needy, he shall, with the wicked, lift up his eyes in hell, being in torment." (D&C 104:17-18.)

The living of these laws brings blessings commensurate with the specific law obeyed, and, in keeping the commandments, the member imparts of his substance in the Lord's own way, the Welfare Program. Furthermore, he knows that by observing the law of the fast, he obtains temporal and spiritual blessings for himself, and, at the same time, he is also imparting of his substance to those in need.

> "And it is my purpose to provide for my saints, for all things are mine.
>
> "But it must needs be done in mine own way . . ." (D&C 104:15-16.)

## Chapter 30

# PREPARING FOR THE REDEMPTION OF ZION

## (Section 105)

The fact that the saints in the early part of this dispensation suffered persecution is consistent with other dispensations of the gospel. A characteristic of the true Church is the persecution that it suffers. Physical persecution causing suffering of body was the lot of the saints who were sent from Jackson County, Missouri. In subsequent years this tribulation did not cease. It is true that the form of persecution has changed today, but it remains, especially in some mission fields of the Church. Furthermore the Savior said:

> "And blessed are all they who are persecuted for my name's sake, for theirs is the kingdom of heaven.
>
> "And blessed are ye when men shall revile you and persecute, and shall say all manner of evil against you falsely, for my sake;
>
> "For ye shall have great joy and be exceeding glad, for great shall be your reward in heaven; for so persecuted they the prophets who were before you." (3 Nephi 12:10-12; cf. Matt. 5:10-12.)

### The Ultimate Blessing

To be persecuted for a cause, though righteous, does not merit the fulness of the Lord's glory. The ultimate blessing comes through obedience to the Lord Jesus Christ. Though one may perform good works for his fellow man, if he does not follow Christ, he can not obtain the ultimate blessing. (D&C 84:49-53.) The things of God are known by the gospel of Jesus Christ. So emphatic was the Nephite prophet Moroni on this truth that he said:

". . . for everything which inviteth to do good, and to persuade to believe in Christ, is sent forth by the power and gift of Christ; wherefore ye may know with a perfect knowledge it is of God.

"But whatsoever thing persuadeth men to do evil, and believe not in Christ, and deny him, and serve not God, then ye may know with a perfect knowledge it is of the devil. . . ." (Moroni 7:16-17.)

The celestial law that provides all glory, all mysteries, and all powers is founded upon the redemptive act of Jesus Christ. Acceptance of his atonement comes through obedience to the principles and ordinances of the gospel of Jesus Christ. (D&C 76:50-62; 1-10.) To be truly accepted of the Lord is to follow this path.

## Zion's Camp

Because of the persecution of the saints in Jackson County in the fall of 1833, the Lord gave a revelation, on February 24, 1834, that called upon the Church to organize a company of men to assist the saints in Missouri by peaceful means. (*Ibid.*, 103:30-36.) The Church was to send agents throughout its branches to collect money for the purchase of lands in Missouri whereon the saints might settle. (*Ibid.*, v. 23.)

What has become known as Zion's Camp was to include five hundred volunteers, but, if fewer than one hundred volunteered, the Camp should not be organized. (*Ibid.*, 30-34.) Leaving in the month of May 1834, the Camp enrolled two hundred and five members, but fewer than this number arrived in Missouri, in June 1834, due to fourteen deaths resulting from cholera which struck the group because of dissensions within the Camp. By divine intervention the Camp was protected by a severe storm which dispersed mobbers who vowed to destroy its members.

While Zion's Camp was located at Fishing River, June 22, 1834, the Prophet received what is known as Section 105.

### "The Transgressions of My People"

Uppermost in the minds of Zion's Camp was the redemption of Zion (Jackson County). For this purpose these brethren had traveled hundreds of miles to assist in that redemption. The cause of the persecutions and drivings from that place is reiterated in this revelation. Six months before this time, the Lord had also revealed some information upon this subject. (D&C 101:1-8.)

Obedience to the commandments given for the redemption of Zion would have brought about her redemptionat that time, said the Lord.

> "Behold, I say unto you, were it not for the transgressions of my people, speaking concerning the Church and not individuals, they might have been redeemed even now. (*Ibid.*, 105:2.)

What brought about the condition that made the Lord speak of the Church as being in transgression? His answer is found in the revelations accounting for the persecutions that came upon the people in Zion. They had "not learned to be obedient to the things which I required at their hands." (D&C 105:3.) What was required? The Church was required not only to live the moral commandments, but also to live the law of consecration as explained principally in Section 42. No one was exempt from living that law in that day. (D&C 70:10; 85:1-8.) The members of the Church had been commanded to gather to appointed places where they could live the laws that would bring a fulness of blessings. But in this commandment the Church failed because the members were not united as required by the law of the celestial kingdom. (*Ibid.*, 105:3-5.) Important for all of us is to live the laws of the Lord that are in force at the time.

## Withholding Assistance

The Church failed to live the law of consecration, and, when persecution came, the commandment was given that the branches of the Church should contribute money that land might be purchased whereon the persecuted saints might settle. (*Ibid.*, 103:23.) The Prophet Joseph Smith and other elders traveled among the branches of the Church to obtain money for this purpose. Their efforts were not always successful. In fact, the Lord reminded the people that the branches of the Church must learn obedience even by chastening, if necessary, for there were many who said: "Where is their God? Behold, he will deliver them in time of trouble, otherwise we will not go up unto Zion, and will keep our moneys." (*Ibid.*, 105:8.)

Whether the circumstance is physical persecution as in the days of Missouri, or poverty caused by other reasons, the saints are still under obligation to assist their fellow Church members.

## A Trial of Faith

There are many times when members of the Church have their faith tried. It may be when they are confronted with the temptation to sin by breaking a commandment. To spend tithing money for some other purpose may be an example. Whatever the temptation, faith is tried.

In the Missouri period of the Church, the members had their trial of faith when the Lord asked for money to help the persecuted saints. The men who were asked to volunteer for Zion's Camp had their faith tested also. Those who accepted this call to service and proved faithful to their responsibilities, were accepted of the Lord. (D&C 105:19.)

Relief Society sisters who show their faith by their works find greater opportunity for service in the kingdom. To assist in the welfare of others as a teacher or leader in the Church is the reward of faith. The trial of faith received by the men in Zion's Camp prepared many for responsible positions in the Church. Most of the twelve apostles and many of the First Council of Seventy were selected from that group.

## What Is Necessary to Redeem Zion

The Lord declared that Zion's redemption, the building of the City of Zion, would not be realized in 1834, due to the transgressions of his people. (D&C 105:9.) It was also said that the elders would have to be endowed "with power from on high" (*Ibid.*, 105:11) before this was possible.

Let us consider the Lord's reasons why Zion was not redeemed in 1834 and think of those reasons as necessary for the preparation of Latter-day Saints today that this goal might yet be attained. First, they must be taught the commandments and their duties more perfectly; second, they must have experience; third, the Church membership must be "very great"; and fourth, they must be sanctified. (D&C 105:10, 31.)

## They Must Be Prepared

The Lord said his people must "wait for a little season for the redemption of Zion" (*Ibid.*, 105:9). In the meantime, however, it was necessary that they make every preparation to fulfill this prophecy.

Before the Church was organized there was a preparation going on in the lives of many people who later would make contributions to the building of Zion upon the earth. One of these was Hyrum Smith, the Prophet's brother. The following advice to him is pertinent to all members of the Church.

Build upon my rock, which is my gospel;

Deny not the spirit of revelation, nor the spirit of prophecy, for wo unto him that denieth these things;

Therefore, treasure up in your heart until the time which is in my wisdom that you shall go forth.

Behold, I speak unto all who have good desires, and have thrust in their sickle to reap. (*Ibid.,* 11:24-27.)

Essential to living the gospel in daily life is to enjoy the spirit of revelation. President Lorenzo Snow suggested in the following words the importance of that spirit:

"There is a way by which persons can keep their consciences clear before God and man, and that is to preserve within them the spirit of God, which is the spirit of revelation to every man and woman. It will reveal to them, even in the simplest of matters, what they shall do, by making suggestions to them. We should try to learn the nature of this spirit, that we may understand its suggestions, and then we will always be able to do right. This is the grand privilege of every Latter-day Saint. We know that it is our right to have the manifestations of the spirit every day of our lives. (*Conference Report* April 1899, p. 52.)

## They Must Be Taught

Contrary to the situation that prevailed in 1834 when all members of the Church were converts, several generations of members have grown up in the Church. There has been time for the teachings of the gospel to become second nature to the member. Though priesthood quorums and auxiliary organizations opportunities for learning are made available from birth to the end of life.

The women of the Relief Society are being prepared in facets of gospel living. There is an abundance of instruction in gospel principles and their application in the lives of members through the organizations of the Church.

As a Relief Society member participates more fully, her ability to understand and apply the principles of the gospel becomes greater. The impress made by these Church organizations depends upon two factors. First, the strength of the desire to learn and, second, the skill and dedication of the teacher. It is well to ask if we are following the counsel of the Lord in the way to become instructed—to "seek learning, even by study and also by faith." (D&C 88:118.)

### They Must Have Experience

Preparation for success in learning duties and commandments is closely related to the second lesson to be learned—to have experience. The law of consecration, called the United Order, is one of the laws to be lived when Zion is redeemed. Insufficient experience in the principles of this order as they apply to individual worthiness and the mechanics of operating the order contributed to the earlier failure.

As an example, since 1936, the Church Welfare Program has given the Church considerable experience in the operation of numerous projects designed to take care of those in need. Not only has this type of experience been gained by Church leaders, but also the members of the Church have learned that obedience to the counsel of the living prophets has brought numerous blessings. They have had the principle of work made more meaningful in their lives. Also, concern for their neighbors has been emphasized as a part of living. It is well to ask ourselves what contribution we have been making to the Welfare Program. Have we contributed to the building of Zion upon the earth by making this kind of offering to the Lord?

### Membership "Very Great"

The number of members of the Church in 1834 is unknown, but 1200 Saints were driven from Jackson County, and a few years later when Nauvoo, Illinois, was at its peak, nearly 20,000 members left that place. With the present Church membership of nearly three million and a steady annual increase of nearly 100,000 converts, it is suggested that the Lord's army is "very great," when compared with the membership of 1834.

How are converts added to the growing kingdom of God? First, by a dedicated missionary corps who are generally supported by parents who are thus contributing to the building of Zion upon the earth. Second, by the referral system of helping missionaries receive "golden" contacts; and third, by living the teachings of the gospel so well that people become attracted to the Church.

## To Become Sanctified

Finally, the Lord told the early saints that, in addition to his Church becoming "very great," the members should become "sanctified before me." (D&C 105:30.) Numerical strength without quality of life would not bring about the Zion which is defined as THE PURE IN HEART. (*Ibid.*, 97:21.) In the beginning of this dispensation, the Lord revealed that men become justified through Jesus Christ. (*Ibid.*, 20:29-31.) This justification is brought about by the atonement that he made for man. When men completely respond to the commandments of the gospel, they may become sanctified.

The principle of sanctification means that one becomes so immersed in the life of the gospel of Jesus Christ that he becomes purified, holy. He yields his heart to God. (Helaman 3:35.) This is not the sanctification interpreted as being filled with the Spirit on a certain occasion, but is the quality of holiness that comes through keeping the Lord's commandments. Moral cleanliness and devotion to responsibilities received as a worker in the kingdom are essential to us as Latter-day Saints.

Keeping one's mind single to God is the way to sanctification. Such single-mindedness involves: (a) walking uprightly before the Lord, seeking to know his will through study, praying unceasingly, recognizing that salvation comes only through Jesus Christ; (b) doing one's duty to bring about a change from the carnal to the spiritual state. To be "born again" (Mosiah 27:25) by the Spirit (Holy Ghost) is a qualification to be sanctified. To become a new creature in Jesus Christ is essential to "inherit the kingdom of God" (Mosiah 27:26). The meaning of being sanctified by the Spirit is expressed in Section 88 in the following words:

> ". . . my voice is Spirit; by Spirit is truth; truth abideth and hath no end; and if it be in you it shall abound.
>
> And if your eye be single to my glory, your whole bodies shall be filled with light, and there shall be no darkness in you; and that body which is filled with light comprehendeth all things.
>
> Therefore, sanctify yourselves that your minds become single to God, and the days will come that you shall see him; for he will unveil his face unto you, and it shall be in his own time, and in his own way, and according to his own will." (D&C 88:66-68.)

To redeem Zion presupposes that members of the Church become dedicated to the objectives of the gospel, receive sanctification, and enjoy the power that comes through righteous living.

## Implementation

Among the many privileges of the member of The Church of Jesus Christ of Latter-day Saints is to be a participant in the events foreseen by prophets of old. One of these is the preparation for the building of the city of Zion, the New Jerusalem, in Jackson County, Missouri.

The following words of President Joseph F. Smith give us a picture of what is needed to help in the redemption of Zion.

> "But when shall I be prepared to go there? Not while I have in my heart the love of this world more than the love of God. Not while I am possessed of that selfishness and greed that would

induce me to cling to the world or my possessions in it, at the sacrifice of a principle or truth. But when I am ready to say, "Father, all that I have, myself included is Thine; my time, my substance, everything that I possess is on the alter, to be used freely, agreeable to Thy holy will, and not my will, but Thine, be done," then perhaps I will be prepared to go and to help redeem Zion. (*Millennial Star*, 56:385-386.)

When a Latter-day Saint is committed to this objective, there is always zeal and enthusiasm for the principles and programs of the Church. His life becomes gospel-centered. He listens to and obeys the voice of the Lord through His servants.

## Chapter 31

# THE GENERAL AUTHORITIES

### (Section 107)

One of the evidences to support the divinity of The Church of Jesus Christ of Latter-day Saints is its organization. With the restoration of the true church, there came into existence a church that included the officers and callings mentioned in the New Testament. (For example: Eph. 4:11; Philip. 1:1.) Of the great many Christian churches that were in existence when the gospel was restored, none had the same organization that existed in the Primitive Church. The Prophet Joseph Smith did not copy from the New Testament, but the Lord revealed to him the structure of the Church.

Before The Church of Jesus Christ of Latter-day Saints was organized, the Lord revealed that there would be twelve apostles in his Church. (D&C 18:27.) At that time the Lord said that they would be known by these two qualifications: (1) the desire to take upon themselves the Savior's name with full purpose of heart and, (2) their works. (*Ibid.*, 18:27-28.)

### Priesthood

In the Church there are two priesthoods, the Melchizedek and the Aaronic, the latter being an appendage to the former. (*Ibid.*, 107:1.) The Melchizedek Priesthood holds the right of presidency; that is, the authority to preside in all matters pertaining to the Church on the earth. (*Ibid.*, v. 9.)

It is not the office that gives power to the priesthood, but the priesthood that gives power and authority to the office. (*Ibid.*, v. 5; Joseph F. Smith, *Conference Report*, October 1903, page 87; *DHC* 2:447.)

## Power of Presidency

Included in the right of presidency held by the Melchizedek Priesthood is the power to administer in "spiritual things" (D&C 107:8). The keys of this power are explained in the revelation as the privilege to: (1) receive the mysteries of the kingdom of heaven; (2) to have the "heavens opened unto them" to receive revelation; and (3) receive the presence of God and his Son Jesus Christ. (*Ibid.*, verses 18-19.)

Since the Melchizedek Priesthood holds the keys to spiritual blessings, spiritual influences are available from the heavens through the administration of that priesthood. Elders may call upon these powers to bless members of their families as they approach major events in their lives, such as school, missions, military service, marriage, etc.; to bless the sick; and to perform other ordinances of the gospel.

While the Melchizedek Priesthood is upon the earth and operating in the lives of the members of the Church, its powers are for the benefit of both man and woman. By right of confirmation in the Church, all have the right to enjoy the gifts of the Holy Ghost; to some it is given by the Holy Ghost to know that Jesus Christ is the Son of God and that he was crucified for the sins of the world. (D&C 46:13.) This same information was stated by the Prophet Joseph Smith as follows:

"No man can receive the Holy Ghost without receiving revelations. The Holy Ghost is a revelator." (*DHC* 6:58.)

## The First Presidency

In March 1832, three years before Section 107 was received, the Lord revealed that the First Presidency of the Church should be organized. To Frederick G. Williams, who was to be a counselor in that Presidency, the Lord said that Joseph Smith had received the "keys of the kingdom, which belong always unto the Presidency of the High Priesthood." (D&C 81:2.) Keys constitute the presiding or directing powers of the priesthood. He who holds the "keys of the kingdom" controls or governs all operations of the Church throughout the world. Unto Joseph Smith, who held these keys, the Lord said that he was "to preside in Council, and set in order all the affairs of this church and kingdom." (*Ibid.*, 90:16.) When the First Presidency of the Church was organized, on March 18, 1833, these powers were then held by that presidency composed of the Prophet Joseph Smith, Sidney Rigdon and Frederick G. Williams. (*Ibid.*, 90:6.)

## The President of the Church

The Lord revealed that there should be a First Presidency that are to be "upheld by the confidence, faith, and prayer of the church." (*Ibid.*, 107:22.) Over the years those who have occupied positions in the First Presidency have had the faith, confidence, and the prayers of the Church.

Each president of the Church has come to his calling prepared of the Lord to lead the saints in the temporal and spiritual phases of their lives. He is appointed by revelation and ordained and set apart by the members of the Council of the Twelve.

Over the years members of the Church have recognized the inspiration that has led the presidents of the Church. As firm believers that revelation continues to lead the Church, they believe with President Wilford Woodruff, who said:

> . . . This is one thing I want to say to my friends and to the Saints of God, that without the Holy Ghost, without direct revelation and the inspiration of God continually, Brigham Young could not have lead this people twenty-four hours. He could not lead them at all. Joseph could not have done it, neither could any man. This power is in the bosom of Almighty God,

and he imparts it to his servants to the prophets as they stand in need of it day to day to build up Zion. (*Journal of Discourses,* 14:33.)

On the day the Church was organized the Lord revealed that the entire Church should uphold the Prophet Joseph Smith and receive his word as the word of the Lord, and, if this was done, the gates of hell would not prevail against the members individually. (D&C 21:4-6.)

## The Apostle

The apostle of the Lord Jesus Christ receives at his ordination all of the keys, powers, and privileges of a prophet, seer, and revelator. (D&C 13; 27:12-13; 110:11-16; *Journal of Discourses*, 9:87.)

The apostle differs from all other offices in the Church in being a special witness for Christ in all the world. (D&C 107:23.) His calling is that of a prophet, seer, and revelator. (*DHC* 2:417.) Although the president of the Church is the only one who may receive revelation for the Church, the responsibility of a prophet, seer, and revelator is explained in D&C 107:33:

> The Twelve are a Traveling Presiding High Council, to officiate in the name of the Lord, under the direction of the Presidency of the Church, agreeable to the institution of heaven; to build up the church, and regulate all the affairs of the same in all nations, first unto the Gentiles and secondly unto the Jews.

The apostle has a special right to receive the inspiration to explain scripture, to instruct, and to counsel the saints. (D&C 28:1-6; 68:2-5.)

Unto the twelve apostles is given the charge to open the door to the preaching of the gospel in all nations. (*Ibid.*, 107:33; 35; 112:21.) In all of their responsibilities, the Twelve are under the jurisdiction of the First Presidency. (*Ibid.*, 107:33; 112:19-20.)

## Assistants to the Twelve

In recent years the First Presidency has called worthy high priests to assist the Council of the Twelve Apostles in their manifold duties. These brethren are not ordained apostles, but, in their calling, they have the necessary authority to represent the First Presidency and the Twelve Apostles when called upon. They attend stake conferences, tour missions of the Church, and, under direction, they serve in many capacities to further the work of the Church. In their official calling, they carry out the assignments given to them. When the first assistants were called in 1941, the First Presidency made this announcement:

In the past history of the Church, especially in President Brigham Young's time, it was found necessary for the First Presidency or the Twelve, or both, to call brethren, frequently designated as Counselors, to help carry on their assigned work in the Church.

The rapid growth of the Church in recent times, the constantly increasing establishment of new Wards and Stakes, the steadily pressing necessity for increasing our missions in numbers and efficiency that the Gospel may be brought to all men, the continual multiplying of Church interests and activities calling for more rigid and frequent observation, supervision, and direction—all have built up an apostolic service of the greatest magnitude.

The First Presidency and Twelve felt that to meet adequately their great responsbilities and to carry on efficiently this service for the Lord, they should have some help.

Accordingly, it has been decided to appoint Assistants to the Twelve, who shall be High Priests, who shall be set apart to act under the direction of the Twelve in the performance of such work as the First Presidency and the Twelve may place upon them.

There will be no fixed number of these Assistants. Their number will be increased or otherwise from time to time as the necessity of carrying on the Lord's work seems to dictate to be wise. (*Conference Report,* April 1941, pp. 94-95.)

## The First Council of Seventy

The revelation informs us that there were to be Seventy who would be called "to preach the gospel, and to be special witnesses unto the Gentiles and in all the world." (D&C 107:25.)

The First Quorum of Seventy had its beginning on February 28, 1835. (*DHC* 2:201.) Not long after this date other quorums of Seventy were organized. All of these quorums were under the direction of the presidents of the First Quorum. On October 8, 1844, there were seventy men in the First Quorum of Seventy who were appointed presidents in the organization of other quorums of Seventy. Today, among the General Authorities there are seven men forming the First Council of Seventy who supervise the Seventy quorums in the Church. (Antoine R. Ivins, "The Calling of the Seventy," *The Instructor*, March 1960, pp. 76-77.)

## Equal in Authority

It is revealed that the Seventy, when fully organized as the First Quorum of Seventy, form a quorum equal in authority to the Twelve, as the Twelve Apostles are also equal in authority with the First Presidency. (D&C 107:24, 26.)

This authority pertains only to the possibility, though improbable, that if the First Presidency and the Twelve Apostles would no longer exist, then the First Quorum of Seventy, when fully organized, would then be equal in authority to those who presided over them. (Joseph Fielding Smith, "The Twelve Apostles," *The Improvement Era*, November 1956, p. 788.)

## The Presiding Bishopric

Matters relating to the office of bishop are given in this revelation. (D&C 107:68-76.) The Presiding Bishopric constitutes the presidency of the Aaronic Priesthood holding the keys of jurisdiction over the Aaronic Priesthood. (*Ibid.*, 107:15-17; 124:141.) As revealed, however, all officers in the Church function under the first Presidency and the Quorum of the Twelve.

## Patriarch to the Church

One of the responsibilities of the Council of the Twelve is to "ordain evangelical ministers, as they shall be designated unto them by revelation." (D&C 107:39.) Joseph Smith said that evangelical ministers are patriarchs (*DHC* 3:381). The Patriarch to the Church gives patriarchal blessings to worthy members of the Church who live in missions, or others who may be recommended to him by their respective proper authorities.

## Stake Patriarchs

When a vacancy occurs in the office of patriarch in a stake, the new patriarch is selected under the direction of a member of the Quorum of the Twelve. In the stakes of Zion, stake members are to receive their blessings from the stake patriarchs, when recommended by their bishops.

## The Law of Unanimity

The members of the Church have learned that the General Authorities are inspired as they have listened to or read their counsel in stake and general conferences. They recognize that one reason for inspired decisions in counsel comes from the manner in which decisions are made. The General Authorities have only the interests of the membership at heart and a dedicated desire to build Zion upon the earth. They exemplify the virtues that are the foundation of making true decisions. (D&C 107:30-31.)

## Implementation

The Latter-day Saint respects those who bear the priesthood, believing that there is no salvation in this life nor in the life to come without that authority. He realizes that those who preside over him and his family are representatives of the Lord. It is his knowledge that the organization of The Church of Jesus Christ of Latter-day Saints has the only true Church organization because he has seen the perfect manner in which it operates, and has a testimony of its divinity. Over the years he has learned and, if observant, he has seen the influence of the Holy Ghost as a revelator guiding the decisions of the leadership of the Church. It is his conviction that the principle of continuous revelation operates daily in leading, directing, and guiding the kingdom of God on the earth. All of these things are known to him by the still, small voice of inspiration that convinces and testifies of the truth.

## Chapter 32

# SUSTAIN THE BRETHREN

## (Section 108)

From the revelations in the Doctrine and Covenants many lessons are learned from the experience of early members of the Church. May we assume that instructions given to an individual at that time apply to members of the Church many decades later? When the Lord reveals a principle of salvation to one or to many, the same principle applies to all of us; provided he has not placed that law in abeyance. (D&C 93:49.)

Important instructions for the benefit of Lyman Sherman are recorded in Section 108. These truths are so essential to every member of the Church that exaltation in the celestial kingdom is impossible without obedience to them.

### Resisting the Voice of the Lord

Lyman Sherman resisted the voice of the Lord by failing to observe the vows he had made with the Lord. (*Ibid.*, 108:3.)

Wherein do Latter-day Saints resist the Lord's voice? It may be as it was with Brother Sherman, that the still, small voice is resisted when it brings assurance that The Church of Jesus Christ of Latter-day Saints is God's organization on the earth. It may be resisted when the Spirit whispers, when a choice must be made between other activities and attending to one's responsibilities in the Church (attendance at appointed meetings, performance of Church activities when scheduled), that one should place the kingdom of God first. It may be resisted when one's inclination to observe the various laws of the gospel, such as the Word of Wisdom, tithing, honesty, and so forth, is ignored in favor of spending the Lord's money for some pleasure, or lying in order to gain some advantage. There are numerous ways in which one may resist the voice of the Lord.

### Repentance

In Brother Sherman's case we have an example of the Lord's concern for the repentant. This principle requires that the individual who has repented of his sins should be prepared to keep the covenants he has made with the Lord. Forgiveness comes from the Lord, as it did to Brother Sherman. (*Ibid.*, verse 1.) It is certain that when the Lord said to him "be more careful henceforth in observing your vows" (*Ibid.*, verse 3), this same counsel could be said to every member of the Church.

### Your Vows

The word *vow* or *vows*, as used in the Doctrine and Covenants, follows the dictionary definition. A vow is a solemn promise or pledge, especially one made to God in which the person dedicates himself to service or a way of life. The word is used in association with words having similar meanings, such as covenants, contracts, bonds, obligations, oaths, and performances. It can be rightly said that every person who has accepted membership into the Church has made vows whereby he will abide by the laws of that kingdom. (*Ibid.*, 41:5.) These covenants are to be observed "in righteousness on all days and at all times." (*Ibid.*, 59:11.)

### Premortal Vows

In the Great Council convened in the heavens before the earth was formed, the plan of salvation was presented to the spirit sons and daughters of God. Those who accepted the plan were permitted to receive a mortal body on the earth where they would "work out their salvation." When we accepted the plan of salvation in the pre-earth life, we committed ourselves to abide by its laws and ordinances. (John A. Widtsoe, *Utah Genealogical and Historical Magazine*, October 1934, p. 289.)

## Vows of the Kingdom

Latter-day Saints begin their contract obligations at baptism. This vow includes the determination that the member will serve the Lord and show this by his works. (D&C 20:37.)

The privilege of partaking of the sacrament to renew the covenants made in baptism is for the member of the Church. (3 Nephi 18:5, 11.) These covenants include the following three things: (1) to take upon oneself the name of Christ; (2) always to remember him; and (3) to keep his commandments. (D&C 20:77-79.) In order to fulfill these vows the Lord said:

> And the members shall manifest before the church, and also before the elders, by a godly walk and conversation, that they are worthy of it, that there may be works and faith agreeable to the holy scriptures—walking in holiness before the Lord. (*Ibid.*, 20:69.)

Those who receive the Melchizedek Priesthood make an "oath and covenant" (*Ibid.*, 84:40) that they will honor that priesthood. (*Ibid.*, 84:33-41.)

In the House of the Lord members of the Church have an additional privilege to make sacred covenants with him. President Joseph F. Smith, sixth President of the Church, in these words mentions some of these vows and the importance of observing them:

> We enter into covenants with the Lord that we will keep ourselves pure and unspotted from the world. We have agreed before God, angels and witnesses, in sacred places, that we will not commit adultery, will not lie, that we will not steal or bear false witness against our neighbor, or take advantage of the

weak, that we will help and sustain our fellow men in the right, and take such a course as will prove effectual in helping the weak to overcome their weaknesses and bring themselves into subjection to the requirements of heaven. We cannot neglect, slight, or depart from the spirit, meaning, intent and purpose, of these covenants and agreements, that we have entered into with our Father in Heaven, without shearing ourselves of our glory, strength, right and title to his blessings, and to the gifts and manifestations of his Spirit. (*Improvement Era* 9:813.)

## Importance of Vows

The Lord has declared by revelation that only those ordinances performed by his priesthood at the time the recipients make vows, contracts, and covenants, remain in force when men are dead. All others "are of no efficacy, virtue, or force in and after the resurrection from the dead." (D&C 132:7.)

The person who turns away from the vow he has made with the Lord will find not only a loss of the promised blessings but cursings. (D&C 41:1; 124:48.) It is man who turns from the covenant, not the Lord.

## Strengthen Your Brethren

On one occasion, when the Israelites were brought out of Egyptian bondage, they were obliged to fight against Amalek. Moses commanded Joshua and some men to fight Amalek. When Moses held up his hands, Israel prevailed, when his hands came down, Amalek prevailed. Victory came to Israel because Moses was insistent in keeping his hands up until Israel won the victory.

But Moses' hands were heavy; and they took a stone, and put it under him, and he sat thereon; and Aaron and Hur stayed up his hands, the one on the one side, and the other on the other side; and his hands were steady until the going down of the sun. (Exodus 17:12.)

And so it has always been. When the Lord's anointed has been supported by the people, the people also progress. When a bearer of the priesthhood acts in his calling to further the kingdom of God on the earth, he is performing service as though the Lord were doing it. (D&C 84:35-38.) Symbolically, the saints covenant to support their leaders when they raise their hands to the square to sustain them.

When a member of the Church refuses to accept the counsel of the First Presidency of the Church, he lays the foundation for insecurity. Such a person in the days of the Prophet Joseph Smith was criticized in a revelation for rejecting such counsel. (*Ibid.*, 124:84.) What does a person lose in his rebellion against the Lord's servants? President Joseph F. Smith answers by saying that the person "cuts himself off from the privileges and blessings of the Priesthood and Church, and severs himself from the people of God." (*Journal of Discourses* 24:193.)

## Counsel to All

If a person enjoys the Spirit of the Lord, it will keep him from losing his faith and turning against the servants of the Lord. Some people, as President Joseph F. Smith said, will become critical because they "consider the small, mostly unintentionally committed errors of its officers, rather than the broader and more important labors" performed by them. (*Gospel Doctrine*, p. 254.)

There are some specific things that members may do in sustaining those who preside over them. The Lord refers to these ways in the revelation to Elder Sherman, as follows:

> Therefore, strengthen your brethren in all your conversation, in all your prayers, in all your exhortations, and in all your doings. (D&C 108:7.)

## In All Your Conversations

True loyalty to our friends and to our leaders is put to the test when we are not with them, when we have the opportunity to express our feelings to others about them. In all our conversations we are admonished to sustain those who preside over us. To speak falsehoods or rumors about someone is contrary to the principle of love of neighbor, a commandment under which we are placed. Surely one is not following this second great commandment if he is telling anything that would hurt another's character. (Matt. 22:36-40; John 13:34-35.) In fact, James said that if one did not bridle his tongue, his religion was vain. (James 1:26.)

It is believed by some that because something is true about a person this thing can be told. Nothing could be further from the truth than to believe that one is justified in speaking the truth about a person regardless of the harm which may come to him because of it. Who knows but what that person has repented of that fault? The gospel teaches us that if we expect to receive forgiveness for sins we must also forgive others. (James E. Talmage, *Articles of Faith*, pp. 110-111.) We have no right to discredit a person before others. If the Lord has accepted one's repentance, who has the right to mention one's faults to someone else? (D&C 58:42; Joseph F. Smith, *Gospel Doctrine*, p. 263.)

When we speak well of our leaders we increase their usefulness. An obligation rests upon the member of the Church to defend the character of an officer when it is assailed by someone. We cannot undo the wrong of bearing false witness against someone. (George F. Richards, *Conference Report*, April 1947, pp. 24, 26.)

Parents who speak adversely against those in authority do harm to their children. Elder Mark E. Petersen related the case of parents who spoke against the bishop regularly in the home with consequent loss of respect for Church authorities by the children and which resulted in their being inactive. (*Conference Report*, October 1952, p. 30.)

Two questions might well be asked by the person who is about to speak against another. First, what good will it do me to speak this thought? Second, what harm will what I say do to the person about whom I am about to speak?

## In All Your Prayers

The person who has received the testimony that prayers are fulfilled, is anxious that the Lord will prosper the leaders of the Church. True love of those who preside in the Church is shown when there is a sincere desire for their physical well-being, their power to accomplish their calling, and their protection against harm. This desire arises out of one's knowledge that the Lord has appointed the leaders and that the kingdom of God will prosper through these divinely appointed servants. With these solicitous feelings, the member of the Church prays that the Lord will bless the leaders. In a revelation the Prophet Joseph Smith prayed that the Lord would remember the presidents of the Church, that they might be exalted before the people, even that their names would be perpetuated through generations of time by what they would be able to accomplish. (D&C 109:71.)

If a member of the Church does not sustain the brethren by praying for them, it would seem that he lacks the welfare of Zion in his heart. On the other hand, by this practice he builds in his own heart a further desire to accomplish his own responsibilities in the Church. The faithful member of the Church knows that the Lord will answer his prayers in behalf of His servants.

## In All Your Exhortations

Among the ways in which a member of the Church may show that he sustains those over him, is to show his loyalty in public. There are occasions when the Latter-day Saint has the opportunity to make such expressions, such as the testimony meeting, or when called upon to teach a class, or when called to speak in the various meetings. In addition to counseling others to sustain the leadership of the Church, appreciation may be expressed for their diligent service. Although men and women must occupy positions of leadership in directing the work of the Lord, it should be remembered that one also honors the position or calling rather than the individual only. (Spencer W. Kimball, *Conference Report*, October 1958, p. 57.)

When one remembers that the person appointed to office has not sought the position, but the Lord through his servants has appointed him, it should be evident that when respect is not shown to the leader, there is a disregard for the priesthood of God. (Matt. 12:30.)

## In All Your Doings

In order that Elder Sherman and all other members of the Church might understand the extent to which one should sustain the brethren over them, the Lord said that this should be done "in all your doings." (D&C 108:7.) Probably one of the additional ways in which this can be done is to accept the calls made upon the member by those in authority.

## Conclusion

The Lord has said that only those who sustain his servants will find the blessings of the gospel.

> And if my people will hearken unto my voice and unto my servants whom I have appointed to lead my people, behold, verily I say unto you, they shall not be moved out of their place.
>
> But if they will not hearken to my voice, nor unto the voice of these men whom I have appointed, they shall not be blest, because they pollute mine holy grounds, and mine holy ordinances,

and charters, and my holy words which I give unto them. (D&C 124:45-46.)

The members of the Church who sustain all of the officers of the stake, ward, and the General Authorities find rich blessings.

## Chapter 33

# THE KIRTLAND TEMPLE (DEDICATORY PRAYER)

## (D&C 109)

As early as 1832, the Lord commanded his people to build a temple in Kirtland, Ohio. (D&C 88:119-120.) A committee was appointed to obtain funds for the construction of the temple. The Lord had told his people that a purpose of this building was that the disciples might go forth to prune the vineyard for the last time. (*Ibid.*, 95:4.) In the circular sent out by the committee, it was said that this house would be the place where the elders might call a solemn assembly and treasure up words of wisdom that they might go to the Gentiles for the last time. (*DHC* 1:349.)

### The Kirtland Temple

On March 27, 1836, the day of the dedication of the Kirtland temple, the structure, consisting of two stories and an attic, was finished except for the second story. The first and second stories each had two pulpits, one at each end, consisting of four different compartments, one consisting of four different compartments, one arising above and a little behind the next one and each capable of seating three persons. One set of the pulpits was for the Melchizedek Priesthood while the one at the other end of the room was for the Aaronic Priesthood. By means of curtains or veils hanging from the ceiling, each room could be divided into four compartments or classes. The doctrine of baptism for the dead had not been revealed at this time, consequently there was no baptismal font in the building. The building was, however, constructed to suit and accommodate the various quorums of the priesthood and the worship of the Church at that time. In the attic, five rooms were built for the holding of school and the use of different quorums of the priesthood.

## Dedicatory Service

The dedicatory service consisted of praying, congregational singing, preaching, testimony bearing, and the dedication of the building by the reading of the prayer given by revelation. Following the prayer the congregation was led in the Hosanna Shout. An important part of the service was the approval of the General Authorities under the law of common consent. It was upon this occasion that the Prophet Joseph Smith asked the people to sustain the twelve apostles as prophets, seers, and revelators. (*DHC* 2:410-428.) Many spiritual manifestations were observed during the day.

## Section 109

Section 109 of the Doctrine and Covenants, the dedicatory prayer for the Kirtland Temple, was received by revelation. (*DHC* 2:420.) Although this prayer was given for a special purpose, there are many elements in it which may assist members of the Church to understand the two following aspects of prayer: (1) prayer form, and (2) prayer content. It is understood that prayer should be appropriate to the occasion and should come from the heart. Particularly where members of the Church are called upon to offer public prayers in behalf of those assembled in meetings, there is suggested the need to use language that expresses the purpose of the prayer. In a study of this dedicatory prayer, one should not consider that all things for which a person should pray are mentioned, because of the special purpose of this prayer. One can learn, however, many important points about prayer that may be beneficial. This revelation is the model for the dedication of temples and other structures in the Church.

## Prayer Content

Some members of the Church are concerned as to how they can keep their daily prayers from becoming formal and trite. If one prays for individual needs only, there is a reason for reviewing the many possibilities for which one might sincerely pray. Section 109 gives many of these points. Some of these elements are as follows: (1) purpose; (2) expression of gratitude; (3) remembrance of others; (4) protection and assistance; (5) forgiveness of sin; (6) the Church and the gospel.

## Purpose

Frequently members of the Church who represent a group or congregation in giving the invocation, mention the purpose for which the meeting is being held. Sometimes reference is made to the faith and diligence of those present.

In the dedicatory prayer one reads a review of the events in the building of the Kirtland Temple. The fulfillment of the commandment to build the temple is mentioned (D&C 109:1-4) and the tribulations experienced amid poverty, "that the Son of Man might have a place to manifest himself to his people." (*Ibid.*, 109:5.) President Sidney Rigdon gave a two and one-half hour address during the service, the purpose of which was to compare the privations and hardships of the people in building the temple with that of the saints during the time of the Savior. (*Life of Heber C. Kimball*, p. 90.) The Prophet also prayed, as we do, for success in a calling, that the solemn assembly commanded to be held, might be acceptable. (*Ibid.*, 109:6-13.)

## Remember the Missionaries

Those members of the Church who have had members of their families serve as missionaries, or who themselves have been on missions for the Church, or who may have been converted through the labors of missionaries, have a strong feeling for the success of those who labor in the mission field. All members of the Church who have a sincere desire for the growth of the Church are anxious to have the Lord's power with his servants. Many verses in the dedicatory prayer are devoted to this subject.

The desire of the Prophet was that nothing which might thwart the progress of the Church would be successful. That those who lied or published slanderous material against the saints might be confounded was a part of that petition. (*Ibid.*, 109:24-33.)

Before the saints had established Kirtland, Ohio, as a gathering place, the Lord promised that when his servants were endowed there would be a gathering to the bosom of the Church. (*Ibid.*, 38:38.) This endowment would be such that they would be taught from on high to perform missionary work. (*Ibid.*, 43:16.) With the temple built, the great missionary program would be inaugurated.

Apparently the endowment referred to in reference to the Kirtland Temple was an outpouring of the Holy Ghost. The Prophet prayed for this blessing for those who would go forth to preach the gospel. (*Ibid.*, 109:22-23, 35, 42.)

## Remember the Suffering Saints

The Prophet prayed that the actions of wicked men against the saints would cease, and that their persecutors might repent of their wicked ways. (D&C 109:45-53.)

The persecution suffered by the saints of the Missouri period consisted of both physical and mental persecution. Although the saints today do not receive persecution from arms or the loss of homes and a lack of the necessities of life, still, in some mission fields, there are possible loss of employment and some forms of ostracism. Latter-day Saints throughout the world may well pray for their fellow members that persecution may cease, but that if tribulations come, they may be able to withstand them.

### Remember the Heads of Governments

Latter-day Saints are known as a peace-loving people. They wait for the day when there will be a permanent peace with the coming of the Savior. (*Ibid.*, 101:26.) They have been commanded, also, to renounce war and to seek peace through the turning of the hearts of the children to the fathers and the hearts of the fathers to the children. (*Ibid.*, 98:16-17.) This admonition to preach the gospel that peace may be generated in the hearts of men is consistent with the truth that surcease from war and calamity is not promised for this dispensation. (*Ibid.*, 1:35; 97:22-23.) Latter-day Saints have the opportunity to pray for the day when the Savior will come, that a new day will dawn upon the world. They also may pray for the rulers of nations, as did the Prophet Joseph Smith, that their hearts and the hearts of their subjects may be softened, that they may accept the servants of the Lord who will preach to them the gospel of peace. (*Ibid.*, 109:54-58.)

### Remember the Leaders of the Church

We have learned that Latter-day Saints, by their prayers, should sustain those who preside over them. (*Ibid.*, 108:7.) In the following words, President George Albert Smith encouraged the saints to do this:

> . . . I hope that we will be found in the lines of our duty, praying for and sustaining our present leaders, blessing them by our kindness and our love, and presenting them before our Heavenly Father in our daily prayers, asking him that he will give them the richness of his love and blessing. (*Conference Report,* October 1934, p. 53.)

Not only did the Prophet Joseph Smith pray that the Lord would remember him, but also his family and relatives, together with the other leaders of the Church. (D&C 109:68-71.)

## Remember the Poor and Afflicted

A purpose of earth life is that man may experience pain, sorrow, and tribulation. (*Ibid.*, 122:7-8.) Through these experiences a sympathetic understanding is developed toward others who suffer.

The dedicatory prayer included the petition to remember the various families of the Church with their sick and afflicted, and also the poor and the meek of the earth. (*Ibid.*, 109:72.)

## Protection and Assistance

Life is precious. We cling to life when sickness or accident threatens the taking of life. The prophecies are abundant that refer to the judgments of the last days, and we see that these predictions are coming to pass. It is our desire that we and our loved ones can withstand these calamities. (*Ibid.*, 29:14-21; 43:22-26; 45:31-33.)

In reference to these judgments, the Prophet indicated that the Lord's predictions would be fulfilled and that we should recognize that the Lord's will would be done. Recognizing that these conditions will prevail on the earth, he prayed that the saints might be delivered from that wickedness. (*Ibid.*, 109:43-46.)

## Forgiveness of Sins

Forgiveness of sins comes through the atonement of Jesus Christ. Latter-day Saints should express to their Heavenly Father appreciation for the gift of repentance through Jesus Christ. (*Ibid.*, 109:34.)

## The Church and the Gospel

In the gospel plan there are many events predicted for the dispensation in which we live. Those mentioned in the dedicatory prayer are events for whose speedy fulfillment Latter-day Saints might well pray. The Prophet prayed on behalf of the membership of the Church that the Lord would have mercy upon the various segments of scattered Israel. He called attention to the need for the Jews to return to their ancient homeland. (*Ibid.*, 109:61-64.) The Lamanites, about whom the Book of Mormon reveals a great destiny, are mentioned as subjects of salvation to be converted to the fulness of the gospel. (*Ibid.*, 109:65-66.) Finally, the Prophet prayed that the rest of scattered Israel might be gathered into the Church from the nations of the earth. (*Ibid.*, 109:67.)

## Thy Will Be Done

Man's understanding is limited. He is unable to see beyond his own vista except through the eye of prophecy. God's sight is an eternal one—from the beginning to the end. He knows all things, and he is all-powerful.

Latter-day Saints have the privilege of learning the will of the Father and of understanding by the light of revelation, insofar as revelation allows. There are times in men's lives when they must accept through faith the unrevealed, and say, as the Prophet Joseph Smith prayed in this dedicatory prayer: "Thy will be done, O Lord, and not ours." (D&C 109:44.)

## Implementation

Latter-day Saints have been counseled from the beginning to express their faith through individual prayer, through family prayer, and, when asked, before the congregations of the saints. They have come to realize that without prayer they cannot receive salvation.

Children reared in Latter-day Saint homes learn to pray. There are times when it seems that there is a need to express oneself beyond the usual requests for individual needs. The possibilities of expressing one's innermost feelings concerning the Church and the gospel are almost limitless. As one comes to understand the plan of salvation better, his desires for success of the kingdom are increased, and his appreciation for what the Lord has provided mankind through the gospel is greatly enlarged.

The dedicatory prayer for the Kirtland Temple, given by revelation, is a source of inspiration for those who seek to enlarge their prayer possibilities. Out of this revelation, one may receive confirmation of matters about which he has prayed and may also learn of other opportunities which, apparently, the Lord would have us understand. Might it not be well seriously to consider further expressions of gratitude for the numerous privileges that are ours? One need not mention all possible prayer elements in a given prayer, but perhaps one or more new items may be spoken, to be replaced by other thoughts in subsequent prayers as the Spirit may direct. The Lord has said that he who obeys his ordinances and prays with a contrite spirit is accepted of him. (D&C 52:15.)

## Chapter 34

# THE RESTORATION OF THE KEYS OF THE PRIESTHOOD

## (Section 110)

Without the priesthood there would not be The Church of Jesus Christ of Latter-day Saints. Although the priesthood was restored by John the Baptist, and Peter, James, and John, it was necessary that the keys of the priesthood be restored to direct the use of the priesthood for salvation purposes.

With the dedication of the Kirtland Temple, on March 27, 1836, a structure known as the House of the Lord was available that priesthood keys might be given to man again. When one considers that the inhabitants of the earth were without divine authority for many centuries and, thus were without the knowledge of God, the importance of restoring the priesthood may be appreciated. (D&C 84:20.) Without the knowledge of God—that is not only the knowledge of the true God, but also the means by which a faithful man may reach his eternal destiny—the purpose of man's earth-life would be thwarted.

### Keys of the Priesthood Restored

On Sunday, April 3, 1836, one week after the dedication of the Kirtland Temple, four personages appeared to Joseph Smith and Oliver Cowdery. These resurrected beings were: Jesus Christ, Moses, Elias, and Elijah. One other account appears in sacred history when beings from the other side of the veil appeared for a similar purpose. During his mortal ministry, the Savior took his apostles, Peter, James, and John, with him on the mount where there appeared Moses and Elias. (Matt. 17:1-8.) For what purpose did the Savior, Moses, and Elijah meet with these apostles? President Joseph Fielding Smith provides us with this answer:

. . . When Moses and Elijah came to the Savior and to Peter, James, and John upon the Mount, what was their coming for? Was it just some spiritual manifestation to strengthen these three apostles? Or did they come merely to give comfort unto the Son of God in his ministry and to prepare him for his crucifixion? No! That was not the purpose. I will read it to you. The Prophet Joseph Smith has explained it as follows:

"The Priesthood is everlasting. The Savior, Moses, and Elias, gave the keys to Peter, James and John, on the mount, when they were transfigured before him. The Priesthood is everlasting—without beginning of days or end of years; without father, mother, etc. If there is no change of ordinances, there is no change of Priesthood. Wherever the ordinances of the Gospel are administered, there is the Priesthood. . . . Christ is the Great High Priest; Adam next." [*Teachings of the Prophet Joseph Smith,* compiled by Joseph Fielding Smith, page 158.]

. . . The Lord preserved him [Moses], so that he could come at the proper time and restore his keys, on the heads of Peter, James, and John, who stood at the head of the dispensation of the meridian of time. He reserved Elijah from death that he might also come and bestow his keys upon the heads of Peter, James, and John and prepare them for their ministry. (*Doctrines of Salvation* 2:110-111.)

## Kirtland Temple Fame

It was prophesied that the fame of the Kirtland Temple would spread to foreign lands and that the blessings available through that temple would be poured out upon the heads of the members of the Church. (D&C 110:10.) Although this temple was repudiated by the Lord when it fell unto unworthy hands following the exodus of the saints from Kirtland, Ohio, the events of April 3, 1836, will continue to bless the lives of both member and nonmember throughout the generations. (*Ibid.*, 124:28; 110:9.)

The Savior as head of his Church upon the earth came to the Kirtland Temple to accept it as his house. (D&C 110:7.) The Church is the kingdom of God upon the earth. (*Ibid.*, 124:27-28.)

## Jesus Christ Lives

In a world gone astray from the principles of the gospel of Jesus Christ, Latter-day Saints stand as testators to the truths restored in that gospel. Paramount above all other truths are the facts that God lives and that his Only Begotten Son is the Redeemer of men.

Joseph Smith and Oliver Cowdery saw the resurrected Jesus Christ in a glorified vision in the Kirtland Temple similar to the vision received by John the Revelator. (Rev. 1:12-18.)

> The veil was taken from our minds, and the eyes of our understanding were opened.
>
> We saw the Lord standing upon the breastwork of the pulpit, before us; and under his feet was a paved work of pure gold, in color like amber.
>
> His eyes were as a flame of fire; the hair of his head was white like the pure snow; his countenance shone above the brightness of the sun; and his voice was as the sound of rushing waters, even the voice of Jehovah. . . . (D&C 110:1-3.)

## Jesus Our Advocate

Following the description of the Savior in the Kirtland Temple, the Lord declared that it was he who was slain for mankind, for he is "your advocate with the Father." (D&C 110:4.) Man alone is neither capable nor does he have the power to save himself from sin. It is the Lord Jesus Christ who pleads the cause of repentant man before the Father. As man's Advocate, he is the spokesman, or intercessor, to bring about salvation from sin. On another occasion, the Savior instructed his Church to listen to him as the Advocate with the Father:

> Saying: Father, behold the sufferings and death of him who did no sin, in whom thou wast well pleased; behold the blood of thy Son which was shed, the blood of him whom thou gavest that thyself might be glorified;
>
> Wherefore, Father, spare these my brethren that believe on my name, that they may come unto me and have everlasting life. (*Ibid.*, 45:4-5.)

By reason of the redeeming sacrifice of Christ, he provides rescue from the effects of sin. Knowing that imperfect man sins, he stands with outstretched arms to all who seek for his pardoning grace. (*Ibid.*, 38:4; 62:1.)

Every member of the Church should be profoundly grateful for the privilege to receive forgiveness of sins through repentance. By entering into spiritual life through baptism, the symbol of the atonement of Christ, the member of Christ's Church need not receive additional baptisms for sins committed. (Repentance is the principle of forgiveness for those in spiritual life.) Every person in the Church needs his Advocate with the Father that he may eventually be clean to be qualified to enter God's presence.

## Moses and His Keys

The second personage to appear to Joseph Smith and Oliver Cowdery was Moses, the ancient lawgiver and leader of captive Israel from Egyptian bondage. In these words, his appearance and purpose are given:

> After this vision closed, the heavens were again opened unto us; and Moses appeared before us, and committed unto us the keys of the gathering of Israel from the four parts of the earth, and the leading of the ten tribes from the land of the north. (D&C 110:11.)

Inasmuch as the ten lost tribes are unknown to us today, we should consider that the use of the conjunction "and" in this verse separates them from the other branches of Israel who are known today; therefore, we should accept the fact that they will return from the land of the north as prophesied, when they are commanded.

Among the other branches of Israel are: (1) the tribes of Ephraim and Manasseh who join The Church of Jesus Christ of Latter-day Saints, including the Lamanites (2 Nephi 30:4-6); and (2) the Jewish people who are returning to the Holy Land.

Five years before the keys of the priesthood were restored in the Kirtland Temple, the Lord promised his people that when they got to the Ohio Valley they would be endowed with power to go forth among the nations to do his work. He also promised them that he would lead them whithersoever he would, for Israel would be saved. (*Ibid.*, 38:31-33.)

## Salvation Through Gathering

There are two concepts of gathering as found in the scriptures. The first is for a people to be gathered out of the world into the kingdom of God. (Rev. 18; D&C 133:4-7, 14.) The second is for those who have accepted the gospel of Jesus Christ to gather into designated places as commanded by the Prophet. (*Ibid.*, 29:7-9.) Later, the Saints were told to gather to holy places called stakes of Zion. (*Ibid.*, 101:20-22.) We are living today in the period prophesied by Nephi when members of the true Church would be scattered among the nations and armed with righteousness and power. (1 Nephi 14:14.)

## Purposes of Gathering

To be gathered into the Church provides the way of salvation. The scriptures and the modern prophets teach several major purposes for the gathering of the saints to designated places. These are: (1) to be instructed in the principles of righteousness and to be obedient to those instructions; (2) to build temples and perform temple ordinances; and (3) to escape the destruction of wars and other calamities.

## To Become Instructed

Anciently, two prophets foretold the time when Israel, in the last days, would gather together to learn of God's ways and to walk in his paths. (Micah 4:1-2; Isaiah 11:11-12.) This fundamental purpose has been taught throughout the dispensation in which we live. President John Taylor once said:

> We stand, then, really in an important position before God and before the world. God has called us from the world. He has told us that we are not of the world.
>
> . . . And you have gathered to Zion that you might be taught and instructed in the laws of life and listen to the words which emanate from God, become one people and one nation, partake of one spirit, and prepare yourselves, your progenitors and posterity for an everlasting inheritance in the celestial kingdom of God. (*Journal of Discourses,* John Taylor, 14:188-189.)

## Temples and Gathering

Temples are commanded to be built that the Lord may reveal to his people principles of exaltation. In these holy edifices the worthy members of the Church are instructed in the ways of God and learn to walk in his paths. It was the Prophet Joseph Smith who declared that the main objective for the gathering of a people together in any age of the world was to build a temple to the Lord where they might be taught the way of salvation. (*DHC* 5:423-424.) Other modern prophets have confirmed this same fact. (Brigham Young, *Journal of Discourses,* 11:161-162; George A. Smith, *Ibid.,* 2:214; John Taylor, *Ibid.,* 26:70.)

## Elias and His Keys

It is recorded that following the visitation of Moses in the Kirtland Temple, the following occurred:

After this, Elias appeared, and committed the dispensation of the gospel of Abraham, saying that in us and our seed all generations after us should be blessed. (D&C 110:12.)

In the dispensation of the fulness of times the keys of all dispensations with their powers, authorities, rights, privileges, and covenants were to be restored. (Acts 3:19-21; Eph. 1:9-10.) Consequently, ancient prophets came to the Prophet Joseph Smith and conferred the keys of their dispensations. (D&C 128:21.)

Elias, who held the keys of the Abrahamic dispensation, conferred upon Joseph Smith and Oliver Cowdery everything that pertained to that dispensation, including the blessings and covenants that were pronounced upon Abraham's head. (Joseph Fielding Smith, *Doctrines of Salvation* 3:127.)

What characterized the dispensation of Abraham, or as it is called in the revelation, the gospel of Abraham? (D&C 110:12.) From the Old Testament and the Pearl of Great Price, we learn of these two promises made to Abraham (Genesis 17:1-9; Abraham 2:6-12): (1) his posterity was to be numerous; (2) through his seed the nations of the earth would be blessed by bearing the priesthood and as custodians of the gospel of Jesus Christ.

With the restoration of the keys brought back to the earth by Elias, Latter-day Saints who seek the highest blessings of the gospel in the temple may receive the same promises made to Abraham. Marriage for eternity provides for the faithful the privilege to have a continuation of the seeds forever; that is the power to beget spirit offspring following the resurrection. This blessing is made possible by the covenant the Lord made with Abraham and his seed. (D&C 132:29-32.) When one considers that exaltation is the purpose for which God made man, and that these keys have been restored through Elias, every Latter-day Saint should be grateful that this power is again on the earth. (Moses 1:39.)

## Elijah and His Keys

The last personage to appear in the Kirtland Temple on April 3, 1836, was Elijah the prophet who lived in the days of King Ahab of Israel. (1 Kings 17; 2 Kings 2.) He was translated in a chariot of fire, but modern revelation states that he was resurrected at the time of Christ's resurrection. (D&C 133:35.)

The importance of his mission in the last days was prophesied by Malachi, who declared that, before the second coming of Christ, Elijah would "turn the heart of the fathers to the children, and the heart of the children to their fathers." (Malachi 4:4-6.) The Angel Moroni told the Prophet Joseph Smith that Elijah would restore the priesthood and would plant in the hearts of the children the promises that were made with their fathers. (D&C Section 2.)

If Elijah restored priesthood keys in our day, what specifically did he restore in view of the fact that before 1836 the Aaronic and Melchizedek Priesthoods were restored? (D&C 27:7-8, 12-13.) The Prophet Joseph Smith gave the answer when he said that Elijah held the key of the fulness of the Melchizedek Priesthood that all ordinances of the gospel might be administered in righteousness. (*DHC* 6:251; 4:211.) These powers are called the sealing powers of the priesthood whereby all ordinances of the gospel become valid by that power. (Joseph Fielding Smith, *The Way to Perfection*, p. 161.)

## Elijah's Powers and Salvation for the Dead

From the discussion above, it is evident that the keys restored by Elijah included more authority than the work of salvation for the dead. It is true, however, that the sealing powers of the priesthood are necessary to make valid all ordinances whether for the dead or the living, but these powers also make possible a welding link between fathers and children. Fathers in the spirit world have the opportunity to hear the gospel, to accept it, and then receive by proxy the ordinances of salvation in the temples. (D&C 128:18.)

### Implementation

In view of the glorious events that occurred in the Kirtland (Ohio) Temple on April 3, 1836, every Latter-day Saint may have the opportunity to work out his salvation in this life and in the life to come.

The appearance of the resurrected Savior to the Prophet Joseph Smith and Oliver Cowdery upon that occasion attests that Jesus Christ is the resurrected Savior. The member of the Church does not have to rely only upon evidence from ancient books; there is modern scripture to affirm his faith. Not only is this information available to him, but he may know of this truth by the power of the Holy Ghost. Furthermore, the Latter-day Saint is grateful that the Lord has committed to man upon the earth certain priesthood keys that make it possible for him to receive salvation. He may participate in missionary work and assist in the instruction of his fellow man in the way of salvation as a part of the gathering process going on in the world. Also, he may receive the promise of eternal increase in the House of the Lord whereby his exaltation in the celestial kingdom is possible. For this intent the gospel of Jesus Christ has been restored in the last days. Finally, through the sealing powers of the priesthood returned to the earth by Elijah, the member of the Church may receive the opportunity to perform a necessary work for his kindred dead. He may also rest assured that the ordinances of the gospel in his behalf are efficacious throughout eternity, provided that his life is lived in accordance with the terms of the covenants he has made with the Lord in The Church of Jesus Christ of Latter-day Saints.

## Chapter 35

# BE THOU HUMBLE

## (D&C 112:10)

The Prophet Joseph Smith wrote that during the year 1837 a spirit of speculation in lands and property of all kinds, which was prevalent throughout the country, took hold of the members of the Church. Out of this practice other evils developed, such as faultfinding, evil-surmising, dissension, and apostasy. He said that no quorum of the Church was entirely exempt from the influence of these evil powers, and that even some of the twelve apostles were overcome with this spirit. Amidst this unrest and apostasy, the Lord revealed to him that "something new must be done for the salvation of His Church." (*DHC* 2:487.) As a result, the first foreign mission of the Church was organized under the leadership of Elder Heber C. Kimball of the Quorum of the Twelve. Consequently, in June 1837, he was set apart to preside over the missionary work in England. The same day the gospel of Jesus Christ was first preached in England, the Lord gave Section 112 for the special benefit of Elder Thomas B. Marsh, President of the Quorum of the Twelve, and also for the other members of that quorum. (*DHC* 2:487-499.)

### A Truth for Everyone

Especially important for Elder Marsh was the following truth:

> Be thou humble; and the Lord thy God shall lead thee by the hand, and give thee answer to thy prayers. (D&C 112:10.)

Throughout the Doctrine and Covenants there are revealed truths which, though addressed to individuals, are nonetheless applicable to all members of the Church. These scriptures are known as universal truths because of their applicability to everyone. Such is the one quoted above.

## Follow the Master

The exemplar of humility was the Savior. He was completely submissive to the will of his Father in heaven. Premortally Jesus was one of the Godhead and was Creator of many worlds before he came to earth. (Moses 2:26; Colossians 1:16-17.) In that life he desired that the fulness of honor be given to the Father at the time of the council in heaven, when decisions were reached concerning the eternal advancement of the spirit children of the Father. (Moses 4:1-4.) In the plan of salvation, Jesus willingly submitted to the will of the Father in becoming the Atoner of man. (John 17:4; Luke 22:39-45.) Every member of the Church should reflect upon the cost of the atonement made by Jesus, for the price was very great in terms of suffering. (D&C 19:15-19.)

During his ministry he became the pattern for all men. In regard to baptism, which he taught was essential, Jesus showed the way by humbling himself before the Father in submitting to baptism. (2 Nephi 31:5-10.)

## Why Humility?

The first answer to a query by the Latter-day Saint as to why he should be humble is that God has commanded men to be humble. The benefits of being humble must also give the answer to the need for this virtue (Mosiah 3:18-19.) What, according to the revelations, makes of this quality the pathway to salvation? Obedience to the commandments is the first essential. (Matt. 7:21.) The Lord blesses the person of humility. In what ways? (1) He "shall lead thee by the hand, and give thee answer to thy prayers." (D&C 112:10.) (2) The Lord's spirit enlightens the humble. (*Ibid.*, 136:33.) (3) "Let him that is ignorant learn wisdom by humbling himself." (*Ibid.*, v. 32.) (4) The promise of seeing and knowing the Lord is made to the humble. (*Ibid.*, 67:10.) (5) His arm of mercy is extended to the humble in freeing them of bondage. (Mosiah 29:18-20.) (6) The weak are made strong and are thus able to fulfill other commandments. (Ether 12:26-27.) (7) The humble receive knowledge. (D&C 1:28.) (8) The blessing of assisting the Lord in his work comes to the humble. (*Ibid.*, 12:8.)

## Lessons in Humility

As the Savior ministered unto all, even to the giving of his life, so we also should become the servants of all in exercising the virtue of humility. (Matt. 20:25-28.) The apostle Paul testified that he had made himself servant of all that he might gain the more. (1 Cor. 9:19.) Might not Latter-day Saints develop the quality of humility, as commanded, in order that they also "might gain the more," even life eternal?

Six months after the Church was organized, the Lord gave a revelation for the benefit of Thomas B. Marsh, the same person who is the subject of the revelation from which the scripture-theme of this chapter is taken. He was counseled to govern his house in meekness. (D&C 31:9.) But he failed to be sufficiently humble when his wife was convicted of a dishonest deed. As a result, Brother Marsh, in a period of disaffection, left the Church because of his lack of humility. Due to his pride and arrogance and unwillingness to follow the leadership of the Church, he apostatized while president of the Quorum of the Twelve in 1838.

## How to Develop Humility

Among the ways by which the virtue of humility may be acquired are the following: (1) by placing one's full trust in Jesus Christ as his Atoner; (2) by fasting and prayer; (3) through diligent study of the plan of salvation; (4) by being teachable; and (5) by elimination of vices opposed to humility.

### Trust in Christ

The first principle of the gospel is faith in Jesus Christ as the Only Begotten Son of God. As the Savior of men through the atonement he satisfies the demands of justice and mercy for all men. (Alma 42:5-15; Moroni 7:39-42.) The humble person recognizes that there is no salvation in this world nor in the world to come without faith in Christ as his Redeemer. (2 Nephi 9:6-13.)

### Fasting and Prayer

One of the most beneficial practices to develop humility is to place oneself in subjection to the Father through fasting and prayer. By fasting one shows his willingness to subject his physical appetite to his own will and to God's will by keeping the commandment. Sometimes one must force himself to obey and thus, in gaining one victory, he is prepared for other accomplishments. President Brigham Young once said that if a person did not feel like praying, he should get down on his knees and stay there until he felt like it. (*Journal of Discourses* 16:28.) By yielding one's heart to God in fasting and praying, one becomes stronger in faith and humility. (Helaman 3:55.)

### Diligent Study

It seems inconsistent to believe that a member of the Church can be ignorant of the principles of the gospel and remain fully subject to the Father. Certainly, no man can be saved in ignorance. (D&C 131:6.) To do the will of the Father, it is necessary to know what his will is. The Prophet Joseph Smith said that if a person did not get knowledge, he would be brought into captivity by some evil power from the other world. (*DHC* 4:588.)

The humble person is he who has a deep, abiding faith in the Lord. Elder John A. Widtsoe has pointed out that,

> . . . The extent of a person's faith depends in part on the amount of his knowledge.
>
> The degree of faith possessed by any man depends not upon the extent of his knowledge, but upon the certainty of his knowledge, which leads to the proper use of his knowledge. (*Joseph Smith,* p. 163.)

An important factor in having the assurance of gospel truth is not only to have an academic knowledge of the gospel, but also to receive the Spirit of the Lord testifying of its truth. President Brigham Young, in this way, admonished the saints to receive this blessing:

> Let us be humble, fervent, submissive, yielding ourselves to the will of the Lord, and there is no danger but that we shall have His Spirit to guide us. (*Journal of Discourses* 13:155.)

## Being Teachable

An important phase of humility is teachableness; that is, the ability to place oneself in harmony with the principles of the gospel. The person who is unteachable, hard to accept revelation, lacks the necessary humility. The comparison between the adult who is saved in the kingdom of God and the little child, best illustrates the quality of teachableness and the need for it. The Savior placed a child before his disciples and gave two requirements for them to enter the kingdom of heaven; (1) to become converted, and (2) to become as little children. His closing point was:

> Whosoever therefore shall humble himself as this little child, the same is greatest in the kingdom of heaven. (Matt. 18:1-4.)

Reliance upon the scriptures was enjoined upon the Church by the Twelve Apostles, in 1838, as follows:

> Be careful that you teach not for the word of God the commandments of men, nor the doctrines of men, nor the ordinances of men, inasmuch as you are God's messengers. Study the word of God, and preach it and not your opinions, for no man's opinion is worth a straw. Advance no principle but what you can prove, for one scriptural proof is worth ten thousand opinions. (*DHC* 3:395-396.)

## Elimination of Vices

The last suggestion as to how one may develop the quality of humility is to eliminate every barrier to one's success in that development. The vice found in the revelations that is opposed to humility is inordinate pride. Inordinate pride has several manifestations, such as boasting and vainglory.

Pride is condemned in the scriptures because it is the opposite of humility. It is self esteem arising out of one's possessions, position, or accomplishments. The apostle John wrote:

> Love not the world, neither the things that are in the world. If any man love the world, the love of the Father is not in him.
>
> For all that is in the world, the lust of the flesh, and the lust of the eyes, and the pride of life, is not of the Father, but is of the world. (1 John 2:15-16.)

Boasting is a manifestation of pride. When people boast about their wealth, education, business ability, physical prowess, or works of righteousness, they lack humility.

Vainglory is extreme self-pride or excessive ostentatious vanity. The apostle Paul counseled nothing be done in vainglory but that all should esteem others better than themselves. (Phil. 2:3.)

## Humility Is Strength

The gospel of Jesus Christ extols humility as a prime requisite to eternal life. Submission to the will of God is the key to happiness here and eternal joys in the life to come. As already mentioned in this lesson, the Savior was the epitome of meekness. In his promise to the faithful he declared that, in accepting him, one would receive rest to his soul, for he was "meek and lowly in heart." (Matt. 11:29.)

Service to others is an integral part of the gospel plan; consequently, one may understand why humility is a basic ingredient of that plan, for without humility the greatest service to man would not be rendered.

Jesus' humility did not conflict with his strong condemnation of the Pharisees and lawyers who ignored the spirit of the law. (Luke 11:37-54.) He vigorously taught the truth without fear, even to the giving of his life for that truth. (Mark 14:43-65.)

The person possessed of humility is strong. Living the gospel gives strength over weakness. Assisted by the Holy Ghost the member of the Church rises above the base, worldly vices and, being armed with truth and righteousness, is possessed of a power that may eventually culminate in the powers of godhood.

## Implementation

To be humble requires submission to the will of the Father as instructed in the gospel of Jesus Christ. The objective of this lesson will be realized when those who come within its influence learn why the Lord requires that his people incorporate this virtue into their lives. It will not be accomplished until each person develops a program of soul searching to determine wherein he lacks the qualities that are found in the truly humble person.

## Chapter 36

# THE CHURCH AND ITS PURPOSES

## (Section 115)

When the Holy Priesthood was restored in the last days, the organization of the true Church upon the earth was effected, on April 6, 1830.

One of the confirmatory evidences of the Lord's instituting his Church in 1830 is its name. Despite the fact that hundreds of "Christian" churches were organized before The Church of Jesus Christ of Latter-day Saints, that Church is the only one that carries the full name of the Founder of the Christian religion.

### The Name of the Church

The word of the Lord, as given in Section 115 of the Doctrine and Covenants, made known the name by which his Church would be known from that time forth:

> And also unto my faithful servants who are of the high council of my church in Zion, for this it shall be called, and unto all the elders and people of my Church of Jesus Christ of Latter-day Saints, scattered abroad in all the world;
>
> For thus shall my church be called in the last days, even The Church of Jesus Christ of Latter-day Saints. (Verses 3-4.)

While ministering among the Nephites, the resurrected Savior gave the most complete information concerning the reason for his Church being named for him. His disciples asked him what name should be given to the Church he was organizing among them. The Lord reminded them that they should take upon themselves his name and those who remained faithful to the end would would be saved. Then this message was given to them:

Therefore, whatsoever ye shall do, ye shall do it in my name; therefore ye shall call the church in my name; and ye shall call upon the father in my name that he will bless the church for my sake.

And how be it my church save it be called in my name? For if a church be called in Moses' name then it be Moses' church; or if it be called in the name of a man then it be the church of a man; but if it be called in my name then it is my church, if it so be that they are built upon my gospel. (3 Nephi 27:7-8.)

## Latter-day Saints

The Savior then promised his disciples that since it was his Church, if they prayed for the Church in his name, the Father would hear them. (3 Nephi 27:9-12.)

Appended to the title, The Church of Jesus Christ, is the important name "Latter-day Saints." Because this Church was organized in the last days, it carries this name. As Elder James E. Talmage points out, the word "Saint" has a very special meaning in this title. The word means "holy" when used as an adjective, but as a noun it means "a holy one." Therefore, members of this Church profess to be holy ones. This definition does not mean that the member of the Church is without blemish or blame, but it does mean, as one definition suggests, that "holy" applies to exclusive service in the cause of God. (*Conference Report*, April 1922, page 72.)

As the saints are set apart from the world by a covenant of baptism, so they are a chosen generation, a holy nation, and a peculiar people, upon whom rests the responsibility of living in accordance with gospel truths. (1 Peter 2:9.) Theirs is the responsibility to learn to live in unity, to be of "one accord, of one mind." (Phil. 2:2.)

Latter-day Saints are not peculiar because of dress, looks, or other characteristics, but, rather, due to their religious beliefs and practices based upon those beliefs. Elder John A. Widtsoe once pointed out the differences that make this people peculiar as follows: (1) the belief that the Church was founded on direct revelation from God; (2) the Church is the only true church upon the earth possessing the Holy Priesthood; (3) the body of doctrine and beliefs constitutes a fulness of the gospel of Jesus Christ; (4) the truth that gospel principles must be applied in one's life; (5) the members of the Church have the courage to live its teachings. (*Evidences and Reconciliations*, pp. 41-45.)

## The Gospel and the Church

In the scriptures the words *gospel* and *church* are synonymous as to their purpose. The gospel consists of principles and ordinances by which salvation may come to the believer. The Church, on the other hand, is the organization of these believers. For all intent and purposes when one speaks of the gospel as a means of salvation, he might also say that the Church is the means by which believers in the gospel receive salvation. Without the gospel there would be no Church, and without the Church there would not be the means by which the gospel could be administered.

When the priesthood is on the earth, the Church is the instrument through which that authority functions. The priesthood makes it possible for men to receive salvation ordinances. (D&C 84:19, 26, 27.)

In this chapter, we will consider that when the scriptures speak of the gospel or the Church, they are the same, for as pointed out, the one without the other will not bring salvation.

## A Divine Commission

After giving the Church its full name, the Lord gave a charge to his Church and its members as follows:

> Verily I say unto you all: Arise and shine forth, that thy light may be a standard for the nations. (D&C 115:5.)

To every member of The Church of Jesus Christ of Latter-day Saints the Lord has given this responsibility. Each one is instructed to exert his influence among men that the accumulative light of all members of the Church may be a standard for all people.

It is destined that the gospel of Jesus Christ should be a light to the world—the means by which the nations would receive direction in governing their people in the ways of security and peace. In addition, the gospel is a standard or guide to the members of the Church, and also to the non-member that may seek it. (D&C 45:9.)

## Purpose of the Church

The scriptures reveal that there are three major responsibilities of The Church of Jesus Christ of Latter-day Saints. They are: (1) to preach the gospel; (2) to perfect the lives of the members of the Church; (3) to make it possible for the member of the Church to save his dead.

There are other purposes for the restoration of the gospel, but they may be included in the three major ones mentioned above. If the member of the Church is to let his light shine forth that others may be influenced by it, then it would seem that his covenant obligation would be fulfilled through these purposes. Not just one of the programs of the Church, but all of them are necessary for salvation.

## Preach the Gospel

Throughout this dispensation the Church has promulgated the gospel through a unique missionary program. The contribution of thousands of missionaries to making the gospel known among the nations of the earth, has produced an energetic and devoted leadership in the Church that has helped the work progress.

If the member of the Church is to fulfill his covenant with the Lord, he will accept the inspired statement of

President David O. McKay: "Every member a missionary." All members of the Church do not have the opportunity for a formal mission, but each member may perform missionary work in these ways: (1) respond to mission service, stake or foreign, if eligible; (2) induce nonmembers of the Church to accept the opportunity to hear the missionaries; (3) live an exemplary life that the fruits of the gospel may be known for what they are intended—a happy and worthwhile life; (4) develop a family life that will shine forth, in parents and children, that is beyond reproach; (5) plan that family members may serve in the mission field.

## Perfect the Lives of Members

The second major purpose for which the Church has been restored is to assist the member of the Church to bring his life into harmony with the principal objective of the gospel—the perfection that will eventually bring eternal life in God's presence. (Matt. 5:48; 3 Nephi 12:48; Moses 1:39.)

Wherein does the gospel provide the means by which the member of the Church may perfect his life? By baptism, by both water and Spirit, there is provided the gift of the Holy Ghost that brings innumerable helps to continue along the way to perfection. Prominent among these are the gifts of the Holy Ghost, which are to be sought for after baptism that one may not be deceived. (D&C 46:7-26.)

Organizationally through the Church, manifold opportunities are provided whereby the person may: (1) have fellowship with fellow members; (2) find strength through partaking of the sacrament worthily; (3) receive opportunities for service to others through teaching and leadership positions.

## Learn the Gospel

How can a member of the Church shine forth that his light may be a standard for his family and associates without knowing how to make or improve that light? From the Lord's Preface to the Doctrine and Covenants we find ways in which the revelations have affected for good the lives of those who sought perfection. (D&C 1:24-28.) In order to relate these points to the commandment to study the gospel, perhaps we could put these ideas in question form: (1) How does one know when he errs or makes mistakes that are contrary to what the Lord has revealed? (2) Unless one knows what it means to observe a commandment, how will one learn of what he is to repent? For example, do you know what the Lord requires of his people in the observance of the Sabbath day? (D&C 59:5-24.) (3) May a person be truly humble without an understanding of the principle of humility, as God requires humility? (4) How will one receive knowledge, from time to time, without seeking for that knowledge? Furthermore, will revelation be received for individual guidance and blessing unless the conditions are met that entitle one to revelation? The Lord has blessed his people with the institutional means by which they may perfect their lives.

## To Save the Dead

The final major responsibility of the Church is to provide the means whereby the members may fulfill their covenant obligation to their kindred dead. Without the Church there would not be the means whereby the dead might be saved. First, the keys of this work are in the Church, and without them there could not be a valid ordinance performed. Second, the physical facilities for baptisms for the dead, endowments, and sealings are possible through the Church. Third, a rich storehouse of genealogical data is in the Church.

The prophet Joseph Smith said that:

> . . . Those Saints who neglect it [baptism for the dead] in behalf of their deceased relatives, do it at the peril of their own salvation. (*DHC* 4:426.)

## Implementation

Latter-day Saints belong to a Church that is God-organized and God-directed. They have taken upon themselves sacred covenants that they will live to merit the name "saint." It is their objective to assist in making the Church independent above all things under heaven. They know that this is possible if they individually and collectively seek to unify their efforts to build Zion upon the earth. When they read the scriptures, they learn how to live to fulfill their purpose in life.

Since Latter-day Saints are citizens of God's kingdom, they know they have privileges and opportunities that are possible because the gospel and the Church have been restored to perform three major functions: (1) to preach the gospel; (2) to perfect their lives; (3) to work for the salvation of their kindred dead. Their lives must be a part of these, for they know it is the sure way to salvation here and in the eternal worlds. Their hearts rejoice in contemplation of the Lord's promises, such as this one:

> Therefore, let your hearts be comforted; for all things shall work together for good to them that walk uprightly, and to the sanctification of the church. (D&C 100:15.)

## Chapter 37

# THE LAW OF TITHING

### (Section 119)

The modern revelations emphasize the need for members of The Church of Jesus Christ of Latter-day Saints to build Zion on the earth. (D&C 6:6-7.) The earliest law of this dispensation to assist in the building of Zion upon the earth was the law of consecration. (D&C 42:33-36.) When this law was placed in abeyance, the Lord revealed the law of tithing as the next method of obtaining revenue for the growth of his kingdom. (*Ibid.*, 105:9-10; 119.)

Before the law of tithing was fully revealed, the Prophet Joseph Smith and Oliver Cowdery, in 1834, committed themselves to the principle of tithing. (*DHC* 2:175.) When this law was made known in 1838 at Far West, Missouri, it came in response to this supplication: "O Lord! Show unto thy servant how much thou requirest of the properties of thy people for a tithing." (*Ibid.*, 3:44.) At an earlier period the law of tithing was prophetically mentioned in a revelation while the law of consecration was in force. The Lord said that it was "a day of sacrifice, and a day for the tithing of my people . . ." (D&C 64:23.) (*Ibid.*, 64:24; *Doctrine and Covenants Commentary*, p. 394.)

### A Lesser Law

The law of tithing became a schoolmaster to bring the members of the Church to the greater law of consecration, as the law of Moses anciently was the lesser law to bring ancient Israel to the fulness of the gospel of Jesus Christ. (Melvin J. Ballard, *Conference Report*, October

1929, pp. 50-51.) Although a law may be thought of as lesser, it does not follow that the lesser of the two laws does not require obedience. In fact, all of God's laws are everlasting or eternal in the same way that the law of tithing is declared to be "a standard law unto them forever . . ." (D&C 119:4.) All laws remain forever, yet they may not all be in force at the same time, some serving as preparation to the living of other laws.

## An Eternal Inheritance

The faithful saint lays claim to an inheritance when the earth is redeemed and sanctified. (D&C 88:19-22.) Those who obey the law of tithing are acquiring an inheritance on the celestialized earth. Malachi said that those whose names are found in the book of remembrance are those "that feared the Lord, and that thought upon his name. . . . And they shall be mine . . . in that day when I make up my jewels. . . ." (Malachi 3:16-18.)

## The Law of Tithing

In answer to the prayer as to what constitutes a tithe, the Lord revealed that the members of the Church should pay "one-tenth of all their interest annually." (D&C 117:4.) As Elder Howard W. Hunter has said:

> Interest means profit, compensation, increase. It is the wage of one employed, the profit from the operation of a business, the increase of one who grows or produces, or the income to a person from any other source . . . (Howard W. Hunter, (*Conference Report,* April 1964, p. 35.)

When the law of tithing was received, the Lord required that his saints should begin their tithing with giving all of their surplus property to the Church, and thereafter to pay one-tenth on their income. (D&C 119:1.)

## A Gift or an Obligation?

Whether or not tithing is a gift or an obligation may be answered with the reply that, since the law is a commandment, it is obligatory upon all members of the Church who receive an income to pay tithing. If tithing were a gift, the saint would not be required to surrender the tithe, but he could pay it whenever he desired or not pay it at all. "Verily, thus saith the Lord, I require . . . one-tenth of all their interest annually . . ." (*Ibid.*, 119:1, 4.)

Tithing is, however, a voluntary offering because the Lord does not compel his people to live a commandment. This law is no different from the law of the Sabbath or any of the laws of the gospel. Each person decides whether or not he wants the blessing arising from obedience to the law. (*Ibid.*, 130:20-21.)

## Debts and Tithing

The Old Testament Prophet Malachi expressed the truth that when a person withheld the tithe from the Lord, he was robbing him.

> Will a man rob God? Yet ye have robbed me. But ye say, Wherein have we robbed thee? In tithes and offerings.
>
> Ye are cursed with a curse: for ye have robbed me, even this whole nation. (Malachi 3:8-9.)

Expressed in the language of Elder Howard W. Hunter, we learn the following:

> The Lord has established the law of tithing, and because it is his law, it becomes our obligation to observe it if we love him and have a desire to keep his commandments and receive his blessings. In this way it becomes a debt. The man who doesn't pay his tithing because he is in debt should ask himself if he is not also in debt to the Lord. The Master said: "But seek ye first the kingdom of God and his righteousness: and all these things shall be added unto you." (Matthew 6:33.)

We can't walk east and west at the same time. We can't serve both God and mammon. The man who rejects the law of the tithe is the man who has not given it a fair try. Of course it costs something. It takes work and thought and effort to live any of the laws of the gospel or any of its principles. (*Conference Report,* April 1964, p. 35.)

## Beware of False Teaching

What would you do if you were told by a good member of the Church that although you have an income from wages, rent, and so forth, you should not pay your tithing? This is the way this question was solved by the widowed mother of President Joseph F. Smith when he was but a boy. When she arrived at the tithing office with a load of potatoes as her tithing, the clerk chided her for paying her tithing. Whereupon she said: "William, you ought to be ashamed of yourself. Would you deny me a blessing? If I did not pay my tithing, I should expect the Lord to withhold his blessings from me. I pay my tithing, not only because it is a law of God, but because I expect a blessing by doing it. By keeping this and other laws, I expect to prosper, and to be able to provide for my family." In relating this story, President Smith testified that she had an abundance to support her family and that her family never lacked. Then he said: "That widow had her name recorded in the book of the law of the Lord . . ." (*Gospel Doctrine*, pp. 228-229.)

## Records in Heaven

The Prophet Joseph Smith said that "Our acts are recorded, and at a future day they will be laid before us . . ." (*DHC* 2:26.)

The Church maintains an accurate record of the tithing paid by the members. Not long after the law of consecration was revealed, the Lord made known that a general Church record of all things that transpired in Zion should be made. The names of those who were not diligent were not to be recorded with the faithful. It was said that the "book of the law of God" (D&C 85:5) would not contain the names of this class. (D&C 85:1-5.) The faithful, on the other hand, were promised that they should have their names recorded in the "Lamb's book of life." (Revelation 21:27; D&C 128:7.) This record is maintained in the heavens and contains the names of those who have kept the commandments, including the law of tithing.

Members of the Church should know that on many occasions during their lives they are judged by their bishops to receive blessings the Church may bestow upon them. The principle of tithing is a measure, with other commandments, to determine a person's worthiness.

## Ancient Promises—Blessings Today?

Malachi's words have profound meaning for today. (Malachi 3:8-18.) His condemnation of the people for their having robbed God in their tithes and offerings reminds one of Elder Howard W. Hunter's characterization of the non-tithe payer in these words:

> . . . In larceny there is an unlawful acquisition of the property, while in embezzlement the property which belongs to another is acquired lawfully and then fraudulently converted to the possessor's use.
>
> In order to memorize these distinctions [while in law school], I pictured in my mind, to represent larceny, a masked burglar, sneaking about under the cover of darkness, taking that which was not his. To represent the theory of embezzlement I thought of a non-tithepayer. The Lord's share came into his hands lawfully, but he misappropriated it to his own use. This seems to be the accusation of Malachi. (*Conference Report,* April 1964, p. 34.)

The Lord has said that every man is only a steward over his earthly possessions, for all that exists belongs to the Lord. (D&C 104:13-14.) One may think of the tithe as the payment of rent for the air one breathes, the clothes one wears, or the food one eats; in fact, for all earthly possessions.

### A Challenge

The challenge of the law of tithing is expressed in these words: "... prove me now herewith, saith the Lord of hosts, if I will not open you the windows of heaven, and pour you out a blessing, that there shall not be room enough to receive it." (Malachi 3:10.)

"Prove me" by living my law and see the results! Elder James E. Talmage expressed the point that since man has a need for the material things of the earth to support himself and family, the Lord has promised that the means of acquiring these things are available, but one's life may not be one of uniform increase in substance and possessions. One pays the rental in accordance with the amount of increase received during a given year. As more is received then more is expected, but if less is received, then less is expected. Consequently, all the faithful, the poor or the rich, may be stockholders in the great corporation of God. (James E. Talmage, *Articles of Faith*, pp. 527-528.)

Elder Melvin J. Ballard observed that one should not pay his tithing with the hope that he will be immediately benefited financially. He said the following:

> ... I have listened to the testimonies of thousands in the mission field, converts to the Church, who have had faith in this law, and who have paid their tithing, and the Lord has manifested His good pleasure towards them by bringing a material increase that greatly relieved them of distresses that were pressing upon them. Do I mean to say that a man who has an income of a hundred dollars and pays ten dollars of it into the Church for the Lord's work, can make the ninety dollars go as far as the hundred? Yes, by wisely spending it, sometimes a good deal farther. I have observed it is not brains nor strength that brings material prosperity altogether. It is simply doing the

right thing at the right time that leads on to success. (*The Deseret News*, December 17, 1927, p. 5.)

## "Windows of Heaven"

One of the stirring episodes in Church history was presented to the Church by film under the title "Windows of Heaven." The event occurred in the year 1899 when President Lorenzo Snow received the inspiration to take many of the General Authorities to St. George, Utah to hold conference. While there he received a revelation on tithing. The saints in that area were discouraged because a severe drought had made it virtually impossible for them to plant their crops. The Church was also heavily in debt. During one of the conference meetings, the Lord revealed to the President of the Church the means by which the people at the Church might be blessed. This account is given of that experience:

> . . . God manifested to him there and then not only the purpose of the call to visit the Saints in the South. He told them that he could see, as he had never realized before, how the law of tithing had been neglected by the people, also that the Saints, themselves, were heavily in debt, as well as the Church, and now through strict obedience to this law—the paying of a full and honest tithing—not only would the Church be relieved of its great indebtedness, but through the blessings of the Lord this would also be the means of freeing the Latter-day Saints from their individual obligations, and they would become a prosperous people. (*The Church News,* January 20, 1934, p. 4.)

Subsequently, events proved that the promise of the Lord through President Snow was literally fulfilled in behalf of the members of the Church who accepted the Lord's challenge, and because of their acceptance of the law of tithing the Church came out of financial bondage. The prosperity of the saints and the accomplishments of the Church have resulted because of obedience to the law of tithing and all other commandments.

## A Warning

A person who has covenanted with the Lord in baptism and then fails to pay his tithing becomes spiritually sick. One of the sure signs of weakened faith and loss of spirituality is due to this cause. The neglect of one principle of the gospel invariably causes neglect in other principles. (Brigham Young, *Journal of Discourses*, 15:163.) A purpose of the law of the tithe is that a person may receive spiritual growth from the practice. The law, faithfully observed, has the effect of uprooting selfishness and demonstrating loyalty to the kingdom of God. It testifies to the fact that one desires to become one with the Lord in working for his purposes on earth and in heaven.

## Build the Kingdom

In addition to the growth of spirituality received by the tithe payer, the Lord's work prospers through the revenue from the tithing. The progress of the Church in the erection of meetinghouses, temples, welfare program, missionary work, and many other programs is provided from the tithes of the people. The dedicated Latter-day Saint works for the building of the kingdom of God through the payment of tithing.

## Implementation

The Latter-day Saint who obeys the law of tithing is living a spiritual law necessary for a successful life. Although tithing funds are used for the construction of material things, such as buildings, nonetheless, the use made of those structures, such as a temple or meeting place, is for spiritual purposes.

Not only is the tithepayer contributing to his own spiritual welfare, but also to the welfare of his fellow Church members. The Lord has said that obedience to this law sanctifies the land of Zion unto him and unto us. (D&C 119:6.) In fact, it is revealed that Zion is those who keep the commandments, including the law of tithing. Since the purpose of the members of the Church is to build Zion on the earth, it is impossible to fulfill this purpose without making a contribution of one's means by which revenue is received to further the Lord's work.

The law of tithing has been called the law of inheritance. He who desires to receive a celestial inheritance must give full obedience to gospel requirements. There is no success in this life that does not include preparation for life eternal with the blessings of perpetual posterity in the celestial kingdom.

President Joseph F. Smith has emphasized the importance of the law of tithing in the following statement:

> By this principle the loyalty of the people of this Church shall be put to the test. By this principle it shall be known who is for the kingdom of God and who is against it. By this principle it shall be seen whose hearts are set on doing the will of God and keeping His commandments, thereby sanctifying the land of Zion unto God, and who are opposed to this principle and have cut themselves off from the blessings of Zion . . . (*Conference Report,* April 1900, p. 47.)

## Chapter 38

# THE BLESSINGS OF THE PRIESTHOOD

## (Section 121:26-46)

From the trials and difficulties of a dungeon cell, the Prophet Joseph Smith wrote an epistle to the saints that has contributed three sections to the Doctrine and Covenants. (Sections 121, 122, 123.) In that part of the letter which makes up Section 121, emphasis is given to the condemnation of the enemies of the Lord's people, including apostates. Then follows a change from these condemnatory statements to the blessings received by the faithful, devoted Latter-day Saint.

### Revelation to All

Aside from salvation itself as a gift of God, probably the greatest gift bestowed upon man in this life is the gift of the Holy Ghost. Without this gift there is no salvation. (D&C 33:10-13; 76:50-53.) In addition to providing remission of sins with water baptism by an authorized servant of God, the Holy Ghost, among other blessings, is the means whereby revelation is communicated to man. (*Ibid.*, 19:31; 2 Nephi 31:17; Moroni 10:5.)

By the gift of the Holy Ghost men learn the truth of the revelations. (Moroni 10:3-4.) Among the other blessings, the power imparts knowledge of the plan of salvation to the member of the Church as well as to the prophet. One learns the meaning of passages of scriptures, always subject, however, to the interpretation of those empowered to interpret the gospel. Although the prophets, seers, and revelators (First Presidency, Apostles, and Patriarch to the Church) have the power to interpret the scriptures, yet they are under the overall power and authority of the President of the Church. (J. Reuben Clark, Jr., Address to Seminary and Institute Faculty, July 7, 1954, at Brigham Young University.) No faithful, devoted Latter-day Saint would contend against these authorities on matters of doctrine.

With the foregoing limitation, every member of the Church should receive revelation. The Prophet Joseph Smith said:

> No man can receive the Holy Ghost without receiving revelations. The Holy Ghost is a revelator. (*DHC* 6:58.)

In this same vein, the Prophet wrote that in this dispensation there would be revealed knowledge that had been kept hidden from before the foundation of the world. Furthermore, this period of time was anxiously desired by the ancients, for all things would be made known. (D&C 121:26-32.)

## Vain Efforts

Men are incapable of preventing the Lord from giving revelation to his people, since man cannot stop the operations of the Holy Ghost. The individual by his unworthy actions may, however, prevent the Holy Spirit from giving him guidance and blessings. (D&C 1:32-33; 130:20-21.)

The numerous attempts to thwart the Lord's work in this dispensation have come to nothing. Although individual apostasies among some in high places have made their impact upon others, the Church has continued to roll forward. President John Henry Smith said the following about the work of the Lord:

> . . . Nothing can stay its progress. You and I may fall by the wayside; we may lack the fortitude and faith to endure and fulfill our part; but the work itself has gone on from the day the announcement was made of the administration of heavenly beings, and it will continue in its onward march until every

nation, kindred, tongue, and people throughout the universe shall hear the glad tidings of great joy and have the privilege of accepting or rejecting the same in the exercise of the agency our Father has given them. . . .

It cannot be expected that its mission will be accomplished without opposition. It must meet adverse elements, it must overcome obstacles, it must secure the ground step by step, without fear and without favor, honoring our Heavenly Father, and maintaining the dignity of that Priesthood God has given to us. . . . (*Conference Report,* October 1905, pp. 13-14.)

## Called and Chosen

The Lord has said that many are called, but few are chosen. (D&C 121:34.) His servants have been calling upon the nations to repent. Many have responded to this call, and those who have accepted the gospel of Jesus Christ are chosen, for they are the salt of the earth. They are the savor of men; that is, they are distinctive among men. (D&C 101:39-40; 1 Peter 2:9.) But all who become members of the kingdom of God do not fulfill the requirements to become chosen. Worthiness of life is the requisite to being chosen. (D&C 105:35-36.) Jesus came into the world that light might lead men to the Father. He is declared to be the Light which lighteth every man that cometh into the world. (D&C 93:2.) Then it follows that those who elect not to receive the light have not become aware of the spiritual influences which may enlighten their lives.

## The Things of This World

In a further explanation of the reason for members of the Church not being chosen, the Lord said that they set their hearts upon the things of this world. (D&C 121:34-35.) When one's heart and mind are upon temporal things only, his spirituality is weakened until the things of God are no longer a part of his daily life. Sometimes this weakening process is hastened when men seek the approbation and praise of men at the cost of principle.

When this happens, the bearer of the priesthood forgets that only upon the principles of righteousness is it possible to call upon the powers of heaven. Former spiritual strength is wasted away, and the individual has lost the power to officiate for the Lord and to bless his family with the divine influence that accompanies righteous conduct. (*Ibid.*, verse 36.)

What are some of the things of this world that lead to this condition? In the same revelation, we learn that pride, vain ambition, and compulsion when used to dominate the souls of men, bring a loss of the Spirit of the Lord. (*Ibid.*, verse 37.)

Inordinate pride prevents a person from being sufficiently humble to acknowledge his weaknesses and faults. A domineering attitude does not allow a husband-wife-child relationship full growth in a home. Compulsion was the plan advocated by Lucifer in the premortal world. It has brought hardship and sorrow from the evil it has created in the lives of the dominated.

The following counsel to Emma Smith is applicable to all:

> And verily I say unto thee that thou shalt lay aside the things of this world, and seek the things of a better. (D&C 25:10.)

## Individual Salvation

Each person is saved upon the same principles. No distinction is made between them, for each is a child of God sent to this earth to receive training in the laws of progress. Men are ordained to the priesthood because this authority is the power to preside in the home and in Church capacities. The woman, on the other hand, has the responsibility to bear and rear children. In this capacity she must give her time and talents that the children receive the best training in principles of righteousness. The husband and wife, together, share the responsibility of rearing the children. The mother is entitled, through her faithfulness, to receive the blessings of the priesthood. For this purpose she is married in the temple, where she rceives the principles of exaltation and, in a real sense, partakes of the greatest blessings of the priesthood that God bestows upon his children. (D&C 124:27-28; 41-42.)

## Priesthood Principles

One of the important purposes for which men exist is to perform service for others. Since all men agreed premortally to sustain the plan of salvation, each one is under covenant to assist in the salvation of all men who also made the same covenant. When men or women use their influence to affect for good the behavior of others, they are fulfilling this obligation. The Lord has said that when bearers of the priesthood attempt to affect the behavior of others, they should do so only upon righteous principles. These are enumerated in the revelation as: persuasion, long-suffering, gentleness, meekness, love unfeigned, kindness, and pure knowledge. (D&C 121:41-42).

Inasmuch as women in the Church seek the same salvation as the men, and the priesthood saves both on the same principles, priesthood principles of conduct must be adhered to by both.

## "Only By Persuasion"

The priesthood bearer and those who receive the blessings of the priesthood are counseled to use their authority only by persuasion, not by force. One persuades to his own belief or actions by appeal to reason, and not by force. In terms of the gospel plan, free agency is the basis for governing the souls of men. Force was rejected in the premortal councils as being opposed to the laws of God. One may urge but not compel.

The mother in the home has the rare opportunity to persuade the children to act in conformity with good principles. She listens to complaints, entreaties, and requests, knowing that at these times correct counsel and instruction may be given. In this process one repeats counsel and also the consequences of disobedience to law. The Prophet Joseph Smith was upbraided by the Lord, on an occasion, for accepting the persuasions of men rather than the counsel of God in the revelations. As a consequence, he was denied the privilege of continuing in the Lord's work until he repented. (D&C 3:5-8.) So also does man forfeit blessings by failing to follow righteous counsel.

### "By Long Suffering"

The saints are called upon to bear patiently the ridicule, insults, or even injuries which may come because of adherence to the truth. The Savior suffered insult, ridicule, and extreme pain as no man has suffered. (D&C 19:15-17.) His life in this respect is a challenge to all.

To teach a child of God that gospel truths are worth taking the insults or tauntings of others is a noble task. To learn that truth is truth and will ever remain so, and that the finest quality of soul is to stand up for truth, is a major lesson to be learned in life.

### "By Gentleness and Meekness"

Authoritarian methods of instruction, where the parent or teacher attempts to impose his will upon someone else, are contrary to the principles of gentleness or meekness. Harsh methods of discipline are rarely effective. Fear of reprisal or correction rarely brings desirable results, for fear may generate hatred for the disciplinarian. Quiet conversation without a display of anger, becomes the rewarding method of obtaining results. Is it not also wise to be a good listener to receive the full story rather than only one side? The gentle, meek person seeks to understand, to use gospel principles as guides to correct solutions to problems. His concern is to make the best judgment in all cases by weighing all evidence and, through prayer, to reach right decisions.

### "By Love Unfeigned and By Kindness"

Love of God is the highest expression of love that is possible. (Deut. 6:4-9.) Can a man love God and not love his fellow man? The apostle John answers this question with a question: ". . . he that loveth not his brother whom he hath seen, how can he love God whom he hath not seen?" (1 John 4:20-21.)

Members of the Church are bound together in a bond created by the Spirit of the Lord. Of all people, their administrations should be characterized by love. This love must be unfeigned; that is sincere, genuine, not pretended.

### "Pure Knowledge"

The dictionary defines *pure* as "faultless, perfect, true, and blameless." Pure knowledge, as used in this revelation, includes all of these adjectives. The knowledge that saves is found in the gospel of Jesus Christ—it is true knowledge. The laws of righteousness are perfect, blameless, and faultless. In view of this information, for what kind of knowledge should the Latter-day Saint seek? Without gospel knowledge, it is impossible to be saved, and it is impossible to assist in the salvation of others. What has already been given in this chapter about the virtues that should govern one's actions in his relationship with others, indicates the need to follow the Lord's counsel.

If true knowledge is to guide our actions, then what principle is given for our guidance after we have reprimanded a son, or daughter, or others? The answer is:

> Reproving betimes with sharpness, when moved upon by the Holy Ghost; and then showing forth afterwards an increase

> of love toward him whom thou hast reproved, lest he esteem thee to be his enemy;
>
> That he may know that thy faithfulness is stronger than the cords of death. (D&C 121:43-44.)

If one desires to be "moved upon by the Holy Ghost," it is necessary that his life conform to "pure knowledge." Would the Holy Ghost inspire and direct the father or mother who did not try to use the principles by which the priesthood operates? (Moroni 8:25-26.)

If we are faithful in bestowing love towards our own and others, this promise is given:

> Let thy bowels also be full of charity towards all men, and to the household of faith, and let virtue garnish thy thoughts unceasingly; then shall thy confidence wax strong in the presence of God; and the doctrine of the priesthood shall distil upon thy soul as the dews from heaven.
>
> The Holy Ghost shall be thy constant companion, and thy scepter an unchanging scepter of righteousness and truth; and thy dominion shall be an everlasting dominion, and without compulsory means it shall flow unto thee forever and ever. (D&C 121:45-46.)

## Conclusion

The Lord promises through his ancient and modern prophets that revelation would be abundant in the last days and that the members of his Church would enjoy its benefits. Men who would endeavor to stop his work would come to naught.

Although those who would affiliate with his church would be the salt of the earth, all would not be chosen, primarily because their desires would be upon the things of this world. Some significant promises were given to the priesthood, among them an everlasting dominion with the blessings of the Holy Ghost. The principles necessary to function in the priesthood were qualities of soul, as important for the women of the Church as for the priesthood.

In training children, instructing youth, and in the numerous relationships that exist among members of the Church and others, counsel was given whereby those relationships would be successful. Among these principles of righteousness were: persuasion, long-suffering, gentleness and meekness, love unfeigned, kindness, and pure knowledge. If these qualities abound when instruction, reprimands, and counsel are given, the Holy Ghost will lead, guide, and direct into meaningful relationships.

## Chapter 39

# ADVERSITY

### (Sections 121:1-10; 122.)

As indicated in other chapters, Sections 121, 122, and 123 are extracts from a letter written by the Prophet Joseph Smith from March 20 to 25, 1839, while he and other brethren were in Liberty Jail, Missouri. (*DHC* 3:289-305.) In the *Doctrine and Covenants Commentary*, we find the following about the contents of this letter:

> In the opening paragraph of the letter, the Prophet refers to the fearful crimes committed against the Saints. He hears the cries of orphans and widows; he sees the innocent blood that stains the soil of the State; he contemplates the inhumanity of the people, that "shocks all nature," and "beggars and defies all description," and then he pours out his soul in lamentation before his God, as Jeremiah of old wept upon the ruins of Jerusalem: "O God! Where art thou?" And he prays, "Remember thy suffering Saints." (*Doctrine and Covenants Commentary,* p. 753.)

### Suffering Saints

Why do members of The Church of Jesus Christ of Latter-day Saints suffer? Why does an Almighty God permit sin, sorrow, disappointments, pain, and suffering? Some unbelievers in God have argued that because he permits suffering, he does not exist. Many others have lost faith in God because of tribulation.

As in all cases, to understand the answer to life's purpose, man's relationship to God, and a multitude of other matters, the answer must come from the source of all truth—revelation.

Admitting the presence of suffering and various adversities in life, a fact which is found on every side, it must be allowed that men are better able to endure tribulation provided they know the reason for the adversity! Recognizing this truth, the Lord has provided enough information to give men strength to withstand tribulations.

The Savior said that in this world there would be tribulation, but his disciples could be of good cheer, for he had overcome the world. (John 16:33.) From the treasury of revealed information, what is this message of good cheer?

## Premortal Agreement

The revelations teach that all mankind lived in a spirit world before this birth. In that existence there was contention over the plan of salvation that should redeem men when they were born in an earth-life. Satan sought the honor of God, to ascend to His throne, through a proposal of his own. This plan was rejected in favor of the plan of the Father espoused by Jesus Christ, the Firstborn in the spirit world. (Moses 4:1-4; D&C 19:36-38.)

When the plan of salvation was accepted by the spirit sons and daughters of God, each person covenanted to abide by that plan. Included in the gospel of Jesus Christ is the Father's plan that his sons and daughters might come to earth to receive bodies that they might live under conditions of mortality. We are here! In what kind of an environment? The kind where we learn good from evil; to struggle against evil; to preserve our lives where we may have disappointments, loss of wealth, death of a loved one, sorrow, pain, and other afflictions. It is a place, also, where we may prove ourselves to see if we will do whatsoever the Lord commands us. (Abraham 3:24-26.)

Admitting the doctrine of premortality, we have the basis for understanding the purpose of afflictions and also the fact that we *elected* to come to the earth where these conditions would exist. In fact, we shouted with joy and sang in the contemplation that we could progress only by earth-life to the eternal life that God promised to the faithful. (Job 38:4, 7; Titus 1:2.)

## Opposition in All Things

Among the purposes of this life is to determine whether or not we will be true to the Lord's commandments. (Abraham 3:24-26.) Also, as the Book of Mormon says, since there is opposition in all things the opportunity to be proved is possible. (2 Nephi 2:11.) We are also here to partake of the bitter as well as the sweet. (D&C 29:39; Moses 6:55-56.) Without these purposes, which include our free agency, there could be no existence. (D&C 93:30.)

In the beginning, Adam and Eve received these truths that they might understand the purpose for which they become mortal. Thus they were cast out into a world of sorrow, trouble, labor, and eventual death. But they were also informed that this path was necessary to receive a fulness of joy. (Moses 5:10; D&C 93:33-34.) Eve expressed her joy in this knowledge, for she could know good and evil and the possibility of eternal life. (Moses 5:11.)

President Brigham Young gave us this information about adversities:

> . . . If Adam had not sinned, and if his posterity had continued upon the earth, they could not have known sin, or the bitter from the sweet, neither would they have known righteousness, for the plain and simple reason that every effect can only be fully manifested by its opposite. If the Saints could realize things as they are when they are called to pass through trials, and to suffer what they call sacrifices, they would acknowledge them to be the greatest blessings that could be bestowed upon them. But put them in possession of true principles and true enjoyments, without the opposite, and they could not know enjoyment, they could not realize happiness. They could not tell light from darkness, because they have no knowledge of

darkness and consequently are destitute of a realizing sense of light. If they should not taste the bitter, how could they realize the sweet? They could not. (*Journal of Discourses,* 2:301-302.)

## Adversities and the Faithful

If one is living according to the commandments, may we believe that he is immune to afflictions? Jacob, the Book of Mormon prophet, was told that his afflictions were consecrated for his gain. (2 Nephi 2:2.) The faithful pass through tests to see if they will remain faithful. (Ether 12:6.)

The greatest example of suffering was the Savior. His trials and the taking of the world's sins upon himself with eventual death on the cross, have become the example for all men. (D&C 19:15-19.)

President Hugh B. Brown said the following about the Master:

"... We cannot think of the history of the past and bring to our minds examples of adversity without thinking of the one who stands as the central figure of all time, the Master, the one who was prophetically referred to before he was born as 'man of sorrows,' (Isaiah 53:3), who was acquainted with grief, the one to whom Paul referred as he who learned obedience by the things he suffered. (See Heb. 5:8.) (Hugh B. Brown, *Eternal Quest,* p. 248.)

## Joseph Smith

The Prophet Joseph Smith learned lessons in affliction throughout his life. (D&C 127:2.) One of the important lessons he learned is given in Section 122, a portion of the letter written in Liberty Jail.

The Lord spoke peace to the Prophet's soul in a prophecy concerning his life. Fools would have his name in derision while the righteous would seek wisdom and counsel from his hand. Although the efforts of the wicked would never turn the saints against him, their influence would cause him great trouble. (D&C 124:1-4.)

The Lord had reminded the Prophet that he was not like Job of old whose friends had forsaken him. (*Ibid.*, 121:9-10.) God said to the Prophet:

"If thou art called to pass through tribulation; if thou art in perils among false brethren; if thou art in perils among robbers; if thou art in perils by land or by sea;

"If thou art accused with all manner of false accusations; if thine enemies fall upon thee; if they tear thee from the society of thy father and mother and brethren and sisters; and if with a drawn sword thine enemies tear thee from the bosom of thy wife, and of thine offspring, and thine elder son, although but six years of age, shall cling to thy garments and shall say, My father, my father, what are the men going to do with you? and if then he shall be thrust from thee by the sword, and thou be dragged to prison, and thine enemies prowl around thee like wolves for the blood of the lamb;

"And if thou shouldst be cast into the pit, or into the hands of murderers, and the sentence of death passed upon thee; if thou be cast into the deep; if the billowing surge conspire against thee; if fierce winds become thine enemy; if the heavens gather blackness, and all the elements combine to hedge up the way . . ." (D&C 122:5-7.)

Following this recital of great afflictions, the Lord gave the purpose of adversity in these words:

". . . know thou, my son, that all these things shall give thee experience, and shall be for thy good.

"The Son of Man hath descended below them all. Art thou greater than he?" (*Ibid.*, 122:7-8.)

## Experiences Are Good

What do the scriptures reveal concerning the value or blessing of tribulations? One of the major purposes of this life is to prove ourselves that we may be worthy of the greatest measure of salvation.

Trials are for our own benefit. President George Q. Cannon pointed out that, in the case of Abraham who was commanded to sacrifice his son Isaac, the Lord wanted to impress upon him a lesson that he could obtain in only this way. It was not for God's benefit that this was done, because he knew what Abraham would do. (D&C 38:2.) So also with others who undergo trials, it is for their own good that they may know for themselves. (*Gospel Truth*, p. 113.)

Calamities mentioned in sacred history have ultimately been blessings. The fall of Adam and Eve brought forth opportunities for God's spirit children to receive bodies and to prove themselves. The great suffering of Christ and his crucifixion were calamities, but man was redeemed from death and hell by that atoning sacrifice. The scattering of Israel throughout the world sprinkled the blood that believes—that many nations might partake of the gospel plan. The history of the Nephites is one of trials, calamities, and sufferings, but through it all the experiences gained brought strength and development.

Elder Orson F. Whitney asks this question and answers it:

> "To whom do we look, in days of grief and disaster, for help and consolation? Who are these friendly neighbors gathered in today? They are men and women who have suffered, and out of their experience in suffering they bring forth the riches of their sympathy and condolences as a blessing to those now in need. Could they do this had they not suffered themselves . . . ? We go to men and women of thought and sympathy, men and women who have suffered themselves and can give us the comfort that we need. Is not this God's purpose in causing his children to suffer? He wants them to become more like himself. God has suffered far more than man ever did or ever will, and is therefore the great source of sympathy and consolation. (*Improvement Era,* Vol. 22, Nov. 1918, p. 7.)

## "Art Thou Greater than He?"

Although adversities are present in this world—and they have their spiritual meaning in our lives—it is not contemplated in the gospel plan that because the Savior died for mankind the saints must give their lives as martyrs. It is true, however, that some of the saints may be required to give their lives in defense of the truth. (D&C 103:27-28.) On the other hand, no man will be required to suffer as the Savior suffered, for no sacrifice would be as great as his. (*Ibid.*, 19:16-19.)

### Afflictions and Punishment

The Prophet Joseph Smith taught that it is a false idea to believe that the saints will escape all the judgments—disease, pestilence, war, etc.—of the last days; consequently, it is an unhallowed principle to say that these adversities are due to transgression. (*Teachings of the Prophet Joseph Smith*, p. 162.)

President Joseph F. Smith taught that it is a feeble thought to believe that the illness and affliction that come to us are attributable either to the mercy or the displeasure of God.

> . . . Sometimes we are prone to charge God with causing our afflictions and our troubles; but if we could see as God sees, if we could understand as he understands, if we could trace the effects back to the cause, and that truly, by the spirit of correct understanding, we would unquestionably discover that our troubles, or suffering, or affliction are the result of our own indiscretion or lack of knowledge, or of wisdom. (*Gospel Doctrine*, p. 57.)

When commandments are not obeyed, the penalties of the law then follow. (D&C 130:20-21.) The saints in Missouri were commanded to live the law of consecration and to redeem Zion, but because of disobedience to commandments, the Lord said they were afflicted, persecuted, and driven from the land. The chastening hand of the Lord fell upon them that they might learn obedience. They were not to be cast off completely, but they would be remembered in the day of mercy. (D&C 101:1-9.)

## Afflictions and Repentance

In these last days various tribulations are present. The fact that they are known widely is one of the signs of the approaching end. (D&C 29:14-20; 45:28, 34.) Should a member of the Church seek to understand these calamitous events as God has revealed their purpose, or think of them only in terms of an immediate perspective? God's law and purposes are eternal.

President Joseph F. Smith gave the following reasons for natural calamities: (1) to quicken people's devotion to others; and (2) to be schoolmasters to teach people to prepare themselves by righteous living for the second coming of Christ. (*Gospel Doctrine*, pp. 54-55.)

## Implementation

Premortally, the Lord presented a plan that provided an opportunity for his spirit children to receive the experience of an earth life. In that life they were to partake of the bitter as well as the sweet. The fact that pain, sorrow, discouragement, and loss of loved ones in death would be a part of that experience would nevertheless be for their good. With this knowledge of what would be, the children of God willingly accepted the opportunity to come to earth because it would provide the way by which they might eventually, if faithful, become as their Heavenly Father.

In order that earth's inhabitants might be successful, the plan of salvation included the opportunity for them to learn of their premortality, the purpose of life, and also the reality of the hereafter. With faith in the word of the Lord, the saint who has accepted these truths is strengthened against adversities. The testimony borne by the Holy Ghost to the soul of the saint also gives strength to withstand the trials of life.

The important truth about adversity is the effect it has upon the person. President David O. McKay said:

"Today there are those who have met disaster, which almost seems defeat, who have become somewhat soured in their natures; but if they stop to think, even the adversity which has come to them may prove a means of spiritual uplift. Adversity itself may lead toward and not away from God and spiritual enlightenment; and privation may prove a source of strength if we can but keep the sweetness of mind and spirit. (David O. McKay, *Treasures of Life,* pp. 107-108.)

## Chapter 40

# THE FRUITS OF APOSTASY

### (Sections 121:11-25; 123)

During the dispensation of the fulness of times, Satan has increased his attempts to destroy the Lord's work because this period of time is destined to be the culminating period when labor for the salvation of men, living and dead, will be accomplished. At the opening of this dispensation when Joseph Smith received the First Vision, Satan's efforts to thwart the work of the Lord were manifest in an attempt to destroy him. (Joseph Smith 2:13-17.)

The wiles of the Adversary have been effective in seducing the unwary. But to entice a covenant son or daughter of God to succumb to his temptations is a great victory; consequently, his efforts are particularly leveled at those who are members of the kingdom of God.

### None Exempt

High office in the Church does not insure that the seeds of apostasy may not be sown in the person's life. (D&C 20:31-34.) Men who stood with the Prophet Joseph Smith amid hardships and persecution subsequently fell away from the Church. The instances are rare, however.

During a period of persecution in Missouri, when the Prophet and several other leaders were in Liberty Jail on trumped-up charges, the Prophet received revelations which are numbered Sections 121, 122, 123 in the Doctrine and Covenants. These revelations were extracted from an epistle written by the Prophet. (*DHC* 3:289-305.) Among other things in Section 121, we find the Lord's answer to those who have persecuted the saints, among whom were some apostates.

Beginning with verse 11, the revelation reminded the Prophet that the hopes of those who sought to charge him with transgression would be blasted and that their hearts were corrupted and retribution would surely come. (Verse 13.) Those who cry against the Lord's anointed do it because they are the servants of sin. (Verses 16-17.) To swear falsely against the Lord's anointed ones and to seek to harm them bring the following severe penalties: (1) they shall not have membership in the Church; (2) their material blessings will diminish; (3) they shall not escape the damnation of hell. (D&C 121:18-23; 124:50.)

## Cause of Apostasy

It is false to assume that the principles of the gospel are at fault when members in high places fall away from the Church. Some people ask why the three special witnesses to the Book of Mormon left the Church, since they had such a marvelous experience. The answer is a simple one: they failed to keep the commandments. So it is with people, high or low, who elect to become apostate.

There are, however, many things which lead people into dark and forbidden paths. Some of these elements will be mentioned in this chapter with their consequent results, as well as ways to overcome these tendencies.

## Indicators of Apostasy

To assemble all of the factors that indicate that the seeds of apostasy are gaining ascendancy in one's life might constitute a long list. Some of these signs may be mentioned briefly from those given by Elder John A. Widtsoe, (*Gospel Interpretations*, pp. 38-39.)

(1) *Failure to pray.* In order to maintain spiritual communion with the Lord, it is essential that one acknowledge his dependency upon him, express gratitude for

blessings received, and seek for wisdom through prayer. The moment one lets other activities or interests interfere with daily, sincere prayer, his faith may be weakened. In ignoring prayer completely, the person places himself in the position desired by the evil one. (Alma 32:8-9; 34:39.) On the other hand, the Lord has said that if we do not observe our prayers we stand for judgment. (D&C 68:33.)

(2) *Neglecting study of the gospel.* To maintain a testimony of the gospel successfully, it is necessary to keep knowledgeable in gospel principles. Faith grows with knowledge.

(3) *Lessened participation in Church life.* The Lord has enjoined upon all to be active in his work. (D&C 38:40.)

(4) *A feeling of superiority.* Personal ambition may lead to a feeling of superiority with possible false interpretation of scripture. The true saint is one who remains humble seeking to learn through that humility. (D&C 112:10.)

(5) *Finding fault with other members or with the leadership of the Church.* These may lead to apostasy. This cause for apostasy is probably one of the most common.

## Recognizable Indicators

In the words of Elder Widtsoe:

The dying testimony is easily recognized. The organizations and practices of the Church are ignored; the radio [television] takes the place of the sacrament meeting; golf or motion pictures, the Sunday worship; the cup of coffee, instead of the Word of Wisdom; the cold, selfish hand instead of helpfulness, charity for the poor, and the payment of tithing.

Soon, the testimony is gone, and the former possessor walks about somewhat sour and discontented, and always in his heart, unhappy. He has lost his most precious possession, and has found nothing to replace it. He has lost inward freedom, the gift of obedience to law. (*Gospel Interpretations,* p. 39.)

## Be Not Deceived

There is no happiness in losing one's most valued possession. When one remembers that losses in this life bring sorrow and want, how much more serious is the loss of an eternity of happiness.

To insure against this possibility for those who would hearken to this word, very early in this dispensation the Lord gave counsel to the members of the Church whereby they might not be deceived by the evil one.

The following categories—taken chronologically from the revelations in the Doctrine and Covenants—give some counsel which, if obeyed, will keep the members of the Church from being deceived: (1) grow in perfection; (2) accept the duties of membership in the Church; (3) obey appointed leaders; (4) seek the gifts of the Holy Ghost; (5) study the scriptures; (6) obey Church regulations; (7) keep the Sabbath day holy; (8) be obedient to health and financial laws.

## Grow in Perfection

When the Latter-day Saint resolves to better his life, he begins to fulfill his covenants with the Lord. "Therefore I would that ye should be perfect even as I, or your Father who is in heaven is perfect." (3 Nephi 12:48.) The ultimate goal is attainable by constant application of the principles of truth.

A list of virtues which might be used to begin, today, in perfecting one's life, is found in the revelation directed to Joseph Smith, Sr. (D&C 4:5-6.)

## Accept Duties

Among the duties of membership in The Church of Jesus Christ of Latter-day Saints, the partaking of the sacrament is most important. The Lord has said that we may have his Spirit with us provided we partake of it worthily. (D&C 20:77, 79.) If we enjoy the influence of the Holy Ghost, it will be the means of keeping us on the path to eternal life. (D&C 20:69.)

Closely associated with the partaking of the sacrament is the opportunity to assemble with other saints in meetings so that the strength of the group will be received by the individual. The Lord told the saints in Kirtland, Ohio, to "assemble yourselves together to agree upon my word." (*Ibid.*, 41:2.) If one desires to resist temptation and keep on the narrow path to salvation, one of the best ways is to be a regular attender at appointed meetings.

### Obey Leadership

Obedience to those who preside over the Church is a certain way to keep from being deceived. (D&C 43:3-7; 124:45-46.) The Prophet Joseph Smith taught that when a person begins to criticize the leaders over him, and considers that he alone is right, then that person is on the road to apostasy. (*Teachings of the Prophet Joseph Smith*, pp. 156-7.)

### The Gifts of the Spirit

Because there are "doctrines of devils, or the commandments of men" (D&C 46:7) taught in the world, the Lord revealed that in order that his people might not be deceived, they should seek for the gifts of the Holy Ghost. (D&C 46:8.) The gifts shown in the revelation are given to those who love the Lord and diligently seek to keep his commandments. (*Ibid.*, 46:9-26.)

### Study the Scriptures

The Doctrine and Covenants sets forth the teachings of the gospel in plainness. Often these teachings were given in response to a question or a situation. One revelation containing doctrinal teachings that correct false teachings is Section 49. It is true that the student of the scriptures is able to discriminate between truth and error because he has not only learned the principles of the gospel, but he has also learned fundamental teachings which point the way to obtaining the answer of the problem.

We have also a more sure word of prophecy; whereunto ye do well that ye take heed, as unto a light that shineth in a dark place, until the day dawn, and the day star arise in your hearts;

Knowing this first, that no prophecy of the scripture is of any private interpretation.

For the prophecy came not in old time by the will of man: but holy men of God spake as they were moved by the Holy Ghost. (2 Peter 1:19-21.)

"No prophecy of the scripture is of any private interpretation." (2 Peter 1:20.) There is official interpretation of the doctrines and standards of the Church, and this knowledge comes from the prophets, seers, and revelators. (President Stephen L Richards, (*Conference Report*, October, 1951, pp. 116-117.)

The revealed word of the Lord is: "And whoso treasureth up my word, shall not be deceived. . . ." (Joseph Smith 1:37.)

### Obey Church Regulations

One of the most powerful means of deception is to teach false doctrines and disobedience to the known rules of the Church. Such a condition existed in the early part of this dispensation, and it was revealed that if a person will obey the ordinances and the rules and regulations of the gospel, he will be accepted of God. (D&C 52:14-16.)

### The Sabbath Day

A commandment which seems to be ignored widely is observance of the Sabbath day. It is inconsistent to believe that disobedience to the laws regarding the Sabbath day will not take its toll of the faith of the member of the Church. The commandment regarding the holy day requires devotion to the Lord. (D&C 59:9, 12-13; 68:29.) The Spirit of the Lord is enjoyed when we keep all the commandments.

Not only is faithful devotion required for the covenant people of the Lord on the Sabbath day, but upon all days. (*Ibid.*, 59:11, 21.)

## Health and Financial Laws

On February 27, 1833, the laws of health known as the Word of Wisdom were made known. This commandment to observe certain health laws and to desist from partaking of things contrary to health, is a spiritual law. Probably the most damaging effects of breaking the Word of Wisdom are spiritual. In order to assist Latter-day Saints to have the Spirit of the Lord with them, the Lord gave this commandment and warned them against the evils and designs of those who would encourage them to break this law. (D&C 89:4.) Observance of this law brings increased faith and the development of more spiritual power and wisdom.

The keeping of the law of tithing is a bulwark against the darts of the Adversary. When one pays one-tenth of his increase to the Lord, he is seeking to sanctify himself and his material possessions.

## Implementation

In a period when gospel teachings are being challenged by "new ideas," there is greater need to take inventory of one's inclinations to accept notions that are contrary to accepted gospel principles. The increase in television and radio propaganda and publications of all sorts has created a condition where it is necessary that the member of the Church be better prepared to distinguish between the genuine and the spurious.

Practices should be encouraged in one's life that keep faith at a high level, while ideas and activities that run counter to gospel principles should be shunned. The Lord has provided sufficient opportunities for the saints to remain faithful by revealing keys against being deceived, which, if applied, will help them to keep the faith.

Constant study of the scriptures and their application in daily life are the keystones of success in eliminating tendencies to apostasy. Important in accomplishing this purpose is to give heed to the Holy Spirit within and to live so that the blessing of possessing the Holy Spirit may be continued.

## Chapter 41

# THE NAUVOO TEMPLE AND ITS HIGHER ORDINANCES

### (Section 124:25-44)

One of the distinguishing features of The Church of Jesus Christ of Latter-day Saints is temple building. Beautiful buildings, some of which are called temples, have been constructed in many parts of the world, but none of these edifices has the same function and purpose as a temple built by The Church of Jesus Christ of Latter-day Saints.

The earliest reference to a structure like a temple is the tabernacle carried by the Israelites in the wilderness after coming out of Egyptian bondage. Because of the nature of the sacred ordinances performed, the Lord referred in a modern revelation to the need for the tabernacle. This tabernacle was to be "with them in the wilderness" (D&C 124:38) until a house of the Lord could be built in the land of Canaan where the Lord would reveal ordinances to his people.

There is little information concerning the actual ordinances performed in the temples of the past. It is evident that a knowledge of temple ordinances was known very early, perhaps, however, not in fulness. (See facsimile No. 2 in the Book of Abraham, figures 3, 7, and 8.)

The apostles Peter and Paul foresaw the day when there would be a restoration of all things spoken of by the prophets in the period known as the dispensation of the fulness of times. (Acts 3:19-21; Eph. 1:9-10.) Since temples were a part of earlier dispensations, they would also be found among the Lord's people in the last days. These temples would be places where people from all nations would assemble to worship the God of Abraham, Isaac, and Jacob. (Isaiah 2:2-3; Micah 4:1-2.)

## Kirtland Temple

The first temple erected in this dispensation was located at Kirtland, Ohio, and dedicated on March 27, 1836. It was in that year, on April 3rd, that the keys of the priesthood were restored. (D&C Section 110.)

The Kirtland Temple was unlike other temples constructed later. Regular and special worship services and the School of the Prophets were conducted in that temple.

## Nauvoo Temple

From Missouri, the saints settled in Illinois at Commerce, later named Nauvoo, on the banks of the Mississippi River. In accordance with the commandment to build a temple at Nauvoo, the cornerstones were laid April 6, 1841. (Joseph Fielding Smith, *Essentials in Church History*, pp. 308-309.) The walls of the temple were up to the windows at the time of the Prophet Joseph's death, but the temple was completed to the attic and dedicated November 30, 1845 (*DHC* 7:534) so that endowments could be administered during the winter of 1845-46. The public dedication of the temple was held on May 1, 1846. (*Essentials in Church History*, p. 400.)

A baptismal font was built in the basement of the Nauvoo Temple, and baptisms for the dead were performed in November 1841. (*Essentials in Church History*, p. 310.) The temple was burned in the fall of 1848, and the walls were blown down by a hurricane, May 27, 1850.

Since the days of the Prophet Joseph Smith, thirteen other temples have been erected in the United States and in foreign countries.

## Higher Ordinances of the Gospel

The higher ordinances of the gospel of Jesus Christ consist of those ceremonies and ordinances that are received in the House of the Lord. The fact that there are ordinances which are called "higher," suggests other principles and ordinances which are "lesser." The first principles and ordinances of salvation are faith in the Lord Jesus Christ, repentance of sins, baptism in water for the remission of sins, and the laying on of hands for the gift of the Holy Ghost. (3 Nephi 27:13-21; D&C 33:10-11.) These principles are to be taught freely to all who will listen, but the higher ordinances are not to be revealed except in a temple.

## Importance of First Principles

The New Testament teaches that without faith in Christ, repentance of sins, baptism by immersion for the remission of sins, and receiving the Holy Ghost, it is impossible to "enter into the kingdom of God." (John 3:5; Acts 2:29-39; Romans 6:3-5.)

## The New Testament and Higher Ordinances

The Savior taught his disciples many things that they were to know but which were not for the world. Similarly, the higher ordinances of the gospel may be received by the faithful, devoted member of the Church, but nonmembers and even some members of the Church are not prepared to receive these temple ordinances.

Wherein does the New Testament reveal that there is a segment of the gospel that is reserved for only the disciples? Upon one occasion the Savior took only Peter, James, and John with him on the mount where a wonderful manifestation was received by them. Concerning this vision, the Savior advised his disciples: "Tell the vision to no man, until the Son of man be risen again from the dead." (Matthew 17:9.) In answer to a question from his disciples as to why he taught the people in parables, the following was given:

> ". . . Because it is given unto you to know the mysteries of the kingdom of heaven, but to them it is not given.
>
> "For whosoever hath, to him shall be given, and he shall have more abundance: but whosoever hath not, from him shall be taken away even that he hath.
>
> "Therefore speak I to them in parables: because they seeing see not; hearing they hear not, neither do they understand." (Matthew 13:11-13.)

The apostle Paul had the experience of being caught up to heaven, and hearing words which were not lawful for man to utter. (2 Corinthians 12:2-4.) Thus the gospel in the meridian dispensation contained information which was not to be revealed to the multitudes, but the disciples were to receive these greater things of the kingdom.

The Book of Mormon also bears testimony to this same truth, as expressed by the Prophet Alma:

> ". . . It is given unto many to know the mysteries of God; nevertheless they are laid under a strict command that they shall not impart only according to the portion of his word which he doth grant unto the children of men, according to the heed and diligence which they give unto him." (Alma 12:9.)

However, what if an individual rejects the greater word? Alma continues:

> "And therefore, he that will harden his heart, the same receiveth the lesser portion of the word; and he that will not harden his heart, to him is given the greater portion of the word, until it is given unto him to know the mysteries of God until he know them in full.
>
> "And they that will harden their hearts, to them is given the lesser portion of the word until they know nothing concerning his mysteries; and then they are taken captive by the devil, and led by his will down to destruction. Now this is what is meant by the chains of hell." (*Ibid.*, verses 10-11.)

## A Promise Fulfilled

In the teachings of the resurrected Christ to the Nephites, it is recorded that only the lesser part of what he taught the Nephites was written that they might be brought forth in the last days. If the people would receive this part, then the greater things would be given them. (3 Nephi 26:6-11.)

Within a year after the Church was organized, the Lord revealed that Joseph Smith held "the keys of the mystery of those things which have been sealed." (D&C 42:65.)

The Lord's promise to his saints is having its fulfillment today, in that those who are keeping the commandments receive the mysteries of the kingdom which lead to everlasting life. (*Ibid.*, 63:23.)

## Higher Ordinances

The higher ordinances, or mysteries of the kingdom, administered in the temple consist of washings, anointings, the priesthood endowment, and marriage for eternity.

When the Kirtland Temple was no longer in the possession of The Church of Jesus Christ of Latter-day Saints, the Lord rejected it as his house and promised that the "fulness of the priesthood" (D&C 124:28) which can be received only in a temple, would be available to the members of the Church with the building of the Nauvoo Temple. (D&C 124:25-28; 40-44.)

In connection with the coming of Elijah in the last days, the Prophet Joseph Smith said that there would be a welding of other dispensations with this one, including the revealing of things from the foundation of the world. (D&C 127:8; 128:18.)

## Melchizedek Priesthood and Ordinances

In September of 1832, the Lord revealed that the Melchizedek Priesthood, sometimes called the "greater priesthood," holds the "keys of the mysteries of the kingdom, even the knowledge of God." (D&C 84:19.) It is also said that when Moses brought the children of Israel from Egyptian bondage, an effort was made to prepare the people to enter into the Lord's rest, which is the fulness of his glory where they could behold the face of God, but they would not, for they had hardened their hearts. (*Ibid.*, verses 19-24.)

Without the knowledge of God there is no salvation in its highest sense. To know God is to ultimately become like him, and thus receive all that the Father hath as an exalted being. (*Ibid.*, 38-89.) As indicated, the means by which both men and women may receive the knowledge of God is received by ordinances; and thus, the faithful member of the Church by obedience to commandments may be exalted. (Joseph Fielding Smith, *Doctrines of Salvation*, 3:142-143.) No person can receive the fulness of the priesthood except in the temple. (D&C 124:27-28; *DHC* 5:242.)

## Priesthood Endowment

The Prophet Joseph Smith spent the day of May 4, 1842, in his private office instructing some of the brethren,

> "... in the principles and order of the Priesthood, attending to washings, annointings, endowments and the communication of keys pertaining to the Aaronic Priesthood, setting forth the order pertaining to the Ancient of Days, and all those plans and principles by which any one is enabled to secure the fulness of those blessings which have been prepared for the Church of the First Born, and come up and abide in the presence of the Eloheim in the eternal worlds ... (*DHC* 5:1, 2.)

Elder James E. Talmage defined the temple endowment, as follows:

"The Temple Endowment, as administered in modern temples, comprises instruction relating to the significance and sequence of past dispensations, and the importance of the present as the greatest and grandest era in human history. This course of instruction includes a recital of the most prominent events of the creative period, the condition of our first parents in the Garden of Eden, their disobedience and consequent expulsion from that blissful abode, their condition in the lone and dreary world when doomed to live by labor and sweat, the plan of redemption by which the great transgression may be atoned, the period of the great apostasy, the restoration of the Gospel with all its ancient powers and privileges, the absolute and indispensable condition of personal purity and devotion to the right in present life, and a strict compliance with Gospel requirements." (*The House of the Lord,* pp. 99-100.)

Embodied in the endowment are opportunities for the participant to receive the necessary knowledge and covenants for eternal advancement. Elder Talmage continues his discussion of the endowment, as follows:

"The ordinances of the endowment embody certain obligations on the part of the individual, such as a covenant and promise to observe the law of strict virtue and chastity, to be charitable, benevolent, tolerant and pure; to devote both talent and material means to the spread of truth and the uplifting of the race; to maintain devotion to the cause of truth; and to seek in every way to contribute to the great preparation that the earth may be made ready to receive her King,—the Lord Jesus Christ. With the taking of each covenant and the assuming of each obligation a promised blessing is pronounced, contingent upon the faithful observance of the conditions." (*Ibid.,* p. 100.)

## Faithful Women

The Lord does not hold responsible those individuals of his Church who do not have the opportunity to fulfill commandments. If circumstances do not, at the present, allow for them to receive all of the ordinances of the gospel, they will probably be found in the situation in which Oliver Cowdery found himself:

> "Behold, thou art Oliver, and I have spoken unto thee because of thy desires; therefore treasure up these words in thy heart. Be faithful and diligent in keeping the commandments of God, and I will encircle thee in the arms of my love." (D&C 6:20.)

Other conditions being equal, desires go to judgment as well as deeds. Elder Harold B. Lee of the Council of the Twelve, in advising young women of the Church who had not the opportunity to marry a worthy member of the Church, said that for these women, by continuing to live worthy lives, the time would come when no blessing would be denied them. (*Youth and the Church*, p. 132.)

## Implementation

The dispensation of the fulness of times was prophesied as a period when the teachings and practices of other dispensations would be restored to the earth. Among these would be the building of temples and the performance of sacred ordinances therein. Without these higher ordinances, known in scripture also as the mysteries of the kingdom, it would be impossible for men and women eventually to enter God's presence to receive the knowledge of God, which is exaltation in the celestial kingdom.

Both men and women receive the blessings of the fulness of the priesthood in the temple, but they are laid under a strict command that they will not talk about this sacred knowledge outside of the temple. This commandment is because of the sacred nature of the higher ordinances of the gospel. The Lord gave his disciples this same instruction because others were not prepared for these mysteries.

The holy endowment received in the House of the Lord qualifies the faithful member of the Church to receive the ordinances, covenants, and knowledge which prepare him for God's presence after the resurrection, and with the eternal marriage covenant, for exaltation.

Some members of the Church, particularly women, because of their circumstances (not being married to a worthy member of the Church or being married to a non-member, or being unmarried) will not be denied their righteous desires, if they remain true to the covenants of baptism.

## Chapter 42

# SALVATION FOR THE DEAD

### (Sections 127; 128)

In September 1842, the Prophet Joseph Smith, at Nauvoo, Illinois, addressed two epistles to the saints concerning record keeping and the subject of baptism for the dead. (D&C 127-128.) The Lord had already revealed some matters regarding baptism for the dead. (*Ibid.*, 124.) The first time this doctrine was mentioned in public was at the funeral of Seymour Brunson, who died in August 1840. (*DHC* 4:179.)

When Elder Wilford Woodruff returned from England in 1841, at which time he heard that this doctrine had been revealed, he was overjoyed in the thought that he could have this ordinance of salvation performed for his mother who was dead. Converts to the gospel have had similar feelings when they learned that they may help in the salvation of their deceased loved ones.

### A Glorious Doctrine

In one of the Prophet's epistles he quoted Paul's letter to the Corinthians wherein he refers to baptism for the dead in relation to the resurrection. (1 Cor. 15:29; D&C 128:17.) In the Prophet's explanation of this doctrine, he said:

> . . . and in an especial manner this most glorious of all subjects belonging to the everlasting gospel . . . (D&C 128:17.)

Every Latter-day Saint who has seriously considered the importance of the doctrine of salvation of the dead has had the assurance that this teaching is in accord with the justice and mercy of God. He understands that the plan of salvation would be woefully incomplete unless there were some provision whereby those who did not have an opportunity to accept the gospel in this life might receive it in the next world. In addition, he realizes that this glorious doctrine gives him a greater appreciation for and interest in his progenitors who made it possible for him to have this earth life. His comprehension of the total plan of life is enlarged in the contemplation that he agreed to this plan in the premortal world where salvation of the dead was a part of that plan. (*Ibid.*, 128:5.) He thrills that he has the opportunity to bring joy into the lives of his departed, as expressed in the words of Joseph Smith:

> . . . Let the dead speak forth anthems of eternal praise to the King Immanuel, who hath ordained, before the world was, that which would enable us to redeem them out of their prison; for the prisoners shall go free.
>
> . . . And again I say, how glorious is the voice we hear from heaven, proclaiming in our ears, glory, and salvation, and honor, and immortality, and eternal life; kingdoms, principalities, and powers! (*Ibid.*, verses 22-23.)

## A Modern Revelation

On October 3, 1918, President Joseph F. Smith was contemplating two New Testament scriptures from the apostle Peter. Both of these scriptures referred to the time when the Savior—between the time of his death and his resurrection—went to preach to the spirits of the dead and thus the dead would be judged as "men in the flesh" (1 Peter 4:6) who had heard the gospel of Jesus Christ. (*Ibid.*, 3:18-20.) He later reported to the counselors in the First Presidency and the twelve apostles and the patriarch, the vision of the Savior's ministry among the dead, and they unanimously accepted it. A brief summary of that vision follows.

President Smith saw the righteous dead in the spirit world filled with gladness awaiting the advent of the

Son of God among them. There was no darkness among the righteous, but peace and rejoicing. He saw that the Savior went to the righteous and commissioned them to take the gospel message to the wicked who were assembled in another part of the spirit world.

> . . . Thus was the gospel preached to those who had died in their sins, without a knowledge of the truth, or in transgression, having rejected the prophets. These were taught faith in God, repentance from sin, vicarious baptism for the remission of sins, the gift of the Holy Ghost by the laying on of hands, and all other principles of the gospel that were necessary for them to know in order to qualify themselves that they might be judged according to men in the flesh, but live according to God in the spirit. (*Gospel Doctrine,* p. 474.)

## Man's Spirit

The Lord has revealed that man is spirit, and he is eternal. (D&C 93:33.) The Prophet Joseph Smith said:

> In tracing the thing to the foundation, and looking at it philosophically, we shall find a very material difference between the body and the spirit; the body is supposed to be organized matter, and the spirit, by many is thought to be immaterial, without substance. With this latter statement we should beg leave to differ, and state that spirit is a substance; that it is material, but that it is more pure, elastic and refined matter than the body; that it existed before the body, can exist in the body; and will exist separate from the body, when the body will be mouldering in the dust; and will in the resurrection, be again united with it. (*DHC* 4:575.)

## A Place of Education

One of the purposes of the spirit world is to provide an opportunity for those who have not heard the ever-lasting gospel to learn it. It is a place of repentance for them. Members of the Church also will have opportunity to further perfect their lives. It is erroneous to assume that the person at death is any different in the spirit world than he was in earth life as far as his beliefs, attitudes, and characteristics are concerned. (Alma 34:34.) Deathbed repentance does not assure salvation after a life of negligence or wickedness. The penitent thief on the cross by the Savior did not go to heaven but to the spirit world for further education. (Luke 23:29-43: John 20:11-18; Joseph Fielding Smith, *Teachings of the Prophet Joseph Smith*, p. 309.) The transition of death does not change one's character. President Brigham Young said that changes must come in the same way that changes come in this life, by desire and effort. (Roy W. Doxey, *The Doctrine and Covenants and the Future*, pp. 83-84.)

The faithful, devoted Latter-day Saint, having accepted the atonement of Jesus Christ through the first principles and ordinances of the gospel, will not be under the influence of Satan after death. (Brigham Young, *Journal of Discourses*, 3:94-95.) On the other hand, the wicked unrepentant will more or less be subject to the Adversary's power. (*Ibid.*, 7:240.)

### Righteous and Wicked

In the world of spirits there are two divisions—paradise and hell. From the day of Adam down to the time Christ ministered to the spirits in prison, there was a great gulf between these two places. (Luke 16:19-31; Nephi 9:12-13; Brigham Young, *Journal of Discourses*, 14:229; *Doctrine and Covenants Commentary*, Revised, 1957, p. 463.) Christ bridged the gulf. Since then the gospel has been taught in both paradise and hell, and there has been consequent intermingling of the righteous and wicked spirits. Thus the Prophet Joseph Smith, speaking of conditions as they now exist in the spirit world, said: "Hades, Sheol, paradise, spirits in prison, are all one: it is a world of spirits. The righteous and the wicked all go to the same world of spirits until the resurrection." (*Teachings of the Prophet Joseph Smith*, p. 310.)

In explaining the words of Alma, who was speaking upon the subject of the spirit world in the day of a sharp cleavage between hell and paradise, President Joseph F. Smith said:

> . . . The spirits of all men, as soon as they depart from this mortal body, whether they are good or evil, we are told in the Book of Mormon, are taken home to that God who gave them life, where there is a separation, a partial judgment, and the spirits of those who are righteous are received into a state of happiness which is called paradise, a state of rest, a state of peace, where they expand in wisdom, where they have respite from all their troubles, and where care and sorrow do not annoy. The wicked, on the contrary, have no part nor portion in the Spirit of the Lord, and they are cast into outer darkness, being led captive, because of their own iniquity, by the evil one. And in this space between death and the resurrection of the body, the two classes of souls remain, in happiness or in misery, until the time which is appointed of God that the dead shall come forth and be re-united both spirit and body, and be brought to stand before God, and be judged according to their works. . . . (*Gospel Doctrine*, p. 448.)

## Missionary Work

Probably one of the most important activities in the spirit world is missionary work. In the "Vision of the Redemption of the Dead" received by President Joseph F. Smith, the following is given:

> I beheld that the faithful elders of this dispensation, when they depart from mortal life, continue their labors in the preaching of the gospel of repentance and redemption, through the sacrifice of the Only Begotten Son of God, among those who are in darkness and under the bondage of sin in the great world of the spirits of the dead. The dead who repent will be redeemed, through obedience to the ordinances of the house of God, and after they have paid the penalty of their transgressions, and are washed clean, shall receive a reward according to their works, for they are heirs of salvation. (*Gospel Doctrine*, p. 476.)

## Basis of Salvation for the Dead

On January 21, 1836, in the Kirtland Temple, the Prophet Joseph received a vision in which he was permitted to see the celestial kingdom. Among those he saw were some people he knew on the earth, one of whom was his brother Alvin, who had passed away before the gospel was restored. The voice of the Lord came to him saying:

> "All who have died without a knowledge of this Gospel, who would have received it if they had been permitted to tarry, shall be heirs of the celestial kingdom of God; also all that shall die henceforth without a knowledge of it, who would have received it with all their hearts, shall be heirs of that kingdom, for I, the Lord, will judge all men according to their works, according to the desire of their hearts. (*DHC* 2:380.)

## Baptism for the Dead

In the merciful plan of the Great Creator, provision was made for the salvation of those who would die without a knowledge of the gospel. The same principles and ordinances that save the living also save the dead. (1 Cor. 15:29; Joseph Smith, *DHC* 5:424.) Since the plan provides that mortals must perform the ordinances on the earth in temples, baptism for the dead is performed by proxy, the living representing the dead. Proxies also stand for the dead in receiving the higher ordinances of the gospel in the temple.

The first baptisms for the dead in this dispensation were performed in the Mississippi River because there was not a temple where the ordinance could be performed. (*Essentials in Church History*, p. 305.) Subsequently, these baptisms were discontinued by revelation until the baptismal font in the Nauvoo Temple was completed. (D&C 124:31-35; Joseph Smith, *DHC* 4:426.)

## Records of the Dead

The Prophet Joseph Smith, by revelation, counseled the saints that their records should be maintained in order, and that proper recordings should be made of baptisms for the dead. (D&C 127:5-9; 128:2-4; Joseph Smith, *DHC* 5:141.)

What is recorded on the earth shall be recorded in the heavens, wrote the Prophet Joseph Smith. (D&C 128:8.) Inasmuch as we shall be judged out of the books that are maintained on the earth it is essential that the Church members maintain a proper record of their dead. By this means records are also kept in the heavens by the binding authority of the priesthood. (D&C 128:14; Orson Pratt, *Journal of Discourses* 7:84.)

## Our Salvation

The prophet Malachi prophesied, and the angel Moroni instructed the Prophet Joseph Smith, regarding the coming of Elijah to the earth before the second coming of Christ. (Malachi 4:5-6; D&C 128:17; 2.) On April 3, 1836, Elijah committed the sealing powers of the priesthood to the Prophet and Oliver Cowdery. This power also included the work for the dead. (D&C 110:13-16; Joseph Smith, *DHC* 6:183-184.)

The Prophet taught that the saints could become saviors on Mount Zion by performing temple ordinances in behalf of their dead. (*DHC* 6:184; Obadiah 21.) In this same sermon, he said:

> The Saints have not too much time to save and redeem their dead, and gather together their living relatives, that they may be saved also, before the earth will be smitten, and the consumption decreed falls upon the world. (*DHC* 6:184.)

The importance of the work of redeeming the dead by identifying them and having the necessary ordinances performed for them is indicated by the following statements from the Prophet:

> . . . For we without them cannot be made perfect. Neither can they nor we be made perfect without those who have died in the gospel also; for it is necessary in the ushering in of the dispensation of the fulness of times, which dispensation is now beginning to usher in, that a whole and complete and perfect union, and welding together of dispensations, and keys, and powers, and glories should take place, and be revealed from the days of Adam even to the present time. (D&C 128:18.)
>
> This doctrine presents in a clear light the wisdom and mercy of God in preparing an ordinance for the salvation of the dead, being baptized by proxy, their names recorded in heaven and they judged according to the deeds done in the body. This doctrine was the burden of the scriptures. Those Saints who neglect it in behalf of their deceased relatives, do it at the peril of their own salvation. (*DHC* 4:426.)

## Implementation

An integral part of the doctrine of salvation of the dead is the subject of the spirit world. Every person at death goes into that sphere of existence where the principles of salvation are taught. Faithful members of Christ's Church will continue their labors in that world in behalf of the dead, preparing them for their final stage of existence, the resurrection.

The Lord has instituted the practice of baptism for the dead and the performance of the higher ordinances in temples that exaltation may come to the dead. This opportunity to perform genealogical research and temple service for one's kindred dead, if accepted, will help the Latter-day Saint to uproot selfishness, greed, and other barriers to his own salvation, as he helps those who cannot help themselves in the spirit world.

The initial step in this program is to enroll in a ward genealogical class to learn the rudiments of genealogical research. With this training, one can complete his four generation family group sheet project, as requested by the Church. Becoming involved in this activity should increase one's desire to continue to become a savior on Mount Zion in fulfilling his obligation to his kindred dead.

The magnanimity of the gospel plan is indicated in this important doctrine revealing God's mercy and justice. Before the final judgment is rendered, every person must receive his chance to have the blessings of accepting the gospel. What the living do or do not do in behalf of their kindred dead will redound to their own everlasting exaltation or condemnation.

## Chapter 43

# THE MINISTRY OF ANGELS

### (Section 129; 130:1-11)

A principal belief of The Church of Jesus Christ of Latter-day Saints is that heavenly messengers minister today. When the mob in Jackson County, Missouri, issued a manifesto invoking the saints to leave that place under threat of death, it stated that the Mormons openly blasphemed God because they believed in direct communication from heaven. (*DHC* 1:374-376.)

Why should professed "Christian" people denounce the basic Bible teaching that communication from heaven may come through various media of revelation: visions, dreams, angels, and so forth? The Bible gives many examples of the ministration of holy beings from the other side of the veil. From the Old Testament we learn of many such examples. (Genesis 16:7-11; 22:11-12; Exodus 3:2; Daniel 6:22.) Several accounts are also recorded in the New Testament. (Luke 1:11-13, 28; 22:43; Acts 1:10; 5:18-19.)

Whenever a gospel dispensation has been on the earth, communication from heaven has been received from angels, as well as by other media of revelation.

### The Restoration of the Gospel

The fundamental Bible belief that God will direct his people today, as well as in the past, was renewed with the restoration of the gospel of Jesus Christ. This doctrine, affirmed by example and by the witness of the Holy Ghost, has given new hope and faith in the Bible and in the justice of God.

Latter-day Saints teach that the Church has been restored by direct revelation from heaven, and that the authority to perform ordinances of salvation has been given by angelic personages from heaven. The Aaronic and Melchizedek Priesthoods were thus restored. (D&C 27:7-8, 12-13.) Elijah, Elias, and Moses conferred their keys of authority upon Joseph Smith and Oliver Cowdery in the Kirtland Temple, on April 3, 1836. Ancient prophets have not only returned to the earth as angels, but they have prophesied the time when angels would minister in the last days. (Malachi 3:1-4; 4:5-6; Revelation 14:6-7.)

The restoration of the ancient records of the Nephites by the angel Moroni has given a new book of scripture, which also records the ministry of angels in times past and their messages concerning today and the future. (1 Nephi 13 and 14.)

The Prophet Joseph Smith became well acquainted with many persons of former dispensations who came as angelic persons to convey messages, powers, and authority. (D&C 128:20-21.)

### Heavenly Beings

In vision the Prophet Joseph Smith and Sidney Rigdon saw the heavenly hosts composed of members of the Godhead and angels. Their testimony is:

> And we beheld the glory of the Son, on the right hand of the Father, and received of his fulness;
>
> And saw the holy angels, and them who are sanctified before his throne, worshipping God, and the Lamb, who worship him forever and ever. (D&C 76:20-21.)

Another revelation speaks of two kinds of beings in heaven, namely, resurrected personages with bodies of flesh and bones, and the spirits of just men made perfect. (D&C 129:1-3.) It is also recorded that translated beings serve as heavenly messengers. An example is

John the Revelator, the apostle of the Lord, who did not die but is engaged in the work of salvation. (D&C 7.)

Among Latter-day Saints, the ministry of the Three Nephites, who are translated beings, is best known. These disciples of the Savior, appointed on the American Continent, desired that they might continue to labor for the salvation of men until the second coming of Christ. (3 Nephi 28.)

## What Is An Angel?

Angels are heavenly beings who act in the capacity of envoys, or messengers, between the heaven and earth. They may be spirits who have never had bodies, or spirits whose bodies lie in the grave, or they may be resurrected beings, or translated beings of flesh and bones who must yet die.

The Prophet said that all angels who minister to this earth have either lived upon it or will live upon it. (D&C 130:5.)

These truths concerning angels point out that angels are individuals with the same body structure as we have, and that they do not have wings, as popularly conceived. (*Teachings of the Prophet Joseph Smith*, p. 162.)

Angels, as translated or resurrected beings, have advanced higher in knowledge and power than spirits, said the Prophet Joseph Smith, and they are subject to God. (*DHC* 6:51; 5:426-427.)

In the meantime, resurrected or translated beings serve as divine messengers, until they receive a greater glory, in bringing authority and instruction from God. (*DHC* 4:575-576.) Such a one was Moroni, the custodian of the plates from which have come the Book of Mormon. The Prophet's description of Moroni's first appearance gives some characteristics of a resurrected angel:

While I was thus in the act of calling upon God, I discovered a light appearing in my room, which continued to increase until the room was lighter than at noonday, when immediately a personage appeared at my bedside, standing in the air, for his feet did not touch the floor.

He had on a loose robe of most exquisite whiteness. It was a whiteness beyond anything earthly I had ever seen; nor do I believe that any earthly thing could be made to appear so exceedingly white and brilliant. His hands were naked, and his arms also, a little above the wrist; so, also, were his feet naked, as were his legs, a little above the ankles. His head and neck were also bare. I could discover that he had no other clothing but this robe, as it was open, so that I could see into his bosom. (Joseph Smith 2:30-31.)

## Fallen Angels

The revelations are clear as to the existence of the devil and his fallen angels. Lucifer rebelled in the premortal world and influenced one-third of the hosts of heaven to follow him; and they thus lost their place among the children of God. (Moses 4:1-3; Revelation 12:4; 2 Peter 2:4; D&C 29:36-38.) These angels of Satan are personal beings, that is, they are in form and shape as human beings are, but of spirit. (D&C 131:7-8.) Evil spirits are sentient beings who have the characteristics of a person. (D&C 10:10-15, 20-27.)

The Lord has revealed the machinations of Satan's host toward mankind in order that Latter-day Saints may understand their operations. All evil comes from Satan, for he persuadeth no man to do good. (Moroni 7:12, 17.) His desire is to deceive, foster contention, encourage hatred, murder, and to incite men to rage against good. (2 Nephi 9:2, 9; 28:7-9, 19-22; 3 Nephi 11:29.)

## Satan and the Saints

Those who have made covenants with the Lord in baptism and in the temples are especial targets of Satan's hosts. To destroy the work of the Lord by deceiving the saints is one means by which Satan hopes to gain the victory. (D&C 76:28.) He has organized his forces, set up his kingdom to simulate the genuine in order to deceive the unwary. (*DHC* 6:364.)

His approaches are many and devious, as well described in the Book of Mormon. (2 Nephi 28.) The Prophet Joseph Smith said:

". . . The punishment of the devil was that he should not have a habitation like men. The devils retaliation is, he comes into this world, binds up men's bodies, and occupies them himself. When the authorities come along, they eject him from a stolen habitation. (*DHC* 5:403.)

During the ministry of the Savior, evil spirits possessing the bodies of two persons were cast into a herd of swine at the request of the devils. (Matthew 8:28-32.)

The first miracle in The Church of Jesus Christ of Latter-day Saints was the casting of an evil spirit out of Newel Knight by the Prophet Joseph Smith. When the Prophet rebuked the spirit, Newel spoke out and said that he saw the devil leave him and vanish from his sight. (*DHC* 1:82-83.) The Prophet recorded the following about this miracle:

"This scene was now entirely changed, for as soon as the devil had departed from our friend, his countenance became natural, his distortions of body ceased, and almost immediately the Spirit of the Lord descended upon him, and the visions of eternity were opened to his view. (*DHC* 1:82-83.)

## Existence of Devils

Shortly after the gospel was introduced in England, Elders Heber C. Kimball, Orson Hyde, Willard Richards, and Isaac Russell, were beset by legions of devils who attempted to overcome and destroy these servants of the Lord. The elders heard and saw these spirits. (*Life of Heber C. Kimball*, pp. 129-132.) President Wilford Woodruff had a similar experience in England, but through the intervention of messengers of God, the evil spirits were unable to accomplish their work of destruction. (*The Deseret Weekly*, November 7, 1896.) Many missionaries have experienced confrontations with evil beings from the unseen world. It seems that the devil is particularly interested in preventing the servants of God from accomplishing their missions.

## Knowledge Is Necessary

The Prophet once said that a man is saved no faster than he gains knowledge. (*DHC* 4:588; D&C 131:6.) Then he said:

> "for if he does not get knowledge, he will be brought into captivity by some evil power in the other world, as evil spirits will have more knowledge, and consequently more power than many men who are on the earth. Hence it needs revelation to assist us, and give us knowledge of the things of God. (*DHC* 4:588.)

## Bishops

The Lord has placed bishops in the stakes and branch presidents in the missions in his Church to preside over the people in their wards and branches. In their calling the Lord said the following:

"And unto the bishop of the church, and unto such as God shall appoint and ordain to watch over the church and to be elders unto the church, are to have it given unto them to discern all those gifts lest there shall be any among you professing and yet be not of God." (D&C 46:27.)

From the First Presidency instructions come to the stake presidents under whom the bishops in the stakes serve and to the branch presidents in the missions from the mission presidents. In the event the bishop or branch presidents may require counsel from their respective presidents, they may receive help. In a letter to these Church officers, the First Presidency so counseled the members of the Church. They further stated that if these stake and mission officers require the assistance of the First Presidency, they may ask for it, but the members should seek counsel from their local officers.

## Implementation

With the restoration of the Church, the same teachings and practices of the gospel were restored. The ministry of angels and the gifts and blessings of the gospel are again on the earth. Ministering angels have come to the earth where a specific need existed. As President Wilford Woodruff, who had received such holy visitants, said, the Lord does not send an angel to a person simply to satisfy curiosity, but, rather, to perform a work that only an angel can perform. (*The Deseret Weekly*, November 7, 1896.)

The members of the Church are principal targets of the Adversary, for if he can deceive them through false doctrines, false practices, and even by the false notion that there is no devil, nor a future existence, nor a judgment, he has gained a tremendous victory. If he can persuade them to believe in the ideas of men rather than the counsel of the leaders of the Church, his ends are attained.

On the other hand, if the saint will seek for the gifts of the Holy Ghost to which he is entitled, he will not be deceived; if he will gain knowledge from the scriptures he will not be deceived; if he will follow the counsel of his Church leaders through the line of authority of the First Presidency, stake presidency, and bishopric, he will find himself on the secure, safe path to peace in this life and eternal life in the world to come. (D&C 59:23.)

## Chapter 44

# DOCTRINAL INSTRUCTIONS

### (Sections 130:8-23; 131:5-8)

The Prophet Joseph Smith made observations upon the public and private remarks of member and nonmember. One time Orson Hyde gave his views on various gospel subjects that called forth corrections by the Prophet. At another time the Prophet corrected some statements made by a Methodist preacher. These corrections have provided the Church with some important doctrinal instructions contained in Sections 130 and 131 of the Doctrine and Covenants.

### Knowledge

Latter-day Saints believe in many scriptures that emphasize the need to acquire knowledge. Important among these are the following:

> It is impossible for a man to be saved in ignorance. (D&C 131:6.)
>
> Whatever principle of intelligence we attain unto in this life, it will rise with us in the resurrection.
>
> And if a person gains more knowledge and intelligence in this life through the diligence and obedience than another, he will have so much the advantage in the world to come. (D&C 130:18-19.)

Since the purpose of life is to understand and live the laws that ultimately give salvation (eternal life), then salvation knowledge is the most important part of learning. If one lacks knowledge of the Savior, the atonement, how to accept the atonement for individual salvation, and also the Church which represents the Lord for salvation, it is impossible to be saved. (*DHC* 5:387.)

The person who fails to live gospel teachings degenerates in knowledge. (*DHC* 4:588.) On the other hand, as one studies by faith, his concepts of God and eternity are enlarged, and his power to do good is increased. (D&C 88:118; Alma 12:9-11; *DHC* 2:8.)

Essential salvation knowledge to be learned by the saint is that which pertains to the preservation of his membership in the Church. The revelations give ways by which one may not be deceived by every wind of doctrine. The Latter-day Saint is well grounded in the path of safety when he accepts the following truth: Everything we know about God and our relationship to him comes from revelation. (D&C 52:9, 36.) The revelations are true, for they come from the Giver of all truth. Knowledge pertaining to this life only is insufficient for salvation. We must learn not only how to overcome our sins here, but we must, as the Prophet Joseph Smith says in the following quotation, learn how to triumph over evil in the world to come.

> Salvation is nothing more nor less than to triumph over all our enemies and put them under our feet. And when we have power to put all enemies under our feet in this world, and a knowledge to triumph over all evil spirits in the world to come, then we are saved. . . . (*DHC* 5:387.)

The member of the Church who learns the principles of salvation and the keys against being deceived while in mortality will have that much advantage in the world to come. What we learn here will help us forever.

## Obedience

There is no true success in this life unless one is obedient to gospel principles. When one considers that this life is man's probationary period, this fact is apparent.

Elder Richard L. Evans of the Council of the Twelve, in discussing Section 130:18-19, has pointed out that if the student will keep in mind that diligence and obedience are the key words in the Lord's admonition for his children to acquire intelligence, he will not leave the faith.

Those words are most meaningful—and I have no fear of learning, of the pursuit of knowledge, for any of our young people, if they will keep in mind *diligence* and *obedience*—obedience to the commandments of God, diligence in keeping close to the Church, in keeping active, keeping prayerful, keeping clean, keeping circumspect in their conduct. (*Conference Report,* April 1956, p. 44.)

This advice concerning learning all truth, religious or secular, is in harmony with the Lord's counsel concerning good books, languages, and people. (D&C 90:15.)

The following two scriptures emphasize the reason for obedience and also the operation of law:

I, the Lord, am bound when ye do what I say; but when ye do not what I say, ye have no promise. (D&C 82:10.)

There is a law, irrevocably decreed in heaven before the foundations of this world, upon which all blessings are predicated—

And when we obtain any blessing from God, it is by obedience to that law upon which it is predicated. (*Ibid.,* 130:20-21.)

In 1831, the Lord gave reasons why the saints should be obedient. Among them are: that we are citizens of the Lord's kingdom; the Lord has given this earth to his saints; lest death overtake us; the Savior pleads our cause as our Advocate; and we are Christ's sons and daughters because of our accepting his atonement. (*Doctrine and Covenants Commentary*, pp. 252-254.)

## The Godhead

The Prophet Joseph Smith said the following about the importance of knowing about God:

If any man does not know God, and inquires what kind of a being he is,—if he will search diligently his own heart—if the declaration of Jesus and the apostles be true, he will realize that he has not eternal life; for there can be eternal life on no other principle." (*Teachings of the Prophet Joseph Smith,* p. 344.)

To know God ultimately is to become like him by obedience to his commandments. (D&C 84:19-23; 132:23-24.) The first step in knowing God is to recognize that God is a personal being of flesh and bones. The doctrine of eternal life, or exaltation in the celestial kingdom, is dependent upon this truth.

The Father has a body of flesh and bones as tangible as man's; the Son also; but the Holy Ghost has not a body of flesh and bones, but is a personage of Spirit. Were it not so, the Holy Ghost could not dwell in us.

A man may receive the Holy Ghost, and it may descend upon him and not tarry with him. (D&C 130:22-23.)

Why is it of value for the Latter-day Saint to know that God is a personal being with body, parts, and passions? First, one may then know that faithful men may become as the Father in every sense of the word. Second, to know that God is personal and that he is our Father gives man the ability to approach Deity in prayer in a meaningful way, rather than to pray to an all-present spirit, as God is conceived in the "Christian" world. Third, the true concept of God and Christ and the Holy Ghost, who is also an individual—a personage of spirit—gives meaning to the scriptures about the members of the Godhead. Fourth, one sees that God has a habitat, and he is not in person throughout all space. (D&C 130:8; Abraham 3:2-4, 9.)

### Eternal Man

Latter-day Saints have the opportunity to know about themselves and their place in the plan of salvation.

Whereas the "Christian" churches teach that man has his beginning in this life, the Lord has revealed that all men had a premortal existence. (Abraham 3:22-23.) Men and women are eternal beings by nature. They are made up of body and spirit, both of which are eternal. (D&C 93:29, 33; 131:7-8.) The following comes from the Prophet Joseph Smith:

> The spirit of man is not a created being; it existed from eternity, and will exist to eternity. Anything created cannot be eternal; and earth, water, etc., had their existence in an elementary state, from eternity. (*DHC* 3:387.)

Latter-day Saints understand that they shall have an eternal existence. They will never experience a time when there is not conscious existence. Through the resurrection man's body will be eternally wedded to his spirit. (D&C 93:33-34.)

With this understanding of man's eternity, how does this information contribute to the Latter-day Saint's understanding of himself and of the need to give obedience to the gospel principles? The following points may contribute to the answer to this question: (1) Since man is an eternal being there will be no end to conscious existence; therefore, he will come to judgment as the Lord has predicted. (D&C 76:110-111.) (2) Man is capable of accepting religious truth when he hears it, unless sin darkens his comprehension. (D&C 93:30-33.) (3) Man is endowed with free agency and is responsible for his actions in mortality. (D&C 93:29-33.) Although man was created by God, the Creator is not responsible for what man does during his earthly probation. (4) Since man was begotten by God, he is capable of becoming as his Heavenly Parent. (5) Because man is eternal, the Latter-day Saint has the basis for making decisions, for he knows that these decisions have their eternal consequences for good or for evil.

## The Earth

The scriptures reveal that the earth is a living organism. (Moses 7:48-50; John A. Widtsoe, *Joseph Smith*, p. 149-150.) Elder James E. Talmage said the following concerning all created things:

> Every created thing has been made for a purpose; and every thing that fills the measure of its creation is to be advanced in the scale of progression, within the bounds of its own kind or kingdom, be it an atom of a world, a protozoan or man. (*The Latter-day Prophets and the Doctrine and Covenants,* 3:162.)

The earth fulfills the purpose for which it was made in obeying a celestial law. (D&C 88:25.) It was created that it might be a habitat for man; in fact, men are born of this earth. Because the earth fulfills this purpose, it will be rewarded by being sanctified and become a celestial planet. (*Ibid.*, 88:26.) In this condition, the earth will be as a Urim and Thummim whereby celestial beings will be able to learn about "all kingdoms of a lower order." (*Ibid.*, 130:9.) Those who receive the highest blessings of the celestial kingdom will receive a white stone which "will become a Urim and Thummim . . . whereby things pertaining to a higher order of kingdoms will be made known." (*Ibid.*, 10-11.)

In one's quest for saving knowledge it is discovered that, as the earth obeys the law by which it progresses to a celestial kingdom, so also the Latter-day Saint understands that full obedience to gospel law is necessary for eventual celestialization.

## Salvation

The purpose of life is to work out one's salvation in this world and in the world to come. (D&C 46:7.) Salvation comes by obedience to the principles and practices of the gospel of Jesus Christ.

Elder Marion G. Romney of the Council of the Twelve reminds us that eternal life is not achieved in this life, but an assurance of it may be received here. (D&C 131:5.) In order to make one's calling and election sure, the following three things are necessary: (1) to receive the testimony of Jesus and be baptized; (2) to receive the Holy Ghost by the laying on of hands; and (3) to be sealed by the Holy Spirit of Promise. Brother Romney proceeded to say:

> . . . What is required is wholehearted devotion to the gospel and unreserved allegiance to the Church of Jesus Christ of Latter-day Saints. Speaking to this point, the Prophet taught ". . . that those who keep the commandments of the Lord and walk in his statutes to the end, are the only individuals who shall receive the blessings. . . . We must be willing to sacrifice everything. Through self-discipline and devotion we must demonstrate to the Lord that we are willing to serve him under all circumstances. When we have done this, we shall receive an assurance that we shall have eternal life in the world to come. Then we shall have peace in this world. (*Conference Report,* September 1949, pp. 41-44.)

## Joseph Smith, The Prophet

The Lord declared that this generation would receive the word of the Lord through his Prophet, Joseph Smith. (D&C 5:10.) As long as the dispensation of the fulness of time continues, the word of the Lord through the modern books of scriptures and the Prophet's writings will continue to go forth to the world.

One of the remarkable evidences to support the mission of Joseph Smith is the prophecy on war. (D&C 87.) This revelation states that the American Civil War should begin with the rebellion of South Carolina, for a "voice" declared to Joseph Smith that there would be armed conflict between the North and the South. It would "probably arise through the slave question." (D&C 130:12-13.) Slavery would be a contributing cause of the Civil War, but not the sole cause of it. This point of view agrees with most historians on the cause of that war, although there are some proponents of the theory that slavery was the single cause.

The important truth is that the Civil War was prophesied, and that the details of that war, mentioned in Section 87, were fulfilled. Out of that truth comes a lesson. As one gains more knowledge through diligent study, its value to him comes through his obedience to what is learned. This blessing comes through studying by faith. (D&C 88:118.)

## The Second Coming of Christ

The Savior told his disciples anciently and today that no man knows the day and the hour of his second coming. (Matthew 24:36; D&C 49:7.)

Preparations are underway and have been since the dispensation began for the return of the Savior. His words to his disciples are pertinent today:

"Watch therefore: for ye know not what hour your Lord doth come." (Matthew 24:42; Joseph Smith 1:46.)

As one gains more knowledge by his *diligence* and *obedience*, his faith is strengthened and his insight into the signs of the times is enlarged. He is obedient to this counsel and finds safety in these words ". . . if ye are prepared ye shall not fear." (D&C 38:30.)

## Implementation

Every Latter-day Saint is counseled to learn the principles of the gospel of Jesus Christ. A regular time each day for study brings many rewarding blessings. Without salvation knowledge it is impossible to be saved. Knowledge in itself is not sufficient for salvation, but knowledge obeyed brings salvation in this life and in the world to come. (D&C 59:23.)

A rewarding experience for a Latter-day Saint is to learn the value or application of each principle or doctrine of the gospel. By doing this he learns that gospel teachings are consistent in themselves, and each principle is harmonious with the other parts of the gospel.

Basic to one's appreciation of the gospel as a motivator for righteous action is the doctrine of man's relationship to God, premortality, purpose of life, man's environment, the assurance of being on the Lord's side, and that Joseph Smith is a prophet of God.

## Chapter 45

# ETERNAL MARRIAGE

### (Sections 131:1-4; 132)

In conversation with William Clayton, the Prophet Joseph Smith told him what is now recorded in verses 1 through 4 of Section 131 of the Doctrine and Covenants pertaining to marriage. Section 132 is the revelation on celestial marriage, which includes plural marriage as well as eternal marriage. It is believed that the revelation on plural marriage was received as early as 1831, but Section 132 was committed to writing on July 12, 1843. (*DHC* 5:xxxi.)

Inasmuch as the Lord by revelation has withdrawn the practice of plural marriage, it is only necessary to mention the principle in this lesson. (*The Discourses of Wilford Woodruff*, pp. 213-18.) It is well to remember that this practice is proper only when the Lord commands it. (D&C 49:15-17; *Teachings of the Prophet Joseph Smith*, pp. 323-24; Jacob 2:27-30.) The penalty for practicing plural marriage by a member of the Church today is excommunication, the same as for others who commit adultery. (Joseph F. Smith, *Gospel Doctrine*, p. 280.)

Exaltation in the celestial kingdom requires eternal marriage but does not require plural marriage. In the revelation regarding eternal marriage, the expression "if a man marry a wife," or a similar expression, is used. (D&C 132:15, 18, 19, 26, 41.)

### In the Beginning

In the beginning God ordained that marriage should be a part of earth experience for his sons and daughters.

The following reveals that truth and also that this principle was intended as a part of the plan of salvation.

And again, verily I say unto you, that whoso forbiddeth to marry is not ordained of God, for marriage is ordained of God unto man.

Wherefore, it is lawful that he should have one wife, and they twain shall be one flesh, and all this that the earth might answer the ends of its creation:

And that it might be filled with the measure of man, according to his creation before the world was made. (D&C 49:15-17.)

In discussing the marriage of Adam and Eve, Elder Harold B. Lee, of the Council of the Twelve, referred to its perpetuity, as follows:

Here [Genesis 2:18, 22-24] was a marriage performed by the Lord between two immortal beings, for until sin entered the world their bodies were not subject to death. He made them one, not merely for time, nor for any definite period; they were to be one throughout the eternal ages. If you were to say that because Adam and Eve transgressed and became subject to death that this eternal union was broken, then just remember that the purpose of the atonement by Jesus Christ was to restore that which was lost by the fall. Their restoration then to each other after the resurrection would not require a re-marriage, for death to them was not a divorce; it was only a temporary separation. Resurrection to immortality meant for them a reunion and an eternal bond never again to be severed. "For as in Adam all die, even so in Christ shall all be made alive." (1 Corinthians 15:22.) (*Youth and the Church,* p. 128.)

## Purpose of Marriage

There are some churches which maintain that celibacy is sanctioned by God. One of these churches in the days of the Prophet Joseph Smith was the Shaking Quakers. It was to a group of Latter-day Saint missionaries that the Lord revealed through the Prophet Joseph Smith, that marriage was ordained of him and that those who taught otherwise did not represent him. (D&C 49:15.)

Marriage makes it possible for the earth to answer the end of its creation. Because man, as a premortal being, was designed to come to earth to work out his salvation, marriage was ordained to bring about this purpose. Consequently, the fundamental purpose of marriage is to beget children that the Lord's purposes may be fulfilled. (D&C 49:16-17.)

## Marriage Outside the Church

Should a Latter-day Saint young man or woman marry someone who is not a member of the Church? Leaders of the Church have counseled members to marry within the Church. (*Discourses of Brigham Young*, pp. 196-97; Joseph F. Smith, *Gospel Doctrine*, p. 279; David O. McKay, *Gospel Ideals*, p. 464.) Where the parties to a marriage are both strong in different faiths, the chances for happiness are greatly diminished. (John A. Widtsoe, *Evidences and Reconciliations*, pp. 237-38.)

Sometimes young people feel that when they marry a nonmember, they will be able to convert him or her to the Church. The chances for conversion and the consequent happiness in marriage are far greater if the conversion is made before marriage. (*Youth and the Church*, p. 132.)

The Lord has said that parents should teach their children correct principles to shape their lives for happiness. (D&C 68:25-28.) The mother has a wonderful opportunity in the home to impress upon her children the importance of marrying within the Church.

## Purpose of Life

To work out one's salvation in this life and in the life to come is the paramount purpose of the earth life. This means that the purpose of God in creating man is to grant to him, through obedience, the greatest measure of salvation—eternal life. (Moses 1:39.) As man is the child of God, so also man may, by obedience to law, become as the Father. (D&C 132:20-22.) The blessing of eternal life comes to those who fulfill all the laws and commandments.

## Obedience to the Gospel

The gospel of Jesus Christ provides the way whereby the sons and daughters of God may return to his presence in the celestial kingdom. Baptism is the gate to that kingdom. (D&C 76:50-53.) There are degrees in the celestial kingdom; therefore, members of his Church should seek for the highest degree.

> In the celestial glory there are three heavens or degrees;
>
> And in order to obtain the highest, a man must enter into this order or priesthood [meaning the new and everlasting covenant of marriage];
>
> And if he does not, he cannot obtain it.
>
> He may enter into the other, but that is the end of his kingdom; he cannot have an increase. (D&C 131:1-4.)

The new and everlasting covenant is the gospel of Jesus Christ. There are many covenants within the gospel, and marriage for eternity is one of them. To be fully obedient to the gospel involves full discipleship.

## Eternal Marriage

After a couple have received the higher ordinances of the priesthood endowment in the temple, they are qualified to receive eternal marriage. Only by the keys of the priesthood held by the president of the Church, who delegates these powers to others, may this union be solemnized. (D&C 132:7.) The blessings available to those who marry for eternity are these:

> . . . they shall pass by the angels, and the gods, which are set there, to their exaltation and glory in all things, as hath been sealed upon their heads, which glory shall be a fulness and a continuation of the seeds forever and ever. (D&C 132:19.)

## Eternal Increase

In Section 131 and in Section 132, verse 19, the Lord has told us that if we are faithful to the eternal marriage vows, the blessing of "increase" and "a continuation of the seeds forever and ever" will be received. The Prophet Joseph Smith gave the following information on this subject:

> Except a man and his wife enter into an everlasting covenant and be married for eternity, while in this probation, by the power and authority of the Holy Priesthood, they will cease to increase when they die; that is, they will not have any children after the resurrection. (*DHC* 5:391.)

The children born to an exalted man and woman after the resurrection are spirit beings. The parents are tangible, resurrected persons referred to in the scriptures as having spiritual bodies; that is, with spirit element in their veins rather than blood as in mortal bodies. (D&C 88:27; Alma 11:45; *Discourses of Brigham Young*, p. 374.)

## The Deaths

When resurrected beings are exalted they receive "eternal lives," the power of eternal increase, which is the opposite of the "deaths," or the lack of such power. (D&C 132:24-25.)

Only exalted beings will be married in the future life because they proved themselves while on the earth in being faithful to all things required of them. (D&C 132:13.) In the following verses the conditions in the world to come are explained, having reference to those who receive marriage for eternity and to others who did not subscribe to the full law:

> Therefore, if a man marry him a wife in the world, and he marry her not by me nor by my word, and he covenant with her so long as he is in the world and she with him, their covenant and marriage are not of force when they are dead, and when they

are out of the world; therefore, they are not bound by any law when they are out of the world.

Therefore, when they are out of the world they neither marry nor are given in marriage; but are appointed angels in heaven, which angels are ministering servants, to minister for those who are worthy of a far more, and an exceeding, and eternal weight of glory.

For these angels did not abide my law; therefore, they cannot be enlarged, but remain separately and singly, without exaltation, in their saved condition, to all eternity; and from henceforth are not gods, but are angels of God forever and ever. (D&C 132:15-17.)

If there are some who may believe that their marriage is in effect beyond the grave, although not solemnized by God's priesthood in the temple, the following verse corrects this belief:

And again, verily I say unto you, if a man marry a wife, and make a covenant with her for time and for all eternity, if that covenant is not by me or by my word, which is my law, and is not sealed by the Holy Spirit of promise, through him whom I have anointed and appointed unto this power, then it is not valid neither of force when they are out of the world, because they are not joined by me, saith the Lord, neither by my word; when they are out of the world it cannot be received there, because the angels and the gods are appointed there, by whom they cannot pass; they cannot, therefore, inherit my glory; for my house is a house of order, saith the Lord God. (D&C 132:18.)

## Marriage in the Resurrection

In reference to a question concerning marriage of a woman to several husbands, the Savior said that "in the resurrection they neither marry, nor are given in marriage, but are as the angels of God in heaven." (Matthew 22:30.) What did the Lord mean when he said that there was no marrying in the resurrection? He was speaking of the Sadducees who had rejected the gospel and its teachings about eternal marriage. As far as they were concerned, there was no marrying or giving in marriage in heaven. But if the persons are worthy to be married for eternity, and the opportunity does not come while on the earth, the opportunity for this blessing will come in the world ahead. The necessary ordinances may, for instance, be performed on the earth in a temple by proxy.

What of Latter-day Saint daughters who have died without being sealed to a man in the temple? Elder Melvin J. Ballard gave this counsel:

> Now, then, what of your daughters who have died and have not been sealed to some man? Unless it is made known to you, let their case rest. They will make known to you the agreements and contracts they have mutually entered into. The sealing power shall be forever and ever with this Church, and provisions will be made for them. We cannot run faster than the Lord has provided the way. Their blessings and privileges will come to them in due time. In the meantime, they are safe. (*Sermons and Missionary Services of Melvin J. Ballard,* p. 260.)

Elder Ballard also gives an answer to the same question concerning little children, who, of course, did not receive the sealing ordinance of marriage:

> I lost a son six years of age, and I saw him a man in the spirit world after his death, and I saw how he had exercised his own freedom of choice and would obtain of his own will and volition a companionship, and in due time to him, and all those who are worthy of it, shall come all of the blessings and sealing privileges of the house of the Lord. Do not worry over it. They are safe; they are all right. (*Ibid.*)

What about young men and women who die without the opportunity for marriage in the temple? Elder Harold B. Lee has said:

> You young women advancing in years who have not yet accepted a proposal of marriage, if you make yourselves worthy and ready to go to the house of the Lord and have faith in this sacred principle, even though the privilege of marriage does not come to you now, the Lord will reward you in due time and no blessing will be denied you. You are not under obligation to

accept a proposal from someone unworthy of you for fear you will fail of your blessings. Likewise you young men who may lose your lives in a terrible conflict before you have had an opportunity for marriage, the Lord knows the intents of your hearts and in his own time will reward you with opportunities made possible through temple ordinances instituted in the Church for that purpose. (*Youth and the Church,* p. 132.)

Many women join the Church although their husbands may not. What of them? Salvation is an individual matter. If one party to the marriage remains true to the covenant of baptism and the opportunity for eternal marriage is not possible, then the righteous desires of that person's heart will eventually be realized.

### Blessings of Temple Marriage

Experience has shown that those who marry in the temple generally find success in their marriage. Elder John A. Widtsoe gave the following nine reasons for a temple marriage:

1. It is the Lord's desire and will.
2. It is in harmony with the sacred nature of the marriage covenant.
3. It tends to insure marital happiness.
4. It permits the association of husband and wife for time and for all eternity.
5. It provides the eternal possession of children and family relationship.
6. It acts as a restraint against evil.
7. It furnishes the opportunity for endless [eternal] progression.
8. It places the family under the protection of the power of the priesthood.
9. It provides a God-like destiny for human beings. (*Evidences and Reconciliations,* pp. 231-36.)

### Happy Homes

The performance of the marriage ceremony in the temple is not sufficient in itself to make a happy home.

President David O. McKay has given six elements that lie at the basis of true home building:

1. Let us substitute the present tendency toward a low view of marriage with the lofty view which God gives it. . . .
2. Teach the young of both sexes in the responsibilities and ideals of marriage so that they may realize that marriage involves obligation and is not an arrangement to be terminated at pleasure. . . .
3. Instruct young girls in the fundamental arts of housekeeping, so that when responsibilities of wifehood come, they may be free from the difficulties and perplexities which arise from ignorance and inexperience.
4. Marriage should be solemnized, as far as possible, in the house of God. . . .
5. Keep religion in home life. . . .
6. Teach the young that the foundations of a happy home are laid before even the bride and bridegroom kneel at the marriage altar. (*Gospel Ideals*, pp. 478-79.)

## Implementation

In the premortal world the plan of salvation was formed whereby the spirit sons and daughters of God could receive an earth life necessary for eternal progression. The relationship between God and his children was a parent-child relationship because his spirit children were born of a Heavenly Father and a Heavenly Mother. (*Youth and the Church*, pp. 126-27.) The eternal round of spirit children being born to exalted beings and the opportunity to reach the heights of exaltation by an earth life require marriage for eternity by mortals. Faithfulness to eternal marriage covenants is a means of proving oneself as a part of the eternal plan.

Marriage was instituted by God for the purpose of bringing to earth life his spirit children for this probationary state. Exaltation is possible only to male and female together. (Joseph F. Smith, *Gospel Doctrine*, p. 276.) Marriage is so essential to salvation in the highest sense that provision is made in the gospel that those who do not have the opportunity in life to receive eternal marriage may have the blessing of temple ordinances by proxy.

Latter-day Saint parents have the responsibility of teaching their children the principles of the gospel in order that they may be prepared for marriage in the temple. They know that success in marriage is enhanced greatly by eternal marriage and that only when sealed by the priesthood of God can contracts remain unbroken when men are dead. (D&C 132:13-14.)

## Chapter 46

# GOVERNMENT AND LAWS

### (Section 134)

Latter-day Saints are known as loyal citizens of the countries in which they live. About eighteen months after The Church of Jesus Christ of Latter-day Saints was organized, the Lord commanded his people not to break the law of the land, for if they kept the laws of God there would be no reason for breaking the laws of the land. (D&C 58: 21-22.) Before this time, instructions were given to the authorities of the Church that in cases of infractions of the moral law, the guilty should be delivered up to the law of the land. (D&C 42:84-87.) Later, in two revelations, the saints came to know that the Constitution of the United States was an inspired document and that they should uphold it. (D&C 98:4-7; 101:76-80.)

### Prophecy Fulfilled

An incident in American political history involving the Prophet Joseph Smith and Stephen A. Douglas, a political figure, emphasized the point that the Lord respects his people when they conform to his laws and to the laws of the land. The prophecy also affirms the truth that Joseph Smith enjoyed the prophetic gift. (B. H. Roberts, *New Witnesses for God* 1:304-13.) On May 18, 1843, the Prophet gave the following prophecy to and about Stephen A. Douglas, a little-known judge in Illinois at that time:

> Judge, you will aspire to the Presidency of the United States; and if you ever turn your hand against me or the Latter-day Saints, you will feel the weight of the hand of the Almighty upon you; and you will live to see and know that I have testified the

truth to you; for the conversation of this day will stick to you through life. (*Ibid.*, p. 305.)

By 1857 Judge Douglas, United States senator from the state of Illinois and then aspirant to the Presidency of the United States, delivered a speech in which he alleged that the Mormons in Utah Territory were disloyal to the federal government and that they incited Indian tribes against that government. He then referred to the saints as a "pestiferous, disgusting cancer which is gnawing into the very vitals of the body politic. It must be cut out by the roots, and seared over by the red hot iron of stern and unflinching law." (*Ibid.*, p. 308.)

Although Senator Douglas knew the Latter-day Saint people as a law-abiding people and knew their persecutions in Missouri, he disregarded the voice of prophecy and, in the presidential election of 1860, was defeated by the Republican candidate, Abraham Lincoln.

## Doctrine and Covenants—1835

When the Church sought to print a compilation of the revelations received by Joseph Smith by 1833, a mob destroyed the printing press and practically all of the printed material. (*DHC* 1:390.) Consequently, the *Book of Commandments* was never available to the members of the Church, except for a very few copies.

On August 17, 1835, a general assembly of the Church met to agree on publishing a second compilation to be known as the Doctrine and Covenants. The priesthood members present testified to the truth of the revelations. Oliver Cowdery read an article entitled "Governments and Laws in General." The article was approved and ordered printed in the volume. (*DHC* 2:243-47.)

In order to present the truth concerning the Church's belief about law, because of accusations that it did not uphold the law, it was felt necessary to prepare this article.

## "Our Opinion"

It was printed in the 1835 edition of the Doctrine and Covenants and appears as Section 134 in the current edition. The following preamble to the article is not a part of Section 134:

> That our belief with regard to earthly governments and laws in general may not be misinterpreted nor misunderstood, we have thought proper to present at the close of this volume our opinion concerning the same. (D&C 134, introduction.)

This article is an "opinion" and not a revelation, and therefore "does not hold the same place in the doctrines of the Church as do the revelations." (*Doctrine and Covenants Commentary*, p. 852.) On the other hand, Section 134 was presented to the Church assembled in 1835 and several times since that year as binding upon the members of the Church.

The laws that now govern the nations of the earth will be supplanted by laws instituted by the Savior when he takes his place to reign as King of kings. (*Ibid.*, pp. 204-05; D&C 38:21-22.)

## God-Ordained Governments

The Lord raised up men to formulate the Constitution of the United States that principles of freedom might be exercised in this promised land. Only in this kind of political climate could the Church of Jesus Christ be established in the last days. The land of America was kept hid from the nations that this land might indeed be a place where divine prophecies might be fulfilled. (Ezra Taft Benson, *Conference Report*, October 1961, p. 69.)

The perfect form of government was instituted in the days of Adam, but later the sons of men rebelled against these principles of righteousness. (Moses 5:12-13.) Although Section 134 suggests that governments were instituted for the benefit of men, it is evident that all governments are not in this category. (D&C 134:1.) The Lord does not originate laws contrary to eternal principles like free agency. As Elder Erastus Snow said, all forms of government are better than none at all, in that order is maintained by governments, though some of them may not be the best forms. (*Journal of Discourses*, 22:151.) Nonetheless, God controls the nations though he is not the originator of those governments. (Brigham Young, *Journal of Discourses*, 6:342.)

## Standard of Judgment

The governments set up by men serve a purpose in the eternal plan by requiring men to govern their lives according to law. (D&C 76:111; 134:1.) The Prophet Joseph Smith said:

> He [God] will award judgment or mercy to all nations according to their several deserts, their means of obtaining intelligence, the laws by which they are governed, the facilities afforded them of obtaining correct information, and His inscrutable designs in relation to the human family. . . . (*DHC* 4:596.)

This statement is recognized to be true when one realizes that God is the author of righteousness and that, woven in the various laws of the nations, there are laws which are also found in the gospel of Jesus Christ. (Stephen L Richards, *Conference Report*, October 1923, p. 47.) Also, there are many laws that are contrary to righteous principles. The framers of laws and governments are held accountable for their acts in relation to them, both in making and administering them. (*Doctrine and Covenants Commentary*, pp. 852-53; D&C 134:1, 6.)

## Section 134

By 1835, when Section 134 of the Doctrine and Covenants was prepared, the saints had suffered persecution, loss of property and lives, and their freedom of religious belief had been challenged. It is understandable why they would want their own beliefs concerning law and governments made known. This section might be divided into the following parts: (1) basic rights; (2) governments and officials; (3) religious societies and beliefs; and (4) noninterference in the rights of others.

### Basic Rights

After the statement that men are accountable to the governments under which they live, man's fundamental rights are stated in these words:

> We believe that no government can exist in peace, except such laws are framed and held inviolate as will secure to each individual the free exercise of conscience, the right and control of property, and the protection of life. (D&C 134:2.)

President David O. McKay has called attention to the fact that "there is innate in man a feeling that will rebel against tyranny." (*Deseret News, Church Section,* January 2, 1952, p. 3.) Men have come up from the oppression to overthrow coercive governments. The Declaration of Independence and the Constitution of the United States are examples of the declared rights of men and the protection afforded.

Where there is an infringement of these basic rights, the following belief is expressed:

> We believe that men should appeal to the civil law for redress of all wrongs and grievances, where personal abuse is inflicted or the right of property or character infringed, where such laws exist as will protect the same; but we believe that all men are justified in defending themselves, their friends, and

property, and the government, from the unlawful assaults and encroachments of all persons in times of exigency, where immediate appeal cannot be made to the laws, and relief afforded. (D&C 134:11.)

## Governments and Officials

Latter-day Saints during this dispensation, and especially during the time of Joseph Smith, have had many unfortunate experiences with government officials who have not upheld the constitutional rights of the saints. The following verse points out the obligation of civil magistrates upholding the law of the land in their decisions:

> We believe that all governments necessarily require civil officers and magistrates to enforce the laws of the same; and that such as will administer the law in equity and justice should be sought for and upheld by the voice of the people if a republic, or the will of the sovereign.
>
> We believe that all men are bound to sustain and uphold the respective governments in which they reside, while protected in their inherent and inalienable rights by the laws of such governments; and that sedition and rebellion are unbecoming every citizen thus protected, and should be punished accordingly; and that all governments have a right to enact such laws as in their own judgments are best calculated to secure the public interest; at the same time, however, holding sacred the freedom of conscience. (D&C 134:3, 5.)

In an earlier revelation the saints were counseled to uphold wise and honest men in public office; otherwise, evil would result. (D&C 98:8-10.) It may not always be possible to determine between the wise and the unwise, but the Lord has given some standards by which to make decisions about principles or political issues. Laws which deny men their agency (D&C 98:4-8) and those which permit them to do evil should be changed. (Moroni 7:14-19.)

By divine commandment the Prophet Joseph Smith appealed to the President of the United States and the

Congress for redress of crimes committed against them in Missouri. (D&C 101:81-95; Joseph Fielding Smith, *Essentials in Church History*, pp. 287-94.)

One is reminded that the Lord counseled his saints who had been driven from Jackson County, Missouri, in 1833 and 1834 that they were not to fight for the redemption of Zion, but that he would, in his time, fight their battles. (D&C 105:14-15.)

### Breakers of the Law

Those who break the law should be punished according to the seriousness of the offense. Governments have the right to regulate their societies for the preservation of peace and order. Latter-day Saints are enjoined to bring offenders against the law to justice. (D&C 134:8.) They should also sustain the law enforcement arms of government that all might have justice.

### Religious Societies and Beliefs

Eleven years after Section 134 was written, the Prophet Joseph Smith wrote the Articles of Faith. The eleventh article is as follows: "We claim the privilege of worshiping Almighty God according to the dictates of our own conscience, and allow all men the same privilege, let them worship how, where, or what they may."

This same statement of belief lies at the basis of what is contained in verse 4 of Section 134. The privilege of religious worship is the right of every man provided it does not infringe upon the rights and liberties of others. Equally so, Latter-day Saints believe that government does not have the right to prescribe rules of worship, nor dictate forms for public or private devotion. (D&C 134:4, 7.)

There should not be favoritism shown for one religion over another. (D&C 134:9.) The following principles were given by the First Presidency of the Church:

We declare that from principle and policy, we favor:
The absolute separation of church and state;
No domination of the state by the church;
No church interference with the functions of the state;
No state interference with the functions of the Church, or with the free exercise of religion;
The absolute freedom of the individual from the domination of ecclesiastical authority in political affairs;
The equality of all churches before the law.
("An Address, The Church of Jesus Christ of Latter-day Saints to the World," *Conference Report,* April 1907, p. 14.)

## Excommunication and Disfellowship

The Church of Jesus Christ of Latter-day Saints maintains that religious societies have the right to deal with their members for disorderly conduct, but the punishment should not extend to taking their property or jeopardizing their lives. The penalties for misconduct in the Church are excommunication and disfellowship. (D&C 134:10.)

To be disfellowshipped means that the person remains a member of the Church, but he is limited in what he may do. He may attend meetings, but he may not participate in the activities of the Church. Excommunication removes one from the records of the Church and thus he loses all of the privileges of Church membership. There are three offenses for which one may be punished: (1) the breaking of the moral law, (2) deliberate disobedience to the regulations of the Church, and (3) incorrect interpretation of doctrine when the correct teachings have been explained and the person is unwilling to accept them. (John A. Widtsoe, *Priesthood and Church Government,* p. 209.)

## Implementation

Not long after The Church of Jesus Christ of Latter-day Saints was organized, a conference of the Church adopted a set of principles regarding governments and laws in general. (D&C 134.) Since then the members of the Church have accepted these beliefs as binding upon themselves. To indicate the consistency and application of that early document to the present, the following statement from President David O. McKay is given:

> . . . I repeat that no greater immediate responsibility rests upon members of the Church, upon all citizens of the Republic and of neighboring Republics than to protect the freedom vouchsafed by the Constitution of the United States.
>
> Let us, by exercising our privileges under the Constitution—
>
> (1) Preserve our right to worship God according to the dictates of our conscience.
>
> (2) Preserve the right to work when and where we choose. No free man should be compelled to pay tribute in order to realize this God-given privilege. Read in the Doctrine and Covenants this statement: ". . . it is not right that any man should be in bondage one to another." (D&C 101:79.)
>
> (3) Feel free to plan and to reap without the handicap of bureaucratic interference.
>
> (4) Devote our time, means, and life if necessary, to hold inviolate those laws which will secure to each individual the free exercise of conscience, the right and control of property, and the protection of life.
>
> To sum up this whole question: In these days of uncertainty and unrest, liberty-loving people's greatest responsibility and paramount duty is to preserve and proclaim the freedom of the individual, his relationship to Deity, and . . . the necessity of obedience to the principles of the gospel of Jesus Christ—only thus will mankind find peace and happiness. (*Conference Report,* April 1950, p. 37.)

## Chapter 47

# EVENTS ASSOCIATED WITH THE SECOND COMING OF CHRIST

## (Section 133)

The Church has come into existence to prepare a people for the second coming of Christ. The elect are gathered out of the world into the kingdom of God to prepare themselves for that coming. (D&C 1:8-23; 45:9; 133:1-10; 10:65; 29: 1-8.) These facts were revealed to the Church early in its history.

The first compilation of revelations received by the Prophet Joseph Smith was approved for printing at the conference held on November 1, 1831, over eighteen months after The Church of Jesus Christ of Latter-day Saints was organized. When it was decided by the conference that the revelations should be published under the title *Book of Commandments*, the Lord gave his preface to that book. This revelation (D&C, Section 1) contains the Lord's reasons for giving revelations to the Prophet. (*DHC* 1:222, 226, 234-36.)

The Lord closes the revelation with these verses concerning the last days:

> And again, verily I say unto you, O inhabitants of the earth: I the Lord am willing to make these things known unto all flesh;
>
> For I am no respecter of persons, and will that all men shall know that the day speedily cometh; the hour is not yet, but is nigh at hand, when peace shall be taken from the earth, and the devil shall have power over his own dominion.
>
> And also the Lord shall have power over his saints, and shall reign in their midst, and shall come down in judgment upon Idumea, or the world. (D&C 1:34-36.)

Finally, the Lord said that the prophecies in these revelations will all be fulfilled, and that the Spirit bears record that the revelations are true. (D&C 1:37-39.)

Section 133, the Appendix to the Doctrine and Covenants, gives additional information concerning the last days and the second coming of Christ. The following subjects in the Appendix indicate the importance of this revelation: (1) the principle of gathering; (2) preparation to meet the Bridegroom when he comes; (3) the return of the lost tribes; (4) a description of the second coming of Christ; (5) reasons for the commandments being given in the dispensation of the fulness of times.

## The Gathering

Two aspects of the gathering have operated in this dispensation: (1) to be gathered out of the world into the Church (D&C 29:4; 33:5; 38:42); and (2) to assemble to designated areas. (D&C 31:7-8.)

By baptism one is gathered out of the world into the Church and forsakes the things of this world and cleaves to the principles of righteousness. (D&C 25:10; 133:14.) The first call to gather in a designated area was that to gather in Ohio where the Church had grown rapidly. (D&C 39:15.) At the same time that Kirtland, Ohio, and its environs was a gathering place, the call went out for the saints to gather in western Missouri. (D&C 45:64-65; 57:1.) With the expulsion of the saints from Jackson County, and later from the state of Missouri, refuge was found in Illinois, where the city of Nauvoo became the central gathering place. In 1846, the members of the Church were expelled from Illinois, and the trek across the plains to the Rocky Mountains resulted in a new gathering place. The expansion of missionary work, despite persecution and the many difficulties confronting the saints in building a commonwealth in the West, brought many stakes into existence in fulfillment of prophecy. (D&C 101:20-21.)

## Preparatory Events

There are several events that were prophesied and which have already occurred that indicate the nearness of the Lord's second coming. First, the restoration of The Church of Jesus Christ and the gospel that it might be preached to all the world. (Rev. 14:6-7; D&C 133:36-40.) Second, the publishing of additional books of scripture. (Isa. 29; 1 Ne. 13:39; 2 Ne. 29:11.) Third, a messenger to prepare the way before the Lord—John the Baptist. (Mal. 3:1-4.) Fourth, the coming of Elijah to restore the sealing powers of the priesthood. (Mal. 4:5-6.) Fifth, the gathering of the remnants of Israel, the Latter-day Saints, and the return of the Jews to the Holy Land. (Isa. 2:1-4; 11:11-12; D&C 133:13; 45:25.) Event number five will continue until the second coming of Christ takes place.

Other preparatory events that are prophesied are: (1) wars and rumors of wars (D&C 87); (2) natural calamities such as earthquakes, tidal waves, fires, diseases, and plagues (D&C 29:14-20; 45:31-35); (3) increased wickedness (D&C 29:17; 63:32-33; Mormon 8:26-41); and (4) the appearance of the sign of the Son of Man.

Concerning the sign of the Son of Man, the Prophet Joseph Smith said:

> There will be wars and rumors of wars, signs in the heavens and on the earth beneath, the sun turned into darkness and the moon to blood, earthquakes in divers places, the seas heaving beyond their bounds; then will appear one grand sign of the Son of Man in heaven. But what will the world do? They will say it is a planet, a comet, etc. But the Son of Man will come as the sign of the coming of the Son of Man, which will be as the light of the morning cometh out of the east. (*Teachings of the Prophet*

*Joseph Smith,* pp. 286-87; Matt. 24:30; Luke 21:25-27; D&C 88:93.)

The Prophet said concerning one Hyrum Redding that he had not seen the sign, for the Lord would make it known to his prophet:

> . . . He has not seen the sign of the Son of Man, as foretold by Jesus; neither has any man, nor will any man, until after the sun shall have been darkened and the moon bathed in blood; for the Lord hath not shown me any such sign; and as the prophet saith, so it must be—"Surely the Lord God will do nothing, but He revealeth His secret unto His servants the prophets." (See Amos 3:7; *Teachings of the Prophet Joseph Smith,* p. 280.)

## The Lost Tribes

Preparatory to the coming of the Lord in power and glory is the return of the ten lost tribes. After the death of King Solomon the ten tribes became a kingdom known as Israel. (James E. Talmage, *Articles of Faith*, p. 325.) The Assyrians took them captive in 721 B.C., and they were led northward and were lost to the world. (Jer. 3:12.) The resurrected Lord told the Nephites that the ten tribes had been led out of the land by the Father and that they were neither in the land of Jerusalem nor in any part of the land where he had ministered. (3 Ne. 15:15; 16:1.) These tribes are lost to us but not to the Lord. He told the Nephites that the lost tribes have their own scriptures. (2 Ne. 29:11-14.) In modern revelation it is said that they will bring their rich treasures with them from the land of the north. (D&C 133:30.) It is further given that a highway will be cast up from the deep, and their enemies will be unable to stop their journey. (D&C 133:26-34.)

## The Second Coming of Christ

The coming of the Lord to which reference is usually made in the scriptures is his coming in great power and glory when the wicked shall be destroyed. There is more than one appearance of the Savior, however, as a part of his second coming.

The Prophet Joseph Smith said that in the last days the inhabitants of the world would be divided into the following three categories: (1) the saints, (2) the Jews, and (3) the wicked world. (*DHC* 4:610.) The second coming of Christ will consist of appearances to these three groups.

The scriptures indicate that the Lord will suddenly come to his temple. (Mal. 3:1.) The Savior came to the Kirtland Temple on April 3, 1836, as a partial fulfillment of this prophecy. (Joseph Fielding Smith, *Doctrines of Salvation* 3:12-13.) The complete fulfillment of this prophecy will come with the appearance of the Lord in the Jackson County, Missouri temple, yet to be built. (D&C 84:1-5; 97:15-16; Brigham Young, *JD* 7:142.)

Another visit of the Lord with the saints will be held at Adam-ondi-Ahman, located in Daviess County, Missouri. (D&C 116; *Teachings of the Prophet Joseph Smith*, p. 157.) This conference will be attended by those who have held the keys of the priesthood during the dispensations of the gospel and others invited to the assemblage. It will apparently be unknown to the world and also to those saints not in attendance. (Joseph Fielding Smith, *The Way to Perfection*, pp. 287-91.)

## Appearance to the Jews and to the World

The Savior will appear to the Jewish people when they are sorely beset by the armies of the earth. Almost overcome militarily (Zech. 14:1-2; Rev. 11:1-13; D&C 77:15), the people will have sought refuge in the Mount of Olives, which will have separated; and then the Lord will appear to them as their Messiah whom their fathers crucified. (D&C 45:51-53; Zech. 13:6; 12:8-14; 13:1.) Judah will be redeemed through acceptance of the fulness of the gospel of Jesus Christ to dwell in the Lord's presence. (D&C 133:35.)

The second coming of Christ in power to destroy the morally wicked will usher in his millennial reign. (D&C 63:54; 101:23-24; 133:63-64; 45:74-75.) The wickedness of men will prevent them from abiding in the presence of the Lord. (D&C 133:41-51.) President Charles W. Penrose describes this coming of the Lord in this manner:

> He comes! The earth shakes, and the tall mountains tremble; the mighty deep rolls back to the north as in fear, and the rent skies glow like molten brass. He comes! The dead saints burst forth from their tombs, and "those who are alive and remain" are "caught up" with them to meet him. [I Thess. 4:17.] The ungodly rush to hide themselves from his presence, and call upon the quivering rocks to cover them. He comes! with all the hosts of the righteous glorified. The breath of his lips strikes death to the wicked. His glory is a consuming fire. The proud and rebellious are as stubble; and they are burned and "left neither root nor branch." He sweeps the earth "as with the besom of destruction." [Isa. 14: 23.] He deluges the earth with the fiery floods of his wrath, and the filthiness and abominations of the world are consumed. Satan and his dark hosts are taken and bound—the prince of the power of the air has lost his dominion, for he whose right it is to reign has come, and "the kingdoms of this world have become the Kingdoms of our Lord and of his Christ." [Rev. 11:15.] (*The Latter Day Prophets and the Doctrine and Covenants,* 4:476.)

## Keys to Preparedness

> Wherefore, prepare ye for the coming of the Bridegroom; go ye, go ye out to meet him. (D&C 133:19.)

Only through The Church of Jesus Christ of Latter-day Saints may one be fully prepared to meet the Lord. (Wilford Woodruff, *Young Woman's Journal,* 5:512-13.) There shall be those among the members of the Church who will not be prepared, some being foolish, while the prepared will be wise. (D&C 63:54; Wilford Woodruff, *JD* 18:110.)

What is there in the gospel that will aid the member of the Church to be among the wise? No other people on the earth have the knowledge successfully to be in this class. Some of the important teachings that prepare one for this blessing are: (1) the knowledge that the gospel with the priesthood has been restored; (2) Joseph Smith is a prophet and his successors have held the same high calling; (3) modern books of scriptures; (4) continuous revelation; (5) relationship of man to God; (6) the doctrine of premortality; (7) the purpose of life; and (8) the knowledge of and reality of the future life.

### What Must Be Done

With so much evidence to support the truth as it has been restored, the Latter-day Saint is well-fortified to follow the Lord's instructions as they have come from his servants. What specific things should one do to be considered wise? The following are suggestions: (1) remain out of the world; (2) accept priesthood programs; and (3) secure one's family.

### Not of the World

Go ye out from among the nations, even from Babylon, from the midst of wickedness, which is spiritual Babylon. (D&C 133:14.)

The call has gone forth that Israel is to gather into the fold of Christ in preparation for the Lord's coming. Members of the kingdom have made covenants that they will not partake of worldly influences or practices. (D&C 20:37, 77, 79.)

How may one prepare oneself so that he will not be deceived by the blandishments of the world? Be close to the Church; find strength by Church attendance; study and live the revealed word of the Lord so that it will be easier to know the genuine from the spurious; seek the Spirit; and acquire the virtue of humility.

## Priesthood Acceptance

Priesthood programs of the Church are: genealogical, home teaching, missionary, and welfare. These programs are as much for the women as for the men. Upon each member of the Church devolves the responsibility to participate in all of them. As an example, although a woman does not do home teaching, she can promote the spirit of this important activity in her home by encouraging the priesthood members to do their duty and also to provide the atmosphere for good home teaching in her own home.

## Secure One's Family

Marriage in the temple provides a stability to a marriage union which the Lord intended. Since the family is designed to be eternal, every step necessary to preserve the marriage bond should be undertaken. Without the sealing ordinance by the priesthood in the temple there is no possibility of exaltation in the celestial kingdom. (D&C 131:1-4; 132:16-17.) The Lord has said that people are to be saved as families; consequently, he commanded that parents should teach their children true principles that they might be saved with them. (D&C 68:25-31; 93:47-49.)

Two practices stand out prominently as necessary to preserve parents and children in righteousness. Family prayer binds families together, provides spiritual strength for the tasks of the day, and fulfills individual opportunities to acknowledge the Lord's hand in all things. (D&C 59:21.)

The second important practice is the family home evening program. Probably no better opportunity is afforded both parents and children to learn together. The outlined course of instruction provided by the Church, if followed, will bring family unity and improved individual character into the lives of all participants.

## Conclusion

Latter-day Saints know that Christ will come to rule and reign on the earth in a period when there is great unrest and tribulation in the world. Many signs indicate that his coming is imminent. He will come in power to destroy the wicked. (D&C 101:23-24.) Before this appearance he will come to the saints and also to the Jews who will have gathered to the Holy Land. The time interval between these three appearances is not indicated in the scriptures. It is probable that the period between the coming of the Lord to the Jewish people and to the world will be short.

## Implementation

The wise Latter-day Saint seeks to learn gospel principles that he may not be deceived by the many ideas that are contrary to the truth. (Joseph Smith 1:37.) By this knowledge about his relationship to God and his fellowman, he receives the incentive and strength to prepare himself to avoid the temptations of the world. By the power of the Holy Ghost further strength and knowledge are received for this purpose.

Specifically, the member of the Church is then qualified to remain out of the world though he lives in the world. His witness of the truth is such that he accepts his covenant responsibilities by being an active member. He makes every effort to receive the Lord's marriage ceremony and to rear his children in light and truth. (D&C 93:36-40.)

The Latter-day Saints remember that they are representatives of the ten virgins mentioned in the Lord's parable, who may be either wise or foolish; consequently, they seek to be numbered among the wise. They will not be cast into the fire, for they look to the day when this promise is fulfilled:

And the earth shall be given unto them for an inheritance; and they shall multiply and wax strong, and their children shall grow up without sin unto salvation.

For the Lord shall be in their midst, and his glory shall be upon them, and he will be their king and their lawgiver. (D&C 45:58-59.)

## Chapter 48

# JOSEPH SMITH EVALUATED

## (Section 135)

One of the inspired documents of the latter days was written by President John Taylor at the time he was a member of the Council of the Twelve. (*Doctrine and Covenants Commentary*, p. 855.)

When a man speaks or writes by the Holy Ghost, it becomes scripture—the will, mind, word, and voice of the Lord, "and the power of God unto salvation." (D&C 68:4-5.) When imbued with the Spirit of the Lord a person can know the truth uttered by that Spirit. In this manner the truth is revealed and known by the honest in heart. Ultimately, this is the final test of religious truth. (D&C 50:19-22.)

Measured by this standard, the member of the Church may know that Elder Taylor was under the inspiration of the Holy Ghost when he penned the document about the martyrdom of Joseph and his brother Hyrum Smith. (D&C 135.)

By his apostolic calling Elder Taylor was qualified for this work, and also because he and Elder Willard Richards, later to be a counselor to President Brigham Young, were with the martyred brothers on June 27, 1844, at Carthage Jail, Illinois.

### Joseph Smith Evaluated

President John Taylor, as guided by the Spirit, wrote the following about Joseph Smith:

> Joseph Smith, the Prophet and Seer of the Lord, has done more, save Jesus only, for the salvation of men in this world, than any other man that ever lived in it. . . . (D&C 135:3.)

Centuries before Joseph Smith was born, Joseph, who was sold into captivity by his brothers, foresaw that the seer of the latter days should be named after him and that his father's name would be Joseph. (2 Ne. 3:15.) Of significance in this prophecy is the Lord's statement about Joseph Smith's work and his appraisal of his faithfulness:

> And I will give unto him a commandment that he shall do none other work, save the work which I shall command him. And I will make him great in mine eyes; for he shall do my work. (2 Ne. 3:8.)

It was the testimony of Joseph of Egypt that his descendant of the latter days would attain an esteemed position in mortal life, for:

> . . . A seer shall the Lord my God raise up, who shall be *a choice seer* unto the fruit of my loins.
>
> Yes, Joseph truly said: Thus saith the Lord unto me: *A choice seer* will I raise up out of the fruit of thy loins; and he shall be esteemed highly among the fruit of thy loins. And unto him will I give commandment that *he shall do a work for the fruit of thy loins, his brethren, which shall be of great worth unto them,* even to the bringing of them to the knowledge of the covenants which I have made with thy fathers. (2 Ne. 3:6-7.) (Italics added.)

The Prophet Joseph Smith knew that as other prophets were foreordained to their callings, so also he received a divine calling before he was born. On one occasion he said:

> I suppose that I was ordained to this very office in that Grand Council. (*DHC* 6:364.)

## Greatness Among the Prophets

The inspired evaluation of Joseph Smith that he has done more, except Jesus, for the salvation of men in this world raises a question as to the position of other prophets of God. Each prophet has attained greatness as he has fulfilled his calling. Special recognition, for example, has been given to the prophet Isaiah, about whom Nephi said his soul delighteth in his words. (2 Ne. 25:5.) The resurrected Savior told the Nephites on this continent that ". . . great are the words of Isaiah." (3 Ne. 23:1.) Why were Isaiah's words great? Primarily, because he foresaw events of the dispensation of the fulness of times. (Isa. 2:1-4; 29.) His greatness as a prophet is also evident because he served faithfully the people of his own generation.

Another Old Testament prophet, Ezekiel, was great because he also fulfilled his calling in his day, as well as fortelling events of the future concerning the last days. (Ezek. 37:15-28.)

## New Testament Prophets

Peter, John, and Paul fulfilled their missions in honor to the people of the meridian dispensation. Also, each one of them was permitted to see the greatest dispensation, that of the last days. (Acts 3:19-21; Rev. 14:6-7; Eph. 1:9-10.)

Although all of the works of the former-day prophets are not known to us, we can see wherein they were great. Their personal ministry was confined, as in the case of Joseph Smith, to a relatively few people, but their influence has been felt through their writings and the significance of their acts in this mortal state.

Admittedly, it is difficult to place one prophet above another, for each preforms his work in a particular situation. Therefore, one might say that the "greatest" prophet to a people is the *living* prophet. The principal reason for this belief is due to the opportunity for the living prophet to present solutions to the problems of his day through divine guidance. The prophets who have succeeded Joseph Smith have each met the particular need of his day; so it was with the ancient prophets.

## Joseph Smith's Greatness

Obviously, a prophet must be judged in relation to the time in which he lives. If we believe that Joseph Smith has done more, save Jesus only, for the salvation of men in this world, upon what basis may we say it? Bear in mind that it is said that Joseph Smith did a greater work for the salvation of men in this world. This statement rules out consideration of Adam, certainly one of the greatest of prophets, for his work involved the premortal state, and will involve the future. (*Teachings of the Prophet Joseph Smith*, p. 157; D&C 88:110-15.) President John Taylor apparently had in mind Joseph Smith's accomplishments during mortal life. It was not that he was greater than any other person in the plan of salvation, but only that his greatness was reflected in his mortal ministry.

What then of Joseph Smith? By virtue of his relationship with other dispensations, and the place of the dispensation ushered in by the Prophet Joseph, we shall discover the reasons for his greatness. Our dispensation is the final period in which God will conclude his work for the salvation for men. In addition, it is to contain the truths revealed in past dispensations. This fact was spoken of by both Peter and Paul as the restoration of all things spoken of by the prophets since the world began. (Acts 3:19-21.) Paul said this period of time would bring together all things God had revealed, consequently, it would be known as the "fulness of times." (Eph. 1:9-10.)

Not only would this work involve the salvation of the living but also the dead. It was necessary that the Savior offer his atonement for man and go into the spirit world to initiate the preaching of the gospel to those who died without a knowledge of it. (1 Peter 3:18-20; D&C 128:5.) As far as is known, little work was performed for the dead during the time of the apostles. Few references appear in the New Testament regarding it. (1 Cor. 15:29; Heb. 11:39-40.)

As far as the salvation of man is concerned, Joseph Smith's period was to include *on a large scale* benefits for the *dead* as well as the *living*.

## A Remarkable Prediction

In Joseph Smith's own account of a visit to him by the Angel Moroni, at the age of seventeen, Joseph Smith said that Moroni said:

> . . . God had a work for me to do; and that my name should be had for good and evil among all nations, kindreds, and tongues, or that it should be both good and evil spoken of among all people. (Joseph Smith 2:33.)

The fulfillment of this divine prediction was realized in Joseph Smith's life and continues to be fulfilled. Great men have been lauded and condemned by their contemporaries. Abraham Lincoln was denounced by many who thought he was unjust and illiterate, while others considered him a great man of destiny.

The same may be said of Joseph Smith. To the unrighteous and prejudiced, he was a subject for persecution. But to his faithful followers he was God's anointed seer. Many, not of his own Church, however, also saw his greatness. One of these wrote for the New York Herald from Nauvoo, Illinois, the home of the saints, this personal description of the Prophet:

> Joseph Smith, the President of the Church, Prophet, Seer and Revelator, is thirty-six years of age, six feet high in pumps, weighing two hundred and twelve pounds. He is a man of the highest order of talents, and great independence of character, firm in his integrity, and devoted to his religion; in one word he is a man *per se* as President Tyler would say. As a public speaker, he is bold, powerful, and convincing—possessing both the *suaviter in modo* and the *fortiter in re;* as a leader, wise and prudent, yet fearless; as a military commander, brave and determined; and,

as a citizen, worthy, affable, and kind-bland in his manners, and noble of bearing. (March 19, 1842.)

Concerning the work being done in Nauvoo by the Latter-day Saints, a correspondent of this same newspaper wrote that the priests and philosophers of the day could well take a lesson from Joseph Smith. Of the Prophet it was said he seemed to have

. . . hit the nail exactly on the head, by uniting faith and practice—fancy and fact—religion and philosophy—heaven and earth, so as to form the term of a new religious civilization, bound together in love and tolerance—in industry and energy—that may revolutionize the whole earth one of these days. (Jan. 19, 1842.)

### Further Evaluation

In support of the evaluation of Joseph Smith as discussed in this lesson, President Taylor gave the following:

To seal the testimony of this book and the Book of Mormon, we announce the martyrdom of Joseph Smith the Prophet, and Hyrum Smith the Patriarch. (D&C 135:1.)

He lived great, and he died great in the eyes of God and his people; and like most of the Lord's anointed in ancient times, has sealed his mission and his work with his own blood; and so has his brother Hyrum. In life they were not divided, and in death they were not separated! (D&C 135:3.)

Does the death and testimony of these two prophets affect the salvation of men in this world? An answer to this question involves an understanding of what President Joseph Fielding Smith, of the First Presidency and President of the Council of the Twelve, has termed the divine law of witnesses. (*Doctrines of Salvation* 1:203-28.) This law was stated by Paul as:

In the mouth of two or three witnesses shall every word be established. (2 Cor. 13:1.)

If we had a perfect record of each dispensation, we would know that there has been more than one witness to testify for the Lord. Methuselah, grandfather of Noah, and Lamech, father of Noah, were righteous men who witnessed with Noah in his dispensation. In the Mosaic dispensation, Moses and his brother Aaron served in a similar capacity.

We have a much more complete account of the divine law of witnesses in the meridian dispensation. In addition to Jesus, his Father testified of the divine Sonship of the Savior upon several occasions. (John 5:30-33; 8:14-19; 12:26-30; Matt. 3:15-17.) The twelve apostles were also witnesses; and of these Peter, James, and John received a special witness when they heard the Father's voice and conversed with Moses and Elijah. (Matt. 17:1-8.)

In our own dispensation there were many witnesses to testify of the Lord. Among these testators was Oliver Cowdery, who served with Joseph Smith as a witness of the restoration of the keys of the priesthood. (D&C 13; 27:12-13; 110.) The three special witnesses to the Book of Mormon and also the Eight Witnesses may also be mentioned as God's witnesses to his truth in the last days.

## A Testimony Sealed

In a special way, however, the principle of witnesses was applied in the martyrdom of Joseph and Hyrum Smith. Hyrum was not only the Patriarch to the Church but also Assistant President of the Church, having taken the place of Oliver Cowdery. The divine law of witnesses is expressed in the New Testament as:

> For where a testament is, there must also of necessity be the death of the testator.
>
> For a testament is of force after men are dead: otherwise, it is of no strength at all while the testator liveth. (Heb. 9:16-17.)

After the martyrdom of these prophets, the Lord revealed to Brigham Young that Joseph Smith had sealed his testimony with his blood ". . . that he might be honored and the wicked might be condemned." (D&C 136:39.)

## Non-LDS Evaluation

In the spring of 1844, Josiah Quincy, mayor of Boston and a non-Latter-day Saint, visited the Prophet in the city of Nauvoo. He later published his observations as follows:

> It is by no means improbable that some future textbook for the use of generations yet unborn will contain a question something like this: What historical American of the nineteenth century has exerted the most powerful influence upon the destinies of his countrymen? And it is by no means impossible that the answer to the interrogatory may be thus written: 'Joseph Smith, the Mormon Prophet.' . . . the wonderful influence which this founder of a religion exerted and still exerts, throws him into relief before us, not as a rogue to be criminated but as a phenomenon to be explained . . . Joseph Smith, claiming to be an inspired teacher, faced adversity such as few men have ever attained, and, finally, forty-three days after I saw him, went cheerfully to a martyr's death.

Josiah Quincy concluded his observations by saying:

> Born in the lowest ranks of poverty, without book-learning and with the homeliest of all human names, he had made himself at the age of thirty-nine a power upon the earth. Of the multitudinous family of Smith, none had so won the hearts and shaped human lives as this Joseph. His influence, whether for good or for evil, is potent today, and the end is not yet.
>
> I have endeavored to give the details of my visit to the Mormon prophet with absolute accuracy. If the reader does not know just what to make of Joseph Smith, I cannot help him out of the difficulty. I myself stand helpless before the puzzle. (*Conference Report,* April 1930, pp. 190-92; *Figures of the Past* by Josiah Quincy, University Press, John Wilson and Sons, Cambridge, Copyrighted 1883.)

## Implementation

Biblical prophets foretold the restoration of the gospel and the Church of Jesus Christ with its priesthood powers.

To initiate this work, the Lord raised up Joseph Smith, Jr. foretold by the Old Testament prophet, Joseph of Egypt, as recorded in the Book of Mormon. It was said he would perform the work of salvation appointed him as a choice seer in the Lord's eyes.

This modern prophet was destined to lead the greatest dispensation of the gospel, for he would perform a work for the salvation of the dead as well as the living. His period of time would see the culmination of all of God's work on this earth for the salvation of men. Mighty in its scope and marvelous in its impact upon the souls of men, the work of the dispensation of the fulness of times would eclipse all other gospel periods.

Latter-day Saints believe that "Joseph Smith, the Prophet and Seer of the Lord has done more, save Jesus only, for the salvation of men in this world, than any other man that ever lived in it."

## Chapter 49

# ONE OF JOSEPH SMITH'S CONTRIBUTIONS—TRANSLATION OF THE BOOK OF MORMON

## (Section 135)

One of Joseph Smith's contributions to the salvation of men in this world was the bringing forth of "... the Book of Mormon, which he translated by the gift and power of God...." (D&C 135:3.)

The Book of Mormon, translated from gold plates received from the resurrected Moroni, an ancient American prophet, is a condensed history of people from the old world who were divinely directed to America. The first of these peoples was the Jaredites from the Tower of Babel. (The Book of Ether.) Toward the end of their existence, a colony of Israelites, under the leadership of the prophet Lehi, came from Jerusalem about 600 B.C. In time the Israelites divided into two factions known as Nephites and Lamanites, the former being white and the latter becoming dark-skinned. Another group, known as Mulekites, came from Palestine about the time of the overthrow of the kingdom of Judah in 589 B.C. A merger of this people with other inhabitants of the land occurred several centuries after Lehi's colony landed in what is now America. (Omni 12-22.)

Prophets of God taught principles of salvation to the Book of Mormon people, warning them of temporal and spiritual destruction if they became unrighteous. The predictions of the prophets were literally fulfilled. The Jaredites destroyed themselves by civil war, and the Nephites were later swept off the earth by the Lamanites. North and South American Indian tribes of today are probably descendants of the Lamanites.

## Purposes of the Book of Mormon

Moroni recorded some purposes of the Book of Mormon as follows: (1) to show unto the house of Israel what the Lord has done for their fathers; (2) to inform latter-day Israel of the covenants of the Lord that they might not be cast off forever; and (3) "to the convincing of the Jew and Gentile that Jesus is the Christ, the Eternal God. . . ." (Title Page, Book of Mormon.)

The Book of Mormon prophet Nephi saw in vision other ways in which this book of scripture would be of utmost value to people in the last days. First, it would constitute another witness with the Bible that God's purposes would be fulfilled in behalf of his covenanted people. (2 Nephi 29:8.) Second, it would establish the truth of the Bible. (1 Nephi 13:40.)

## The Bible and the Book of Mormon

Not only does the Book of Mormon witness to the truth of the Bible, but the Bible testifies to the truth of the Nephite record. This testimony came to many Bible prophets who were inspired to prophesy concerning the Book of Mormon. Ezekiel foresaw that the "stick of Judah" (Bible) would in the last days be joined with the "stick of Ephraim" or "Joseph" (Book of Mormon) when the gathering of Israel would take place. These two records of different continents would be one in bringing people to an acceptance of Jesus Christ as their Savior. (Ezekiel 37:16-21.)

Significant among the prophecies regarding the Book of Mormon is the one recorded in chapter 29 of Isaiah. A "book," or the writings of a people who should speak from the dust, would be "delivered to him that is not learned (Joseph Smith)." The words of the book, however, would be taken ". . . to one that is learned (Prof. Charles Anthon). . . . who would fulfill Isaiah's prophecy that he could not read a sealed book. (Verses 11-12.) The

"Book" would be in the world and then the Holy Land would "be turned into a fruitful field." (Verse 17.)

The Bible and the Book of Mormon testify of each other as God's people recorded scripture on the eastern and western continents.

## Contributions of the Book of Mormon

The Book of Mormon shows men the way to salvation in the following three ways:

1. It imparts a knowledge of the true gospel of Jesus Christ.
2. It proclaims the reality of the resurrection of Jesus Christ and of the future life of all men.
3. It assists men to live the gospel plan by witnessing to them, by the power of the Holy Ghost, that the book is true.

## The Book Imparts Knowledge

The Prophet Joseph Smith gave the following evaluation of the Book of Mormon:

> . . . I told the brethren [twelve apostles] that the Book of Mormon was the most correct of any book on earth, and the keystone of our religion, and a man would get nearer to God by abiding by its precepts, than by any other book. (*Teachings of the Prophet Joseph Smith,* p. 194.)

The Three Witnesses to the truth of this book testified that it had been ". . . translated by the gift and power of God. . . ." and that "we know of a surety that the work is true." (Book of Mormon, "The Testimony of Three Witnesses.")

The Lord revealed that the Book of Mormon contains the fulness of the gospel of Jesus Christ. (D&C 20:9; 27:5.) What is the gospel? It is the principles, doctrines, and ordinances revealed from God for the salvation of those who will accept them. The Book of Mormon contains the fulness of the gospel because it is a record of God's dealings with a people who had the gospel fulness and because it records what men must do to gain salvation.

A brief summary of some fundamental Book of Mormon doctrines, found in the Doctrine and Covenants, is as follows: (1) The existence, eternal nature, and creative power of God are demonstrated. (2) The creation of man in God's image and likeness is taught. (3) Man should love, serve, and worship the only living and true God and no other being. (4) The fall of man came by transgression of God's commandments. (5) Because of the fall, Christ's sacrifice was made, as foretold in scriptures. (6) Jesus, though tempted, was sinless. (7) Jesus was crucified, resurrected, and ascended into heaven. (8) Salvation in the kingdom of God is dependent upon acceptance of the gospel and endurance in faith to the end. (9) Salvation is for faithful believers who lived before, as well as during and after, the earthly ministry of Jesus. (10) The "Father, Son, and Holy Ghost are one God, infinite and eternal, without end." (D&C 20:28.) (11) Justification and sanctification through the grace of Jesus Christ are just and true. (12) Man may fall from grace and depart from God. (D&C 20:17-34.)

## Clarification of Gospel Truths

The Book of Mormon adds to our understanding of Bible teachings. The following beatitudes from Jesus' discourse to the Nephites, compared with the rendition in the Bible, are examples. First read the verses without the italicized words as given in the Bible and then the entire verse as it appears in the Book of Mormon.

> Yea, blessed are the poor in spirit *who come unto me,* for theirs is the kingdom of heaven. (3 Nephi 12:3; c. f. Matt. 5:3.) (emphasis added)

And blessed are all they who do hunger and thirst after righteousness, for they shall be filled *with the Holy Ghost.* (3 Nephi 12:6; c. f. Matt. 5:6.) (emphasis added)

## Prophecies of the Last Days

The condition of the apostate religious world is clearly depicted in prophecy, a condition which will eventually bring great destruction at the time of the second coming of Christ. (2 Nephi 28.)

The role of the house of Israel in the last days as an instrument in bringing about God's purposes for man, and the gathering of the Jewish people to the Holy Land, are other parts of these events. (2 Nephi 30:2-10; 3 Nephi 20:29-36; 1 Nephi 22:1-12.)

## The Reality of the Future Life

The title page of the Book of Mormon states that it is to convince every man that Jesus is the Christ, the Eternal God. What does this mean? Essentially, it means that Jesus Christ is divine, the literal Son of God, who has provided the means through his atonement that man may be saved. It also provides the answer to the principal need of the world today—a faith in the reality of the future existence. The Book of Mormon stands as a witness of the divinity of Jesus Christ as the being who made it possible for all people to be resurrected from the dead. Moroni, the last historian-prophet of the Nephite nation, having died about 1500 years before, came to the Prophet Joseph Smith as a resurrected being. Of him, the Prophet wrote:

Moroni, the person who deposited the plates, from whence the Book of Mormon was translated, in a hill in Manchester, Ontario County, New York, being dead, and raised again therefrom, appeared unto me. . . . (*Elders' Journal,* Far West, Mo., July 1838.)

Nephite prophets upon the American continent were inspired to witness to the continued conscious existence of man. The spirit world, or the place where the departed dead live as conscious, living beings, prior to the resurrection, is described and attested to. Alma testifies that at death the spirit enters the world of spirits where the righteous enter paradise and the wicked are in prison. Happiness is the reward of those who have accepted the atonement of Christ, while those who chose evil works are in a state of sorrow because of their iniquity. (Alma 40:11-14.) The last testimony of the prophet Moroni was that at death his spirit would ". . . rest in the paradise of God, until my spirit and body shall again reunite. . . ." (Moroni 10:34.)

The resurrection of Jesus, as the first to receive this blessing on this earth, is related in the Book of Mormon. His dramatic appearance to the Nephites begins with the people hearing a voice from heaven which pierced them to the center, causing their hearts to burn. They heard these words:

> Behold my Beloved Son, in whom I am well pleased, in whom I have glorified my name—hear ye him. (3 Nephi 11:7.)

They saw a man descending out of heaven, clothed in a white robe, who said:

> Behold, I am Jesus Christ, whom the prophets testified shall come into the world.
>
> And behold, I am the light and the life of the world; and I have drunk out of that bitter cup which the Father hath given me, and have glorified the Father in taking upon me the sins of the world, in the which I have suffered the will of the Father in all things from the beginning. (3 Nephi 11:10-11.)

Thereafter, the multitude felt the prints of the nails in his hands and the wound in his side, witnessing the reality of his resurrection with flesh and bones.

Man lives as a spirit entity at death awaiting the resurrection of his body and its uniting with his spirit, never to be divided again in death. This message the world needs today. Unbelief in the reality of life after death does not alter the truth.

## A Power for Salvation

The greatest evidence of religious truth is the knowledge that comes through the Holy Ghost. This power not only affects the mind but also the heart. The process of testimony is the Spirit speaking to man's spirit. The impression of the Spirit upon man's soul is so powerful that the knowledge continues as long as the person is worthy.

To seal the validity of the Book of Mormon for those to whom this record would come, the prophet Moroni gave the following promise:

> And when ye shall receive these things, I would exhort you that ye would ask God, the Eternal Father, in the name of Christ, if these things are not true; and if ye shall ask with a sincere heart, with real intent, having faith in Christ, he will manifest the truth of it unto you, by the power of the Holy Ghost.
>
> And by the power of the Holy Ghost ye may know the truth of all things. (Moroni 10:4-5.)

The fulfillment of this promise is known to thousands of members of The Church of Jesus Christ of Latter-day Saints.

The Savior promised that if one would accept his doctrine, he would know of its truth. (John 7:16-17.) The Holy Ghost has operated in the lives of those who seek diligently as they strive to keep the commandments.

## The Book of Mormon and Salvation

What place does the testimony of the Book of Mormon have in one's personal salvation? The answer to this question is found both in the scriptures and in the lives of hundreds of thousands of people. Basically, when one learns by the power of the Holy Ghost that the Book of Mormon is true, he also receives the knowledge that Jesus Christ lives as an immortal, resurrected being. (Moroni 10:7.)

### Implementation

The Book of Mormon stands as a convincing witness that Joseph Smith is a prophet of God. Not only do its teachings bear testimony of the gospel of Jesus Christ, but they impress their divinity by the spirit that accompanies scripture. There is power in truth which the spiritually minded recognize. (*DHC* 6:273.)

The Book of Mormon is a powerful book. It convinces men of the truth of the gospel of Jesus Christ through its clarification of the doctrines and ordinances that save. Great truths that affect the intellect and the heart are found throughout its pages.

The Book of Mormon is a witness for Jesus Christ as the literal Son of God who was the firstborn from the dead. Not only does it attest to his divinity and resurrection, but to the truth that all men shall receive their bodies again, never to be separated in death. Faith in the reality of this experience—conscious existence forever, eternally—is the present need of an unbelieving world. The Book of Mormon is in the world for this express purpose—a testifier.

This divine record has stood the test of time and will continue to stand as a bulwark of strength for those who have learned from its pages eternal truth by which they guide their lives.

Above all else, this book of scripture has instilled faith in God and in his Son Jesus Christ. The Holy Ghost has borne testimony of the truth of the Book of Mormon, making it one of the greatest of all books in influencing the lives of people. They have endured hardships, trials, and great difficulties because the Spirit has continued to motivate them through the truths of this ancient record.

All men may know the truth for themselves. To know what the Lord requires of man and then to apply that knowledge from the scriptures is a rewarding experience for the faithful. Elder John A. Widtsoe expressed it this way:

> The degree of faith possessed by any man depends not upon the extent of his knowledge, but upon the certainty of his knowledge, which leads to the proper use of his knowledge. . . . (*Joseph Smith*, p. 163.)

## Chapter 50

# ANOTHER OF JOSEPH SMITH'S CONTRIBUTIONS—DOCTRINE AND COVENANTS

## (Section 135)

The Doctrine and Covenants gives direction to the fulfilling of the Lord's promises unto the ancient prophets. The importance of this book in the plan of salvation was given at the November 1831 conference of the Church, in the following words of the Prophet Joseph Smith:

> Being the foundation of the Church in these last days, and a benefit to the world, showing that the keys of the mysteries of the kingdom of our Savior are again entrusted to man; and the riches of eternity within the compass of those who are willing to live by every word that proceedeth out of the mouth of God—therefore the conference voted that they prize the revelations to be worth to the Church the riches of the whole earth, speaking temporally.

In appreciation for the books of scripture received from the Lord by that time the following was also indicated by that conference:

> The great benefits to the world which result from the Book of Mormon and the revelations which the Lord has seen fit in His infinite wisdom to grant unto us for our salvation, and for the salvation of all that will believe, were duly appreciated. . . . (*DHC* 1:235-236.)

### The Salvation of Men in This World

Among the reasons for the evaluation that Joseph Smith had done more for the salvation of men in this world than any other, except Jesus, was his bringing "forth the revelations and commandments which compose this book of Doctrine and Covenants." (D&C 135:3.)

As a modern book of revelation, the Doctrine and Covenants is directed to the people of this generation. It is the voice of the Lord Jesus Christ revealing the way of salvation, both in this life and in the world to come. There are three ways in which the Doctrine and Covenants makes this contribution. (1) It warns individuals and nations of impending destruction if repentance is not forthcoming. (2) It sets forth, in plainness, the gospel of salvation. (3) It witnesses to the truth that there is a life beyond the grave.

## A Voice of Warning

When the revelations received up to 1831 were presented to a conference of the Church, the Lord gave his "preface" to these commandments. In that revelation, reference is made to the apostate condition of the religious world and the nearness of the second coming of Christ. (D&C 1:11-12.) His word is to be known to all men in this life, and in the life to come. The turning away from and the changing of the gospel of Jesus Christ in the past have brought many to seek after false gods. (D&C 1:15-16.) Despite the fact that the gospel has been restored in its fulness, men will continue in error until, as Isaiah said, they are desolate: ". . . therefore the inhabitants of the earth are burned, and few men left." (Isaiah 24:5-6.)

In consequence of these conditions, the Lord said that his servants should declare a "voice of warning" unto all people. (D&C 1:4-5.)

The greatest responsibility resting upon the inhabitants of the earth is to accept the way of salvation. The revelation says:

> And the rebellious shall be pierced with much sorrow; for their iniquities shall be spoken upon the housetops, and their secret acts shall be revealed.
>
> And the voice of warning shall be unto all people, by the mouths of my disciples, whom I have chosen in these last days. (D&C 1:3-4.)

As stated in another revelation, the people of the world are under the bondage of sin, and, like ancient Israel, they have hardened their hearts; therefore, if they continue in this condition, they shall not enter into the Lord's rest, which is the fulness of his glory. (D&C 84:49-50, 24.)

The second reason for raising a warning voice in our day is to let all people know of the frightening events which will engulf the world preceding and at the time of the second coming of Christ. (D&C 1:11-14, 34-35.) Almost every page of the Doctrine and Covenants makes specific reference to or related reference to the judgments that will be poured out upon the earth because of gross wickedness.

## Wars and Other Calamities

Before the Church was organized, the angel Moroni quoted several biblical prophecies pertaining to the last days and said that they would soon be fulfilled. (Joseph Smith, 2:36-41.) Among these prophecies was Malachi's regarding the time when the wicked would be consumed by fire. (Joseph Smith, 2:36-37.) In 1831 it was revealed that peace would be taken from the earth in that generation. (D&C 1:34-35.) Subsequently, these warnings were given:

> Ye hear of wars in far countries, and you say that there will soon be great wars in far countries, but ye know not the hearts of men in your own land. (D&C 38:29.)
>
> Ye hear of wars in foreign lands; but, behold, I say unto you, they are nigh, even at your doors, and not many years hence ye shall hear of wars in your own lands. (D&C 45:63.)

On Christmas day 1832, the Lord revealed some specific information about the wars of the last days. He said that after the war between the North and the South in the United States, war would be poured out upon all nations. (D&C 87:1-3.) Furthermore, conditions would develop whereby slaves would rise up against their masters, and the remnants of the land of America (Indians) would vex the United States with a sore vexation. (D&C 87:4-5.) The inhabitants of the earth would mourn because of plagues, famine, and earthquake until the chastening hand of the Almighty would make "a full end of all nations." (D&C 87:6.)

The word of the Lord concerning the American Civil War and subsequent wars is being fulfilled. Can anyone doubt the "voice of warning" of wars among the nations of the earth in these last days?

## The Plainness of the Gospel

That man might escape the judgments of the last days and also the more enduring judgment of the future life, the Lord has given the plan of salvation anew in plainness and simplicity. Elder Harold B. Lee of the Council of the Twelve suggested the following four things to be done to prepare a people for the second coming of Christ: They should be taught: (1) the personality and nature of God and his Son, Jesus Christ; (2) the divinity of the mission of Jesus as the Savior; (3) the necessity of being cleansed and purified and sanctified to be made worthy to receive the Lord; and (4) acceptance of the divine mission of the Prophet Joseph Smith. (*Conference Report*, October 1956, pp. 61-62.) The Doctrine and Covenants makes a significant contribution to our understanding of these truths.

## The Personality of God

To know God is to receive eternal life, to be like him, and to be in his presence forever. (John 17:3; D&C 132:24.)

Elder Harold B. Lee indicates in the following passage what one great thinker has believed concerning the need to know God as a personal being:

Professor Hacking of Harvard in his "Meaning of God in Human Experience," made even a more significant statement when he wrote: "The alternative to the thought of God as a person is the thought of Him as a substance, as mere energy, and chiefly as law. Just stop and consider for a moment what it would mean for us to try to obey the will of substance, of love, of energy, or worship law, and you will have some idea at least of how near this question of the personality of God comes to the heart of true religion." (*Conference Report,* October 1956, p. 61.)

When the "Christian" religious world was teaching that God is a spirit only, without body, parts, and passions, the Lord revealed to the Prophet Joseph Smith that the Father and the Son are personal beings of flesh and bones. (Joseph Smith 2:17; D&C 130:22-23.) With the knowledge of the true personality and nature of God restored, believing men know what and how to worship. (D&C 93:19.)

## The Divinity of Jesus Christ

In the "Christian" world belief in Jesus Christ as the divine Son of God, who died for man's sins and who was resurrected, has lost ground over the past several decades. People agree that he was a great teacher, but there are those who will not accept his divinity. The irrationality of such a belief is expressed by President Stephen L Richards in the following passage:

There is certainly no consistency in accepting Christ as Lord, without accepting the whole of his Gospel as divine. I have never been able to understand how intelligent, educated men could reconcile the logic or illogic of accepting the authenticity of that portion of the record of the Savior which sets forth his incomparable teachings and philosophy, and at the same time, deny the correctness of the same record which proclaims his Divine Sonship and Lordship. What justification is there for credance in a part of the record and not all of it; or believing some of the things the Master said and not all that he said? I admit that it may be easier, in that it requires less faith, to accept some parts, rather than other parts, but from the standpoint of the authenticity and validity of the record itself, which is admittedly the source from which we obtain our knowledge and information of the Christ, how can one part be true without all being true? To that question I have never been able to discover a satisfactory answer? (*Conference Report,* April 1935, pp. 29-30.)

Latter-day Saints know by revelation that Jesus Christ is divine, the literal Son of God. Jesus Christ was the sinless Son of God, and therefore the only person who could make an atonement for man. The prophesied atonement gave these two benefits: (1) redemption from the grave through the resurrection; and (2) redemption from sins committed by the individual during the years of accountability. (2 Nephi 2:6-16.)

## Cleansed and Purified

Salvation from sin comes only through Jesus Christ, for man cannot be saved in his sins. (Alma 11:37, 40.)

There is no exaltation without the acceptance of Christ as the Savior by faith in him, repentance of sin, baptism by immersion by one having authority, and the receiving of the gift of the Holy Ghost. (3 Nephi 11:31-41; D&C 20:25; 29:17.) In addition, keeping all the other commandments provides a retention of the remission of sins. (Mosiah 4:25-30.)

## Accept the Divine Mission of Joseph Smith

The fourth and final point Elder Lee believes is necessary to prepare a people for the second coming of Christ is the acceptance of Joseph Smith as a prophet. Latter-day Saints do not worship Joseph Smith, but they believe that he received revelations from God to perform a work that is greater than any other's except that of Jesus Christ. (D&C 135:3.)

Missionaries of the Church teach investigators of the gospel to pray that the Holy Ghost will testify to them that Joseph Smith is a prophet of God, that the work established by him, under divine guidance, is God's plan. When a person learns by the Spirit that God has restored his Church and gospel through Joseph Smith, then he is prepared to accept *all* of the restored gospel. The convert's knowledge may not be extensive, but by the testimony of the Spirit he *knows* the fundamental truth that The Church of Jesus Christ of Latter-day Saints is the "only true and living church upon the face of the whole earth." (D&C 1:30.)

God sent his holy angels to Joseph Smith and Oliver Cowdery to confer upon them the Aaronic and Melchizedek Priesthoods so that saving ordinances could be performed by men holding the priesthood, which ordinances would be accepted by God. (D&C 27:7-8, 12-13.) The Doctrine and Covenants not only contributes information on the restoration of God's authority, but it also affirms the fact that without this authority the ordinances of salvation are invalid. (D&C 20:18-20; 84:18-22.)

In several other ways the Doctrine and Covenants attests to the divine mission of Joseph Smith. Detailed information on Church organization and government is a unique contribution to the validity of this mission. (D&C 1:35; 49:24-25; 87; 130:12-13.)

The Doctrine and Covenants contributes to the salvation of man by reaffirming and clarifying doctrines that are obscure or fragmentary in the Bible. Outstanding are the revelations concerning man's nature, the purpose of his life on earth, and his future.

It affirms that man is a child of God, born of divine Parents in a premortal world. (D&C 76:24; 93:29.) The Doctrine and Covenants reveals that by the spirit and body becoming a soul in mortality, the resurrection through the atonement is assured; and through obedience to the principles of the gospel, many may receive a fulness of joy. (D&C 88:15-16; 93; 76:58-60; 132:20-21; 93:33-34.) Among some of the unique teachings of this book of scripture are tithing and the Word of Wisdom. (D&C 89; 119.) It is learned from these revelations that men may reach the divine destiny of godhood by obedience to gospel principles and ordinances, including marriage for eternity. (D&C 131:1-4; 132:15-21.)

## Reality of the Future Life

The third major way in which the modern revelations contribute to the salvation of men in this world is their attestation to the truth that man lives beyond the grave. They do this in two ways: (1) by testifying to the reality of the resurrection; and (2) by the testimonies of men who have seen the resurrected Christ.

Man will be resurrected with a body of flesh and bones, never to experience death again. (D&C 88:27-32, 96-102; 130:18.) In addition to considerable light being given on man's resurrection, specific information is given concerning the appearance of resurrected beings in our day. (D&C 27:5, 7-8, 12-13; 110; 128:19-21.) Thus, further enlightenment is given concerning messages from, or the appearance of, individuals who have lived upon the earth, died, and then have been raised to immortal life.

In the Doctrine and Covenants three persons testify to a sight-knowledge of the Savior. Joseph Smith, Oliver Cowdery, and Sidney Rigdon beheld the resurrected Lord. The first two were in the Kirtland Temple, on April 3, 1836, when they saw the glorified Lord. (D&C 110:1-10.) Joseph Smith and Sidney Rigdon beheld God, Jesus Christ, and the angels in vision at Hiram, Ohio, on February 16, 1832. (D&C 76:19-24.)

## Implementation

The Doctrine and Covenants was given by the Lord for this generation. Its message is intended to save people from their sins and to exalt them in the celestial kingdom. When one considers the great truths of salvation found in this book of scripture, he is impelled to exclaim that it is truly of God. In the words of President Wilford Woodruff:

> . . . we have the Book of Doctrine and Covenants, our Testament, which contains the most glorious, godlike, solemn and eternal truths ever recorded within the lids of a book of the earth. (*Journal of Discourses* 22:331.)

Joseph Smith was the mortal instrument, under divine guidance, to bring forth this book of revelations.

Blessings come not only by acquiring the understanding of doctrines and principles through study, but also by faith. (D&C 88:118.)

## Chapter 51

# ANOTHER OF JOSEPH SMITH'S CONTRIBUTIONS—PEARL OF GREAT PRICE

### (Section 135)

In evaluating the work of the Prophet Joseph Smith, Elder John Taylor said that the Prophet had done more for the salvation of men in this world than any man in it except Jesus Christ. (D&C 135:3.) Among the reasons for this evaluation were the Book of Mormon and the Doctrine and Covenants, and, as Elder Taylor added: "many other wise documents and instructions for the benefit of the children of men." Among these wise documents is the Pearl of Great Price, a book of modern and ancient scripture. It consists of four parts: the Book of Moses, the Book of Abraham, Writings of Joseph Smith (consisting of two parts), and the Articles of Faith.

### The Book of Moses

In June 1830, the Lord revealed some visions received by Moses anciently. (Moses 1.) The remaining seven chapters of the Book of Moses were given to the Prophet Joseph Smith in December 1830. Much is restored in this book that is not recorded in the Bible.

The Lord revealed to Moses his dealings with Adam, Adam's fall and redemption, the premortality of men, the period in which Enoch reared a generation in righteousness, and Noah's ministry. From this revelation has come renewed information about the plan of salvation.

### The Book of Abraham

The Book of Abraham, the second book of scripture in the Pearl of Great Price, came into Joseph Smith's possession in an unusual way. Some Egyptian mummies were purchased by members of the Church in July 1835, from their owner, Michael H. Chandler, who was exhibiting them in the United States. With these mummies were some papyrus rolls upon which were inscribed ancient hieroglyphics. To the great joy of the Prophet it was learned that one of the rolls contained the writings of Abraham, another the writings of Joseph of Egypt. Joseph Smith translated the ancient writings of Abraham, which now constitute the Book of Abraham. (*DHC* 2:235-236, 348-351.)

On Monday, November 27, 1967, in a special ceremony at the New York Metropolitan Museum of Art, eleven papyrus pieces once owned by the Prophet Joseph Smith were presented to President N. Eldon Tanner of the First Presidency. (*Church News*, December 2, 1967, p. 7.) The best information available to the Church for almost one hundred years was that the papyri and the mummies upon which they were found were destroyed in the Chicago Fire of 1871. The recovered papyri are only portions of the material possessed by the Prophet Joseph Smith. The well-preserved Facsimile No. 1 of the Book of Abraham is a part of the collection. The Book of Joseph was not translated completely by the Prophet.

An interesting incident in connection with Joseph Smith and the papyrus rolls occurred upon their discovery by Mr. Chandler in the United States Customs house at New York City.

> "He was immediately told, while yet in the custom house, that there was no man in that city who could translate his roll: but was referred, by the same gentleman, (a stranger,) to Mr. Joseph Smith, Jun., who, continued he, possesses some kind of power or gifts, by which he had previously translated similar characters." (*DHC* 2:349.)

For thousands of years the Lord had preserved these writings that this dispensation might have the testimony of the Abrahamic dispensation concerning such important doctrines as the premortal existence of man, the creation, and the priesthood of God.

### Writings of Joseph Smith

This division of the Pearl of Great Price contains material relating to a revision of the twenty-fourth chapter of Matthew and the story of Joseph Smith's ancestry and early visions. In the revision of the twenty-fourth chapter of Matthew, clarification is given to the events mentioned by the Savior in the New Testament about the signs of the times heralding the destruction of the Jews in the meridian dispensation and the calamities preceding the second coming of Christ in our dispensation. The difference between the two periods is clearly indicated in the revision of this chapter. (verses 21-23.)

### The Articles of Faith

In the *Times and Seasons*, a publication of the Church at Nauvoo, Illinois, on March 1, 1842, an article by the Prophet Joseph Smith appeared giving a short history of his life and also what are known as the Articles of Faith. This account was written to Mr. John Wentworth, editor and publisher of the *Chicago Democrat*, and has become known to the Church as the "Wentworth Letter." Elder James E. Talmage wrote an outstanding book discussing these Articles of Faith. Elder B. H. Roberts gave the following comment regarding them:

> Millions of these "Articles of Faith" have been published; they have been translated into many languages and carried to all the nations of the earth and tribes of men where the New Dispensation of the gospel has been preached. They were not produced by the labored efforts and the harmonized contentions of scholastics, but were struck off by one mind at a single effort to make a declaration of that which is most assuredly believed by the church, for one making earnest inquiry about her history

and her fundamental doctrines. The combined directness, perspicuity, simplicity and comprehensiveness of this statement of the doctrine of the church is regarded as strong evidence of a divine inspiration operating upon the mind of Joseph Smith. (*A Comprehensive History of the Church,* 2:131.)

## Joseph Smith's First Vision

When one considers the claim of Joseph Smith to having been called of God to open the last dispensation of the gospel, one must believe that in the Prophet's works one will find inspiration and guidance to fulfill the purpose of life. The devout Latter-day Saint learns through his study that the contributions of the Prophet to the salvation of men in this world are significant because they raise men to greater heights of understanding and faith. The First Vision is one of the important revelations from God. Its message to all men is such that few can reasonably doubt the authenticity of the Vision. When compared with other recorded accounts of visions of God, this one stands out preeminently as of great worth, not only because of its value as a witness to an unbelieving world of the reality of God's existence. Joseph Smith's testimony of the reality of the First Vision is convincing. (Joseph Smith 2:24-25.)

We learn of the following saving principles from the First Vision:

First, God the Father exists as a personal Being. Joseph Smith saw God the Father, "whose brightness and glory defy all description, standing above me in the air." (Joseph Smith 2:17.) To know God as a personal Being is a prerequisite to eternal life. (John 17:31.)

Second, Jesus is a resurrected Personage, separate and distinct from the Father. "One of them spake unto me, calling me by name and said, pointing to the other—*This is My Beloved Son. Hear Him!*" (Joseph Smith 2:17.)

Third, there is only one true Church. Joseph was told that he should join no church for they had all gone astray. (Joseph Smith 2:18-20.)

Fourth, men may have the assurance that sincere prayer is answered.

> I was one day reading the Epistle of James, first chapter and fifth verse, which reads: *If any of you lack wisdom, let him ask of God, that giveth to all men liberally, and upbraideth not; and it shall be given him.*
>
> At length I came to the conclusion that I must either remain in darkness and confusion, or else I must do as James directs, that is, ask of God.
>
> I had found the testimony of James to be true—that a man who lacked wisdom might ask of God, and obtain, and not be upbraided. (Joseph Smith 2:11-13, 26.)

In order to achieve salvation, man must "ask God" for knowledge by which he may walk uprightly before him. (Moroni 10:3-7; D&C 103:36.) Joseph Smith's testimony of prayer and the reality of the future life furnish further reasons for faith in the efficacy of prayer in leading one to salvation.

## The Gospel of Jesus Christ

Among the contributions to salvation-knowledge from the Book of Moses and the Book of Abraham is the fact that the gospel principles of salvation taught by Jesus Christ were known from the days of Adam. Moses learned that faith, repentance, baptism by immersion, and the receiving of the gift of the Holy Ghost were taught by Adam and his posterity. (Moses 6:52.) The authority conferred upon worthy men to administer gospel ordinances gave the same validity to those ordinances anciently as it does today. (Abraham 1:2-4, 18, 31; 2:8-11.)

Although the New Testament refers to the gospel among the Old Testament people, most "Christian" theologies have not held that people before the time of Christ had these saving principles and ordinances. Thus, the Pearl of Great Price makes a contribution to man's understanding of God's relationship with his children. If one knows that God is a personal Being, the Father of men, he accepts the truth that God is just and merciful because he blessed Adam and his posterity by providing them with salvation teachings. As revealed, God created man and gave him commandments, and when man broke those laws, the means was provided whereby man might be saved from the effects of sin. (D&C 20:17-29.) Men are saved by the same gospel in all ages of the world.

Because of similarities in the "Christian" religion and non-Christian religions, some have claimed that Jesus "borrowed" from other religions to formulate his own. Since the gospel of Jesus Christ was known to Adam, it is no doubt true that other religions "borrowed" from those teachings.

### A Witness to Other Scriptures

In a world of doubt and skepticism, many witnesses are provided to aid and assist those who will be helped. The consistency of teachings throughout the four standard books of scriptures is a testimony of the truths spoken therein. Each book of scripture may give a certain emphasis to one doctrine or teaching above another one, yet the similarity of teachings is remarkable.

The scriptures testify that God lives. The Pearl of Great Price contributes to this truth because of the experiences of Enoch, Moses, and Abraham, who saw and talked with God. (Moses 7:3-4; 1:2; Abraham 3:11-12.)

### Creation Understood

Man's purpose on the earth is to receive greater faith in God and to increase his ability to live the commandments. The Book of Moses and the Book of Abraham are plain in establishing these truths: (1) that every person is a child of God, created after his image as a spirit before the earth was created; and (2) that man's purpose in earth life is to receive a body and then work out his salvation.

An account of the spiritual creation of all things, including man, before they were temporally created, is as follows:

> . . . I, the Lord God, made the heaven and the earth;
>
> And every plant of the field before it was in the earth, and every herb of the field before it grew. For I, the Lord God, created all things, of which I have spoken, spiritually, before they were naturally upon the face of the earth. . . . And I, the Lord God, had created all the children of men . . . for in heaven created I them. . . . (Moses 3:4-5.)

It was Abraham's privilege to behold all of the spirit children of God before the earth was created as their future abode. Among these spirits he was numbered as one who was chosen to perform a mission of responsibility upon the earth. (Abraham 3:22-23.)

An understanding of man's purpose in life is known from the revelations to Moses, as revealed to Joseph Smith. Probably one of the most enlightening scriptures in all sacred literature follows:

> For behold, this is my work and my glory—to bring to pass the immortality and eternal life of man. (Moses 1:39.)

This truth means that God brings about man's resurrection (immortality) through the atonement of his Son Jesus Christ, and also makes man's exaltation (eternal life) possible in the celestial kingdom. Earth life provides the spirit with a body that will become immortal through the atonement of Christ. Without a resurrected body, the attainment of godhood would not be possible. (D&C 93:33-34.) To give immortality to his spirit sons and daughters is the work of God; to give them eternal life is his glory. (D&C 132:31.)

Man, however, may not enjoy his full potential as a child of God unless he proves himself worthy of an exaltation with God his Father. Abraham learned that the earth was the place where man might be proved.

> And there stood one among them that was like unto God, and he said unto those who were with him: We will go down, for there is space there, and we will take of these materials, and we will make an earth whereon these may dwell;
>
> And we will prove them herewith, to see if they will do all things whatsoever the Lord their God shall command them;
>
> . . . and they who keep their second estate shall have glory added upon their heads for ever and ever. (Abraham 3:24-26.)

## Joseph Smith—Restorer of Truth

The prophet Moses foresaw that in the last days, the Lord would raise up another prophet who would be like him. This prophecy is given in these words:

> And in a day when the children of men shall esteem my words as naught and take many of them from the book which thou shalt write, behold, I will raise up another like unto thee; and they shall be had again among the children of men—among as many as shall believe. (Moses 1:41.)

Joseph Smith is that prophet. (D&C 28:2; 107:91.) Many plain and precious truths were removed from the Bible during the period of the great apostasy (1 Nephi 13:23-29.) The restoration of those parts of the gospel of Jesus Christ is found in the three modern books of scripture accepted by Latter-day Saints. Not the least of these is the Pearl of Great Price, from which we learn of revelations to Moses and to Abraham.

Joseph Smith was the instrument in the Lord's hands in restoring ancient salvation truths for modern people. He stands as a witness to the world of those truths. It was his mission to do a work for the salvation of men that would eclipse the work of earlier prophets. (2 Nephi 3:6-9; D&C 135:3.)

## Implementation

The Pearl of Great Price, consisting of four major divisions, gives material from the ancient writings of Abraham and Moses, as well as information from the Prophet Joseph Smith. The divinity of these scriptures is attested in their consistency with other divine scriptures. They give an enlarged view of such fundamental teachings as the purpose of earth life, man's premortality, and the antiquity of the gospel of Jesus Christ.

Since all scripture comes into existence by the power of the Holy Ghost, by that same power one may know that it is divine truth. (D&C 68:2-4; 50:21-22.) Therefore, the person who desires to learn of the truth of the Pearl of Great Price may receive this knowledge by sincere prayer, as did the Prophet Joseph Smith when he sought truth in the Sacred Grove.

An individual value from acceptance of this divine record is the application of its truth regarding the purpose of earth life based upon the doctrine of pre-mortality. To know that a pre-earth life as a child of God gave opportunities for progress to immortality unto eternal life provides motivation for working out one's salvation in this life. Inasmuch as this concept includes the fact that man shall live forever, it provides for decision-making in this life. Every decision ought to be made in terms of the consequences of that decision in the eternity ahead, not for the present life only. The reason for and the fundamental cause as to why man may eventually attain godhood resides in the origin of man's spirit—he has within him the spark of divinity.

Every person who sincerely seeks for the fulness of religious truth will find by accepting the Pearl of Great Price a treasure house of revealed ancient truths that bring him to a better understanding of the questions: Where did I come from? Why am I here?

## Chapter 52

# ZION AND ITS FUTURE

## (Section 136)

Before The Church of Jesus Christ of Latter-day Saints was organized, the Lord gave this counsel to individuals interested in Joseph Smith's work:

> Now, as you have asked, behold, I say unto you, keep my commandments, and seek to bring forth and establish the cause of Zion. (D&C 6:6; 12:6; 14:6.)

*Zion* has several meanings when the foregoing counsel is considered in its context—a time when the Book of Mormon and the modern revelations had not yet been received and the Church was not yet established upon the earth. The marvelous and wondrous work to be restored was not only the Book of Mormon spoken of by Isaiah, not only the building up of a certain geographical area, but the accomplishment of all God's purposes on the earth. (Isa. 29:13-14; D&C 105:31-32.) True it is that Zion in the scriptures refers to Jerusalem, to the ancient city of Enoch's people, to North and South America, to the center place—Jackson County, Missouri—as geographical areas. (2 Kings 19:21; Ps. 48; Moses 7:18-21; *DHC* 6:318-319; D&C 57:1-2.) But Zion also has significance in that it means: (1) the Church of Jesus Christ, and (2) the pure in heart. (D&C 105:32; 97:21.)

### The Fulness of Times

Prophets saw in vision the time when God's work for man would culminate in the dispensation of the fulness of times. They were given the assurance that the Savior would come to usher in a millennial reign of peace. (D&C

29:10-11.) The restoration of the gospel with the priesthood would begin the restitution of all things spoken of by the prophets. (Acts 3:19-21.) Thus this dispensation might be termed a gathering period in which all dispensations are gathered into one culminating period when the purposes of God for man's salvation are completed. (Eph. 1:7-10; D&C 77:12.)

For it is necessary in the ushering in of the dispensation of the fulness of times, which dispensation is now beginning to usher in, that a whole and complete and perfect union, and welding together of dispensations, and keys, and powers, and glories should take place, and be revealed from the days of Adam even to the present time. And not only this, but those things which never have been revealed from the foundation of the world, but have been kept hid from the wise and prudent, shall be revealed unto babes and sucklings in this, the dispensation of the fulness of times. (D&C 128:18.)

## The Gathering and Temple Building

One of the unique teachings of the restitution of all things is the gathering of the tribes of Israel in the last days. The prophets looked with joyful anticipation to the time when this gathering would take place. (Isa. 11:10-16.) Among the branches of Israel to participate in the gathering are: (1) the Jewish people to modern Israel (D&C 133:35; 109:62-64); (2) the ten lost tribes from the land of the north to receive their blessings at the hands of the Latter-day Saints (D&C 133:26-34); (3) the tribe of Joseph through Ephraim and Manasseh, who are the Latter-day Saints. (D&C 103:17; 133:30.) Included in this latter group are those known as the "remnants of Jacob," the American Indian and those on the islands of the Pacific. (D&C 109:65-67.)

Leaders in the salvation of those gathered are the Latter-day Saints, to whom the Lord has said:

Therefore, thus saith the Lord unto you, with whom the priesthood hath continued through the lineage of your fathers—

> For ye are lawful heirs, according to the flesh, and have been hid from the world with Christ in God—
>
> Therefore your life and the priesthood have remained, and must needs remain through you and your lineage until the restoration of all things spoken of by the mouths of all the holy prophets since the world began. (D&C 86:8-10.)

In the words of President Wilford Woodruff:

> I say to the brethren and sisters—you have your appointment; the Lord has raised up these Elders of Israel, and I can prove from the Book of Doctrine and Covenants that you received the Priesthood from eternity, and your lives have been hid with Christ in God, and you knew it not. You are literally and lawfully heirs of the Priesthood through the lineage of your fathers, and that Priesthood will continue throughout eternity, therefore you have received your appointment, and the Lord looks to you to build up his Zion and kingdom upon the earth. (*Journal of Discourses,* 18:120.)

The Prophet Joseph Smith said that the main object of the gathering of the Saints is to build temples. (*Teachings of the Prophet Joseph Smith*, pp. 307-308.) In these sacred edifices where the Lord may come to visit his people, principles of exaltation are administered. (D&C 124:28-31, 37-42.) Thus, the purpose of all activities and programs of the Church should prepare the people for these blessings.

With the keys of the gathering restored, the way was prepared for the instruction of the people in wards and stakes preparatory to their receiving the higher ordinances of the gospel. Also, the way was provided for them to administer saving ordinances for their dead. (D&C 128:5-9.)

### The Catalyst

The Church of Jesus Christ of Latter-day Saints exists for the purpose of bringing men to exaltation. In order that the saints may be assisted in achieving this goal, the Lord has placed within their reach the witness of the Holy Ghost to motivate them to righteousness. As the dedicated, loyal Latter-day Saint becomes acquainted with the essential purpose of the dispensation of the fulness of times—preparation for the second coming of Christ—he learns that his efforts are to build Zion upon the earth. It was for the Prophet Joseph Smith, divinely directed, to restore to the earth the unique concept of Zion. From his own words we learn about Zion and the mission of the Latter-day Saints:

> The building up of Zion is a cause that has interested the people of God in every age; it is a theme upon which prophets, priests and kings have dwelt with peculiar delight; they have looked forward with joyful anticipation to the day in which we live; and fired with heavenly and joyful anticipations they have sung and written and prophesied of this our day; but they died without the sight; we are the favored people that God has made choice of to bring about the Latter-day glory; it is left for us to see, participate in and help to roll forward the Latter-day glory, "the dispensation of the fulness of times, when God will gather together all things that are in heaven, and all things that are upon the earth, "even in one". . . . (*DHC* 4:609-10.)

United with the saints in this noble endeavor will be those of other dispensations who also worked for the accomplishments of God's purpose on the earth. As the Prophet said:

> The heavenly Priesthood will unite with the earthly, to bring about those great purposes; and whilst we are thus united in the one common cause, to roll forth the kingdom of God, the heavenly Priesthood are not idle spectators, the Spirit of God will be showered down from above, and it will dwell in our midst. (*DHC* 4:610.)

## The Holy Ghost (Holy Spirit)

The Holy Ghost (Holy Spirit) is a revelator. The promise of the Lord is that his people will receive, through appointed channels, knowledge by the Holy Spirit—even that which has not been revealed since the world began. In fact, in the fulness of times nothing shall be withheld. (D&C 121:26-28.)

As one views the history of the Church since its organization, the overriding conviction is that the voice of God has been with this Church in all its travels and tribulations. (D&C 128:21.) The efforts of men to thwart the kingdom of God have been futile, although attempts have been made to destroy and to dispossess this people. (D&C 136:17.)

## Challenge to Build

From the beginning of the dispensation, the Lord's servants have admonished the saints to accept the challenge of the dispensation, as given in the words of President Wilford Woodruff:

> We are called to build up Zion, and to establish righteousness and truth; called to build up the kingdom of God. . . . (*Journal of Discourses,* 12:279.)

To build Zion means to participate in all the activities that will further the work of God's kingdom, his Church. (D&C 38:40.) Whatever contribution is made to this goal is a step to the fulfillment of Zion's glory. (D&C 101:17-19.)

## A Center Place

The early saints were given the objective of building a center place from which the wisdom of God would flow to the nations. (John Taylor, *Journal of Discourses,* 6:169.) The temple of the Lord will be built in the New Jerusalem as prophesied, for therein the Lord will dwell, and righteous laws will go forth to govern the nations, as well as from the Old Jerusalem. (D&C 84:1-5; 38:21-22; Isa. 2:1-2.) In that city of Zion, to be located in Jackson County, Missouri, there shall be found peace, safety, and refuge from the wickedness of the world where strife, unrest, and war exist. Zion's people will be free from these acts of violence as they gather from the nations of the earth to serve the Lord. (D&C 45:66-75.)

## In the Meantime

Zion, as envisioned by the prophets, is not here. But the preparation continues for that blessed day. Though some may not realize Zion in its fulness in this life, each saint who assumes his responsibility in building Zion will find eternal joys and happiness. He will, following the resurrection, enjoy the presence of the Lord with other faithful saints. (D&C 27:5-14.)

What of the scattered saints? Members of the Church in parts of the world other than where the headquarters of the Church are found wonder when they should gather to Zion. They have already been gathered out of the world, and as covenant sons or daughters of God they must become pure in heart in order to become Zion. Zion is where the pure in heart dwell. (D&C 97:21; 101:21.)

Although the saints are scattered throughout the world, as foreseen by Nephi, they are to stand in holy places (Zion) until the prophet of the Lord calls them to gather in appointed places. (1 Ne. 14:14; Harold B. Lee, *Conference Report*, April 1948, p. 55.)

The day will come when the leaders of the Church will call the faithful, devoted members to build the New Jerusalem; but the call will come only when the revelation is received by the prophet. (D&C 101:16-21; 105:13.)

## What Is Required?

When the effort to build the center place of Zion failed in 1834, the Lord gave the reasons for the failure. He also indicated through revelation the way whereby that plan will not fail.

> That they themselves may be prepared, and that my people may be taught more perfectly, and have experience, and know

more perfectly concerning their duty, and the things which I require at their hands. (D&C 105:10.)

### The Future of Zion

They who have the testimony of the Spirit that Joseph Smith is a true prophet, that the revelations through him are from God, that The Church of Jesus Christ of Latter-day Saints is the only true and living Church upon the face of the earth, and that the successors of Joseph Smith have also been divinely called, know that all of the prophecies concerning this dispensation will be fulfilled. (D&C 1:37-39.) The Lord has decreed that: (1) his kingdom is on the earth for the last time, and it will stand forever (Daniel 2:44; D&C 65:2); (2) he will raise up a people who will serve him in righteousness (D&C 100:16); and (3) Zion will be redeemed. (D&C 100:13; 136:18.)

Although the future of Zion is assured, the individual member of the Church may not find the blessings of Zion except upon condition of obedience to the commandments.

### Implementation

From the last revelation in the Doctrine and Covenants, given to President Brigham Young, we learn about Zion and her people:

> My people must be tried in all things, that they may be prepared to receive the glory that I have for them, even the glory of Zion; and he that will not bear chastisement is not worthy of my kingdom. (D&C 136:31.)

The trials of present-day saints, compared with those of members of the decades following the organization of the Church, may be quite different, yet the basis for faith and devotion remains the same.

President Heber C. Kimball once said:

"Let me say to you, that many of you will see the time when you will have all the trouble, trial and persecution that you can stand, and plenty of opportunities to show that you are true to God and his work. This Church has before it many close places through which it will have to pass before the work of God is crowned with victory. To meet the difficulties that are coming, it will be necessary for you to have a knowledge of the truth of this work for yourselves. The difficulties will be of such a character that the man or women who does not possess this personal knowledge or witness will fall. If you have not got the testimony, live right and call upon the Lord and cease not till you obtain it. If you do not you will not stand.

Remember these sayings, for many of you will live to see them fulfilled. The time will come when no man nor woman will be able to endure on borrowed light. Each will have to be guided by the light within himself. If you do not have it, how can you stand? Do you believe it?" (*Life of Heber C. Kimball*, pp. 449-50.)

If the saints failed to observe the words of the Lord, the kingdoms of the world would prevail against them, for they were assigned to be a light to the world. (D&C 103:5-13.)

Ample provision has been made whereby the saint may learn his duties from attendance at appointed meetings, study of the scriptures, and by the Holy Ghost as an interpreter and guide to truth; yet there is one sure and practical way to keep on the Lord's side. Expressed in the words of the Prophet Joseph Smith, it is:

"Look to the Presidency and receive instruction." (*DHC* 3:391; D&C 124:45-46.)

The First Presidency of the Church teach only the way of righteousness whereby exaltation will come to those who obey. The revelations of the Lord come to them for the members of the Church. They are inspired to solve the problems of the day and to give the correct interpretation of what the Lord has revealed in the books of scripture.

The Lord has said through the Prophet Joseph Smith concerning the goal for which the saints should strive:

> And your whole labor shall be in Zion, with all your soul, from henceforth; yea, you shall ever open your mouth in my cause, not fearing what man can do, for I am with you. Amen. (D&C 30:11.)

" We ought to have the building up of Zion as our greatest object." (Joseph Smith, *DHC* 3:390.)

If one accepts this charge, then he will accept in deed the closing words of the Doctrine and Covenants:

> Be diligent in keeping all my commandments, lest judgments come upon you, and your faith fail you, and your enemies triumph over you. So no more at present. Amen and amen. (D&C 136:42.)

# Bibliography

## Newspapers and Periodicals

*Conference Report* (Annual and Semi-annual) of the Church of Jesus Christ of Latter-day Saints. Salt Lake City.

*Deseret Weekly.* Salt Lake City, 1896.

*The Improvement Era.* Salt Lake City, 1926, 1942, 1956.

*The Juvenile Instructor.* Salt Lake City, 1928.

*The Millennial Star.* Liverpool, 1895.

*The Utah Genealogical and Historical Magazine.* Salt Lake City, 1931.

*The Young Women's Journal.* Vol. 5. Salt Lake City.

## Articles and Books

Argow, Waldemar. *What Do Religious Liberals Believe?* Yellow Springs, Ohio: Antioch Press Co., 1957.

Brown, Hugh B. *Eternal Quest.* Salt Lake City: Bookcraft, Inc., 1956.

Bowen, Albert E. *Constancy Amid Change.* Salt Lake City: Deseret News Press, 1944.

*Doctrine and Covenants.* Salt Lake City: The Church of Jesus Christ of Latter-day Saints. (Designated in footnotes as D&C.)

Doxey, Roy W. *The Doctrine and Covenants and the Future.* Salt Lake City: Deseret Book Co., 1957.

Doxey, Roy W. *The Doctrine and Covenants Speaks.* Vol. 1. Salt Lake City: Deseret Book Co., 1964.

Doxey, Roy W. *Zion in the Last Days.* Salt Lake City: Bookcraft Inc., 1968.

Doxey, Roy W. *The Latter-day Prophets and the Doctrine and Covenants.* Vol. 1, 3. Salt Lake City: Deseret Book Co., 1963, 1964.

Durham, Dr. G. Homer comp. *Gospel Standards.* Salt Lake City: Deseret News Press, 1941.

Evans, John Henry. *Joseph Smith An American Prophet.* New York: Macmillan Co., 1942.

Fuller, J.F.C. *A Military History of the Western World.* Vol. 3. New York: Funk & Waggnalls Co., 1956.

Gates, Susan (Young). *Lydia Knight's History . . .* by "Homespun." Salt Lake City: Juvenile Instructor Office, 1883.

Hesseltine, William B. and Smiley, David L. *The South in American History.* 2nd ed. Englewood Cliffs, New Jersey: Prentice-Hall, 1960.

Hinckley, Bryant S. *Sermons and Missionary Services of Melvin Joseph Ballard.* Salt Lake City: Deseret Book Co., 1949.

*Journal of Discourses.* 26 Vol. The Church of Jesus Christ of Latter-day Saints. London: F. D. and S. W. Richards.

Lee, Harold B. *Youth and the Church.* Salt Lake City: Deseret News Press, 1955.

Link, Henry C. *The Way to Security.* Garden City, New York: Doubleday and Co., 1951.

McKay, David O. *Treasures of Life.* Salt Lake City: Deseret Book Co., 1962.

Newquist, Jarreld L. comp. *Gospel Truth.* Vol. 1. Salt Lake City: Zion's Book Store, 1957.

Petersen, Mark E. *Your Faith and You.* Salt Lake City: Bookcraft Inc., 1953.

Pratt, Parley P. ed. *Autobiography of Parley Parker Pratt.* 4th ed. Salt Lake City: Deseret Book Co., 1950.

Roberts, B. H. *A Comprehensive History of the Church.* Vol 2. Salt Lake City: Deseret News Press, 1930.

Roberts, B. H. "Divine Immanance and the Holy Ghost," *The Seventy's Course in Theology.* Fifth Year. Salt Lake City: The Deseret News, 1912.

Roberts, B. H. "The Doctrine of Deity," *The Seventy's Course in Theology.* Third Year. Salt Lake City: The Caxton Press, 1910.

Roberts, B. H. *Discourses of B. H. Roberts.* Salt Lake City: Deseret Book, 1948.

Rozwenc, Edwin C. ed. *Slavery As A Cause of the Civil War.* Boston: D. C. Heath and Co., 1949.

Smith, Hyrum and Sjodahl, Janne M. *Doctrine and Covenants* Commentary. Salt Lake City: Deseret Book Co., 1957.

Smith, Joseph. *History of the Church.* The Church of Jesus Christ of Latter-day Saints. Salt Lake City: Deseret News Press, 1902. (Designated as *DHC* in the footnotes.)

Smith, Joseph F. *Gospel Doctrine.* 6th ed. Salt Lake City: Deseret Book Co., 1943.

Smith, Joseph Fielding. *Church History and Modern Revelation.* Series 2, 3. A Course of Study for the Melchizedek Priesthood Quorums. Salt Lake City: Deseret News Press, 1948, 1949.

Smith, Joseph Fielding. *Doctrines of Salvation.* Vol. 2. Salt Lake City: Bookcraft, Inc.

Smith, Joseph Fielding. *Essentials in Church History.* 13th ed. Salt Lake City: Deseret Book Co., 1953.

Smith, Joseph Fielding. *The Progress of Man.* Salt Lake City: Deseret Book Co., 1964.

Smith, Joseph Fielding. comp. *Teachings of the Prophet Joseph Smith.* 3rd ed. Salt Lake City: Deseret News Press, 1942.

Smith, Joseph Fielding. *The Way to Perfection.* 4th ed. Independence, Missouri: Zion's Printing and Publishing Co., 1943.

Talmage, James E., *The House of the Lord.* Salt Lake City: Deseret Book Co., 1968.

Talmage, James E. *The Articles of Faith.* 23rd ed. Salt Lake City: 1942.

Talmage, James E. *The Great Apostasy.* Salt Lake City: Deseret News, 1909.

Talmage, James E. *Jesus The Christ.* 3rd ed. Salt Lake City: Deseret News, 1916.

Talmage, James E. *The Vitality of Mormonism.* Boston: The Gotham Press, 1919.

Taylor, John. *Mediation and Atonement.* Salt Lake City: Stevens & Wallis, Inc., 1950.

Van Doren, Carl. *The Great Rehearsal.* New York: Viking Press, 1948.

Whitney, Orson F. *Life of Heber C. Kimball.* 2nd ed. Salt Lake City: Stevens and Wallis, 1945.

Whitney, Orson F. *Saturday Night Thoughts.* Salt Lake City: Deseret News, 1921.

Widtsoe, John A. comp. *Discourses of Brigham Young.* Salt Lake City: Deseret Book Co., 1954.

Widtsoe, John A. *Evidences and Reconciliations.* Salt Lake City: Stevens and Wallis, Inc., 1943.

Widtsoe, John A. *Gospel Interpretations.* Salt Lake City: Bookcraft, Inc., 1947.

Widtsoe, John A. *Joseph Smith Seeker After Truth Prophet of God.* Salt Lake City: Bookcraft, Inc., 1957.

Widtsoe, John A. *Priesthood and Church Government.* Salt Lake City: Deseret Book Co., 1939.

# Index to Sections of the Doctrine and Covenants

# Index

Y



Z